THE WILL TO LIVE:

Selected Writings of

ARTHUR SCHOPENHAUER

RICHARD TAYLOR was born in Charlotte, Michigan, in 1919. He received his B.A. from the University of Illinois and was attending the University of Chicago when World War II interrupted his studies. His interest in philosophy began when he read Plato and Schopenhauer on board a submarine tender in the Pacific. After the War Professor Taylor received his M.A. from Oberlin College and, in 1951, his Ph.D. from Brown University. He is now Chairman, Department of Philosophy, University of Rochester.

THE WILL TO LIVE:

Selected Writings of
ARTHUR SCHOPENHAUER

Edited by
RICHARD TAYLOR
University of Rochester

FREDERICK UNGAR PUBLISHING CO.
NEW YORK

Republished 1967
by arrangement with Doubleday & Company, Inc.

Copyright © 1962 by Doubleday & Company, Inc.

Third Printing, 1975

Printed in the United States of America

ISBN 0-8044-6847-8
Library of Congress Catalog Card No.: 67-17822

ARTHUR SCHOPENHAUER

1788	Born in the free city of Danzig, son of a wealthy merchant and a popular novelist
1793	Family moved to Hamburg
1793–1805	Studied and traveled throughout Europe, finally returning to Hamburg to enter business with his father
1805	Released from the family business by his father's death
1809	Entered the University at Göttingen
1811–1813	Studied at [the University of] Berlin where he heard Fichte and Schleiermacher
1813	*On the Fourfold Root of the Principle of Sufficient Reason* (his doctoral thesis)
1816	*On Vision and Colors* (inspired by his attachment to Goethe)
1818	*The World as Will and Idea*
1819	Unsuccessfully tried teaching at Berlin
1833	Settled permanently in Frankfurt
1836	*On the Will in Nature*
1839	*On the Freedom of the Will*
1841	*The Two Main Problems of Ethics*
1844	*The World as Will and Idea* (second edition, published with fifty new supplementary essays)
1851	*Parerga and Paralipomena*
1860	Died in Frankfurt

CONTENTS

INTRODUCTION

Perhaps no philosopher ever looked at the world, and at human nature, more penetratingly than Schopenhauer, and probably none has equaled him in relating metaphysical speculation to the detailed, seemingly heterogeneous and unconnected phenomena of that world. No significant aspect of experience escaped his metaphysical interpretation, and things ordinarily thought to be unrelated to each other, and sometimes beneath the notice of philosophy—such as noise, sex, and the anatomy of animals—fall into place in his clear and beautiful thought. Speculative philosophy is usually considered to be arid, detached from life, cultivated only by the scholar in the study or academic hall, and such it in fact has been at the hands of many who have pursued it, including most of the philosophers, like Hegel, contemporary with Schopenhauer. But Schopenhauer's philosophy is filled with life, and concerned from the start, not merely with concepts and categories of traditional thought, but with the meaning and purpose of existence.

Arthur Schopenhauer was born on February 22, 1788, in Danzig, and was intended by his father to follow the life of commerce, for which he had no temperament. He was educated partly in England, and forever exhibited some of the intellectual habits characteristic of British thought. He followed the odious life of commerce for a time, but was released from it, to devote himself wholly to learning, by his father's death. His mother, Johanna Schopenhauer, was a novelist of considerable reputation in her day, and between her and her son there arose a spirit of competition that grew into pronounced enmity, Schopenhauer declaring, rightly, that she would be remembered by the world only as his mother. Among philosophers he venerated Immanuel Kant, acknowledged a debt to Plato, but heaped scorn on most of the rest, particularly those of his own time and culture, whom he dismissed with such mordacious epithets as "windbags." Hegel's thought in particular he despised, and contemptuously scheduled his own lectures, at Berlin, at the same hour as the older man's. Hegel, however, drew the crowds, while Schopenhauer was ignored, providing a painful confirmation of his conviction in the utter worthlessness of mankind. His philosophy attracted little attention through most of his life, but in his last years it began to receive some of the admiration it so richly deserved, and there was even created a demand for his popular essays which were, and have been ever since, widely read. He died, having finally tasted a bit of the recognition he craved, at the age of seventy-two.

Schopenhauer's philosophy rests upon the Kantian distinction between what *is*, and what is *rationally knowable*. The world that one knows, the "phenomenal" world, is comprised entirely of one's own sensations and his rational interpretations of these. Such interpretations, according to Kant, are the result of the mind itself building into its experience certain kinds of order. If our experience were to lack this order, imposed by the mind, it would be chaotic and unintelligible. Since this order is the natural contribution of the mind itself, or of reason, we cannot reason about, or rationally know, anything that is not thus ordered. If there is anything in the "noumenal" world, or the world as it is "in itself," that either corresponds or fails to correspond with this order, we cannot rationally know it. Our own thought, however, together with the sensations which are its materials, exists entirely within us; that is, according to Schopenhauer, within our brains. Efface these, and for us no world exists at all. This is what Schopenhauer means by asserting that the world, as it exhibits itself to our senses, is "an idea," an appearance within the knower himself, and that, considered independently of any reality lying beyond it, it is, in all its vastness and diversity, nothing.

Now Kant had declared that reality, being rationally unknowable, is not knowable at all, though he conceded that we could *guess* what it *ought* to be on the basis of clues afforded by our moral notions. He noted, however, that a man is himself both an appearance, or phenomenon, insofar as he is a perceivable body, and a reality, or noumenon, insofar as he is a subject that perceives, thinks, wills, and acts. Seizing upon this, Schopenhauer pointed out that we can in fact know what is the reality underlying appearances, because each of us is, in his own true nature, that reality. Certainly we do not know our true nature by rational inference, but we can be—and indeed are, if we but reflect on it—perfectly aware of it. And what we *are* is not just thought, but *will;* indeed, our thoughts, no less than our bodily activities, are nothing but the expression of this will which is our innermost nature. This was Schopenhauer's basic principle. We know what reality is, as will, because we are ourselves not merely the expression of will but identical with that will which underlies all phenomena. The greatness of Schopenhauer's thought consists in the ease with which he seemed able to confirm this voluntarism, explaining what rationalism could not explain. Without it, the world and life are but a conglomeration of unrelated things, but, understood as the expression of will, not only human nature but all nature becomes intelligible. Schopenhauer's speculations are, accordingly, not independent discussions of this thing and that, but a unified metaphysics into which all those things that have always been of intense interest to men fit like the pieces of a puzzle.

That will of which the world (and most clearly the organic world, and hence, our own individual lives) is the expression is essentially a primordial, ungrounded force, and a blind one. Standing in the intellectual tradition of Greek philosophy and Renaissance science, and in the moral tradition of Christian theology, we are apt to think of ourselves as guided by rational thought towards those ends that we have examined and found to be good; in short, we think of our will as guided by our thought and reason. But the exact opposite is true. It is because we first, by our very natures, and prior to all knowing, will, that we declare our ends to be good, without further thought, and cast about for the means to gain them. Every man naturally wills life, and the perpetuation of life, before ever giving thought to whether or not it is a good, and he still wills it in the face of any proof that it is not. The beggar, oppressed by want, his body riddled by sickness, some of his senses destroyed, still clings to life, grasping for it with the eagerness of youth. No less does he who has gratified all his life's aims and is now reduced to boredom and meaninglessness crave to perpetuate his effete existence, for its own sake. We view with instinctive awe and terror preparations for the deliberate destruction of any man, and do not pause to consider the worth of that life; we are gripped with fascination and dread at the sight of an impending suicide, even in the knowledge that hundreds are perishing daily all around us; and sometimes a nation is held in suspense while men and machines struggle against time and overwhelming odds to rescue the life of a child who was hitherto unknown, and who will never be heard of again. Without reflecting on it, we see in these other lives the expression of our own nature, and when they are extinguished we experience frustration—not of a desire for one of the world's tempting goods, which do not then even occur to us, but just of the will itself, that will which is identical in each of us.

That this will is blind means only that it has no further end than the mere perpetuation of existence—and bare existence, contrasted with existing *for* something, is the essence of meaninglessness. This fact eludes us so long as we have great designs and purposes to claim our attention; we assume that these motivate us, and do not consider that they are themselves the arbitrary product of a will that has no design or purpose. This pointlessness of life, even of life that is filled with striving and achievement, becomes particularly apparent when we contemplate the vast panorama of non-human life, see the restless determination with which it is pursued, and then inquire into the purpose of it all.

In spring the woods are filled with mayflies, more appropiately called the ephemeral flies, which appear of a sudden from the lakes and streams, and in a few days litter the ground and foliage with their corpses, meanwhile having done the only thing they were born for, to scatter countless eggs, that the same scene may be briefly repeated another year. The cicadas burrow in the darkness of the earth for years, a few of them to emerge finally for a short flight in the sun and to deposit their eggs, only that more may burrow for years, repeating the pointless episode through an eternity. We observe the herrings as they appear from the ocean in the spring, turning the totally foreign and shallow fresh-water streams into a violent turbulence, struggling against the torrents and every obstacle, tumbling over each other in their desperation, oblivious to a hundred predators lining the shore to scoop them at pleasure by the dozens, goaded to the spawning for nothing else than to insure that this meaningless spectacle may never cease. Certain birds span half the globe to nest. The same drama, the same law, the same primordial will to perpetual existence is repeated in every species, every living thing responding as though inspired by some god to fill the whole of nature with its own kind, and wholly indifferent to any other end which will not subserve this one.

The blindness or purposelessness of this striving does not become wholly apparent, however, until we note that the fate of individual things has not the slightest significance in the general design. As Schopenhauer expressed it, deriving the suggestion from Plato, nature cares only for the form or the species, and is wholly indifferent to its members. Life, both human and subhuman, arises in such profusion as to stagger our wits, yet it is all swept into nothingness as if by whim. The insects and fishes of which we just spoke perish in masses, sometimes as if at a signal, but without notice, and it is shortly as if nothing had happened, the species persisting unaltered, and nature as a whole presenting the same general appearance. Were we to step afresh into our world, with the faculties to appreciate what we would find, we could not but contemplate one of nature's living works, whether it be a man or a fly, with awesome admiration—it seems so exquisitely formed, so painstakingly and beautifully harmonized in its parts, so delicately adjusted to its manifold functions, a work of artifice so complex as to make it seem of unique worth to which all else should be subservient. Yet that individual thing is nothing but the expression of will, and as such, counts for utterly nothing, being obliterated by the slightest vagary. Numberless creatures perish in the woodlands from a chance spark, and birds play guilelessly amidst innumerable threats. We are so accustomed to viewing animal life in this light that we no longer see any incongruity in it, or any disparity between the annihilation of this wonder and the cause of it, to which we cannot possibly attach any significance. Yet it is not otherwise with human life. If we declare the individual human life to have some transcendent worth, it is not from the study of nature and history that we have learned to do so; indeed, both nature and history contradict us daily. A man is felled, at the height of his powers, by a bacterium, cities are abolished by an earthquake or typhoon, millions are annihilated at the caprice of a tyrant, their bodies piled into pits and burned like grasshoppers. Yet when the dust has settled, everything is much as it was before, as though nothing had happened. We declare life, or at least human life, or at least our own human life, to be a unique good, even the image of something divine, hardly realizing, in spite of the testimony that is before us constantly, that this very declaration issues from a will or *conatus* which is our true nature, that this will itself has no goal beyond bare existence, and that to it neither our own individual lives, nor any collection of such individuals, is of any importance.

Such is the witness of our experience, and yet virtually all of man's popular metaphysics, in which Schopenhauer includes religion, has amounted to the denial of it. Theologians declare that man, alone among creatures, has a transcendent worth, that every single man has a soul, fashioned from nothing by a god, that this soul not only blesses each of us with a spark of divinity, thus setting us apart from the rest of nature as the images of God, but also guarantees him, alone among creatures, a chance for an immortal existence. Philosophers, meanwhile, invent arguments to convince us that what we find in the world is no true indication of what is going on there. They busy themselves with morality, contending that man's soul endows him with a freedom possessed by no other thing, that he may use it for good or evil, his moral sense (which, again, he alone possesses) making known to him this particular distinction. They further attempt to reconcile what we do find with what religion asserts we ought to find, the former being said to be somehow illusory, this world being, as Leibniz would have us believe, the very best of all possible ones, precisely what we ought to expect a god to make, in case he makes anything. What we find, in short, in virtually all religion and metaphysics, is the denial, resting on no experience whatever, of the most pervasive and ineradicable facts of experience, a denial which must, of course, render *faith*, or the belief in things unseen, a virtue, by all means to be nurtured—which in fact Christianity does declare it to be. And even when the founders of world religions, as in the case of the Buddha, or the Christ, penetrate beyond human wish and pronounce the world to be infected with suffering and evil, and man's selfish will to be the source of much of that evil, their teaching is soon wrapped in a rosy optimism by successive generations of disciples and epigones, so that it becomes, at their hands, very nearly the opposite of what it originally was.

This religious distortion of things, and the ease with which the vast majority of unthinking men embrace the faith to receive it, can be explained, however, in terms of the same will from which it is the business of established religions to divert our attention. For that will, we noted, is essentially, and in fact nothing more than, a force for existence, and cannot be satisfied with less than the promise of endless existence. That we should cease to exist, that we should live and so profoundly will our existence, only to face annihilation a few years hence, is a thought from which men recoil, not pausing to ask *why* such simple non-existence should be filled with such dread for them, but dreading it nonetheless. It is from this calamity that religion promises salvation, and upon this promise its strength and appeal entirely rest. It is thus an utter distortion, and a naïve one, to think of religion as filling the gaps in our speculative *knowledge*, as though our primary need were to learn the things we do not yet know, things that have no bearing upon what we will. The thought of a divine being does not arise in men's minds as the answer to questions of physics and astronomy put by their intellects, but as the precondition of what men instinctively crave—perpetual existence. Nature declares most forcibly that the existence of any particular individual is of no account and is quite plainly temporary; but each individual man, or the will which is his innermost nature, declares that this shall not be so. Finding, however, no promise from nature that it shall not be so, and finding, in fact, the clear assurance that it *is* so, men everywhere believe in gods, as just those beings who alone can overturn the verdict of nature, theologians and metaphysicians forthwith endowing these gods with whatever powers would render this possible. If, Schopenhauer observes, it should ever be proved that immortality, or indeed any life after death, were a flat impossibility, and if, which is not really possible, men should become convinced of this, then their lively interest in their gods would evaporate, religion no longer answering to the need which gave it birth. And similarly, if it should somehow be scientifically discovered that, as a matter of course, all men are automatically guaranteed an endless existence by their very nature, men's interest in their gods would vanish just as quickly, religion then being superfluous to the need that evoked it.

The death of the individual, from which religion promises to redeem one, cannot, however, possibly be represented to reason as an evil, for, as Lucretius long since pointed out, death can be nothing but the beginning of an eternal nonexistence, and it is obvious that nothing can suffer evil merely because of its non-being. That an eternity should elapse, during which this or that individual man no longer exists, cannot in itself be any more a reasonable source of fear or dread to that person than that an eternity should elapse, during which he exists not yet, the two states being perfectly identical. Yet each of us knows that there *was* an endless time during which we were not, and we view this eternal non-existence with perfect equanimity. Clerics and poets who declaim upon the sorrow, or even injustice, in the thought of the mind or soul of a man forever sinking with him into the grave, and who thus proclaim that it somehow must not be so, fail to see that the same sorrow or injustice, if there were any, would likewise attend the thought that this same soul or mind should have lacked existence throughout that eternity before it arose in birth—yet they feel no impulse to say that *this* must not be so.

Death is the dissolution of the individual organism, Schopenhauer noted, and this individual is but a phenomenal thing. The inner nature of that being, the will that underlies its expression in the individual, is not touched by death, and is evidently indestructible in its very nature. We men are like dreams that arise and pass away in the night, the dreamer meanwhile remaining quite unaffected by this procession across the stage of his consciousness. In the birth of a man we see the objectification of will in an animal organism, in a phenomenon that has no fundamental significance. In death, we find the dissolution of that particular expression of will—but there is no termination of the will itself which was thus momentarily expressed. In imagining, then, that in death one's *ego* or self or true nature perishes while the world remains, one turns the true state of things upside down; it is one's world, as an idea, that perishes with his brain, while his true nature, which is no individual thing, is untouched. Certain plants and simple organisms, as well as the cell-constituents of all higher organisms, multiply simply by splitting in half, and here it is perfectly plain that nothing new has been *created*, but only that there has arisen a phenomenal variation upon what existed already. And if one of these halves, now an individual in its own right, should dissolve, the other dividing again—which is the rule throughout nature—we do not imagine that anything has been annihilated or created, but only that what already *was*, has re-expressed itself, and in such a way as to leave things essentially no different than before.

This endless proliferation and dissolution of life, this ceaseless multiplication and division of parts, cannot but strike the contemplative mind as a mystery, a question that cries for an answer; but how quickly the mystery vanishes, and the answer leaps up, when we penetrate beyond the phenomena to the reality that lies within each of us. Every living thing, we find, is like ourselves moved by the irrational impulse, whether conscious or not, to perpetuate itself, but vastly exceeding that is the determination to perpetuate its kind—for many a creature perishes in the very act of procreation, and there is hardly one, including men and women, to whom its own life is not a small thing in comparison with the life of the species. Thus did Plato rightly regard *eros* or sexual passion as part of the impulse to immortality. We look with amusement and fascination upon animals as they respond to the sexual instinct, so manifest is their bondage to something they know not what, and we view in the same way the behavior of adolescents as it begins to engulf them. It has been the primary ingredient of poetry, song, story, and humor since these things began. Rain,

snow, and bitter cold, as well as thirst and the arid heat of
the desert, are battled with the urgency of life and death as
this or that poor animal presses towards a goal of which it has
no real conception, which it seldom even knows, and which
could only, from the standpoint of its own interest, be considered trivial in comparison to its cost. Nor can a reflective
man regard it as otherwise on the human level—except that
here we have a clear idea of the goal, the act of procreation,
which we think of as an end but which is in fact only a means;
and we have idealized it as a sublime thing, plainly deserving
all effort and sacrifice, even deluding ourselves to suppose that
we *first*, by our intellects, perceived it as an inestimable good,
and *then* directed our wills to its attainment, as though the
very opposite were not perfectly obvious. The sexual desire
expresses itself before there is any clear concept of the means
to its gratification. The claims of famine and war subside in
its presence, and everything that moralists and preachers have
exhorted men to treat as having absolute claim on their conduct—such as honor, reputation, and family—are almost cas-
ually jettisoned in favor of this prior claim, made upon us by
nature, the moment the chance for its fulfillment is seen.
Thrones have been abandoned to it, fortunes squandered, and
hardly any man can think without shame upon how his own
petty business has been ceaselessly muddled by it, Cupid finding ways, Schopenhauer notes, of slipping locks of hair even
into the portfolios of cabinet ministers and the manuscripts of
philosophers.

So long as we view this turmoil from the standpoint of the
individual man and his private interests and aims, it appears
senseless; but as soon as we regard the individual as the expression of a will that cares nothing for him, but only for existence as such and, accordingly, for its perpetuation, then
what before was mysterious becomes familiar, and the riddles
of passionate love are unfolded. Thus do we find that a man,
at peace with the world and beholden to no one, multiplies
his burdens and responsibilities without limit, lightly and
with a gay heart, for the sake, he imagines, of possessing that
woman so lovely as to deserve all such sacrifice and more—
and hardly has he gained this one, than every other woman
charms him more. Not so with a woman, whose chief impulse

is to cleave to him whom she has—not, as she imagines, in her own interests, but in the interests of her children, born and unborn. A man, Schopenhauer observes, is by nature prone to inconstancy, a woman to constancy—precisely because he can sire a hundred children in a year, and she bear only one. Thus does every woman react, initially and instinctively, to every other woman with enmity and the competitive spirit, even though that other may pose no threat, and may even be unknown to her; whereas a man's initial impulse is to gallantry and ingratiation towards every nubile woman, and to any other man his first reaction is one of total indifference. The delights that passionate love holds out, which are the underlying theme of all romance and song, are in fact the most nebulous and evanescent of any, being wholly extinguished in the very act of their ultimate momentary achievement; and what before overwhelmed one as a sublime appearance to be won at all effort is found to be an illusion in its reality—just because the means was mistaken for the end, and was misconceived as the goal of the individual himself. The true end, the perpetuation of the species, which is of no passionate concern to the individual and which he, in fact, endeavors by ingenious machination to frustrate if he can, is nonetheless achieved most effectively, and with total unconcern for its cost to him who is the instrument of it. We tend to condemn marriages of convenience, or of wealth, or those arranged by parents in their wisdom, for in these passionate love is assumed to be at best a subordinate motive, and we in our hearts consider the interest of the race as paramount, as something that should not be disregarded in the interests of the rational desires of its individual members. Yet it is those unions that are generally happiest and most durable, and that do in time usually produce a genuine affection, just because they are made in the explicit interests of the two persons immediately affected. Passionate love, on the other hand, which serves no real interest of individuals and more often than not disdains these in its determination to achieve its own impersonal end, forms the basis of the least stable and most unhappy unions of wedlock, because its interests are not those of the individuals immediately concerned. We nevertheless, sensing the overwhelming importance of the ultimate end and the relative insignificance of those who are its means, approve this passion as the only proper motive. We cheer on the elopers as they flout wisdom and prudence, and congratulate them when every rational consideration and all cool deliberation have been irrevocably swept aside. It is, Schopenhauer perceived, the immortal part of a man, his true nature or will, that gazes longingly into the eyes of his loved one, and in this longing each of us finds himself. What is mortal in him, his own individuality, desires everything else, but counts for absolutely nothing.

Schopenhauer's notorious pessimism, implied in all the foregoing, must not be understood as an attitude with which he approaches speculation, to be endorsed or rejected according to individual temperament, but rather as a solemn, rational conclusion drawn from our common experience. The whole world contradicts optimism, and if one is an optimist nonetheless, it is in deference to the claims of the heart rather than of the understanding. The minimum requirements of optimism would be, first, that life, or at least human life, has a rational purpose beyond the mere perpetuation of life which we share with the brutes; that we can apprehend this purpose intellectually, are free to pursue it, and that it is worthy of our endeavor—but not one of these claims can be borne out with any conviction. And second, in order for optimism to be true there must be genuine, positive goods in the world, and these must prevail, or give some promise of prevailing, over their opposites—but nothing seems less likely to be true. Theologians and philosophers following them have indeed tried to convince us by ingenious reasoning that goodness prevails, that it is even identical with all existence, and that evil is only an illusion—but the slightest sense of reality contradicts this. Things are lovely throughout nature in exact proportion to their rarity; ugliness is the norm towards which all things tend. Flowers appear briefly and wither quickly, but the dirt and manure from which they spring and to which they at once return endure indestructibly. Genius appears here and there, accidentally, among men, but it is forever engulfed in the ocean of stupidity that gives no hint of being accidental. And indeed, a man of genius can be rendered an idiot by the slightest physiological disturbance, but a dolt cannot be rendered a genius by all the powers of heaven and earth, so durable is that state. Hideous caterpillars transform themselves at last, and after appalling decimation of foliage, into moths whose loveliness moves us to gasp, but so brief is their tenure of nocturnal existence that nature has not bothered to give them mouths or tongues wherewith to eat, and their beauty perishes with them in hardly a few short hours. Health and the joy of life are nowhere so apparent as in infants, who know nothing, and who are in the fullest sense protected from the world that we are supposed to believe is a refulgent and unadulterated goodness. A man who, in the fullness of years, exhibited the joyousness of a child could not but appear to us as an utter fool, as one who by that time should have learned better. Pain is what is positive, being actually felt, while pleasure is the negative, illusory thing, being identified simply with the absence of pain. Youth and health are good—but we do not feel them, nor attach any positive qualities to them, nor in any way sense them until they are lost in sickness and age—and the loss of them is felt most acutely. Similarly, in the realm of desire it is our wants and cravings that we feel; their satisfactions are felt only indirectly as the temporary quiescence of these wants, which were positive and real. And such is exactly what we should expect if we understand our true nature, which is to will, blindly and without rational purpose, and thus to be made miserable by the most trifling frustrations and annoyances, but to be made wholly happy and satisfied by nothing at all, not even the pleasures and gratifications of a lifetime. When one views his life in this context and perspective, and sees it as that tiny expression of the life and existence unfolding itself throughout all time, he can say with conviction, "I understand, and I know," and this knowledge quenches the protest of his craving and desire.

The ethical theory Schopenhauer derives from such considerations stands unique in the history of thought. Traditionally, and particularly in the present day, moralists address themselves to the refined analyses of ethical concepts such as justice, goodness, and right—but in so doing they limit themselves from the outset to that framework of thought conventional to our own culture, or even to the spontaneous appraisals made by unreflective men whose habits of thought are simply the distillation of that culture. The slightest knowledge of metaphysics teaches us, however, that this enterprise is misconceived from the start, for such words as "ought" and "duty" have no rational force whatever except on the assumption that men's wills are free to choose among alternatives, to decide which of various competing motives shall determine behavior —an assumption to which, once formulated, it is difficult to attach any clear meaning. Our behavior is the product of our motives, and the most general and pervasive of these—such as greed, altruism, vanity, the love of honor or of possession— are in their various combinations fairly fixed in every man from the start, a fact that is usually quite evident to everyone so long as he is viewing the behavior of others. Our motives, in turn, are not chosen by our intellects, and cannot even be thought of in that way by anyone having the barest acquaintance with human nature without the absurdity of such a conception leaping up. They are the product of our wills, and our wills are but part of a larger will that is ungrounded and irrational from the start. The vain and greedy man was vain and greedy long before he ever gave thought to vanity and greed, or weighed them in his understanding against their opposites. So likewise the sweet and compassionate soul's sweetness has sprung not from reflection, nor from the quiet study of moral treatises, but from something far deeper, from the original will or inner nature of that person himself. Thus we find that learning and the gifts of intellect bear no correlation at all to virtue and rectitude. A man of sense, accordingly, before putting his trust in another, knows well enough to inquire into that man's heart, that is, his intentions or will, rather than his reason, and regards with correct indifference his achievements in learning, which have no influence upon this.

Even so, there is a task for the philosopher to do in the realm of morals, and it is one that Schopenhauer performs with such skill as to leave him almost without competitors. That task is not to delineate our duties, or spin out the nuances of meanings in moral appraisals as they flow from the tongues of unthinking men, but to establish the very *basis* of morality; that is, to distinguish what it is in human nature that moves us to such profound condemnation and commendation. This he finds in the three basic springs, or pervasive motives, of conduct; namely, *egoism,* or self-love, which is the impulse to one's own weal or good; *malice,* or the impulse to others' woe or hurt; and *compassion,* or the impulse to others' weal and well-being. Now each of these is a distinct and basic motive, and not one which—like the love of gain, for example—is derivative from something more basic. Egoism, whose role in determining behavior is so pervasive that the absence of it in any man would render him an anomaly in our eyes, is selfishness for its own sake, that is, the impulse to one's own good as an end in itself, rather than as a means to something ulterior to that. Malice, similarly, is disinterested nastiness, that is, the impulse to hurt others without any expectation of actual benefit to oneself. And pure compassion—which like all lovely things is above all rare—is sweetness, sympathy, or what Schopenhauer calls loving-kindness, without ulterior motive; that is, the impulse to the weal or joy of other creatures, without hope of any gain to oneself thereby.

Now each of these motives is a fundamental ingredient of human nature, such that the total absence of any one of them would be viewed as an aberration. Yet egoism or concern for oneself is the most reliable of them. We find it unhesitatingly allowed, for example, as the presupposition of all laws and prescriptions of penalties, and indeed of everything pertaining to human relationships, even those, such as within the family, wherein it would be expected to have least force. Marriage, which is officially a union of love, is nonetheless realistically assumed to be a union of two self-regarding wills, each with its own jealously guarded rights and prerogatives, and such it in fact almost invariably is. Nor does the most egregious egoism or self-concern ever strike us as really abnormal. A wealthy man, for instance, walks past a beggar whose plight he could relieve effortlessly, and then bends down to pick a trivial coin from the walk for himself. When some poor soul is felled on the streets of a metropolis, whether from illness or drink, it can by no means be assumed that any of the indurate multitude who must step over him to get on with their rounds will stop to assist him, although he is eventually removed as an obstruction to traffic.

There is, however, nothing inherently immoral in egoism, which is entirely self-regarding, nor anything necessarily pernicious in its fruits; the impulse to one's own weal and well-being ordinarily results, at worst, in indifference to others, while it often, quite incidentally, brings benefits to them. As an incentive to action, it is neither uniquely moral nor immoral, but simply amoral.

Malice, on the other hand, is the very *basis* of immorality, and evidently exists only in human nature, being quite foreign to all other creatures. We do indeed find pain and suffering throughout nature, but only in men do we sometimes find these the very purposes of action, such that malice becomes deliberate and disinterested. The cruelty of one animal towards another is the product of uncomprehending indifference, not of deliberate choice, whereas in men it is sometimes a chosen aim. Thus has a public execution always drawn crowds—not, surely, for the moral lesson they hope to derive, which is the pretended justification for its publicity, but for the satisfaction of seeing the deliberately and legally imposed suffering that they have been promised. A man who has in his dementia resolved to leap from a high building always attracts onlookers in whom the emotions of dread and fascination are curiously mingled, and, from the pure malice of some of these, chants and exhortations to jump invariably arise. Nor can this impulse to cruelty possibly be regarded as an artificial product of social life and culture; it is, in the strictest sense, an *original* sin, which advanced civilization endeavors to combat, but never implants. Children feel malice long before they have any capacity for compassion, delighting in the shortcomings, stupidity or deformity of others, teasing and tormenting whatever is within reach, without any hope of benefit thereby, and often at some cost to themselves. Thus does every natural or feral animal rightly and instinctively fear and flee from men, being cajoled to approach even the friendliest human gesture only after long and patient training, and even then with distrust. The instinct to hunt is an original one which, though often conjoined with the love of the out-of-doors, has nevertheless an independent motivation; for many who care nothing for the out-of-doors still go to great cost and preparation for the pleasures of hooks, traps, and guns. Nor can the impulse to gossip, which is the delighted sharing with friends of the defects of others, be regarded as springing from anything but an original incentive. One must be *taught* to praise, and only with effort does one find satisfaction in the achievements of others, while epithets of scorn and execration rise spontaneously to the lips.

That this malice is the very basis of immorality follows from the fact that it is the one and only common element in all acts that are the source of immediate moral revulsion. A man might—in fact usually does—hurt others in response to his own insatiable selfishness, and this we disparage, but our sense of morality is not outraged. The pain he causes is the result of his unfeeling indifference, and he appears to us more as an insensitive animal, or one who knows no better, than as a satan. But that one should, *knowing* what pain is, make pain in another creature the very object of his interest and will, always evokes the deepest moral repugnance.

Now when we look at human nature, so generously endowed with egoism and augmented by malice, it might seem that any incentive directly opposed to these would be impossible. Yet it does actually exist, here and there, and rarely. Sympathy or compassion, as the words themselves suggest, is the identification of oneself, that is, of one's will, with the sufferings of others; the imaginative feeling, with them, of their pain and anxiety; and as such it overcomes and cancels both egoism and malice, with which it is wholly incompatible. Tender souls are sometimes appalled at the suffering of some poor and perhaps worthless creature, and in highly civilized nations there are even founded societies devoted to the alleviation of the sufferings of all animals, entirely without hope of gratitude or reward. There sometimes even appears a holy man—a Buddha or a Christ—who, by a dramatic act or otherwise, identifies himself with the very sufferings of the world, and thus is planted the seed of a religion. We look at a child, whose feelings have been senselessly crushed by some trivial or grave incident, or at the lover, whether in fact or fiction, suffering the torment of rejection, and we *know* what it is like. Our own ego is momentarily extinguished, we become identical in our thought and feeling with the suffering self or will before us, and loving-kindness wells up, in spite of ourselves. Or we see a man, bent upon revenge, even justified in his thirst for it, having the power of it in his hands, immune to all fear of reprisal—who nevertheless hesitates at the last moment, restrained by a power within him; and we see that he envisaged the suffering he was about to inflict, that he imaginatively identified himself with it, that he *felt compassion* and this compassion prevailed. Here we are in the presence of something with which the precepts of moralists and clerics have nothing to do, yet our hearts are filled with profound approbation. Here, and here alone, we see the basis of genuinely moral conduct. Without it, we have at best civilized behavior, motivated by hope of gain, fear of penalty, or sometimes mere habit. But in the presence of genuine compassion, even if faint and faltering, we find ourselves constrained to approval that has no regard for our own interests, and our own selfishness bows helplessly before it; not from high expectations of its consequences, which may be trivial, nor from the perception that here some moral rule is embodied—for compassion is a feeling and thus subject to no rule—but from the transcendent beauty of the motive itself, and the truth expressed in it, dimly perceived, that the inner nature or will of all living things is the same. "Ought" and "ought not," categorical imperatives, commandments of gods, considerations of public utility, and all else that moralists have tried to make so central, have here no relevance. There is only the command of the heart, which knows no philosophy, but before which every system of morals gives way and collapses.

The role that Schopenhauer assigns to compassion in ethics gives also the clue to his scheme of salvation. Compassion is a prompting of the heart, that is, of the will, and not of the intellect and senses, which only see but do not feel. Its effect is the partial and momentary extinguishing of the will itself, resulting from the perception of the same suffering will in others. And this is clearly the first step of deliverance—to see beyond the phenomena of individuality separating the "me" from the "thou," to penetrate the veil of illusion and grasp the reality beneath it, the common will that unites all things. Compassion, however, accomplishes this to a very limited extent, for it is rare, fleeting, and quite at the mercy of external circumstances. Nevertheless in this experience we do find the partial extinction of the individual will, that will being itself, paradoxically, the instrument of its own destruction; we know, therefore, that it is possible, and that at least here one can be in a small measure released from his bondage to the groundless source of existence and, what is the same thing, from suffering. We find this same quiescence of the will, albeit a temporary one, in the contemplation of beauty, for aesthetic contemplation and restless craving are impossible to combine, yet the former is sometimes possible to a sensitive soul. In the quiet perception of painting, of natural beauty, and above all of music, which has a metaphysic of its own, the ground of existence is lost, suffering is put far behind, and the mind approaches an awareness of something eternal and immutable, something that ordinarily eludes us just because it has no reference to our will, and hence no bearing upon individual cravings and goals. Final deliverance, however, could only consist in a total and permanent release from this bondage, an ideal which is not a possible one in life, for life is itself the expression of will. We do nevertheless find it achieved to a very high degree in the lives of the saints, particularly in ancient Buddhism; for it is the teaching of this religion, as it is Schopenhauer's, that life is essentially suffering, that this suffering arises from craving, particularly the craving for existence, and that the release from this suffering can only come from the release from blind craving itself. The Buddhist ideal is the state of Nirvana, wherein all desire, willing, and craving are put to rest, and with them, individuality. It is an ideal the Buddhists represent as realizable, though perhaps not in a natural life. Now to us this overcoming and transcendence of the will appears as the abnegation of life, and thus, we are apt to think, of all of life's goods; but this is only because we imagine that these goods are desirable independently of our craving for them. For Schopenhauer, as for the Buddhist, salvation is the victory over, and the annihilation of, the world, which is nothing; of life, which is suffering; and of the individual ego, which is an illusion.

R. T.

A NOTE ON THE SELECTIONS

Most of the writings in this collection are taken from the second edition of Schopenhauer's greatest book, *The World as Will and Idea,* and were considered by their author to be addenda and notes to the main body of that work. They are, nonetheless, complete and independent in their own right, and embody some of Schopenhauer's most penetrating insights. Several other selections are from Schopenhauer's better known essays which he wrote for general appeal, and one, "Comparative Anatomy," is a chapter from his remarkable book, *On the Will in Nature.* His concept of the will emerges clearly from some of the first writings that follow; the remaining selections trace the implications and ramifications of this fundamental idea. For the extracts from *The World as Will and Idea,* the 1883 translation of R. B. Haldane and J. Kemp was used. "Comparative Anatomy" is from *On the Will in Nature* translated by Mme. Karl Hillebrand in 1889. The remaining pieces are taken from *The Essays of Arthur Schopenhauer* translated by T. Bailey Saunders.

THE WILL TO LIVE:

Selected Writings of

ARTHUR SCHOPENHAUER

I

ON MAN'S NEED OF METAPHYSICS[1]

(CHAPTER XVII *from* SUPPLEMENTS TO THE FIRST BOOK OF THE WORLD AS WILL AND IDEA)

With the exception of man, no being wonders at its own existence; but it is to them all so much a matter of course that they do not observe it. The wisdom of nature speaks out of the peaceful glance of the brutes; for in them the will and the intellect are not yet so widely separated that they can be astonished at each other when they meet again. Thus here the whole phenomenon is still firmly attached to the stem of nature from which it has come, and is partaker of the unconscious omniscience of the great mother. Only after the inner being of nature (the will to live in its objectification) has ascended, vigorous and cheerful, through the two series of unconscious existences, and then through the long and broad series of animals, does it attain at last to reflection for the first time on the entrance of reason, thus in man. Then it marvels at its own works, and asks itself what it itself is. Its wonder however is the more serious, as it here stands for the first time consciously in the presence of *death*, and besides the finiteness of all existence, the vanity of all effort forces itself more or less upon it. With this reflection and this wonder there arises therefore for man alone, the *need for a metaphysic;* he is accordingly an *animal metaphysicum.* At the beginning of his consciousness certainly he also accepts himself as a matter of course. This does not last long however, but very early, with the first dawn of reflection, that wonder already appears, which is some day to become the mother of metaphysics. Moreover, the special philosophical disposition consists primarily in this, that a man

[1] This selection is connected with § 15 of THE WORLD AS WILL AND IDEA, Dolphin Books, Doubleday & Company, Inc., 1961.

is capable of wonder beyond the ordinary and everyday degree, and is thus induced to make the *universal* of the phenomenon his problem, while the investigators in the natural
sciences wonder only at exquisite or rare phenomena, and their
problem is merely to refer these to phenomena which are better known. The lower a man stands in an intellectual regard
the less of a problem is existence itself for him; everything,
how it is, and that it is, appears to him rather a matter of
course. This rests upon the fact that his intellect still remains
perfectly true to its original destiny of being serviceable to
the will as the medium of motives, and therefore is closely
bound up with the world and nature, as an integral part of
them. Consequently it is very far from comprehending the
world in a purely objective manner, freeing itself, so to speak,
from the whole of things, opposing itself to this whole, and so
for a while becoming as if self-existent. On the other hand, the
philosophical wonder which springs from this is conditioned in
the individual by higher development of the intellect, yet in
general not by this alone; but without doubt it is the knowledge of death, and along with this the consideration of the
suffering and misery of life, which gives the strongest impulse
to philosophical reflection and metaphysical explanation of the
world. If our life were endless and painless, it would perhaps
occur to no one to ask why the world exists, and is just the
kind of world it is; but everything would just be taken as a
matter of course. In accordance with this we find that the
interest which philosophical and also religious systems inspire
has always its strongest hold in the dogma of some kind of
existence after death; and although the most recent systems
seem to make the existence of their gods the main point, and
to defend this most zealously, yet in reality this is only because
they have connected their special dogma of immortality with
this, and regard the one as inseparable from the other: only
on this account is it of importance to them. For if one could
establish their doctrine of immortality for them in some other
way, their lively zeal for their gods would at once cool, and it
would give place almost to complete indifference if, conversely,
the absolute impossibility of immortality were proved to them;
for the interest in the existence of the gods would vanish with
the hope of a closer acquaintance with them, to the residuum

which might connect itself with their possible influence on the events of this present life. But if one could prove that continued existence after death is incompatible with the existence of gods, because, let us say, it pre-supposes originality of being, they would soon sacrifice the gods to their own immortality and become zealous for Atheism. The fact that the materialistic systems, properly so-called, and also absolute scepticism, have never been able to obtain a general or lasting influence, depends upon the same grounds.

Temples and churches, pagodas and mosques, in all lands and in all ages, in splendour and vastness, testify to the metaphysical need of man, which, strong and ineradicable, follows close upon his physical need. Certainly whoever is satirically inclined might add that this metaphysical need is a modest fellow who is content with poor fare. It sometimes allows itself to be satisfied with clumsy fables and insipid tales. If only imprinted early enough, they are for a man adequate explanations of his existence and supports of his morality. Consider, for example, the Koran. This wretched book was sufficient to found a religion of the world, to satisfy the metaphysical need of innumerable millions of men for twelve hundred years, to become the foundation of their morality, and of no small contempt for death, and also to inspire them to bloody wars and most extended conquests. We find in it the saddest and the poorest form of Theism. Much may be lost through the translations; but I have not been able to discover one single valuable thought in it. Such things show that metaphysical capacity does not go hand in hand with the metaphysical need. Yet it will appear that in the early ages of the present surface of the earth this was not the case, and that those who stood considerably nearer than we do to the beginning of the human race and the source of organic nature, had also both greater energy of the intuitive faculty of knowledge, and a truer disposition of mind, so that they were capable of a purer, more direct comprehension of the inner being of nature, and were thus in a position to satisfy the metaphysical need in a more worthy manner. Thus originated in the primitive ancestors of the Brahmans, the Rishis, the almost superhuman conceptions which were afterwards set down in the Upanishads of the Vedas.

On the other hand, there have never been wanting persons who were interested in deriving their living from that metaphysical need, and in making the utmost they could out of it. Therefore among all nations there are monopolists and farmers-general of it—the priests. Yet their trade had everywhere to be assured to them in this way, that they received the right to impart their metaphysical dogmas to men at a very early age, before the judgment has awakened from its morning slumber, thus in early childhood; for then every well-impressed dogma, however senseless it may be, remains for ever. If they had to wait till the judgment is ripe, their privileges could not continue.

A second, though not a numerous class of persons, who derive their support from the metaphysical need of man, is constituted by those who live by *philosophy*. By the Greeks they were called Sophists, by the moderns they are called Professors of Philosophy. Aristotle (*Metaph.*, ii. 2) without hesitation numbers Aristippus among the Sophists. In Diogenes Laertius (ii. 65) we find that the reason of this is that he was the first of the Socratics who accepted payment for his philosophy; on account of which Socrates also returned him his present. Among the moderns also those who live *by* philosophy are not only, as a rule, and with the rarest exceptions, quite different from those who live *for* philosophy, but they are very often the opponents, the secret and irreconcilable enemies of the latter. For every true and important philosophical achievement will overshadow their own too much, and, moreover, cannot adapt itself to the views and limitations of their guild. Therefore it is always their endeavour to prevent such a work from making its way; and for this purpose, according to the age and circumstances in each case, the customary means are suppressing, concealing, hushing up, ignoring and keeping secret, or denying, disparaging, censuring, slandering and distorting, or, finally, denouncing and persecuting. Hence many a great man has had to drag himself wearily through life unknown, unhonoured, unrewarded, till at last, after his death, the world became undeceived as to him and as to them. In the meanwhile they had attained their end, had been accepted by preventing him from being accepted, and, with wife and child, had lived *by* philosophy, while he lived *for* it. But if he is dead, then the thing is reversed; the new generation of the former class, which always exists, now becomes heir to his achievements, cuts them down to its own measure, and now lives *by* him. That Kant could yet live both *by* and *for* philosophy depended on the rare circumstance that, for the first time since *Divus Antoninus* and *Divus Julianus,* a philosopher sat on the throne. Only under such auspices could the "Critique of Pure Reason" have seen the light. Scarcely was the king dead than we see that Kant also, seized with fear, because he belonged to the guild, modified, expurgated, and spoiled his masterpiece in the second edition, and yet was soon in danger of losing his place; so that Campe invited him to come to him, in Brunswick, and live with him as the instructor of his family (Ring., *Ansichten aus Kant's Leben,* p. 68). University philosophy is, as a rule, mere juggling. Its real aim is to impart to the students, in the deepest ground of their thought, that tendency of mind which the ministry that appoints to the professorships regards as consistent with its views. The ministry may also be perfectly right in this from a statesman's point of view; only the result of it is that such philosophy of the chair is a *nervis alienis mobile lignum,* and cannot be regarded as serious philosophy, but as the mere jest of it. Moreover, it is at any rate just that such inspection or guidance should extend only to the philosophy of the chair, and not to the real philosophy that is in earnest. For if anything in the world is worth wishing for—so well worth wishing for that even the ignorant and dull herd in its more reflective moments would prize it more than silver and gold—it is that a ray of light should fall on the obscurity of our being, and that we should gain some explanation of our mysterious existence, in which nothing is clear but its misery and its vanity. But even if this is in itself attainable, it is made impossible by imposed and compulsory solutions.

We shall now subject to a general consideration the different ways of satisfying this strong metaphysical need.

By *metaphysics* I understand all knowledge that pretends to transcend the possibility of experience, thus to transcend nature or the given phenomenal appearance of things, in order to give an explanation of that by which, in some sense or other, this experience or nature is conditioned; or, to speak in popular language, of that which is behind nature, and makes it pos-

sible. But the great original diversity in the power of understanding, besides the cultivation of it, which demands much
leisure, makes so great a difference between men, that as soon
as a people has emerged from the state of savages, no *one*
metaphysic can serve for them all. Therefore among civilised
nations we find throughout two different kinds of metaphysics,
which are distinguished by the fact that the one has its evidence *in itself*, the other *outside itself*. Since the metaphysical
systems of the first kind require reflection, culture, and leisure
for the recognition of their evidence, they can be accessible
only to a very small number of men; and, moreover, they can
only arise and maintain their existence in the case of advanced
civilisation. On the other hand, the systems of the second kind
exclusively are for the great majority of men who are not capable of thinking, but only of believing, and who are not accessible to reasons, but only to authority. These systems may therefore be called metaphysics of the people, after the analogy of
poetry of the people, and also wisdom of the people, by which
is understood proverbs. These systems, however, are known
under the name of religions, and are found among all nations,
not excepting even the most savage. Their evidence is, as has
been said, external, and as such is called revelation, which is
authenticated by signs and miracles. Their arguments are principally threats of eternal, and indeed also temporal evils, directed against unbelievers, and even against mere doubters.
As *ultima ratio theologorum,* we find among many nations the
stake or things similar to it. If they seek a different authentication, or if they make use of other arguments, they already make
the transition into the systems of the first kind, and may degenerate into a mixture of the two, which brings more danger
than advantage, for their invaluable prerogative of being imparted to *children* gives them the surest guarantee of the permanent possession of the mind, for thereby their dogmas grow
into a kind of second inborn intellect, like the twig upon the
grafted tree; while, on the other hand, the systems of the first
kind only appeal to grown-up people, and in them always find
a system of the second kind already in possession of their con-
victions. Both kinds of metaphysics, whose difference may be
briefly expressed by the words reasoned conviction and faith,
have this in common, that every one of their particular systems

stands in a hostile relation to all the others of its kind. Between those of the first kind war is waged only with word and pen; between those of the second with fire and sword as well. Several of the latter owe their propagation in part to this last kind of polemic, and all have by degrees divided the earth between them, and indeed with such decided authority that the peoples of the earth are distinguished and separated more according to them than according to nationality or government. They alone *reign*, each in its own province. The systems of the first kind, on the contrary, are at the most *tolerated*, and even this only because, on account of the small number of their adherents, they are for the most part not considered worth the trouble of combating with fire and sword—although, where it seemed necessary, these also have been employed against them with effect; besides, they occur only in a sporadic form. Yet in general they have only been endured in a tamed and subjugated condition, for the system of the second kind which prevailed in the country ordered them to conform their teaching more or less closely to its own. Sometimes it not only subjugated them, but even employed their services and used them as a support, which is however a dangerous experiment. For these systems of the first kind, since they are deprived of power, believe they may advance themselves by craft, and never entirely lay aside a secret ill-will which at times comes unexpectedly into prominence and inflicts injuries which are hard to heal. For they are further made the more dangerous by the fact that all the real sciences, not even excepting the most innocent, are their secret allies against the systems of the second kind, and without themselves being openly at war with the latter, suddenly and unexpectedly do great mischief in their province. Besides, the attempt which is aimed at by the enlistment referred to of the services of the systems of the first kind by the second—the attempt to add an inner authentication to a system whose original authentication was external, is in its nature perilous; for, if it were capable of such an authentication, it would never have required an external one. And in general it is always a hazardous thing to attempt to place a new foundation under a finished structure. Moreover, how should a religion require the suffrage of a philosophy? It has everything upon its side—revelation, tradition, miracles, prophecies, the protection of the government, the highest rank, as is due to the truth, the consent and reverence of all, a thousand temples in which it is proclaimed and practised, bands of sworn priests, and, what is more than all, the invaluable privilege of being allowed to imprint its doctrines on the mind at the tender age of childhood, whereby they became almost like innate ideas. With such wealth of means at its disposal, still to desire the assent of poor philosophers it must be more covetous, or to care about their contradiction it must be more fearful, than seems to be compatible with a good conscience.

To the distinction established above between metaphysics of the first and of the second kind, we have yet to add the following:—A system of the first kind, thus a philosophy, makes the claim, and has therefore the obligation, in everything that it says, *sensu stricto et proprio*, to be true, for it appeals to thought and conviction. A religion, on the other hand, being intended for the innumerable multitude who, since they are incapable of examination and thought, would never comprehend the profoundest and most difficult truths *sensu proprio*, has only the obligation to be true *sensu allegorico*. Truth cannot appear naked before the people. A symptom of this *allegorical* nature of religions is the *mysteries* which are to be found perhaps in them all, certain dogmas which cannot even be distinctly thought, not to speak of being literally true. Indeed, perhaps it might be asserted that some absolute contradictions, some actual absurdities, are an essential ingredient in a complete religion, for these are just the stamp of its allegorical nature, and the only adequate means of making the ordinary mind and the uncultured understanding *feel* what would be incomprehensible to it, that religion has ultimately to do with quite a different order of things, with an order of *things in themselves*, in the presence of which the laws of this phenomenal world, in conformity with which it must speak, vanish; and that therefore not only the contradictory but also the comprehensible dogmas are really only allegories and accommodations to the human power of comprehension. It seems to me that it was in this spirit that Augustine and even Luther adhered to the mysteries of Christianity in opposition to Pelagianism, which sought to reduce everything to the dull level of comprehensibility. From this point of view it is also conceivable how Tertullian could say in all seriousness: *"Prorsus credibile est, quia ineptum est: . . . certum est, quia impossibile"* (*De Carne Christi*, c. 5). This *allegorical* nature of religions makes them independent of the proofs which are incumbent on philosophy, and in general withdraws them from investigation. Instead of this they require faith, that is, a voluntary admission that such is the state of the case. Since, then, faith guides action, and the allegory is always so framed that, as regards the practical, it leads precisely to that which the truth *sensu proprio* would also lead to, religion is justified in promising to those who believe eternal salvation. Thus we see that in the main, and for the great majority, who cannot apply themselves to thought, religions very well supply the place of metaphysics in general, the need of which man feels to be imperative. They do this partly in a practical interest, as the guiding star of their action, the unfurled standard of integrity and virtue, as Kant admirably expresses it; partly as the indispensable comfort in the heavy sorrows of life, in which capacity they fully supply the place of an objectively true metaphysic, because they lift man above himself and his existence in time, as well perhaps as such a metaphysic ever could. In this their great value and indeed necessity shows itself very clearly. On the other hand, the only stumbling-stone is this, that religions never dare to confess their allegorical nature, but have to assert that they are true *sensu proprio*. They thereby encroach on the province of metaphysics proper, and call forth the antagonism of the latter, which has therefore expressed itself at all times when it was not chained up. The controversy which is so perseveringly carried on in our own day between supernaturalists and rationalists also rests on the failure to recognise the allegorical nature of all religion. Both wish to have Christianity true *sensu proprio;* in this sense the former wish to maintain it without deduction, as it were with skin and hair; and thus they have a hard stand to make against the knowledge and general culture of the age. The latter wish to explain away all that is properly Christian; whereupon they retain something which is neither *sensu proprio* nor *sensu allegorico* true, but rather a mere platitude, little better than Judaism, or at the most a shallow Pelagianism, and, what is worst, an abject optimism, absolutely foreign to Christianity proper.

Moreover, the attempt to found a religion upon reason removes it into the other class of metaphysics, that which has its authentication *in itself,* thus to the foreign ground of the philosophical systems, and into the conflict which these wage against each other in their own arena, and consequently exposes it to the light fire of scepticism and the heavy artillery of the "Critique of Pure Reason"; but for it to venture there would be clear presumption.

It would be most beneficial to both kinds of metaphysics that each of them should remain clearly separated from the other and confine itself to its own province, that it may there be able to develop its nature fully. Instead of which, through the whole Christian era, the endeavour has been to bring about a fusion of the two, for the dogmas and conceptions of the one have been carried over into the other, whereby both are spoiled. This has taken place in the most open manner in our own day in that strange hermaphrodite or centaur, the so-called philosophy of religion, which, as a kind of gnosis, endeavours to interpret the given religion, and to explain what is true *sensu allegorico* through something which is true *sensu proprio.* But for this we would have to know and possess the truth *sensu proprio* already; and in that case such an interpretation would be superfluous. For to seek first to find metaphysics, *i.e.,* the truth *sensu proprio,* merely out of religion by explanation and interpretation would be a doubtful and dangerous undertaking, to which one would only make up one's mind if it were proved that truth, like iron and other base metals, could only be found in a mixed, not in a pure form, and therefore one could only obtain it by reduction from the mixed ore.

Religions are necessary for the people, and an inestimable benefit to them. But if they oppose themselves to the progress of mankind in the knowledge of the truth, they must with the utmost possible forbearance be set aside. And to require that a great mind—a Shakspeare; a Goethe—should make the dogmas of any religion implicitly, *bonâ fide et sensu proprio,* his conviction is to require that a giant should put on the shoe of a dwarf.

Religions, being calculated with reference to the power of comprehension of the great mass of men, can only have indirect, not immediate truth. To require of them the latter is as if one wished to read the letters set up in the form-chase, instead of their impression. The value of a religion will accordingly depend upon the greater or less content of truth which it contains under the veil of allegory, and then upon the greater or less distinctness with which it becomes visible through this veil, thus upon the transparency of the latter. It almost seems that, as the oldest languages are the most perfect, so also are the oldest religions. If I were to take the results of my philosophy as the standard of truth, I would be obliged to concede to Buddhism the pre-eminence over the rest. In any case it must be a satisfaction to me to see my teaching in such close agreement with a religion which the majority of men upon the earth hold as their own; for it numbers far more adherents than any other. This agreement, however, must be the more satisfactory to me because in my philosophising I have certainly not been under its influence. For up till 1818, when my work appeared, there were very few, exceedingly incomplete and scanty, accounts of Buddhism to be found in Europe, which were almost entirely limited to a few essays in the earlier volumes of "Asiatic Researches," and were principally concerned with the Buddhism of the Burmese. Only since then has fuller information about this religion gradually reached us, chiefly through the profound and instructive essays of the meritorious member of the St. Petersburg Academy, J. J. Schmidt, in the proceedings of his Academy, and then little by little through several English and French scholars, so that I was able to give a fairly numerous list of the best works on this religion in my work, "On the Will in Nature," under the heading *Sinology*. Unfortunately Csoma Körösi, that persevering Hungarian, who, in order to study the language and sacred writings of Buddhism, spent many years in Tibet, and for the most part in Buddhist monasteries, was carried off by death just as he was beginning to work out for us the results of his researches. I cannot, however, deny the pleasure with which I read, in his provisional accounts, several passages cited directly from the Kahgyur itself; for example, the following conversation of the dying Buddha with Brahma, who is doing him homage: "There is a description of their conversation on the subject of creation,—by whom was the world made?

Shakya asks several questions of Brahma,—whether was it he who made or produced such and such things, and endowed or blessed them with such and such virtues or properties,—whether was it he who caused the several revolutions in the destruction and regeneration of the world. He denies that he had ever done anything to that effect. At last he himself asks Shakya how the world was made,—by whom? Here are attributed all changes in the world to the moral works of the animal beings, and it is stated that in the world all is illusion, there is no reality in the things; all is empty. Brahma, being instructed in his doctrine, becomes his follower" (Asiatic Researches, vol. xx. p. 434).

I cannot place, as is always done, the fundamental difference of all religions in the question whether they are monotheistic, polytheistic, pantheistic, or atheistic, but only in the question whether they are optimistic or pessimistic, that is, whether they present the existence of the world as justified by itself, and therefore praise and value it, or regard it as something that can only be conceived as the consequence of our guilt, and therefore properly ought not to be, because they recognise that pain and death cannot lie in the eternal, original, and immutable order of things, in that which in every respect ought to be. The power by virtue of which Christianity was able to overcome first Judaism, and then the heathenism of Greece and Rome, lies solely in its pessimism, in the confession that our state is both exceedingly wretched and sinful, while Judaism and heathenism were optimistic. That truth, profoundly and painfully felt by all, penetrated, and bore in its train the need of redemption.

I turn to a general consideration of the other kind of metaphysics, that which has its authentication in itself, and is called *philosophy*. I remind the reader of its origin, mentioned above, in a *wonder* concerning the world and our own existence, inasmuch as these press upon the intellect as a riddle, the solution of which therefore occupies mankind without intermission. Here, then, I wish first of all to draw attention to the fact that this could not be the case if, in Spinoza's sense, which in our own day has so often been brought forward again under modern forms and expositions as pantheism, the world were an "*absolute substance*," and therefore an *absolutely necessary existence.* For this means that it exists with so great a necessity that beside it every other necessity comprehensible to our understanding as such must appear as an accident. It would then be something which comprehended in itself not only all actual but also all possible existence, so that, as Spinoza indeed declares, its possibility and its actuality would be absolutely one. Its non-being would therefore be impossibility itself; thus it would be something the non-being or other-being of which must be completely inconceivable, and which could therefore just as little be thought away as, for example, space or time. And since, further, *we ourselves* would be parts, modes, attributes, or accidents of such an absolute substance, which would be the only thing that, in any sense, could ever or anywhere exist, our and its existence, together with its properties, would necessarily be very far from presenting itself to us as remarkable, problematical, and indeed as an unfathomable and ever-disquieting riddle, but, on the contrary, would be far more self-evident than that two and two make four. For we would necessarily be incapable of thinking anything else than that the world is, and is, as it is; and therefore we would necessarily be as little conscious of its existence *as such, i.e.,* as a problem for reflection, as we are of the incredibly fast motion of our planet.

All this, however, is absolutely not the case. Only to the brutes, who are without thought, does the world and existence appear as a matter of course; to man, on the contrary, it is a problem, of which even the most uneducated and narrow-minded becomes vividly conscious in certain brighter moments, but which enters more distinctly and more permanently into the consciousness of each one of us the clearer and more enlightened that consciousness is, and the more material for thought it has acquired through culture, which all ultimately rises, in minds that are naturally adapted for philosophising, to that *wonder* which comprehends in its whole magnitude that problem which unceasingly occupies the nobler portion of mankind in every age and in every land, and gives it no rest. In fact, the pendulum which keeps in motion the clock of metaphysics, that never runs down, is the consciousness that the non-existence of this world is just as possible as its existence. Thus, then, the Spinozistic view of it as an absolutely necessary existence, that is, as something that absolutely and in every sense ought to and must be, is a false one. Even simple Theism, since in its cosmological proof it tacitly starts by inferring the previous non-existence of the world from its existence, thereby assumes beforehand that the world is something contingent. Nay, what is more, we very soon apprehend the world as something the non-existence of which is not only conceivable, but indeed preferable to its existence. Therefore our wonder at it easily passes into a brooding over the *fatality* which could yet call forth its existence, and by virtue of which such stupendous power as is demanded for the production and maintenance of such a world could be directed so much against its own interest. The philosophical astonishment is therefore at bottom perplexed and melancholy; philosophy, like the overture to "Don Juan," commences with a minor chord. It follows from this that it can neither be Spinozism nor optimism. The more special nature, which has just been indicated, of the astonishment which leads us to philosophise clearly springs from the sight of the *suffering and the wickedness* in the world, which, even if they were in the most just proportion to each other, and also were far outweighed by good, are yet something which absolutely and in general ought not to be. But since now nothing can come out of nothing, these also must have their germ in the origin or in the kernel of the world itself. It is hard for us to assume this if we look at the magnitude, the order and completeness, of the physical world, for it seems to us that what had the power to produce such a world must have been able to avoid the suffering and the wickedness. That assumption (the truest expression of which is Ormuzd and Ahrimines), it is easy to conceive, is hardest of all for Theism. Therefore the freedom of the will was primarily invented to account for wickedness. But this is only a concealed way of making something out of nothing, for it assumes an *Operari* that proceeded from no *Esse* (see *Die beiden Grundprobleme der Ethik*, p. 58, *et seq.*; second edition, p. 57 *et seq.*). Then it was sought to get rid of evil by attributing it to matter, or to unavoidable necessity, whereby the devil, who is really the right *Expediens ad hoc*, was unwillingly set aside. To evil also belongs *death;* but wickedness is only the throwing of the existing evil from oneself on to another. Thus, as was said

above, it is wickedness, evil, and death that qualify and inten-
sify the philosophical astonishment. Not merely that the world
exists, but still more that it is such a wretched world, is the
punctum pruriens of metaphysics, the problem which awakens
in mankind an unrest that cannot be quieted by scepticism
nor yet by criticism.

We find *physics* also (in the widest sense of the word)
occupied with the explanation of the phenomena in the world.
But it lies in the very nature of its explanations themselves that
they cannot be sufficient. Physics cannot stand on its own
feet, but requires a metaphysic to lean upon, whatever airs it
may give itself towards the latter. For it explains the phenomena by something still more unknown than they are themselves; by laws of nature, resting upon forces of nature, to
which the power of life also belongs. Certainly the whole present condition of all things in the world, or in nature, must
necessarily be explicable from purely physical causes. But such
an explanation—supposing one actually succeeded so far as to
be able to give it—must always just as necessarily be tainted
with two imperfections (as it were with two sores, or like
Achilles with the vulnerable heel, or the devil with the horse's
hoof), on account of which everything so explained really remains still unexplained. First with this imperfection, that the
beginning of every explanatory chain of causes and effects,
i.e., of connected changes, can absolutely *never* be reached,
but, just like the limits of the world in space and time, unceasingly recedes *in infinito*. Secondly with this, that the whole
of the efficient causes out of which everything is explained
constantly rest upon something which is completely inexplicable, the original *qualities* of things and the *natural forces* which
play a prominent part among them, by virtue of which they
produce a specific kind of effect, *e.g.*, weight, hardness, impulsive force, elasticity, warmth, electricity, chemical forces
&c., and which now remain in every explanation which is
given, like an unknown quantity, which absolutely cannot be
eliminated, in an otherwise perfectly solved algebraical equa-
tion. Accordingly there is no fragment of clay, however little
worth, that is not entirely composed of inexplicable qualities.
Thus these two inevitable defects in every purely physical,
i.e., causal, explanation show that such an explanation can only

be *relative*, and that its whole method and nature cannot be
the only one, the ultimate and thus the sufficient one, *i.e.*,
cannot be the method of explanation that can ever lead to the
satisfactory solution of the difficult riddle of things, and to the
true understanding of the world and existence; but that the
physical explanation in general and as such requires further a
metaphysical explanation, which affords us the key to all its
assumptions, but just on this account must necessarily follow
quite a different path. The first step to this is that one should
bring to distinct consciousness and firmly retain the difference
of the two, hence the difference between *physics* and *meta-*
physics. It rests in general on the Kantian distinction between
phenomenon and *thing in itself*. Just because Kant held the
latter to be absolutely unknowable, there was, according to
him, no *metaphysics*, but merely immanent knowledge, *i.e.*,
physics, which throughout can speak only of phenomena, and
also a critique of the reason which strives after metaphysics.
Here, however, in order to show the true point of connection
between my philosophy and that of Kant, I shall anticipate
the second book, and give prominence to the fact that Kant,
in his beautiful exposition of the compatibility of freedom and
necessity (Critique of Pure Reason, first edition, p. 532–554;
and Critique of Practical Reason, p. 224–231 of Rosenkranz's
edition), shows how one and the same action may in one aspect be perfectly explicable as necessarily arising from the
character of the man, the influence to which he has been
subject in the course of his life, and the motives which are
now present to him, but yet in another aspect must be regarded as the work of his free will; and in the same sense he
says, § 53 of the "Prolegomena": "Certainly natural necessity
will belong to every connection of cause and effect in the world
of sense; yet, on the other hand, freedom will be conceded to
that cause which is not itself a phenomenon (though indeed
it is the ground of phenomena), thus nature and freedom
may without contradiction be attributed to the same thing,
but in a different reference—in the one case as a phenomenon,
in the other case as a thing in itself." What, then, Kant teaches
of the phenomenon of man and his action my teaching extends
to *all* phenomena in nature, in that it makes the *will* as a
thing in itself their foundation. This proceeding is justified first

of all by the fact that it must not be assumed that man is specifically *toto genere* radically different from the other beings and things in nature, but rather that he is different only in degree. I turn back from this premature digression to our consideration of the inadequacy of physics to afford us the ultimate explanation of things. I say, then, everything certainly is physical, but yet nothing is explicable physically. As for the motion of the projected bullet, so also for the thinking of the brain, a physical explanation must ultimately be in itself possible, which would make the latter just as comprehensible as is the former. But even the former, which we imagine we understand so perfectly, is at bottom as obscure to us as the latter; for what the inner nature of expansion in space may be —of impenetrability, mobility, hardness, elasticity, and gravity remains, after all physical explanations, a mystery, just as much as thought. But because in the case of thought the inexplicable appears most immediately, a spring was at once made here from physics to metaphysics, and a substance of quite a different kind from all corporeal substances was hypostatised —a soul was set up in the brain. But if one had not been so dull as only to be capable of being struck by the most remarkable of phenomena, one would have had to explain digestion by a soul in the stomach, vegetation by a soul in the plant, affinity by a soul in the reagents, nay, the falling of a stone by a soul in the stone. For the quality of every unorganised body is just as mysterious as the life in the living body. In the same way, therefore, the physical explanation strikes everywhere upon what is metaphysical, by which it is annihilated, *i.e.*, it ceases to be explanation. Strictly speaking, it may be asserted that no natural science really achieves anything more than what is also achieved by Botany: the bringing together of similars, classification. A physical system which asserted that its explanations of things—in the particular from causes, and in general from forces—were really sufficient, and thus exhausted the nature of the world, would be the true *Naturalism*. From Leucippus, Democritus, and Epicurus down to the *Système de la Nature*, and further, to Delamark, Cabanis, and to the materialism that has again been warmed up in the last few years, we can trace the persistent attempt to set up a *system of physics without metaphysics*, that is, a system which would make the phenomenon the thing in itself. But all their explanations seek to conceal from the explainers themselves and from others that they simply assume the principal matter without more ado. They endeavour to show that all phenomena, even those of mind, are physical. And they are right; only they do not see that all that is physical is in another aspect also metaphysical. But, without Kant, this is indeed difficult to see, for it presupposes the distinction of the phenomenon from the thing in itself. Yet without this Aristotle, much as he was inclined to empiricism, and far as he was removed from the Platonic hyperphysics, kept himself free from this limited point of view. Such an *absolute system of physics* as is described above, which leaves room for no *metaphysics*, would make the *Natura naturata* into the *Natura naturans;* it would be physics established on the throne of metaphysics, yet it would comport itself in this high position almost like Holberg's theatrical would-be politician who was made burgomaster. Indeed behind the reproach of atheism, in itself absurd, and for the most part malicious, there lies, as its inner meaning and truth, which gives it strength, the obscure conception of such an absolute system of physics without metaphysics. Certainly such a system would necessarily be destructive of ethics; and while Theism has falsely been held to be inseparable from morality, this is really true only of *metaphysics in general, i.e.,* of the knowledge that the order of nature is not the only and absolute order of things. Therefore we may set up this as the necessary *Credo* of all just and good men: "I believe in metaphysics." In this respect it is important and necessary that one should convince oneself of the untenable nature of an *absolute system of physics,* all the more as this, the true *naturalism,* is a point of view which of its own accord and ever anew presses itself upon a man, and can only be done away with through profound speculation. In this respect, however, all kinds of systems and faiths, so far and so long as they are accepted, certainly serve as a substitute for such speculation. But that a fundamentally false view presses itself upon man of its own accord, and must first be skilfully removed, is explicable from the fact that the intellect is not originally intended to instruct us concerning the nature of things, but only to show us their relations, with reference to our will; it is, as we shall find in the second book, only the medium of motives. Now, that the world schematises itself in the intellect in a manner which exhibits quite a different order of things from the absolutely true one, because it shows us, not their kernel, but only their outer shell, happens accidentally, and cannot be used as a reproach to the intellect; all the less as it nevertheless finds in itself the means of rectifying this error, in that it arrives at the distinction between the phenomenal appearance and the inner being of things, which distinction existed in substance at all times, only for the most part was very imperfectly brought to consciousness, and therefore was inadequately expressed, indeed often appeared in strange clothing. The Christian mystics, when they call it the *light of nature*, declare the intellect to be inadequate to the comprehension of the true nature of things. It is, as it were, a mere surface force, like electricity, and does not penetrate to the inner being.

The insufficiency of pure naturalism appears, as we have said, first of all, on the empirical path itself, through the circumstance that every physical explanation explains the particular from its cause; but the chain of these causes, as we know *a priori*, and therefore with perfect certainty, runs back to infinity, so that absolutely no cause could ever be the first. Then, however, the effect of every cause is referred to a law of nature, and this finally to a force of nature, which now remains as the absolutely inexplicable. But this inexplicable, to which all phenomena of this so clearly given and naturally explicable world, from the highest to the lowest, are referred, just shows that the whole nature of such explanation is only conditional, as it were only *ex concessis*, and by no means the true and sufficient one; therefore I said above that physically everything and nothing is explicable. That absolutely inexplicable element which pervades all phenomena, which is most striking in the highest, *e.g.*, in generation, but yet is just as truly present in the lowest, *e.g.*, in mechanical phenomena, points to an entirely different kind of order of things lying at the foundation of the physical order, which is just what Kant calls the order of things in themselves, and which is the goal of metaphysics. But, secondly, the insufficiency of pure naturalism comes out clearly from that fundamental philosophical truth, which we have fully considered in the first half of this book, and which is also the theme of the "Critique of Pure Reason"; the truth that every *object*, both as regards its objective existence in general and as regards the manner (forms) of this existence, is throughout conditioned by the knowing *subject*, hence is merely a phenomenon, not a thing in itself. This is explained in § 7 of the first volume, and it is there shown that nothing can be more clumsy than that, after the manner of all materialists, one should blindly take the objective as simply given in order to derive everything from it without paying any regard to the subjective, through which, however, nay, in which alone the former exists. Samples of this procedure are most readily afforded us by the fashionable materialism of our own day, which has thereby become a philosophy well suited for barbers' and apothecaries' apprentices. For it, in its innocence, matter, assumed without reflection as absolutely real, is the thing in self, and the one capacity of a thing in itself is impulsive force, for all other qualities can only be manifestations of this.

With naturalism, then, or the purely physical way of looking at things, we shall never attain our end; it is like a sum that never comes out. Causal series without beginning or end, fundamental forces which are inscrutable, endless space, beginningless time, infinite divisibility of matter, and all this further conditioned by a knowing brain, in which alone it exists just like a dream, and without which it vanishes—constitute the labyrinth in which naturalism leads us ceaselessly round. The height to which in our time the natural sciences have risen in this respect entirely throws into the shade all previous centuries, and is a summit which mankind reaches for the first time. But however great are the advances which *physics* (understood in the wide sense of the ancients) may make, not the smallest step towards *metaphysics* is thereby taken, just as a plane can never obtain cubical content by being indefinitely extended. For all such advances will only perfect our knowledge of the *phenomenon;* while *metaphysics* strives to pass beyond the phenomenal appearance itself, to that which so appears. And if indeed it had the assistance of an entire and complete experience, it would, as regards the main point, be in no way advantaged by it. Nay, even if one wandered through all the planets and fixed stars, one would thereby have made no step in *metaphysics*. It is rather the case that the greatest advances of physics will make the need of metaphysics ever more felt; for it is just the corrected, extended, and more thorough knowledge of nature which, on the one hand, always undermines and ultimately overthrows the metaphysical assumptions which till then have prevailed, but, on the other hand, presents the problem of metaphysics itself more distinctly, more correctly, and more fully, and separates it more clearly from all that is merely physical; moreover, the more perfectly and accurately known nature of the particular thing more pressingly demands the explanation of the whole and the general, which, the more correctly, thoroughly, and completely it is known empirically, only presents itself as the more mysterious. Certainly the individual, simple investigator of nature, in a special branch of physics, does not at once become clearly conscious of all this; he rather sleeps contentedly by the side of his chosen maid, in the house of Odysseus, banishing all thoughts of Penelope. Hence we see at the present day the *husk of nature* investigated in its minutest details, the intestines of intestinal worms and the vermin of vermin known to a nicety. But if some one comes, as, for example, I do, and speaks of the *kernel of nature*, they will not listen; they even think it has nothing to do with the matter, and go on sifting their husks. One finds oneself tempted to call that over-microscopical and micrological investigator of nature the cotquean of nature. But those persons who believe that crucibles and retorts are the true and only source of all wisdom are in their own way just as perverse as were formerly their antipodes the Scholastics. As the latter, absolutely confined to their abstract conceptions, used these as their weapons, neither knowing nor investigating anything outside them, so the former, absolutely confined to their empiricism, allow nothing to be true except what their eyes behold, and believe they can thus arrive at the ultimate ground of things, not discerning that between the phenomenon and that which manifests itself in it, the thing in itself, there is a deep gulf, a radical difference, which can only be cleared up by the knowledge and accurate delimitation of the subjective element of the phenomenon, and the insight that the ultimate and most important conclusions concerning the nature of things can only be drawn from self-consciousness; yet without all this one cannot advance a step beyond what is directly given to the senses, thus can get no further than to the problem. Yet, on the other hand, it is to be observed that the most perfect possible knowledge of nature is the corrected *statement of the problem* of metaphysics. Therefore no one ought to venture upon this without having first acquired a knowledge of all the branches of natural science, which, though general, shall be thorough, clear, and connected. For the problem must precede its solution. Then, however, the investigator must turn his glance inward; for the intellectual and ethical phenomena are more important than the physical, in the same proportion as, for example, animal magnetism is a far more important phenomenon than mineral magnetism. The last fundamental secret man carries within himself, and this is accessible to him in the most immediate manner; therefore it is only here that he can hope to find the key to the riddle of the world and gain a clue to the nature of all things. The special province of metaphysics thus certainly lies in what has been called mental philosophy.

> The ranks of living creatures thou dost lead
> Before me, teaching me to know my brothers
> In air and water and the silent wood:
>
> .   .   .   .
>
> Then to the cave secure thou leadest me,
> Then show'st me mine own self, and in my breast
> The deep, mysterious miracles unfold.
>
> —FAUST

Finally, then, as regards the *source or the foundation* of metaphysical knowledge, I have already declared myself above to be opposed to the assumption, which is even repeated by Kant, that it must lie *in mere conceptions*. In no knowledge can conceptions be what is first; for they are always derived from some perception. What has led, however, to that assumption is probably the example of mathematics. Mathematics can leave perception altogether, and, as is especially the case in algebra, trigonometry, and analysis, can operate with purely abstract conceptions, nay, with conceptions which are represented only by signs instead of words, and can yet

arrive at a perfectly certain result, which is still so remote
that any one who adhered to the firm ground of perception
could not arrive at it. But the possibility of this depends, as
Kant has clearly shown, on the fact that the conceptions of
mathematics are derived from the most certain and definite
of all perceptions, from the *a priori* and yet intuitively known
relations of quantity, and can therefore be constantly realised
again and controlled by these, either arithmetically, by performing the calculations which are merely indicated by those
signs, or geometrically, by means of what Kant calls the construction of the conceptions. This advantage, on the other
hand, is not possessed by the conceptions out of which it was
believed metaphysics could be built up; such, for example, as
essence, being, substance, perfection, necessity, reality, finite,
infinite, absolute, ground, &c. For such conceptions are by no
means original, as fallen from heaven, or innate; but they also,
like all conceptions, are derived from perceptions; and as, unlike the conceptions of mathematics, they do not contain the
mere form of perception, but more, empirical perceptions must
lie at their foundation. Thus nothing can be drawn from them
which the empirical perceptions did not also contain, that is,
nothing which was not a matter of experience, and which,
since these conceptions are very wide abstractions, we would
receive with much greater certainty at first hand from experience. For from conceptions nothing more can ever be drawn
than the perceptions from which they are derived contain. If
we desire pure conceptions, *i.e.*, such as have no empirical
source, the only ones that can be produced are those which
concern space and time, *i.e.*, the merely formal part of perception, consequently only the mathematical conceptions, or
at most also the conception of causality, which indeed does
not originate in experience, but yet only comes into consciousness by means of it (first in sense-perception); therefore experience indeed is only possible by means of it; but it also is
only valid in the sphere of experience, on which account Kant
has shown that it only serves to communicate the connection
of experience, and not to transcend it; that thus it admits only
of physical application, not of metaphysical. Certainly only its
a priori origin can give apodictic certainty to any knowledge;
but this limits it to the mere *form* of experience in general, for

it shows that it is conditioned by the subjective nature of the intellect. Such knowledge, then, far from taking us beyond experience, gives only one *part* of experience itself, the *formal* part, which belongs to it throughout, and therefore is universal, consequently mere form without content. Since now metaphysics can least of all be confined to this, it must have also *empirical* sources of knowledge; therefore that preconceived idea of a metaphysic to be found purely *a priori* is necessarily vain. It is really a *petitio principii* of Kant's, which he expresses most distinctly in § 1 of the Prolegomena, that metaphysics must not draw its fundamental conceptions and principles from experience. In this it is assumed beforehand that only what we knew *before* all experience can extend beyond all possible experience. Supported by this, Kant then comes and shows that all such knowledge is nothing more than the form of the intellect for the purpose of experience, and consequently can never lead beyond experience, from which he then rightly deduces the impossibility of all metaphysics. But does it not rather seem utterly perverse that in order to discover the secret of experience, *i.e.*, of the world which alone lies before us, we should look quite away from it, ignore its content, and take and use for its material only the empty forms of which we are conscious *a priori?* Is it not rather in keeping with the matter that *the science of experience in general,* and as such, should also be drawn from experience? Its problem itself is given it empirically; why should not the solution of it call in the assistance of experience? Is it not senseless that he who speaks of the nature of things should not look at things themselves, but should confine himself to certain abstract conceptions? The task of metaphysics is certainly not the observation of particular experiences, but yet it is the correct explanation of experience as a whole. Its foundation must therefore, at any rate, be of an empirical nature. Indeed the *a priori* nature of a part of human knowledge will be apprehended by it as a given *fact,* from which it will infer the subjective origin of the same. Only because the consciousness of its *a priori* nature accompanies it is it called by Kant *transcendental* as distinguished from *transcendent,* which signifies "passing beyond all possibility of experience," and has its opposite in *immanent, i.e.*, remaining within the limits of experience. I gladly recall the original meaning of this expression introduced by Kant, with which, as also with that of the Categories, and many others, the apes of philosophy carry on their game at the present day. Now, besides this, the source of the knowledge of metaphysics is not *outer* experience alone, but also *inner*. Indeed, what is most peculiar to it, that by which the decisive step which alone can solve the great question becomes possible for it, consists, as I have fully and thoroughly proved in "On the Will in Nature," under the heading, "Physical Astronomy," in this, that at the right place it combines outer experience with inner, and uses the latter as a key to the former.

The origin of metaphysics in empirical sources of knowledge, which is here set forth, and which cannot fairly be denied, deprives it certainly of that kind of apodictic certainty which is only possible through knowledge *a priori*. This remains the possession of logic and mathematics—sciences, however, which really only teach what every one knows already, though not distinctly. At most the primary elements of natural science may also be deduced from knowledge *a priori*. By this confession metaphysics only surrenders an ancient claim, which, according to what has been said above, rested upon misunderstanding, and against which the great diversity and changeableness of metaphysical systems, and also the constantly accompanying scepticism, in every age has testified. Yet against the possibility of metaphysics in general this changeableness cannot be urged, for the same thing affects just as much all branches of natural science, chemistry, physics, geology, zoology, &c., and even history has not remained exempt from it. But when once, as far as the limits of human intellect allow, a true system of metaphysics shall have been found, the unchangeableness of a science which is known *a priori* will yet belong to it; for its foundation can only be *experience in general*, and not the particular and special experiences by which, on the other hand, the natural sciences are constantly modified and new material is always being provided for history. For experience as a whole and in general will never change its character for a new one.

The next question is: How can a science drawn from experience pass beyond it and so merit the name of metaphysics?

It cannot do so perhaps in the same way as we find a fourth number from three proportionate ones, or a triangle from two sides and an angle. This was the way of the pre-Kantian dogmatism, which, according to certain laws known to us *a priori*, sought to reason from the given to the not given, from the consequent to the reason, thus from experience to that which could not possibly be given in any experience. Kant proved the impossibility of a metaphysic upon this path, in that he showed that although these laws were not drawn from experience, they were only valid for experience. He therefore rightly taught that in such a way we cannot transcend the possibility of all experience. But there are other paths to metaphysics. The whole of experience is like a cryptograph, and philosophy the deciphering of it, the correctness of which is proved by the connection appearing everywhere. If this whole is only profoundly enough comprehended, and the inner experience is connected with the outer, it must be capable of being *interpreted, explained* from itself. Since Kant has irrefutably proved to us that experience in general proceeds from two elements, the forms of knowledge and the inner nature of things, and that these two may be distinguished in experience from each other, as that of which we are conscious *a priori* and that which is added *a posteriori*, it is possible, at least in general, to say, what in the given experience, which is primarily merely phenomenal, belongs to the *form* of this phenomenon, conditioned by the intellect, and what, after deducting this, remains over for the *thing in itself*. And although no one can discern the thing in itself through the veil of the forms of perception, on the other hand every one carries it in himself, indeed is it himself; therefore in self-consciousness it must be in some way accessible to him, even though only conditionally. Thus the bridge by which metaphysics passes beyond experience is nothing else than that analysis of experience into phenomenon and thing in itself in which I have placed Kant's greatest merit. For it contains the proof of a kernel of the phenomenon different from the phenomenon itself. This can indeed never be entirely separated from the phenomenon and regarded in itself as an *ens extramundanum*, but is always known only in its relations to and connections with the phenomenon itself. But the interpretation and explanation of the latter, in relation to the former, which is its inner kernel, is capable of affording us information with regard to it which does not otherwise come into consciousness. In this sense, then, metaphysics goes beyond the phenomenon, *i.e.*, nature, to that which is concealed in or behind it, always regarding it, however, merely as that which manifests itself in the phenomenon, not as independent of all phenomenal appearance; it therefore remains immanent, and does not become transcendent. For it never disengages itself entirely from experience, but remains merely its interpretation and explanation, since it never speaks of the thing in itself otherwise than in its relation to the phenomenon. This at least is the sense in which I, with reference throughout to the limitations of human knowledge proved by Kant, have attempted to solve the problem of metaphysics. Therefore his Prolegomena to future metaphysics will be valid and suitable for mine also. Accordingly it never really goes beyond experience, but only discloses the true understanding of the world which lies before it in experience. It is neither, according to the definition of metaphysics which even Kant repeats, a science of mere conceptions, nor is it a system of deductions from *a priori* principles, the uselessness of which for the *end* of metaphysics has been shown by Kant. But it is rational knowledge, drawn from perception of the external actual world and the information which the most intimate fact of self-consciousness affords us concerning it, deposited in distinct conceptions. It is accordingly the science of experience; but its subject and its source is not particular experiences, but the totality of all experience. I completely accept Kant's doctrine that the world of experience is merely phenomenal, and that the *a priori* knowledge is valid only in relation to phenomena; but I add that just as phenomenal appearance, it is the manifestation of that which appears, and with him I call this the thing in itself. This must therefore express its nature and character in the world of experience, and consequently it must be possible to interpret these from this world, and indeed from the matter, not the mere form, of experience. Accordingly philosophy is nothing but the correct and universal understanding of experience itself, the true exposition of its meaning and content. To this the metaphysical, *i.e.*, that which is merely clothed in the phenomenon and veiled in its forms, is that which is related to it as thought to words.

Such a deciphering of the world with reference to that which manifests itself in it must receive its confirmation from itself, through the agreement with each other in which it places the very diverse phenomena of the world, and which without it we do not perceive. If we find a document the alphabet of which is unknown, we endeavour to make it out until we hit upon an hypothesis as to the significance of the letters in accordance with which they make up comprehensible words and connected sentences. Then, however, there remains no doubt as to the correctness of the deciphering, because it is not possible that the agreement and connection in which all the letters of that writing are placed by this explanation is merely accidental, and that by attributing quite a different value to the letters we could also recognise words and sentences in this arrangement of them. In the same way the deciphering of the world must completely prove itself from itself. It must throw equal light upon all the phenomena of the world, and also bring the most heterogeneous into agreement, so that the contradiction between those which are most in contrast may be abolished. This proof from itself is the mark of genuineness. For every false deciphering, even if it is suitable for some phenomena, will conflict all the more glaringly with the rest. So, for example, the optimism of Leibnitz conflicts with the palpable misery of existence; the doctrine of Spinoza, that the world is the only possible and absolutely necessary substance, is incompatible with our wonder at its existence and nature; the Wolfian doctrine, that man obtains his *Existentia* and *Essentia* from a will foreign to himself, is contradicted by our moral responsibility for the actions which proceed with strict necessity from these, in conflict with the motives; the oft-repeated doctrine of the progressive development of man to an ever higher perfection, or in general of any kind of becoming by means of the process of the world, is opposed to the *a priori* knowledge that at any point of time an infinite time has already run its course, and consequently all that is supposed to come with time would necessarily have already existed; and in this way an interminable list might be given of the contradictions of dogmatic assumptions with the given reality of things. On the other hand, I must deny that any doctrine of my philosophy could fairly be added to such a list, because each of them has been thought out in the presence of the perceived reality, and none of them has its root in abstract conceptions alone. There is yet in it a fundamental thought which is applied to all the phenomena of the world as their key; but it proves itself to be the right alphabet at the application of which all words and sentences have sense and significance. The discovered answer to a riddle shows itself to be the right one by the fact that all that is said in the riddle is suitable to it. In the same way my doctrine introduces agreement and connection into the confusion of the contrasting phenomena of this world, and solves the innumerable contradictions which, when regarded from any other point of view, it presents. Therefore, so far, it is like a sum that comes out right, yet by no means in the sense that it leaves no problem over to solve, no possible question unanswered. To assert anything of that sort would be a presumptuous denial of the limits of human knowledge in general. Whatever torch we may kindle, and whatever space it may light, our horizon will always remain bounded by profound night. For the ultimate solution of the riddle of the world must necessarily be concerned with the things in themselves, no longer with the phenomena. But all our forms of knowledge are adapted to the phenomena alone; therefore we must comprehend everything through coexistence, succession, and causal relations. These forms, however, have meaning and significance only with reference to the phenomenon; the things in themselves and their possible relations cannot be apprehended by means of those forms. Therefore the actual, positive solution of the riddle of the world must be something that human intellect is absolutely incapable of grasping and thinking; so that if a being of a higher kind were to come and take all pains to impart it to us, we would be absolutely incapable of understanding anything of his expositions. Those, therefore, who profess to know the ultimate, *i.e.*, the first ground of things, thus a primordial being, an absolute, or whatever else they choose to call it, together with the process, the reasons, motives, or whatever it may be, in consequence of which the world arises from it, or springs, or falls, or is produced, set in existence, "discharged," and ushered forth, are playing tricks, are vain boasters, when indeed they are not charlatans.

I regard it as a great excellence of my philosophy that all its truths have been found independently of each other, by contemplation of the real world; but their unity and agreement, about which I had been unconcerned, has always afterwards appeared of itself. Hence also it is rich, and has widespreading roots in the ground of perceptible reality, from which all nourishment of abstract truths springs; and hence, again, it is not wearisome—a quality which, to judge from the philosophical writings of the last fifty years, one might regard as essential to philosophy. If, on the other hand, all the doctrines of a philosophy are merely deduced the one out of the other, and ultimately indeed all out of one first principle, it must be poor and meagre, and consequently wearisome, for nothing can follow from a proposition except what it really already says itself. Moreover, in this case everything depends upon the correctness of *one* proposition, and by a single mistake in the deduction the truth of the whole would be endangered. Still less security is given by the systems which start from an intellectual intuition, *i.e.*, a kind of ecstasy or clairvoyance. All knowledge so obtained must be rejected as subjective, individual, and consequently problematical. Even if it actually existed it would not be communicable, for only the normal knowledge of the brain is communicable; if it is abstract, through conceptions and words; if purely perceptible or concrete, through works of art.

If, as so often happens, metaphysics is reproached with having made so little progress, it ought also to be considered that no other science has grown up like it under constant oppression, none has been so hampered and hindered from without as it has always been by the religion of every land, which, everywhere in possession of a monopoly of metaphysical knowledge, regards metaphysics as a weed growing beside it, as an unlicensed worker, as a horde of gipsies, and as a rule tolerates it only under the condition that it accommodates itself to serve and follow it. For where has there ever been true freedom of thought? It has been vaunted sufficiently; but whenever it wishes to go further than perhaps to differ about the subordinate dogmas of the religion of the country, a holy shudder seizes the prophets of tolerance, and they say: "Not a step further!" What progress of metaphysics was possible under such oppression? Nay, this constraint which the privileged metaphysics exercises is not confined to the *communication* of thoughts, but extends to *thinking* itself, for its dogmas are so firmly imprinted in the tender, plastic, trustful, and thoughtless age of childhood, with studied solemnity and serious airs, that from that time forward they grow with the brain, and almost assume the nature of innate thoughts, which some philosophers have therefore really held them to be, and still more have pretended to do so. Yet nothing can so firmly resist the comprehension of even the *problem* of metaphysics as a previous solution of it intruded upon and early implanted in the mind. For the necessary starting-point for all genuine philosophy is the deep feeling of the Socratic: "This one thing I know, that I know nothing." The ancients were in this respect in a better position than we are, for their national religions certainly limited somewhat the imparting of thoughts; but they did not interfere with the freedom of thought itself, because they were not formally and solemnly impressed upon children, and in general were not taken so seriously. Therefore in metaphysics the ancients are still our teachers.

Whenever metaphysics is reproached with its small progress, and with not having yet reached its goal in spite of such sustained efforts, one ought further to consider that in the meanwhile it has constantly performed the invaluable service ·of limiting the boundless claims of the privileged metaphysics, and yet at the same time combating naturalism and materialism proper, which are called forth by it as an inevitable reaction. Consider to what a pitch the arrogance of the priesthood of every religion would rise if the belief in their doctrines was as firm and blind as they really wish. Look back also at the wars, disturbances, rebellions, and revolutions in Europe from the eighth to the eighteenth century; how few will be found that have not had as their essence, or their pretext, some controversy about beliefs, thus a metaphysical problem, which became the occasion of exciting nations against each other. Yet is that whole thousand years a continual slaughter, now on the battlefield, now on the scaffold, now in the streets, in metaphysical interests! I wish I had an authentic list of all crimes which Christianity has really prevented, and all good deeds it has really performed, that I might be able to place them in the other scale of the balance.

Lastly, as regards the *obligations* of metaphysics, it has only one; for it is one which endures no other beside it—the obligation to be *true*. If one would impose other obligations upon it besides this, such as to be spiritualistic, optimistic, monotheistic, or even only to be moral, one cannot know beforehand whether this would not interfere with the fulfilment of that first obligation, without which all its other achievements must clearly be worthless. A given philosophy has accordingly no other standard of its value than that of truth. For the rest, philosophy is essentially *world-wisdom:* its problem is the world. It has to do with this alone, and leaves the gods in peace —expects, however, in return, to be left in peace by them.

II

TRANSCENDENT CONSIDERATIONS CONCERNING THE WILL AS THING IN ITSELF

(CHAPTER XXV *from* SUPPLEMENTS TO THE SECOND
BOOK OF THE WORLD AS WILL AND IDEA)

Even the merely empirical consideration of nature recognises a constant transition from the simplest and most necessary manifestation of a universal force of nature up to the life and consciousness of man himself, through gentle gradations, and with only relative, and for the most part fluctuating, limits. Reflection, following this view, and penetrating somewhat more deeply into it, will soon be led to the conviction that in all these phenomena, the inner nature, that which manifests itself, that which appears, is one and the same, which comes forth ever more distinctly; and accordingly that what exhibits itself in a million forms of infinite diversity, and so carries on the most varied and the strangest play without beginning or end, this is one being which is so closely disguised behind all these masks that it does not even recognise itself, and therefore often treats itself roughly. We, however, have now entered even deeper into the secret, since by what has already been said we have been led to the insight that when in any phenomenon a *knowing consciousness* is added to that inner being which lies at the foundation of all phenomena, a consciousness which when directed inwardly becomes *self-consciousness,* then that inner being presents itself to this self-consciousness as that which is so familiar and so mysterious, and is denoted by the word *will.* Accordingly we have called that universal fundamental nature of all phenomena *the will,* after that manifestation in which it unveils itself to us most fully; and by this word nothing is further from our intention than to denote an unknown *x;* but, on the contrary, we denote that which at least on one side is infinitely better known and more intimate than anything else.

Let us now call to mind a truth, the fullest and most thorough proof of which will be found in my prize essay on the freedom of the will—the truth that on account of the absolutely universal validity of the law of causality, the conduct or the action of all existences in this world is always strictly *necessitated* by the causes which in each case call it forth. And in this respect it makes no difference whether such an action has been occasioned by causes in the strictest sense of the word, or by stimuli, or finally by motives, for these differences refer only to the grade of the susceptibility of the different kinds of existences. On this point we must entertain no illusion: the law of causality knows no exception; but everything, from the movement of a mote in a sunbeam to the most deeply considered action of man, is subject to it with equal strictness. Therefore, in the whole course of the world, neither could a mote in a sunbeam describe any other line in its flight than it has described, nor a man act any other way than he has acted; and no truth is more certain than this, that all that happens, be it small or great, happens with absolute *necessity*. Consequently, at every given moment of time, the whole condition of all things is firmly and accurately determined by the condition which has just preceded it, and so is it with the stream of time back to infinity and on to infinity. Thus the course of the world is like that of a clock after it has been put together and wound up; thus from this incontestable point of view it is a mere machine, the aim of which we cannot see. Even if, quite without justification, nay, at bottom, in spite of all conceivability and its conformity to law, one should assume a first beginning, nothing would thereby be essentially changed. For the arbitrarily assumed first condition of things would at its origin have irrevocably determined and fixed, both as a whole and down to the smallest detail, the state immediately following it; this state, again, would have determined the one succeeding it, and so on *per secula seculorum,* for the chain of causality, with its absolute strictness—this brazen bond of necessity and fate—introduces every phenomenon irrevocably and unalterably, just as it is. The difference merely amounts to this, that in the case of the one assumption we would have before us a piece of clockwork which had once been wound up, but in the case of the other a perpetual motion; the necessity of the course, on the other hand, would remain the same. In the prize essay already referred to I have irrefutably proved that the action of man can make no exception here, for I showed how it constantly proceeds with strict necessity from two factors—his character and the motives which come to him. The character is inborn and unalterable; the motives are introduced with necessity under the guidance of causality by the strictly determined course of the world.

Accordingly then, from one point of view, which we certainly cannot abandon, because it is established by the objective laws of the world, which are *a priori* valid, the world, with all that is in it, appears as an aimless, and therefore incomprehensible, play of an eternal necessity. Now, what is objectionable, nay, revolting, in this inevitable and irrefutable view of the world cannot be thoroughly done away with by any assumption except this, that as in one aspect every being in the world is a phenomenon, and necessarily determined by the laws of the phenomenon, in another aspect it is in itself *will*, and indeed absolutely *free will*, for necessity only arises through the forms which belong entirely to the phenomenon, through the principle of sufficient reason in its different modes. Such a will, then, must be self-dependent, for, as free, *i.e.*, as a thing in itself, and therefore not subject to the principle of sufficient reason, it cannot depend upon another in its being and nature any more than in its conduct and action. By this assumption alone will as much *freedom* be supposed as is needed to counterbalance the inevitable strict *necessity* which governs the course of the world. Accordingly one has really only the choice either of seeing that the world is a mere machine which runs on of necessity, or of recognising a free will as its inner being whose manifestation is not directly the action but primarily the *existence and nature* of things. This freedom is therefore transcendental, and consists with empirical necessity, in the same way as the transcendental ideality of phenomena consists with their empirical reality. That only under this assumption the action of a man, in spite of the necessity with which it proceeds from his character and the motives, is yet *his own* I have shown in my prize essay on the freedom of the will; with this, however, self-dependency is attributed to his nature. The same relation holds good of all things in the world. The strictest *necessity*, carried out honestly with rigid consistency, and the most perfect *freedom*, rising to omnipotence, had to appear at once and together in philosophy; but, without doing violence to truth, this could only take place by placing the whole *necessity* in the *acting and doing* (*Operari*), and the whole *freedom* in the *being and nature* (*Esse*). Thereby a riddle is solved which is as old as the world, simply because it has hitherto always been held upside down and the freedom persistently sought in the *Operari*, the necessity in the *Esse*. I, on the contrary, say: Every being without exception *acts* with strict necessity, but it *exists* and is what it is by virtue of its *freedom*. Thus with me freedom and necessity are to be met with neither more nor less than in any earlier system; although now one and now the other must be conspicuous according as one takes offence that *will* is attributed to processes of nature which hitherto were explained from necessity, or that the same strict necessity is recognised in motivation as in mechanical causality. The two have merely changed places: freedom has been transferred to the *Esse*, and necessity limited to the *Operari*.

In short, *Determinism* stands firm. For fifteen hundred years men have wearied themselves in vain to shake it, influenced by certain crotchets, which are well known, but dare scarcely yet be called by their name. Yet in accordance with it the world becomes a mere puppet-show, drawn by wires (motives), without it being even possible to understand for whose amusement. If the piece has a plan, then fate is the director; if it has none, then blind necessity. There is no other deliverance from this absurdity than the knowledge that the *being and nature* of all things is the manifestation of a really *free will*, which knows itself in them; for their *doing and acting* cannot be delivered from necessity. To save freedom from fate and chance, it had to be transferred from the action to the existence.

As now necessity only affects the phenomenon, not the thing in itself, *i.e.*, the true nature of the world, so also does *multiplicity*. This is sufficiently explained in § 25 of THE WORLD AS WILL AND IDEA. I have only to add here one remark in confirmation and illustration of this truth.

Every one knows only *one* being quite immediately—his own will in self-consciousness. Everything else he knows only indi-

rectly, and then judges it by analogy with this; a process
which he carries further in proportion to the grade of his reflective powers. Even this ultimately springs from the fact that
there really is *only one being;* the illusion of multiplicity
(*Maja*), which proceeds from the forms of external, objective
comprehension, could not penetrate to inner, simple consciousness; therefore this always finds before it only one being.

If we consider the perfection of the works of nature, which
can never be sufficiently admired, and which even in the lowest
and smallest organisms, for example, in the fertilising parts of
plants or in the internal construction of insects, is carried out
with as infinite care and unwearied labour as if each work of
nature had been its only one, upon which it was therefore able
to expend all its art and power; if we yet find this repeated an
infinite number of times in each one of innumerable individuals
of every kind, and not less carefully worked out in that one
whose dwelling-place is the most lonely, neglected spot, to
which, till then, no eye had penetrated; if we now follow the
combination of the parts of every organism as far as we can,
and yet never come upon one part which is quite simple, and
therefore ultimate, not to speak of one which is inorganic; if,
finally, we lose ourselves in calculating the design of all those
parts of the organism for the maintenance of the whole by
virtue of which every living thing is complete in and for itself; if we consider at the same time that each of these masterpieces, itself of short duration, has already been produced
anew an innumerable number of times, and yet every example
of a species, every insect, every flower, every leaf, still appears
just as carefully perfected as was the first of its kind; thus that
nature by no means wearies and begins to bungle, but, with
equally patient master-hand, perfects the last like the first:
then we become conscious, first of all, that all human art is
completely different, not merely in degree, but in kind, from
the works of nature; and, next, that the working force, the
natura naturans, in each of its innumerable works, in the least
as in the greatest, in the last as in the first, *is immediately
present whole and undivided,* from which it follows that, as
such and in itself, it knows nothing of space and time. If we
further reflect that the production of these hyperboles of all
works of art costs nature absolutely nothing, so that, with in-

conceivable prodigality, she creates millions of organisms which never attain to maturity, and without sparing exposes every living thing to a thousand accidents, yet, on the other hand, if favoured by chance or directed by human purpose, readily affords millions of examples of a species of which hitherto there was only one, so that millions cost her no more than one; this also leads us to see that the multiplicity of things has its root in the nature of the knowledge of the subject, but is foreign to the thing in itself, *i.e.*, to the inner primary force which shows itself in things; that consequently space and time, upon which the possibility of all multiplicity depends, are mere forms of our perception; nay, that even that whole inconceivable ingenuity of structure associated with the reckless prodigality of the works upon which it has been expended ultimately springs simply from the way in which things are apprehended by us; for when the simple and indivisible original effort of the will exhibits itself as object in our cerebral knowledge, it must appear as an ingenious combination of separate parts, as means and ends of each other, accomplished with wonderful completeness.

The *unity of that will,* here referred to, which lies beyond the phenomenon, and in which we have recognised the inner nature of the phenomenal world, is a metaphysical unity, and consequently transcends the knowledge of it, *i.e.*, does not depend upon the functions of our intellect, and therefore can not really be comprehended by it. Hence it arises that it opens to the consideration an abyss so profound that it admits of no thoroughly clear and systematically connected insight, but grants us only isolated glances, which enable us to recognise this unity in this and that relation of things, now in the subjective, now in the objective sphere, whereby, however, new problems are again raised, all of which I will not engage to solve, but rather appeal here to the words *est quadam prodire tenus,* more concerned to set up nothing false or arbitrarily invented than to give a thorough account of all;—at the risk of giving here only a fragmentary exposition.

If we call up to our minds and distinctly go through in thought the exceedingly acute theory of the origin of the planetary system, first put forth by Kant and later by Laplace, a theory of which it is scarcely possible to doubt the correct-

ness, we see the lowest, crudest, and blindest forces of nature
bound to the most rigid conformity to law, by means of their
conflict for one and the same given matter, and the accidental
results brought about by this produce the framework of the
world, thus of the designedly prepared future dwelling-place
of innumerable living beings, as a system of order and harmony, at which we are the more astonished the more distinctly
and accurately we come to understand it. For example, if we
see that every planet, with its present velocity, can only maintain itself exactly where it actually has its place, because if
it were brought nearer to the sun it would necessarily fall into
it, or if placed further from it would necessarily fly away from
it; how, conversely, if we take the place as given, it can only
remain there with its present velocity and no other, because
if it went faster it would necessarily fly away from the sun,
and if it went slower it would necessarily fall into it; that thus
only one definite place is suitable to each definite velocity of a
planet; and if we now see this solved by the fact that the same
physical, necessary, and blindly acting cause which appointed
it its place, at the same time and just by doing so, imparted to
it exactly the only velocity suitable for this place, in consequence of the law of nature that a revolving body increases its
velocity in proportion as its revolution becomes smaller; and,
moreover, if finally we understand how endless permanence is
assured to the whole system, by the fact that all the mutual
disturbances of the course of the planets which unavoidably
enter, must adjust themselves in time; how then it is just the
irrationality of the periods of revolution of Jupiter and Saturn
to each other that prevents their respective perturbations from
repeating themselves at one place, whereby they would become dangerous, and brings it about that, appearing seldom
and always at a different place, they must sublate themselves
again, like dissonances in music which are again resolved into
harmony. By means of such considerations we recognise a design and perfection, such as could only have been brought
about by the freest absolute will directed by the most penetrating understanding and the most acute calculation. And yet,
under the guidance of that cosmogony of Laplace, so well
thought out and so accurately calculated, we cannot prevent
ourselves from seeing that perfectly blind forces of nature, act-

ing according to unalterable natural laws, through their conflict and aimless play among themselves, could produce nothing else but this very framework of the world, which is equal
to the work of an extraordinarily enhanced power of combination. Instead now, after the manner of Anaxagoras, of dragging
in the aid of an *intelligence* known to us only from animal nature, and adapted only to its aims, an intelligence which, coming from without, cunningly made use of the existing forces of
nature and their laws in order to carry out its ends, which are
foreign to these,—we recognise in these lowest forces of nature
themselves that same, one will, which indeed first manifests itself in them, and already in this manifestation striving after its
goal, through its original laws themselves works towards its
final end, to which therefore all that happens according to
blind laws of nature must minister and correspond. And this
indeed cannot be otherwise, because everything material is
nothing but just the phenomenal appearance, the visibility, the
objectivity of the will to live which is one. Thus even the lowest
forces of nature themselves are animated by that same will,
which afterwards, in the individual beings provided with intelligence, marvels at its own work, as the somnambulist wonders in the morning at what he has done in his sleep; or, more
accurately, which is astonished at its own form which it beholds in the mirror. This unity which is here proved of the
accidental with the intentional, of the necessary with the free,
on account of which the blindest chances, which, however,
rest upon universal laws of nature, are as it were the keys
upon which the world-spirit plays its melodies so full of significance,—this unity, I say, is, as has already been remarked, an
abyss in the investigation into which even philosophy can
throw no full light, but only a glimmer.

But I now turn to a *subjective* consideration belonging to
this place, to which, however, I am able to give still less distinctness than to the objective consideration which has just
been set forth; for I shall only be able to express it by images
and similes. Why is our consciousness brighter and more distinct the further it extends towards without, so that its greatest
clearness lies in sense perception, which already half belongs
to things outside us,—and, on the other hand, grows dimmer
as we go in, and leads, if followed to its inmost recesses, to a

darkness in which all knowledge ceases? Because, I say, consciousness presupposes *individuality;* but this belongs to the mere phenomenon, for it is conditioned by the forms of the phenomenon, space and time, as multiplicity of the similar. Our inner nature, on the other hand, has its root in that which is no longer phenomenon, but thing in itself, to which, therefore, the forms of the phenomenon do not extend; and thus the chief conditions of individuality are wanting, and with these the distinctness of consciousness falls off. In this root of existence the difference of beings ceases, like that of the radii of a sphere in the centre; and as in the sphere the surface is produced by the radii ending and breaking off, so consciousness is only possible where the true inner being runs out into the phenomenon, through whose forms the separate individuality becomes possible upon which consciousness depends, which is just on that account confined to phenomena. Therefore all that is distinct and thoroughly comprehensible in our consciousness always lies without upon this surface of the sphere. Whenever, on the contrary, we withdraw entirely from this, consciousness forsakes us,—in sleep, in death, to a certain extent also in magnetic or magic influences; for these all lead through the centre. But just because distinct consciousness, being confined to the surface of the sphere, is not directed towards the centre, it recognises other individuals certainly as of the same kind, but not as identical, which yet in themselves they are. Immortality of the individual might be compared to a point of the surface flying off at a tangent. But immortality, by virtue of the eternal nature of the inner being of the whole phenomenon, may be compared to the return of that point, on the radius, to the centre, of which the whole surface is just the extension. The will as the thing in itself is whole and undivided in every being, as the centre is an integral part of every radius; while the peripherical end of this radius is in the most rapid revolution, with the surface, which represents time and its content, the other end, at the centre, which represents eternity, remains in the profoundest peace, because the centre is the point of which the rising half is not different from the sinking. Therefore in the Bhagavad-gita it is said: *"Haud distributum animantibus, et quasi distributum tamen insidens, animantiumque sustentaculum id cognoscendum, edax et rursus gen-*

itale" (Lect. 13, 16 vers. Schlegel). Certainly we fall here into mystical and figurative language, but it is the only language in which anything can be said on this entirely transcendent theme. So this simile also may pass. The human race may be imagined as an *animal compositum,* a form of life of which many polypi, especially those which swim, such as *Veretillum, Funiculina,* and others, afford examples. As in these the head isolates each individual animal, and the lower part, with the common stomach, combines them all in the unity of one life process, so the brain with its consciousness isolates the human individual, while the unconscious part, the vegetative life with its ganglion system, into which in sleep the brain-consciousness disappears, like a lotus which nightly sinks in the flood, is a common life of all, by means of which in exceptional cases they can even communicate, as, for example, occurs when dreams communicate themselves directly, the thoughts of the mesmeriser pass into the somnambulist, and finally also in the magnetic or generally magical influence proceeding from intentional willing. Such an influence, if it occurs, is *toto genere* different from every other on account of the *influxus physicus* which takes place, for it is really an *actio in distans* which the will, certainly proceeding from the individual, yet performs in its metaphysical quality as the omnipresent substratum of the whole of nature. One might also say that as in the *generatio æquivoca* there sometimes and as an exception appears a weak residue of the original *creative power* of the will, which in the existing forms of nature has already done its work and is extinguished, so there may be, exceptionally, acting in these magical influences, as it were, a surplus of its original *omnipotence,* which completes its work and spends itself in the construction and maintenance of the organisms. I have spoken fully of this magical property of the will in "The Will in Nature," and I gladly omit here discussions which have to appeal to uncertain facts, which yet cannot be altogether ignored or denied.

III

CHARACTERISATION OF THE
WILL TO LIVE[1]

(CHAPTER XXVIII *from* SUPPLEMENTS TO THE SECOND
BOOK OF THE WORLD AS WILL AND IDEA)

Our second book closed with the question as to the goal and aim of that will which had shown itself to be the inner nature of all things in the world. The following remarks may serve to supplement the answer to this question given there in general terms, for they lay down the character of the will as a whole.

Such a characterisation is possible because we have recognised as the inner nature of the world something thoroughly real and empirically given. On the other hand, the very name "world-soul," by which many have denoted that inner being, gives instead of this a mere *ens rationis;* for "soul" signifies an individual unity of consciousness which clearly does not belong to that nature, and in general, since the conception "soul" supposes knowing and willing in inseparable connection and yet independent of the animal organism, it is not to be justified, and therefore not to be used. The word should never be applied except in a metaphorical sense, for it is much more insidious than *psyche* or *anima,* which signify breath.

Much more unsuitable, however, is the way in which so-called pantheists express themselves, whose whole philosophy consists chiefly in this, that they call the inner nature of the world, which is unknown to them, "God"; by which indeed they imagine they have achieved much. According to this, then, the world would be a theophany. But let one only look at it: this world of constantly needy creatures, who continue for a time only by devouring one another, fulfil their existence

[1] This selection is connected with § 29 of THE WORLD AS WILL AND IDEA, Dolphin Books, Doubleday & Company, Inc., 1961.

in anxiety and want, and often suffer terrible miseries, till at last they fall into the arms of death; whoever distinctly looks upon this will be obliged to confess that a God who could think of changing Himself into such a world as this must certainly have been tormented by the devil. I know well that the pretended philosophers of this century follow Spinoza in this, and think themselves thereby justified. But Spinoza had special reasons for thus naming his one substance, in order, namely, to preserve at least the word, although not the thing. The stake of Giordano Bruno and of Vanini was still fresh in the memory; they also had been sacrificed to that God for whose honour incomparably more human sacrifices have bled than on the altars of all heathen gods of both hemispheres together. If, then, Spinoza calls the world God, it is exactly the same thing as when Rousseau in the *"Contrat social,"* constantly and throughout denotes the people by the word *le souverain;* we might also compare it with this, that once a prince who intended to abolish the nobility in his land, in order to rob no one of his own, hit upon the idea of ennobling all his subjects. Those philosophers of our day have certainly one other ground for the nomenclature we are speaking of, but it is no more substantial. In their philosophising they all start, not from the world or our consciousness of it, but from God, as something given and known; He is not their *quæsitum*, but their *datum*. If they were boys I would then explain to them that this is a *petitio principii,* but they know this as well as I do. But since Kant has shown that the path of the earlier dogmatism, which proceeded honestly, the path from the world to a God, does not lead there, these gentlemen now imagine they have found a fine way of escape and made it cunningly. Will the reader of a later age pardon me for detaining him with persons of whom he has never heard.

Every glance at the world, to explain which is the task of the philosopher, confirms and proves that *will to live,* far from being an arbitrary hypostasis or an empty word, is the only true expression of its inmost nature. Everything presses and strives towards *existence,* if possible *organised existence,* i.e., *life,* and after that to the highest possible grade of it. In animal nature it then becomes apparent that *will to live* is the keynote of its being, its one unchangeable and unconditioned quality.

Let any one consider this universal desire for life, let him see the infinite willingness, facility, and exuberance with which the will to live presses impetuously into existence under a million forms everywhere and at every moment, by means of fructification and of germs, nay, when these are wanting, by means of *generatio æquivoca*, seizing every opportunity, eagerly grasping for itself every material capable of life: and then again let him cast a glance at its fearful alarm and wild rebellion when in any particular phenomenon it must pass out of existence; especially when this takes place with distinct consciousness. Then it is precisely the same as if in this single phenomenon the whole world would be annihilated for ever, and the whole being of this threatened living thing is at once transformed into the most desperate struggle against death and resistance to it. Look, for example, at the incredible anxiety of a man in danger of his life, the rapid and serious participation in this of every witness of it, and the boundless rejoicing at his deliverance. Look at the rigid terror with which a sentence of death is heard, the profound awe with which we regard the preparations for carrying it out, and the heartrending compassion which seizes us at the execution itself. We would then suppose there was something quite different in question than a few less years of an empty, sad existence, embittered by troubles of every kind, and always uncertain: we would rather be amazed that it was a matter of any consequence whether one attained a few years earlier to the place where after an ephemeral existence he has billions of years to be. In such phenomena, then, it becomes visible that I am right in declaring that *the will to live* is that which cannot be further explained, but lies at the foundation of all explanations, and that this, far from being an empty word, like the absolute, the infinite, the idea, and similar expressions, is the most real thing we know, nay, the kernel of reality itself.

But if now, abstracting for a while from this interpretation drawn from our inner being, we place ourselves as strangers over against nature, in order to comprehend it objectively, we find that from the grade of organised life upwards it has only one intention—that of the *maintenance of the species*. To this end it works, through the immense superfluity of germs, through the urgent vehemence of the sexual instinct, through

its willingness to adapt itself to all circumstances and oppor-
tunities, even to the production of bastards, and through the
instinctive maternal affection, the strength of which is so great
that in many kinds of animals it even outweighs self-love, so
that the mother sacrifices her life in order to preserve that of
the young. The individual, on the contrary, has for nature only
an indirect value, only so far as it is the means of maintaining
the species. Apart from this its existence is to nature a matter
of indifference; indeed nature even leads it to destruction as
soon as it has ceased to be useful for this end. Why the individual exists would thus be clear; but why does the species
itself exist? That is a question which nature when considered
merely objectively cannot answer. For in vain do we seek by
contemplating her for an end of this restless striving, this ceaseless pressing into existence, this anxious care for the maintenance of the species. The strength and time of the individuals
are consumed in the effort to procure sustenance for themselves and their young, and are only just sufficient, sometimes
even not sufficient, for this. Even if here and there a surplus
of strength, and therefore of comfort—in the case of the *one*
rational species also of knowledge—remains, this is much too
insignificant to pass for the end of that whole process of nature. The whole thing, when regarded thus purely objectively,
and indeed as extraneous to us, looks as if nature was only
concerned that of all her (Platonic) *Ideas, i.e.,* permanenet
forms, none should be lost. Accordingly, as if she had so thoroughly satisfied herself with the fortunate discovery and combination of these Ideas (for which the three preceding occasions on which she stocked the earth's surface with animals
were only the preparation), that now her only fear is lest any
one of these beautiful fancies should be lost, *i.e.,* lest any one
of these forms should disappear from time and the causal
series. For the individuals are fleeting as the water in the
brook; the Ideas, on the contrary, are permanent, like its eddies: but the exhaustion of the water would also do away with
the eddies. We would have to stop at this unintelligible view
if nature were known to us only from without, thus were given
us merely *objectively,* and we accepted it as it is comprehended
by knowledge, and also as sprung from knowledge, *i.e.,* in the
sphere of the idea, and were therefore obliged to confine our-

selves to this province in solving it. But the case is otherwise, and a glance at any rate is afforded us into the *interior of nature*; inasmuch as this is nothing else than *our own inner being*, which is precisely where nature, arrived at the highest grade to which its striving could work itself up, is now by the light of knowledge found directly in self-consciousness. Here the will shows itself to us as something *toto genere* different from the idea, in which nature appears unfolded in all her (Platonic) Ideas; and it now gives us, at one stroke, the explanation which could never be found upon the objective path of the idea. Thus the subjective here gives the key for the exposition of the objective. In order to recognise, as something original and unconditioned, that exceedingly strong tendency of all animals and men to retain life and carry it on as long as possible—a tendency which was set forth above as characteristic of the subjective, or of the will—it is necessary to make clear to ourselves that this is by no means the result of any objective *knowledge* of the worth of life, but is independent of all knowledge; or, in other words, that those beings exhibit themselves, not as drawn from in front, but as impelled from behind.

If with this intention we first of all review the interminable series of animals, consider the infinite variety of their forms, as they exhibit themselves always differently modified according to their element and manner of life, and also ponder the inimitable ingenuity of their structure and mechanism, which is carried out with equal perfection in every individual; and finally, if we take into consideration the incredible expenditure of strength, dexterity, prudence, and activity which every animal has ceaselessly to make through its whole life; if, approaching the matter more closely, we contemplate the untiring diligence of wretched little ants, the marvellous and ingenious industry of the bees, or observe how a single burying-beetle (*Necrophorus vespillo*) buries a mole of forty times its own size in two days in order to deposit its eggs in it and insure nourishment for the future brood (*Gleditsch, Physik. Bot. Œkon. Abhandl.*, iii. 220), at the same time calling to mind how the life of most insects is nothing but ceaseless labour to prepare food and an abode for the future brood which will arise from their eggs, and which then, after they have consumed the food and passed through the chrysalis state, enter upon life merely to begin again from the beginning the same labour; then also how, like this, the life of the birds is for the most part taken up with their distant and laborious migrations, then with the building of their nests and the collecting of food for the brood, which itself has to play the same rôle the following year; and so all work constantly for the future, which afterwards makes bankrupt;—then we cannot avoid looking round for the reward of all this skill and trouble, for the end which these animals have before their eyes, which strive so ceaselessly—in short, we are driven to ask: What is the result? what is attained by the animal existence which demands such infinite preparation? And there is nothing to point to but the satisfaction of hunger and the sexual instinct, or in any case a little momentary comfort, as it falls to the lot of each animal individual, now and then in the intervals of its endless need and struggle. If we place the two together, the indescribable ingenuity of the preparations, the enormous abundance of the means, and the insufficiency of what is thereby aimed at and attained, the insight presses itself upon us that life is a business, the proceeds of which are very far from covering the cost of it. This becomes most evident in some animals of a specially simple manner of life. Take, for example, the mole, that unwearied worker. To dig with all its might with its enormous shovel claws is the occupation of its whole life; constant night surrounds it; its embryo eyes only make it avoid the light. It alone is truly an *animal nocturnum;* not cats, owls, and bats, who see by night. But what, now, does it attain by this life, full of trouble and devoid of pleasure? Food and the begetting of its kind; thus only the means of carrying on and beginning anew the same doleful course in new individuals. In such examples it becomes clear that there is no proportion between the cares and troubles of life and the results or gain of it. The consciousness of the world of perception gives a certain appearance of objective worth of existence to the life of those animals which can see, although in their case this consciousness is entirely subjective and limited to the influence of motives upon them. But the *blind* mole, with its perfect organisation and ceaseless activity, limited to the alternation of insect larvæ and hunger, makes the disproportion of the means to the end apparent. In this respect the consideration of the animal world left to itself in lands uninhabited by men is also specially instructive. A beautiful picture of this, and of the suffering which nature prepares for herself without the interference of man, is given by Humboldt in his *"Ansichten der Natur"* (second edition, p. 30 *et seq.*); nor does he neglect to cast a glance (p. 44) at the analogous suffering of the human race, always and everywhere at variance with itself. Yet in the simple and easily surveyed life of the brutes the emptiness and vanity of the struggle of the whole phenomenon is more easily grasped. The variety of the organisations, the ingenuity of the means, whereby each is adapted to its element and its prey contrasts here distinctly with the want of any lasting final aim; instead of which there presents itself only momentary comfort, fleeting pleasure conditioned by wants, much and long suffering, constant strife, *bellum omnium*, each one both a hunter and hunted, pressure, want, need, and anxiety, shrieking and howling; and this goes on *in secula seculorum*, or till once again the crust of the planet breaks. Yunghahn relates that he saw in Java a plain far as the eye could reach entirely covered with skeletons, and took it for a battlefield; they were, however, merely the skeletons of large turtles, five feet long and three feet broad, and the same height, which come this way out of the sea in order to lay their eggs, and are then attacked by wild dogs (*Canis rutilans*), who with their united strength lay them on their backs, strip off their lower armour, that is, the small shell of the stomach, and so devour them alive. But often then a tiger pounces upon the dogs. Now all this misery repeats itself thousands and thousands of times, year out, year in. For this, then, these turtles are born. For whose guilt must they suffer this torment? Wherefore the whole scene of horror? To this the only answer is: it is thus that the will to live objectifies itself. Let one consider it well and comprehend it in all its objectifications; and then one will arrive at an understanding of its nature and of the world; but not if one frames general conceptions and builds card houses out of them. The comprehension of the great drama of the objectification of the will to live, and the characterisation of its nature, certainly demands somewhat more accurate consideration and greater thoroughness than the dismissal of the world by attributing to it the title of God, or, with a silliness which only the German fatherland offers and knows how to enjoy, explaining it as the "Idea in its other being," in which for twenty years the simpletons of my time have found their unutterable delight. Certainly, according to pantheism or Spinozism, of which the systems of our century are mere travesties, all that sort of thing reels itself off actually without end, straight on through all eternity. For then the world is a God, *ens perfectissimum, i.e.,* nothing better can be or be conceived. Thus there is no need of deliverance from it; and consequently there is none. But why the whole tragi-comedy exists cannot in the least be seen; for it has no spectators, and the actors themselves undergo infinite trouble, with little and merely negative pleasure.

Let us now add the consideration of the human race. The matter indeed becomes more complicated, and assumes a certain seriousness of aspect; but the fundamental character remains unaltered. Here also life presents itself by no means as a gift for enjoyment, but as a task, a drudgery to be performed; and in accordance with this we see, in great and small, universal need, ceaseless cares, constant pressure, endless strife, compulsory activity, with extreme exertion of all the powers of body and mind. Many millions, united into nations, strive for the common good, each individual on account of his own; but many thousands fall as a sacrifice for it. Now senseless delusions, now intriguing politics, incite them to wars with each other; then the sweat and the blood of the great multitude must flow, to carry out the ideas of individuals, or to expiate their faults. In peace industry and trade are active, inventions work miracles, seas are navigated, delicacies are collected from all ends of the world, the waves engulf thousands. All strive, some planning, others acting; the tumult is indescribable. But the ultimate aim of it all, what is it? To sustain ephemeral and tormented individuals through a short span of time in the most fortunate case with endurable want and comparative freedom from pain, which, however, is at once attended with ennui; then the reproduction of this race and its striving. In this evident disproportion between the trouble and the reward, the will to live appears to us from this point of view, if taken objectively, as a fool, or subjectively, as a delusion, seized by which everything living works with the utmost exertion of its strength for something that is of no value. But when we consider it more closely, we shall find here also that it is rather a blind pressure, a tendency entirely without ground or motive.

The law of motivation, as was shown in § 29 of THE WORLD AS WILL AND IDEA only extends to the particular actions, not to willing *as a whole and in general.* It depends upon this, that if we conceive of the human race and its action *as a whole and universally,* it does not present itself to us, as when we contemplate the particular actions, as a play of puppets who are pulled after the ordinary manner by threads outside them; but from this point of view, as puppets which are set in motion by internal clockwork. For if, as we have done above, one compares the ceaseless, serious, and laborious striving of men with what they gain by it, nay, even with what they ever can gain, the disproportion we have pointed out becomes apparent, for one recognises that that which is to be gained, taken as the motive-power, is entirely insufficient for the explanation of that movement and that ceaseless striving. What, then, is a short postponement of death, a slight easing of misery or deferment of pain, a momentary stilling of desire, compared with such an abundant and certain victory over them all as death? What could such advantages accomplish taken as actual moving causes of a human race, innumerable because constantly renewed, which unceasingly moves, strives, struggles, grieves, writhes, and performs the whole tragi-comedy of the history of the world, nay, what says more than all, *perseveres* in such a mock-existence as long as each one possibly can? Clearly this is all inexplicable if we seek the moving causes outside the figures and conceive the human race as striving, in consequence of rational reflection, or something analogous to this (as moving threads), after those good things held out to it, the attainment of which would be a sufficient reward for its ceaseless cares and troubles. The matter being taken thus, every one would rather have long ago said, "*Le jeu ne vaut pas la chandelle,*" and have gone out. But, on the contrary, every one guards and defends his life, like a precious pledge intrusted to him under heavy responsibility, under infinite cares and abundant misery, even under which life is tolerable. The wherefore and the why, the reward for this, certainly he does not see; but he has accepted the worth of that pledge without seeing it, upon trust and faith, and does not know what it consists in. Hence I have said that these puppets are not pulled from without, but each bears in itself the clockwork from which its movements result. This is *the will to live,* manifesting itself as an untiring machine, an irrational tendency, which has not its sufficient reason in the external world. It holds the individuals firmly upon the scene, and is the *primum mobile* of their movements; while the external objects, the motives, only determine their direction in the particular case; otherwise the cause would not be at all suitable to the effect. For, as every manifestation of a force of nature has a cause, but the force of nature itself none, so every particular act of will has a motive, but the will in general has none: indeed at bottom these two are one and the same. The will, as that which is metaphysical, is everywhere the boundary-stone of every investigation, beyond which it cannot go. From the original and unconditioned nature of the will, which has been proved, it is explicable that man loves beyond everything else an existence full of misery, trouble, pain, and anxiety, and, again, full of ennui, which, if he considered and weighed it purely objectively, he would certainly abhor, and fears above all things the end of it, which is yet for him the one thing certain.[2] Accordingly we often see a miserable figure, deformed and shrunk with age, want, and disease, implore our help from the bottom of his heart for the prolongation of an existence, the end of which would necessarily appear altogether desirable if it were an objective judgment that determined here. Thus instead of this it is the blind will, appearing as the tendency to life, the love of life, and the sense of life; it is the same which makes the plants grow. This sense of life may be compared to a rope which is stretched above the puppet-show of the world of men, and on which the puppets hang by invisible threads, while apparently they are supported only by the ground beneath them (the objective value of life). But if the rope becomes weak the puppet sinks; if it

[2] *"Augustini de civit. Dei,"* L. xi. c. 27, deserves to be compared as an interesting commentary on what is said here.

breaks the puppet must fall, for the ground beneath it only seemed to support it: *i.e.*, the weakening of that love of life shows itself as hypochondria, spleen, melancholy: its entire exhaustion as the inclination to suicide, which now takes place on the slightest occasion, nay, for a merely imaginary reason, for now, as it were, the man seeks a quarrel with himself, in order to shoot himself dead, as many do with others for a like purpose;—indeed, upon necessity, suicide is resorted to without any special occasion. (Evidence of this will be found in Esquirol, *Des maladies mentales,* 1838.) And as with the persistence in life, so is it also with its action and movement. This is not something freely chosen; but while every one would really gladly rest, want and ennui are the whips that keep the top spinning. Therefore the whole and every individual bears the stamp of a forced condition; and every one, in that, inwardly weary, he longs for rest, but yet must press forward, is like his planet, which does not fall into the sun only because a force driving it forward prevents it. Therefore everything is in continual strain and forced movement. Men are only apparently drawn from in front; really they are pushed from behind; it is not life that tempts them on, but necessity that drives them forward. The law of motivation is, like all causality, merely the form of the phenomenon. We may remark in passing that this is the source of the comical, the burlesque, the grotesque, the ridiculous side of life; for, urged forward against his will, every one bears himself as best he can, and the straits that thus arise often look comical enough, serious as is the misery which underlies them.

In all these considerations, then, it becomes clear to us that the will to live is not a consequence of the knowledge of life, is in no way a *conclusio ex præmissis,* and in general is nothing secondary. Rather, it is that which is first and unconditioned, the premiss of all premisses, and just on that account that from which philosophy must *start,* for the will to live does not appear in consequence of the world, but the world in consequence of the will to live.

I scarcely need to draw attention to the fact that the considerations with which we now conclude the second book already point forcibly to the serious theme of the fourth book, indeed would pass over into it directly if it were not that my architectonic symmetry makes it necessary that the third book, with its fair contents, should come between, as a second consideration of *the world as idea*, the conclusion of which, how-ever, again points in the same direction.

IV

ON THE OBJECTIFICATION OF THE WILL IN UNCONSCIOUS NATURE[1]

(CHAPTER XXIII *from* SUPPLEMENTS TO THE SECOND BOOK OF THE WORLD AS WILL AND IDEA)

That the will which we find within us does not proceed, as philosophy has hitherto assumed, first from knowledge, and indeed is a mere modification of it, thus something secondary, derived, and, like knowledge itself, conditioned by the brain; but that it is the *prius* of knowledge, the kernel of our nature, and that original force itself which forms and sustains the animal body, in that it carries out both its unconscious and its conscious functions;—this is the first step in the fundamental knowledge of my metaphysics. Paradoxical as it even now seems to many that the will in itself is without knowledge, yet the scholastics in some way already recognised and confessed it; for Jul. Cæs. Vaninus (that well-known sacrifice to fanaticism and priestly fury), who was thoroughly versed in their philosophy, says in his *"Amphitheatro,"* p. 181: *"Voluntas potentia cœca est, ex scholasticorum opinione."* That, further, it is that same will which in the plant forms the bud in order to develop the leaf and the flower out of it; nay, that the regular form of the crystal is only the trace which its momentary effort has left behind, and that in general, as the true and only automaton, in the proper sense of the word, it lies at the foundation of all the forces of unorganised nature, plays, acts, in all their multifarious phenomena, imparts power to their laws, and even in the crudest mass manifests itself as gravity;—this insight is the second step in that fundamental knowledge, and is brought about by further reflection. But it would be the grossest misunderstanding to suppose that this is a mere

[1] This selection is connected with § 23 of THE WORLD AS WILL AND IDEA, Dolphin Books, Doubleday & Company, Inc., 1961.

question of a word to denote an unknown quantity. It is rather the most real of all real knowledge which is here expressed in language. For it is the tracing back of that which is quite inaccessible to our immediate knowledge, and therefore in its essence foreign and unknown to us, which we denote by the words *force of nature,* to that which is known to us most accurately and intimately, but which is yet only accessible to us in our own being and directly, and must therefore be carried over from this to other phenomena. It is the insight that what is inward and original in all the changes and movements of bodies, however various they may be, is in its nature identical; that yet we have only one opportunity of getting to know it more closely and directly, and that is in the movements of our own body. In consequence of this knowledge we must call it *will.* It is the insight that that which acts and strives in nature, and exhibits itself in ever more perfect phenomena, when it has worked itself up so far that the light of knowledge falls directly upon it, *i.e.,* when it has attained to the state of self-consciousness—exists as that *will,* which is what is most intimately known to us, and therefore cannot be further explained by anything else, but rather affords the explanation of all other things. It is accordingly the *thing in itself* so far as this can ever be reached by knowledge. Consequently it is that which must express itself in some way in everything in the world, for it is the inner nature of the world and the kernel of all phenomena.

As my essay, "On the Will in Nature," specially refers to the subject of this chapter, and also adduces the evidence of unprejudiced empiricists in favour of this important point of my doctrine, I have only to add now to what is said there a few supplementary remarks, which are therefore strung together in a somewhat fragmentary manner.

First, then, with reference to plant life, I draw attention to the remarkable first two chapters of Aristotle's work upon plants. What is most interesting in them, as is so often the case with Aristotle, are the opinions of earlier profound philosophers quoted by him. We see there that Anaxagoras and Empedocles quite rightly taught that plants have the motion of their growth by virtue of their indwelling *desires;* nay, that they also attributed to them pleasure and pain, therefore

sensation. But Plato only ascribed to them desires, and that on
account of their strong appetite for nutrition (*cf.* Plato in the
"Timæus," p. 403, Bip.) Aristotle, on the other hand, true to
his customary method, glides on the surface of things, confines
himself to single characteristics and conceptions fixed by current expressions, and asserts that without sensation there can
be no desires, and that plants have not sensation. He is, however, in considerable embarrassment, as his confused language
shows, till here also, "where fails the comprehension, a word
steps promptly in as deputy," namely, the faculty of nourishing. Plants have this, and thus a part of the so-called soul,
according to his favourite division into *anima vegetativa, sensi-
tiva,* and *intellectiva.* This, however, is just a scholastic *Quid-
ditas,* and signifies *plantæ nutriuntur quia habent facultatem
nutritivam.* It is therefore a bad substitute for the more profound research of his predecessors, whom he is criticising. We
also see, in the second chapter, that Empedocles even recognised the sexuality of plants; which Aristotle then also finds
fault with, and conceals his want of special knowledge behind
general propositions, such as this, that plants could not have
both sexes combined, for if so they would be more complete
than animals. By quite an analogous procedure he displaces
the correct astronomical system of the world of the Pythagoreans, and by his absurd fundamental principles, which he
specially explains in the books *de Cœlo,* introduces the system
of Ptolemy, whereby mankind was again deprived of an already discovered truth of the greatest importance for almost
two thousand years.

I cannot refrain from giving here the saying of an excellent
biologist of our own time who fully agrees with my teaching.
It is G. R. Treviranus, who, in his work, *"Ueber die Erschein-
ungen und Gesetze des organischen Lebens,"* 1832, Bd. 2,
Abth. 1, § 49, has said what follows: "A form of life is, however, conceivable in which the effect of the external upon the
internal produces merely feelings of desire or dislike. Such is
the life of plants. In the higher forms of animal life the external
is felt as something objective." Treviranus speaks here from
pure unprejudiced comprehension of nature, and is as little
conscious of the metaphysical importance of his words as of
the *contradictio in adjecto* which lies in the conception of

something "felt as objective," a conception which indeed he works out at great length. He does not know that all feeling is essentially subjective, and all that is objective is, on the other hand, perception, and therefore a product of the understanding. Yet this does not detract at all from the truth and importance of what he says.

In fact, in the life of plants the truth that will can exist without knowledge is apparent—one might say palpably recognisable. For here we see a decided effort, determined by wants, modified in various ways, and adapting itself to the difference of the circumstances, yet clearly without knowledge. And just because the plant is without knowledge it bears its organs of generation ostentatiously in view, in perfect innocence; it knows nothing about it. As soon, on the other hand, as in the series of existences knowledge appears the organs of generation are transferred to a hidden part. Man, however, with whom this is again less the case, conceals them intentionally: he is ashamed of them.

Primarily, then, the vital force is identical with the will, but so also are all other forces of nature; though this is less apparent. If, therefore, we find the recognition of a desire, *i.e.*, of a will, as the basis of *plant life*, expressed at all times, with more or less distinctness of conception, on the other hand, the reference of the forces of *unorganised* nature to the same foundation is rarer in proportion as their remoteness from our own nature is greater. In fact, the boundary between the organised and the unorganised is the most sharply drawn in the whole of nature, and perhaps the only one that admits of no transgressions; so that *natura non facit saltus* seems to suffer an exception here. Although certain crystallisations display an external form resembling the vegetable, yet even between the smallest lichen, the lowest fungus, and everything unorganised there remains a fundamental and essential difference. In the *unorganised* body that which is essential and permanent, thus that upon which its identity and integrity rests, is the material, the *matter*; what is unessential and changing is, on the other hand, the *form*. With the *organised* body the case is exactly reversed; for its life, *i.e.*, its existence as an organised being, simply consists in the constant change of the *material*, while the *form* remains permanent. Its being and its identity thus lies in the *form* alone. Therefore the continuance of the *un-organised* body depends upon *repose* and exclusion from external influences: thus alone does it retain its existence; and if this condition is perfect, such a body lasts for ever. The continuance of the *organised* body, on the contrary, just depends upon continual *movement* and the constant reception of external influences. As soon as these are wanting and the movement in it stops it is dead, and thereby ceases to be organic, although the trace of the organism that has been still remains for a while. Therefore the talk, which is so much affected in our own day, of the life of what is unorganised, indeed of the globe itself, and that it, and also the planetary system, is an organism, is entirely inadmissible. The predicate life belongs only to what is organised. Every organism, however, is throughout organised, is so in all its parts; and nowhere are these, even in their smallest particles, composed by aggregation of what is unorganised. Thus if the earth were an organism, all mountains and rocks, and the whole interior of their mass, would necessarily be organised, and accordingly really nothing unorganised would exist; and therefore the whole conception of it would be wanting.

On the other hand, that the manifestation of a *will* is as little bound up with life and organisation as with knowledge, and that therefore the unorganised has also a will, the manifestations of which are all its fundamental qualities, which cannot be further explained,—this is an essential point in my doctrine; although the trace of such a thought is far seldomer found in writers who have preceded me than that of the will in plants, where, however, it is still unconscious.

In the forming of the crystal we see, as it were, a tendency towards an attempt at life, to which, however, it does not attain, because the fluidity of which, like a living thing, it is composed at the moment of that movement is not enclosed in a *skin*, as is always the case with the latter, and consequently it has neither vessels in which that movement could go on, nor does anything separate it from the external world. Therefore, rigidity at once seizes that momentary movement, of which only the trace remains as the crystal.

The thought that the will, which constitutes the basis of our own nature, is also the same will which shows itself even in the lowest unorganised phenomena, on account of which the conformity to law of both phenomena shows a perfect analogy, lies at the foundation of Goethe's *"Wahlverwandt-schaften,"* as the title indeed indicates, although he himself was unconscious of this.

Mechanics and astronomy specially show us how this will conducts itself so far as it appears at the lowest grade of its manifestation merely as gravity, rigidity, and inertia. Hydraulics shows us the same thing where rigidity is wanting and the fluid material is now unrestrainedly surrendered to its predominating passion, gravity. In this sense hydraulics may be conceived as a characteristic sketch of water, for it presents to us the manifestations of will to which water is moved by gravity; these always correspond exactly to the external influences, for in the case of all non-individual existences there is no particular character in addition to the general one; thus they can easily be referred to fixed characteristics, which are called laws, and which are learned by experience of water. These laws accurately inform us how water will conduct itself under all different circumstances, on account of its gravity, the unconditioned mobility of its parts, and its want of elasticity. Hydrostatics teaches how it is brought to rest through gravity; hydrodynamics, how it is set in motion; and the latter has also to take account of hindrances which adhesion opposes to the will of water: the two together constitute hydraulics. In the same way Chemistry teaches us how the will conducts itself when the inner qualities of materials obtain free play by being brought into a fluid state, and there appears that wonderful attraction and repulsion, separating and combining, leaving go of one to seize upon another, from which every precipitation originates, and the whole of which is denoted by "elective affinity" (an expression which is entirely borrowed from the conscious will). But Anatomy and Physiology allow us to see how the will conducts itself in order to bring about the phenomenon of life and sustain it for a while. Finally, the poet shows us how the will conducts itself under the influence of motives and reflection. He exhibits it therefore for the most part in the most perfect of its manifestations, in rational beings, whose character is individual, and whose conduct and suffering he brings before us in the Drama, the Epic, the Romance,

&c. The more correctly, the more strictly according to the laws of nature his characters are there presented, the greater is his fame; hence Shakspeare stands at the top. The point of view which is here taken up corresponds at bottom to the spirit in which Goethe followed and loved the natural sciences, although he was not conscious of the matter in the abstract. Nay more, this not only appears from his writings, but is also known to me from his personal utterances.

If we consider the will, where no one denies it, in conscious beings, we find everywhere, as its fundamental effort, the *self-preservation* of every being: *omnis natura vult esse conservatrix sui*. But all manifestations of this fundamental effort may constantly be traced back to a seeking or pursuit and a shunning or fleeing from, according to the occasion. Now this also may be shown even at the lowest grades of nature, that is, of the objectification of the will, where the bodies still act only as bodies in general, thus are the subject-matter of mechanics, and are considered only with reference to the manifestations of impenetrability, cohesion, rigidity, elasticity, and gravity. Here also the *seeking* shows itself as gravitation, and the *shunning* as the receiving of motion; and the *movableness* of bodies by pressure or impact, which constitutes the basis of mechanics, is at bottom a manifestation of the effort after *self-preservation*, which dwells in them also. For, since as bodies they are impenetrable, this is the sole means of preserving their cohesion, thus their continuance at any time. The body which is impelled or exposed to pressure would be crushed to pieces by the impelling or pressing body if it did not withdraw itself from its power by flight, in order to preserve its cohesion; and when flight is impossible for it this actually happens. Indeed, one may regard *elastic* bodies as the more *courageous*, which seek to repel the enemy, or at least to prevent him from pursuing further. Thus in the one secret which (besides gravity) is left by mechanics otherwise so clear, in the communicability of motion, we see a manifestation of the fundamental effort of the will in all its phenomena, the effort after self-preservation, which shows itself even at the lowest grades as that which is essential.

In unorganised nature the will objectifies itself primarily in the universal forces, and only by means of these in the phe-

nomena of the particular things which are called forth by
causes. In § 26 of THE WORLD AS WILL AND IDEA I have fully
explained the relation between cause, force of nature, and will
as thing in itself. One sees from that explanation that metaphysics never interrupts the course of physics, but only takes
up the thread where physics leaves it, at the original forces in
which all causal explanation has its limits. Only here does the
metaphysical explanation from the will as the thing in itself
begin. In the case of every physical phenomenon, of every
change of material things, its cause is primarily to be looked
for; and this cause is just such a particular *change* which has
appeared immediately before it. Then, however, the original
force of nature is to be sought by virtue of which this cause
was capable of acting. And first of all the *will* is to be recognised as the inner nature of this force in opposition to its manifestation. Yet the will shows itself just as directly in the fall
of a stone as in the action of the man; the difference is only
that its particular manifestation is in the one case called forth
by a motive, in the other by a mechanically acting cause, for
example, the taking away of what supported the stone; yet in
both cases with equal necessity; and that in the one case it
depends upon an individual character, in the other upon an
universal force of nature. This identity of what is fundamentally essential is even made palpable to the senses. If, for instance, we carefully observe a body which has lost its equilib-
rium, and on account of its special form rolls back and forward
for a long time till it finds its centre of gravity again, a certain
appearance of life forces itself upon us, and we directly feel
that something analogous to the foundation of life is also active
here. This is certainly the universal force of nature, which,
however, in itself identical with the *will*, becomes here, as it
were, the soul of a very brief *quasi* life. Thus what is identical
in the two extremes of the manifestation of the will makes itself
faintly known here even to direct perception, in that this raises
a feeling in us that here also something entirely original, such
as we only know in the acts of our own will, directly succeeded
in manifesting itself.

We may attain to an intuitive knowledge of the existence
and activity of the will in unorganised nature in quite a different and a sublime manner if we study the problem of the

three heavenly bodies, and thus learn more accurately and specially the course of the moon round the earth. By the different combinations which the constant change of the position of these three heavenly bodies towards each other introduces, the course of the moon is now accelerated; now retarded, now it approaches the earth, and again recedes from it; and this again takes place differently in the perihelion of the earth from in its aphelion, all of which together introduces such irregularity into the moon's course that it really obtains a capricious appearance; for, indeed, Kepler's third law is no longer constantly valid, but in equal times it describes unequal areas. The consideration of this course is a small and separate chapter of celestial mechanics, which is distinguished in a sublime manner from terrestrial mechanics by the absence of all impact and pressure, thus of the *vis a tergo* which appears to us so intelligible, and indeed of the actually completed case, for besides *vis inertiæ* it knows no other moving and directing force, except only gravitation, that longing for union which proceeds from the very inner nature of bodies. If now we construct for ourselves in imagination the working of this given case in detail, we recognise distinctly and directly in the moving force here that which is given to us in self-consciousness as will. For the alterations in the course of the earth and the moon, according as one of them is by its position more or less exposed to the influence of the sun, are evidently analogous to the influence of newly appearing motives upon our wills, and to the modifications of our action which result.

The following is an illustrative example of another kind. Liebig (*Chemie in Anwendung auf Agrikultur*, p. 501), says: "If we bring moist copper into air which contains carbonic acid, the affinity of the metal for the oxygen of the air will be increased by the contact with this acid to such a degree that the two will combine with each other; its surface will be coated with green carbonic oxide of copper. But now two bodies which have the capacity of combining, the moment they meet assume opposite electrical conditions. Therefore if we touch the copper with iron, by producing a special electrical state, the capacity of the copper to enter into combination with the oxygen is destroyed; even under the above conditions it remains bright." The fact is well known and of technical use. I

quote it in order to say that here the will of the copper, laid
claim to and occupied by the electrical opposition to iron,
leaves unused the opportunity which presents itself for its
chemical affinity for oxygen and carbonic acid. Accordingly
it conducts itself exactly as the will in a man who omits an
action which he would otherwise feel himself moved to in
order to perform another to which a stronger motive urges
him.

I have shown in THE WORLD AS WILL AND IDEA that the
forces of nature lie outside the chain of causes and effects, because they constitute their accompanying condition, their
metaphysical foundation, and therefore prove themselves to be
eternal and omnipresent, *i.e.*, independent of time and space.
Even in the uncontested truth that what is essential to a *cause*
as such consists in this, that it will produce the same effect at
any future time as it does now, it is already involved that something lies in the cause which is independent of the course of
time, *i.e.*, is outside of all time; this is the force of nature which
manifests itself in it. One can even convince oneself to a certain
extent empirically and as a matter of fact of the *ideality* of
this form of our perception by fixing one's eyes upon the
powerlessness of time as opposed to natural forces. If, for example, a rotatory motion is imparted to a planet by some external cause, if no new cause enters to stop it, this motion
will endure for ever. This could not be so if time were something in itself and had an objective, real existence; for then it
would necessarily also produce some effect. Thus we see here,
on the one hand, the *forces of nature,* which manifest themselves in that rotation, and, if it is once begun, carry it on for
ever without becoming weary or dying out, prove themselves
to be eternal or timeless, and consequently absolutely real and
existing in themselves; and, on the other hand, *time* as something which consists only in the manner in which we apprehend that phenomenon, since it exerts no power and no influence upon the phenomenon itself; for *what does not act is
not.*

We have a natural inclination whenever it is possible to explain every natural phenomenon *mechanically;* doubtless because mechanics calls in the assistance of the fewest original,
and hence inexplicable, forces, and, on the other hand, con-

tains much that can be known *a priori,* and therefore depends upon the forms of our own intellect, which as such carries with it the highest degree of comprehensibility and clearness. However, in the "Metaphysical First Principles of Natural Science" Kant has referred mechanical activity itself to a dynamical activity. On the other hand, the application of mechanical explanatory hypotheses, beyond what is demonstrably mechanical, to which, for example, Acoustics also belongs, is entirely unjustified, and I will never believe that even the simplest chemical combination or the difference of the three states of aggregation will ever admit of mechanical explanation, much less the properties of light, of heat, and electricity. These will always admit only of a dynamical explanation, *i.e.,* one which explains the phenomenon from original forces which are entirely different from those of impact, pressure, weight, &c., and are therefore of a higher kind, *i.e.,* are more distinct objectifications of that will which obtains visible form in all things. I am of opinion that light is neither an emanation nor a vibration; both views are akin to that which explains transparency from pores, and the evident falseness of which is proved by the fact that light is subject to no mechanical laws. In order to obtain direct conviction of this one only requires to watch the effects of a storm of wind, which bends, upsets, and scatters everything, but during which a ray of light shooting down from a break in the clouds is entirely undisturbed and steadier than a rock, so that with great directness it imparts to us the knowledge that it belongs to another order of things than the mechanical: it stands there unmoved like a ghost. Those constructions of light from molecules and atoms which have originated with the French are indeed a revolting absurdity. An article by Ampère, who is otherwise so acute, upon light and heat, which is to be found in the April number of the *"Annales de chimie et physique,"* of 1835, may be considered as a flagrant expression of this, and indeed of the whole of atomism in general. There the solid, the fluid, and the elastic consist of the same atoms, and all differences arise solely from their aggregation; nay, it is said that space indeed is infinitely divisible, but not matter; because, if the division has been carried as far as the atoms, the further division must fall in the spaces between the atoms! Light and heat, then, are here vibrations of the atoms; and sound, on the other hand, is a vibration of the molecules composed of the atoms. In truth, however, these atoms are a fixed idea of the French savants, and therefore they just speak of them as if they had seen them. Otherwise one would necessarily marvel that such a matter-of-fact nation as the French can hold so firmly to a completely transcendent hypothesis, which is quite beyond the possibility of experience, and confidently build upon it up to the sky. This is just a consequence of the backward state of the metaphysics they shun so much, which is poorly represented by M. Cousin, who, with all good will, is shallow and very scantily endowed with judgment. At bottom they are still Lockeians, owing to the earlier influence of Condillac. Therefore for them the thing in itself is really matter, from the fundamental properties of which, such as impenetrability, form, hardness, and the other primary qualities, everything in the world must be ultimately explicable. They will not let themselves be talked out of this, and their tacit assumption is that matter can only be moved by mechanical forces. In Germany Kant's teaching has prevented the continuance of the absurdities of the atomistic and purely mechanical physics for any length of time; although at the present moment these views prevail here also, which is a consequence of the shallowness, crudeness, and folly introduced by Hegel. However, it cannot be denied that not only the evidently porous nature of natural bodies, but also two special doctrines of modern physics, apparently render assistance to the atomic nuisance. These are, Hauz's Crystallography, which traces every crystal back to its kernel form, which is an ultimate form, though only *relatively* indivisible; and Berzelius's doctrine of chemical atoms, which are yet mere expressions for combining proportions, thus only arithmetical quantities, and at bottom nothing more than counters. On the other hand, Kant's thesis in the second antinomy in defence of atoms, which is certainly only set up for dialectical purposes, is a mere sophism, as I have proved in my criticism of his philosophy, and our understanding itself by no means leads us necessarily to the assumption of atoms. For just as little as I am obliged to think that the slow but constant and uniform *motion* of a body before my eyes is composed of innumerable motions which are absolutely quick, but broken and interrupted by just as many absolutely short moments of rest, but, on the contrary, know very well that the stone that has been thrown flies more slowly than the projected bullet, yet never pauses for an instant on the way, so little am I obliged to think of the mass of a body as consisting of atoms and the spaces between them, *i.e.,* of absolute density and absolute vacuity; but I comprehend those two phenomena without difficulty as constant *continua,* one of which uniformly fills time and the other space. But just as the one motion may yet be quicker than another, *i.e.,* in an equal time can pass through more space, so also one body may have a greater specific gravity than another, *i.e.,* in equal space may contain more matter: in both cases the difference depends upon the intensity of the acting force; for Kant (following Priestley) has quite correctly reduced matter to forces. But even if the analogy here set up should not be admitted as valid, and it should be insisted upon that the difference of specific gravity can only have its ground in porosity even this assumption would always lead, not to atoms, but only to a perfectly dense matter, unequally distributed among different bodies; a matter which would certainly be no longer *compressible,* when no pores ran through it, but yet, like the space which it fills, would always remain infinitely *divisible.* For the fact that it would have no pores by no means involves that no possible force could do away with the continuity of its spatial parts. For to say that everywhere this is only possible by extending the already existing intervals is a purely arbitrary assertion.

The assumption of atoms rests upon the two phenomena which have been touched upon, the difference of the specific gravity of bodies and that of their compressibility, for both are conveniently explained by the assumption of atoms. But then both must also always be present in like measure, which is by no means the case. For, for example, water has a far lower specific gravity than all metals properly so called. It must thus have fewer atoms and greater interstices between them, and consequently be very compressible: but it is almost entirely incompressible.

The defence of atoms might be conducted in this way. One may start from porosity and say something of this sort: All bodies have pores, and therefore so also have all parts of a body: now if this were carried out to infinity, there would ultimately be nothing left of a body but pores. The refutation would be that what remained over would certainly have to be assumed as without pores, and so far as absolutely dense, yet not on that account as consisting of absolutely indivisible particles, atoms; accordingly it would certainly be absolutely incompressible, but not absolutely indivisible. It would therefore be necessary that it should be asserted that the division of a body is only possible by penetrating into its pores; which, however, is entirely unproved. If, however, this is assumed, then we certainly have atoms, *i.e.*, absolutely indivisible bodies, thus bodies of such strong cohesion of their spatial parts that no possible power can separate them: but then one may just as well assume such bodies to be large as small, and an atom might be as big as an ox, if it only would resist all possible attacks upon it.

Imagine two bodies of very different kinds, entirely freed from all pores by compression, as by means of hammering, or by pulverisation;—would their specific gravity then be the same? This would be the criterion of dynamics.

V

THE METAPHYSICS OF THE LOVE OF THE SEXES

(CHAPTER XLIV *from* SUPPLEMENTS TO THE FOURTH
BOOK OF THE WORLD AS WILL AND IDEA)

> Ye wise men, highly, deeply learned,
> Who think it out and know,
> How, when, and where do all things pair?
> Why do they kiss and love?
> Ye men of lofty wisdom, say
> What happened to me then;
> Search out and tell me where, how, when,
> And why it happened thus.
>
> —BÜRGER.

We are accustomed to see poets principally occupied with describing the love of the sexes. This is as a rule the chief theme
of all dramatic works, tragical as well as comical, romantic as
well as classical, Indian as well as European. Not less is it the
material of by far the largest part of lyrical and also of epic
poetry, especially if we class with the latter the enormous piles
of romances which for centuries every year has produced in all
the civilised countries of Europe as regularly as the fruits of
the earth. As regards their main contents, all these works are
nothing else than many-sided brief or lengthy descriptions of
the passion we are speaking of. Moreover, the most successful
pictures of it—such, for example, as Romeo and Juliet, *La
Nouvelle Hélöise*, and *Werther*—have gained immortal fame.
Yet, when Rochefoucauld imagines that it is the same with
passionate love as with ghosts, of which every one speaks, but
which no one has seen; and Lichtenberg also in his essay,
"Ueber die Macht der Liebe," disputes and denies the reality
and naturalness of that passion, they are greatly in error. For
it is impossible that something which is foreign and contrary

to human nature, thus a mere imaginary caricature, could be unweariedly represented by poetic genius in all ages, and received by mankind with unaltered interest; for nothing that is artistically beautiful can be without truth:—

Rien n'est beau que le vrai; le vrai seul est aimable.
—BOILEAU

Certainly, however, it is also confirmed by experience, although not by the experience of every day, that that which as a rule only appears as a strong yet still controllable inclination may rise under certain circumstances to a passion which exceeds all others in vehemence, and which then sets aside all considerations, overcomes all obstacles with incredible strength and perseverance, so that for its satisfaction life is risked without hesitation, nay, if that satisfaction is still withheld, is given as the price of it. Werthers and Jacopo Ortis exist not only in romance, but every year can show at least half a dozen of them in Europe: *Sed ignotis perierunt mortibus illi;* for their sorrows find no other chroniclers than the writers of official registers or the reporters of the newspapers. Yet the readers of the police news in English and French journals will attest the correctness of my assertion. Still greater, however, is the number of those whom the same passion brings to the madhouse. Finally, every year can show cases of the double suicide of a pair of lovers who are opposed by outward circumstances. In such cases, however, it is inexplicable to me how those who, certain of mutual love, expect to find the supremest bliss in the enjoyment of this, do not withdraw themselves from all connections by taking the extremest steps, and endure all hardships, rather than give up with life a pleasure which is greater than any other they can conceive. As regards the lower grades of that passion, and the mere approaches to it, every one has them daily before his eyes, and, as long as he is not old, for the most part also in his heart.

So then, after what has here been called to mind, no one can doubt either the reality or the importance of the matter; and therefore, instead of wondering that a philosophy should also for once make its own this constant theme of all poets, one ought rather to be surprised that a thing which plays throughout so important a part in human life has hitherto practically been disregarded by philosophers altogether, and lies before us as raw material. The one who has most concerned himself with it is Plato, especially in the "Symposium" and the "Phædrus." Yet what he says on the subject is confined to the sphere of myths, fables, and jokes, and also for the most part concerns only the Greek love of youths. The little that Rousseau says upon our theme in the *"Discours sur l'inégalité"* (p. 96, ed. Bip.) is false and insufficient. Kant's explanation of the subject in the third part of the essay, *"Ueber das Gefühl des Schönen und Erhabenen"* (p. 435 *seq.* of Rosenkranz's edition), is very superficial and without practical knowledge, therefore it is also partly incorrect. Lastly, Platner's treatment of the matter in his "Anthropology" (§ 1347 *seq.*) every one will find dull and shallow. On the other hand, Spinoza's definition, on account of its excessive naïveté, deserves to be quoted for the sake of amusement: *"Amor est titillatio, concomitante idea causæ externæ (Eth.* iv., prop. 44, *dem.*).* Accordingly I have no predecessors either to make use of or to refute. The subject has pressed itself upon me objectively, and has entered of its own accord into the connection of my consideration of the world. Moreover, least of all can I hope for approbation from those who are themselves under the power of this passion, and who accordingly seek to express the excess of their feelings in the sublimest and most ethereal images. To them my view will appear too physical, too material, however metaphysical and even transcendent it may be at bottom. Meanwhile let them reflect that if the object which to-day inspires them to write madrigals and sonnets had been born eighteen years earlier it would scarcely have won a glance from them.

For all love, however ethereally it may bear itself, is rooted in the sexual impulse alone, nay, it absolutely is only a more definitely determined, specialised, and indeed in the strictest sense individualised sexual impulse. If now, keeping this in view, one considers the important part which the sexual impulse in all its degrees and nuances plays not only on the stage and in novels, but also in the real world, where, next to the love of life, it shows itself the strongest and most powerful of motives, constantly lays claim to half the powers and

thoughts of the younger portion of mankind, is the ultimate
goal of almost all human effort, exerts an adverse influence
on the most important events, interrupts the most serious occupations every hour, sometimes embarrasses for a while even
the greatest minds, does not hesitate to intrude with its trash
interfering with the negotiations of statesmen and the investigations of men of learning, knows how to slip its love letters
and locks of hair even into ministerial portfolios and philosophical manuscripts, and no less devises daily the most entangled
and the worst actions, destroys the most valuable relationships,
breaks the firmest bonds, demands the sacrifice sometimes of
life or health, sometimes of wealth, rank, and happiness, nay,
robs those who are otherwise honest of all conscience, makes
those who have hitherto been faithful, traitors; accordingly,
on the whole, appears as a malevolent demon that strives to
pervert, confuse, and overthrow everything;—then one will be
forced to cry, Wherefore all this noise? Wherefore the straining and storming, the anxiety and want? It is merely a question
of every Hans finding his Grethe.[1] Why should such a trifle
play so important a part, and constantly introduce disturbance
and confusion into the well-regulated life of man? But to the
earnest investigator the spirit of truth gradually reveals the
answer. It is no trifle that is in question here; on the contrary,
the importance of the matter is quite proportionate to the seriousness and ardour of the effort. The ultimate end of all love
affairs, whether they are played in sock or cothurnus, is really
more important than all other ends of human life, and is therefore quite worthy of the profound seriousness with which every
one pursues it. That which is decided by it is nothing less
than *the composition of the next generation*. The *dramatis
personæ* who shall appear when we are withdrawn are here
determined, both as regards their existence and their nature,
by these frivolous love affairs. As the being, the *existentia*, of
these future persons is absolutely conditioned by our sexual
impulse generally, so their nature, *essentia*, is determined by
the individual selection in its satisfaction, *i.e.*, by sexual love,
and is in every respect irrevocably fixed by this. This is the

[1] I have not ventured to express myself distinctly here: the
courteous reader must therefore translate the phrase into Aris-
tophanic language.

key of the problem: we shall arrive at a more accurate knowledge of it in its application if we go through the degrees of love, from the passing inclination to the vehement passion, when we shall also recognise that the difference of these grades arises from the degree of the individualisation of the choice.

The collective love affairs of the present generation taken together are accordingly, of the whole human race, the serious *meditatio compositionis generationis futuræ, e qua iterum pendent innumeræ generationes.* This high importance of the matter, in which it is not a question of individual weal or woe, as in all other matters, but of the existence and special nature of the human race in future times, and therefore the will of the individual appears at a higher power as the will of the species;—this it is on which the pathetic and sublime elements in affairs of love depend, which for thousands of years poets have never wearied of representing in innumerable examples; because no theme can equal in interest this one, which stands to all others which only concern the welfare of individuals as the solid body to the surface, because it concerns the weal and woe of the species. Just on this account, then, is it so difficult to impart interest to a drama without the element of love, and, on the other hand, this theme is never worn out even by daily use.

That which presents itself in the individual consciousness as sexual impulse in general, without being directed towards a definite individual of the other sex, is in itself, and apart from the phenomenon, simply the will to live. But what appears in consciousness as a sexual impulse directed to a definite individual is in itself the will to live as a definitely determined individual. Now in this case the sexual impulse, although in itself a subjective need, knows how to assume very skilfully the mask of an objective admiration, and thus to deceive our consciousness; for nature requires this stratagem to attain its ends. But yet that in every case of falling in love, however objective and sublime this admiration may appear, what alone is looked to is the production of an individual of a definite nature is primarily confirmed by the fact that the essential matter is not the reciprocation of love, but possession, *i.e.,* the physical enjoyment. The certainty of the former can therefore by no means console us for the want of the latter;

on the contrary, in such a situation many a man has shot himself. On the other hand, persons who are deeply in love, and can obtain no return of it, are contented with possession, *i.e.*, with the physical enjoyment. This is proved by all forced marriages, and also by the frequent purchase of the favour of a woman, in spite of her dislike, by large presents or other sacrifices, nay, even by cases of rape. That this particular child shall be begotten is, although unknown to the parties concerned, the true end of the whole love story; the manner in which it is attained is a secondary consideration. Now, however loudly persons of lofty and sentimental soul, and especially those who are in love, may cry out here about the gross realism of my view, they are yet in error. For is not the definite determination of the individualities of the next generation a much higher and more worthy end than those exuberant feelings and supersensible soap bubbles of theirs? Nay, among earthly aims, can there be one which is greater or more important? It alone corresponds to the profoundness with which passionate love is felt, to the seriousness with which it appears, and the importance which it attributes even to the trifling details of its sphere and occasion. Only so far as this end is assumed as the true one do the difficulties encountered, the infinite exertions and annoyances made and endured for the attainment of the loved object, appear proportionate to the matter. For it is the future generation, in its whole individual determinateness, that presses into existence by means of those efforts and toils. Nay, it is itself already active in that careful, definite, and arbitrary choice for the satisfaction of the sexual impulse which we call love. The growing inclination of two lovers is really already the will to live of the new individual which they can and desire to produce; nay, even in the meeting of their longing glances its new life breaks out, and announces itself as a future individuality harmoniously and well composed. They feel the longing for an actual union and fusing together into a single being, in order to live on only as this; and this longing receives its fulfilment in the child which is produced by them, as that in which the qualities transmitted by them both, fused and united in one being, live on. Conversely, the mutual, decided and persistent aversion between a man and a maid is a sign that what they could produce would only be a badly organised, in itself inharmonious and unhappy being. Hence there lies a deeper meaning in the fact that Calderon, though he calls the atrocious Semiramis the daughter of the air, yet introduces her as the daughter of rape followed by the murder of the husband.

But, finally, what draws two individuals of different sex exclusively to each other with such power is the will to live, which exhibits itself in the whole species, and which here anticipates in the individual which these two can produce an objectification of its nature answering to its aims. This individual will have the will, or character, from the father, the intellect from the mother, and the corporisation from both; yet, for the most part, the figure will take more after the father, the size after the mother,—according to the law which comes out in the breeding of hybrids among the brutes, and principally depends upon the fact that the size of the fœtus must conform to the size of the uterus. Just as inexplicable as the quite special individuality of any man, which is exclusively peculiar to him, is also the quite special and individual passion of two lovers; indeed at bottom the two are one and the same: the former is *explicite* what the latter was *implicite*. The moment at which the parents begin to love each other—to fancy each other, as the very happy English expression has it—is really to be regarded as the first appearance of a new individual and the true *punctum saliens* of its life, and, as has been said, in the meeting and fixing of their longing glances there appears the first germ of the new being, which certainly, like all germs, is generally crushed out. This new individual is to a certain extent a new (Platonic) Idea; and now, as all Ideas strive with the greatest vehemence to enter the phenomenal world, eagerly seizing for this end upon the matter which the law of causality divides among them all, so also does this particular Idea of a human individuality strive with the greatest eagerness and vehemence towards its realisation in the phenomenon. This eagerness and vehemence is just the passion of the two future parents for each other. It has innumerable degrees; in its nature, however, it is everywhere the same. On the other hand, it will be in degree so much the more powerful the more *individualised* it is; that is, the more the loved individual is exclusively suited, by virtue of all his or her parts and qualities, to satisfy the desire of the lover and the need established by his or her own individuality. What is really in question here will become clear in the further course of our exposition. Primarily and essentially the inclination of love is directed to health, strength, and beauty, consequently also to youth; because the will first of all seeks to exhibit the specific character of the human species as the basis of all individuality: ordinary amorousness does not go much further. To these, then, more special claims link themselves on, which we shall investigate in detail further on, and with which, when they see satisfaction before them, the passion increases. But the highest degrees of this passion spring from that suitableness of two individualities to each other on account of which the will, *i.e.*, the character, of the father and the intellect of the mother, in their connection, make up precisely that individual towards which the will to live in general which exhibits itself in the whole species feels a longing proportionate to this its magnitude, and which therefore exceeds the measure of a mortal heart, and the motives of which, in the same way, lie beyond the sphere of the individual intellect. This is thus the soul of a true and great passion. Now the more perfect is the mutual adaptation of two individuals to each other in each of the many respects which have further to be considered, the stronger will be their mutual passion. Since there do not exist two individuals exactly alike, there must be for each particular man a particular woman—always with reference to what is to be produced— who corresponds most perfectly. A really passionate love is as rare as the accident of these two meeting. Since, however, the possibility of such a love is present in every one, the representations of it in the works of the poets are comprehensible to us. Just because the passion of love really turns about that which is to be produced, and its qualities, and because its kernel lies here, a friendship without any admixture of sexual love can exist between two young and good-looking persons of different sex, on account of the agreement of their disposition, character, and mental tendencies; nay, as regards sexual love there may even be a certain aversion between them. The reason of this is to be sought in the fact that a child produced by them would have physical or mental qualities which were

inharmonious; in short, its existence and nature would not answer the ends of the will to live as it exhibits itself in the
species. On the other hand, in the case of difference of disposition, character, and mental tendency, and the dislike, nay,
enmity, proceeding from this, sexual love may yet arise and
exist; when it then blinds us to all that; and if it here leads
to marriage it will be a very unhappy one.

Let us now set about the more thorough investigation of
the matter. Egoism is so deeply rooted a quality of all individuals in general, that in order to rouse the activity of an
individual being egoistical ends are the only ones upon which
we can count with certainty. Certainly the species has an earlier, closer, and greater claim upon the individual than the
perishable individuality itself. Yet when the individual has to
act, and even make sacrifices for the continuance and quality
of the species, the importance of the matter cannot be made
so comprehensible to his intellect, which is calculated merely
with regard to individual ends, as to have its proportionate
effect. Therefore in such a case nature can only attain its ends
by implanting a certain illusion in the individual, on account
of which that which is only a good for the species appears to
him as a good for himself, so that when he serves the species
he imagines he is serving himself; in which process a mere
chimera, which vanishes immediately afterwards, floats before
him, and takes the place of a real thing as a motive. This
illusion is instinct. In the great majority of cases this is to be
regarded as the sense of the species, which presents what is
of benefit to *it* to the will. Since, however, the will has here
become individual, it must be so deluded that it apprehends
through the sense of the individual what the sense of the species presents to it, thus imagines it is following individual ends
while in truth it is pursuing ends which are merely general
(taking this word in its strictest sense). The external phenomenon of instinct we can best observe in the brutes where its
rôle is most important; but it is in ourselves alone that we
arrive at a knowledge of its internal process, as of everything
internal. Now it is certainly supposed that man has almost no
instinct; at any rate only this, that the new-born babe seeks for
and seizes the breast of its mother. But, in fact, we have a
very definite, distinct, and complicated instinct, that of the

selection of another individual for the satisfaction of the sexual
impulse, a selection which is so fine, so serious, and so arbitrary. With this satisfaction in itself, *i.e.*, so far as it is a sensual
pleasure resting upon a pressing want of the individual, the
beauty or ugliness of the other individual has nothing to do.
Thus the regard for this which is yet pursued with such ardour, together with the careful selection which springs from
it, is evidently connected, not with the chooser himself—although he imagines it is so—but with the true end, that which
is to be produced, which is to receive the type of the species
as purely and correctly as possible. Through a thousand physical accidents and moral aberrations there arise a great variety
of deteriorations of the human form; yet its true type, in all
its parts, is always again established: and this takes place under the guidance of the sense of beauty, which always directs
the sexual impulse, and without which this sinks to the level
of a disgusting necessity. Accordingly, in the first place, every
one will decidedly prefer and eagerly desire the most beautiful individuals, *i.e.*, those in whom the character of the species is most purely impressed; but, secondly, each one will
specially regard as beautiful in another individual those per-
fections which he himself lacks, nay, even those imperfections
which are the opposite of his own. Hence, for example, little
men love big women, fair persons like dark, &c. &c. The delusive ecstasy which seizes a man at the sight of a woman
whose beauty is suited to him, and pictures to him a union
with her as the highest good, is just the *sense of the species*,
which, recognising the distinctly expressed stamp of the same,
desires to perpetuate it with this individual. Upon this decided
inclination to beauty depends the maintenance of the type of
the species: hence it acts with such great power. We shall
examine specially further on the considerations which it follows. Thus what guides man here is really an instinct which
is directed to doing the best for the species, while the man
himself imagines that he only seeks the heightening of his own
pleasure. In fact, we have in this an instructive lesson concerning the inner nature of all instinct, which, as here, almost
always sets the individual in motion for the good of the species.
For clearly the pains with which an insect seeks out a particular flower, or fruit, or dung, or flesh, or, as in the case of

the ichneumonidæ, the larva of another insect, in order to deposit its eggs there only, and to attain this end shrinks neither from trouble nor danger, is thoroughly analogous to the pains with which for his sexual satisfaction a man carefully chooses a woman with definite qualities which appeal to him individually, and strives so eagerly after her that in order to attain this end he often sacrifices his own happiness in life, contrary to all reason, by a foolish marriage, by love affairs which cost him wealth, honour, and life, even by crimes such as adultery or rape, all merely in order to serve the species in the most efficient way, although at the cost of the individual, in accordance with the will of nature which is everywhere sovereign. Instinct, in fact, is always an act which seems to be in accordance with the conception of an end, and yet is entirely without such a conception. Nature implants it wherever the acting individual is incapable of understanding the end, or would be unwilling to pursue it. Therefore, as a rule, it is given only to the brutes, and indeed especially to the lowest of them which have least understanding; but almost only in the case we are here considering it is also given to man, who certainly could understand the end, but would not pursue it with the necessary ardour, that is, even at the expense of his individual welfare. Thus here, as in the case of all instinct, the truth assumes the form of an illusion, in order to act upon the will. It is a voluptuous illusion which leads the man to believe he will find a greater pleasure in the arms of a woman whose beauty appeals to him than in those of any other; or which indeed, exclusively directed to a single individual, firmly convinces him that the possession of her will ensure him excessive happiness. Therefore he imagines he is taking trouble and making sacrifices for his own pleasure, while he does so merely for the maintenance of the regular type of the species, or else a quite special individuality, which can only come from these parents, is to attain to existence. The character of instinct is here so perfectly present, thus an action which seems to be in accordance with the conception of an end, and yet is entirely without such a conception, that he who is drawn by that illusion often abhors the end which alone guides it, procreation, and would like to hinder it; thus it is in the case of almost all illicit love affairs. In accordance with the character of the matter which has been explained, every lover will experience a marvellous disillusion after the pleasure he has at last attained, and will wonder that what was so longingly desired accomplishes nothing more than every other sexual satisfaction; so that he does not see himself much benefited by it. That wish was related to all his other wishes as the species is related to the individual, thus as the infinite to the finite. The satisfaction, on the other hand, is really only for the benefit of the species, and thus does not come within the consciousness of the individual, who, inspired by the will of the species, here served an end with every kind of sacrifice, which was not his own end at all. Hence, then, every lover, after the ultimate consummation of the great work, finds himself cheated; for the illusion has vanished by means of which the individual was here the dupe of the species.

But all this reflects light on the instincts and mechanical tendencies of the brutes. They also are, without doubt, involved in a kind of illusion, which deceives them with the prospect of their own pleasure, while they work so laboriously and with so much self-denial for the species, the bird builds its nest, the insect seeks the only suitable place for its eggs, or even hunts for prey which, unsuited for its own enjoyment, must be laid beside the eggs as food for the future larvæ, the bees, the wasps, the ants apply themselves to their skilful dwellings and highly complicated economy. They are all guided with certainty by an illusion, which conceals the service of the species under the mask of an egotistical end. This is probably the only way to comprehend the inner or subjective process that lies at the foundation of the manifestations of instinct. Outwardly, however, or objectively, we find in those creatures which are to a large extent governed by instinct, especially in insects, a preponderance of the ganglion system, *i.e.*, the *subjective* nervous system, over the objective or cerebral system; from which we must conclude that they are moved, not so much by objective, proper apprehension as by subjective ideas exciting desire, which arise from the influence of the ganglion system upon the brain, and accordingly by a kind of illusion; and this will be the *physiological* process in the case of all instinct. For the sake of illustration

I will mention as another example of instinct in the human species, although a weak one, the capricious appetite of women who are pregnant. It seems to arise from the fact that the nourishment of the embryo sometimes requires a special or definite modification of the blood which flows to it, upon which the food which produces such a modification at once presents itself to the pregnant woman as an object of ardent longing, thus here also an illusion arises. Accordingly woman has one instinct more than man; and the ganglion system is also much more developed in the woman. That man has fewer instincts than the brutes and that even these few can be easily led astray, may be explained from the great preponderance of the brain in his case. The sense of beauty which instinctively guides the selection for the satisfaction of sexual passion is led astray when it degenerates into the tendency to pederasty; analogous to the fact that the blue-bottle (*Musca vomitoria*), instead of depositing its eggs, according to instinct, in putrefying flesh, lays them in the blossom of the *Arum dracunculus*, deceived by the cadaverous smell of this plant.

Now that an instinct entirely directed to that which is to be produced lies at the foundation of all sexual love will receive complete confirmation from the fuller analysis of it, which we cannot therefore avoid. First of all we have to remark here that by nature man is inclined to inconstancy in love, woman to constancy. The love of the man sinks perceptibly from the moment it has obtained satisfaction; almost every other woman charms him more than the one he already possesses; he longs for variety. The love of the woman, on the other hand, increases just from that moment. This is a consequence of the aim of nature which is directed to the maintenance, and therefore to the greatest possible increase, of the species. The man can easily beget over a hundred children a year; the woman, on the contrary, with however many men, can yet only bring one child a year into the world (leaving twin births out of account). Therefore the man always looks about after other women; the woman, again, sticks firmly to the one man; for nature moves her, instinctively and without reflection, to retain the nourisher and protector of the future offspring. Accordingly faithfulness in marriage is with the man artificial, with the woman it is natural, and thus adultery on the part of the woman is much less pardonable than on the part of the man, both objectively on account of the consequences and also subjectively on account of its unnaturalness.

But in order to be thorough and gain full conviction that the pleasure in the other sex, however objective it may seem to us, is yet merely disguised instinct, *i.e.*, sense of the species, which strives to maintain its type, we must investigate more fully the considerations which guide us in this pleasure, and enter into the details of this, rarely as these details which will have to be mentioned here may have figured in a philosophical work before. These considerations divide themselves into those which directly concern the type of the species, *i.e.*, beauty, those which are concerned with physical qualities, and lastly, those which are merely relative, which arise from the requisite correction or neutralisation of the one-sided qualities and abnormities of the two individuals by each other. We shall go through them one by one.

The first consideration which guides our choice and inclination is age. In general we accept the age from the years when menstruation begins to those when it ceases, yet we give the decided preference to the period from the eighteenth to the twenty-eighth year. Outside of those years, on the other hand, no woman can attract us: an old woman, *i.e.*, one who no longer menstruates, excites our aversion. Youth without beauty has still always attraction; beauty without youth has none. Clearly the unconscious end which guides us here is the possibility of reproduction in general: therefore every individual loses attraction for the opposite sex in proportion as he or she is removed from the fittest period for begetting or conceiving. The second consideration is that of health. Acute diseases only temporarily disturb us, chronic diseases or cachexia repel us, because they are transmitted to the child. The third consideration is the skeleton, because it is the basis of the type of the species. Next to age and disease nothing repels us so much as a deformed figure; even the most beautiful face cannot atone for it; on the contrary, even the ugliest face when accompanied by a straight figure is unquestionably preferred. Further, we feel every disproportion of the skeleton most strongly; for example, a stunted, dumpy, short-boned figure, and many such; also a halting gait, where it is not the result of an extraneous accident. On the other hand, a strikingly beautiful figure can make up for all defects: it enchants us. Here also comes in the great value which all attach to the smallness of the feet: it depends upon the fact that they are an essential characteristic of the species, for no animal has the tarsus and the metatarsus taken together so small as man, which accords with his upright walk; he is a plantigrade. Accordingly Jesus Sirach also says (xxvi. 23, according to the revised translation by Kraus): "A woman with a straight figure and beautiful feet is like columns of gold in sockets of silver." The teeth also are important; because they are essential for nourishment and quite specially hereditary. The fourth consideration is a certain fulness of flesh; thus a predominance of the vegetative function, of plasticity; because this promises abundant nourishment for the fœtus; hence great leanness repels us in a striking degree. A full female bosom exerts an exceptional charm upon the male sex; because, standing in direct connection with the female functions of propagation, it promises abundant nourishment to the new-born child. On the other hand, excessively fat women excite our disgust: the cause is that this indicates atrophy of the uterus, thus barrenness; which is not known by the head, but by instinct. The last consideration of all is the beauty of the face. Here also before everything else the bones are considered; therefore we look principally for a beautiful nose, and a short turned-up nose spoils everything. A slight inclination of the nose downwards or upwards has decided the happiness in life of innumerable maidens, and rightly so, for it concerns the type of the species. A small mouth, by means of small maxillæ, is very essential as specifically characteristic of the human countenance, as distinguished from the muzzle of the brutes. A receding or, as it were, cut-away chin is especially disagreeable, because *mentum prominulum* is an exclusive characteristic of our species. Finally comes the regard for beautiful eyes and forehead; it is connected with the psychical qualities, especially the intellectual which are inherited from the mother.

The unconscious considerations which, on the other hand, the inclination of women follows naturally cannot be so exactly assigned. In general the following may be asserted: They give the preference to the age from thirty to thirty-five years, especially over that of youths who yet really present the height of human beauty. The reason is that they are not guided by taste but by instinct, which recognises in the age named the acme of reproductive power. In general they look less to beauty, especially of the face. It is as if they took it upon themselves alone to impart this to the child. They are principally won by the strength of the man, and the courage which is connected with this; for these promise the production of stronger children, and also a brave protector for them. Every physical defect of the man, every divergence from the type, may with regard to the child be removed by the woman in reproduction, through the fact that she herself is blameless in these respects, or even exceeds in the opposite direction. Only those qualities of the man have to be excepted which are peculiar to his sex, and which therefore the mother cannot give to the child: such are the manly structure of the skeleton, broad shoulders, slender hips, straight bones, muscular power, courage, beard, &c. Hence it arises that women often love ugly men, but never an unmanly man, because they cannot neutralise his defects.

The second class of the considerations which lie at the foundation of sexual love are those which regard psychical qualities. Here we shall find that the woman is throughout attracted by the qualities of the heart or character in the man, as those which are inherited from the father. The woman is won especially by firmness of will, decision, and courage, and perhaps also by honesty and goodheartedness. On the other hand, intellectual gifts exercise no direct and instinctive power over her, just because they are not inherited from the father. Want of understanding does a man no harm with women; indeed extraordinary mental endowment, or even genius, might sooner influence them unfavourably as an abnormality. Hence one often sees an ugly, stupid, and coarse fellow get the better of a cultured, able, and amiable man with women. Also marriages from love are sometimes consummated between natures which are mentally very different: for example, the man is rough, powerful, and stupid; the woman tenderly sensitive, delicately thoughtful, cultured, æsthetic, &c.; or the man is a genius and learned, the woman a goose:

Sic visum Veneri; cui placet impares
Formas atque animos sub juga aënea
Sævo mittere cum joco.

The reason is, that here quite other considerations than the intellectual predominate,—those of instinct. In marriage what is looked to is not intellectual entertainment, but the production of children: it is a bond of the heart, not of the head. It is a vain and absurd pretence when women assert that they have fallen in love with the mind of a man, or else it is the over-straining of a degenerate nature. Men, on the other hand, are not determined in their instinctive love by the qualities of character of the woman; hence so many Socrateses have found their Xantippes; for example, Shakspeare, Albrecht Dürer, Byron, &c. The intellectual qualities, however, certainly influence here, because they are inherited from the mother. Yet their influence is easily outweighed by that of physical beauty, which acts directly, as concerning a more essential point. However, it happens, either from the feeling or the experience of that influence, that mothers have their daughters taught the fine arts, languages, and so forth in order to make them attractive to men, whereby they wish to assist the intellect by artificial means, just as, in case of need, they assist the hips and the bosom. Observe that here we are speaking throughout only of that entirely immediate instinctive attraction from which alone love properly so called grows. That a woman of culture and understanding prizes understanding and intellect in a man, that a man from rational reflection should test and have regard to the character of his bride, has nothing to do with the matter with which we are dealing here. Such things lie at the bottom of a rational choice in marriage, but not of the passionate love, which is our theme.

Hitherto I have only taken account of the *absolute* considerations, *i.e.*, those which hold good for every one: I come now to the *relative* considerations, which are individual, because in their case what is looked to is the rectification of the type of the species, which is already defectively presented, the correction of the divergences from it which the chooser's own person already bears in itself, and thus the return to the pure presentation of the type. Here, then, each one loves what he lacks. Starting from the individual constitution, and directed to the individual constitution, the choice which rests upon such relative considerations is much more definite, decided, and exclusive than that which proceeds merely from the absolute considerations; therefore the source of really passionate love will lie, as a rule, in these relative considerations, and only that of the ordinary and slighter inclination in the absolute considerations. Accordingly it is not generally precisely correct and perfect beauties that kindle great passions. For such a truly passionate inclination to arise something is required which can only be expressed by a chemical metaphor: two persons must neutralise each other, like acid and alkali, to a neutral salt. The essential conditions demanded for this are the following. First: all sex is one-sided. This one-sidedness is more distinctly expressed in one individual than in another; therefore in every individual it can be better supplemented and neutralised by one than by another individual of the opposite sex, for each one requires a one-sidedness which is the opposite of his own to complete the type of humanity in the new individual that is to be produced, the constitution of which is always the goal towards which all tends. Physiologists know that manhood and womanhood admit of innumerable degrees, through which the former sinks to the repulsive gynander and hypospadæus, and the latter rises to the graceful androgyne; from both sides complete hermaphrodism can be reached, at which point stand those individuals who, holding the exact mean between the two sexes, can be attributed to neither, and consequently are unfit to propagate the species. Accordingly, the neutralisation of two individualities by each other, of which we are speaking, demands that the definite degree of *his* manhood shall exactly correspond to the definite degree of *her* womanhood; so that the one-sidedness of each exactly annuls that of the other. Accordingly, the most manly man will seek the most womanly woman, and *vice versa,* and in the same way every individual will seek another corresponding to him or her in degree of sex. Now how far the required relation exists between two individuals is instinctively felt by them, and, together with the other relative considerations, lies at the foundation of the higher degrees of love. While, therefore, the lovers speak pathetically of the harmony of their souls, the heart of the matter is for the most part the agreement or suitableness pointed out here with reference to the being which is to be produced and its perfection, and which is also clearly of much more importance than the harmony of their souls, which often, not long after the marriage, resolves itself into a howling discord. Now, here come in the further relative considerations, which depend upon the fact that every one endeavours to neutralise by means of the other his weaknesses, defects, and deviations from the type, so that they will not perpetuate themselves, or even develop into complete abnormities in the child which is to be produced. The weaker a man is as regards muscular power the more will he seek for strong women; and the woman on her side will do the same. But since now a less degree of muscular power is natural and regular in the woman, women as a rule will give the preference to strong men. Further, the size is an important consideration. Little men have a decided inclination for big women, and *vice versa;* and indeed in a little man the preference for big women will be so much the more passionate if he himself was begotten by a big father, and only remains little through the influence of his mother; because he has inherited from his father the vascular system and its energy, which was able to supply a large body with blood. If, on the other hand, his father and grandfather were both little, that inclination will make itself less felt. At the foundation of the aversion of a big woman to big men lies the intention of nature to avoid too big a race, if with the strength which *this* woman could impart to them they would be too weak to live long. If, however, such a woman selects a big husband, perhaps for the sake of being more presentable in society, then, as a rule, her offspring will have to atone for her folly. Further, the consideration as to the complexion is very decided. Blondes prefer dark persons, or brunettes; but the latter seldom prefer the former. The reason is, that fair hair and blue eyes are in themselves a variation from the type, almost an abnormity, analogous to white mice, or at least to grey horses. In no part of the world, not even in the vicinity of the pole, are they indigenous, except in Europe, and are clearly of Scandinavian origin. I may here express my opinion in passing that the white colour of the skin is not natural to man, but that by nature he has a black or brown skin, like our forefathers the Hindus; that consequently a white man has never originally sprung from the womb of nature, and that thus there is no such thing as a white race, much as this is talked of, but every white man is a faded or bleached one. Forced into the strange world, where he only exists like an exotic plant, and like this requires in winter the hothouse, in the course of thousands of years man became white. The gipsies, an Indian race which immigrated only about four centuries ago, show the transition from the complexion of the Hindu to our own. Therefore in sexual love nature strives to return to dark hair and brown eyes as the primitive type; but the white colour of the skin has become a second nature, though not so that the brown of the Hindu repels us. Finally, each one also seeks in the particular parts of the body the corrective of his own defects and aberrations, and does so the more decidedly the more important the part is. Therefore snub-nosed individuals have an inexpressible liking for hooknoses, parrot-faces; and it is the same with regard to all other parts. Men with excessively slim, long bodies and limbs can find beauty in a body which is even beyond measure stumpy and short. The considerations with regard to temperament act in an analogous manner. Each will prefer the temperament opposed to his own; yet only in proportion as his one is decided. Whoever is himself in some respect very perfect does not indeed seek and love imperfection in this respect, but is yet more easily reconciled to it than others; because he himself insures the children against great imperfection of this part. For example, whoever is himself very white will not object to a yellow complexion; but whoever has the latter will find dazzling whiteness divinely beautiful. The rare case in which a man falls in love with a decidedly ugly woman occurs when, besides the exact harmony of the degree of sex explained above, the whole of her abnormities are precisely the opposite, and thus the corrective, of his. The love is then wont to reach a high degree.

The profound seriousness with which we consider and ponder each bodily part of the woman, and she on her part does the same, the critical scrupulosity with which we inspect a woman who begins to please us, the capriciousness of our choice, the keen attention with which the bridegroom observes his betrothed, his carefulness not to be deceived in any part, and the great value which he attaches to every excess or defect in the essential parts, all this is quite in keeping with the importance of the end. For the new being to be produced will have to bear through its whole life a similar part. For example, if the woman is only a little crooked, this may easily impart to her son a hump, and so in all the rest. Consciousness of all this certainly does not exist. On the contrary, every one imagines that he makes that careful selection in the interest of his own pleasure (which at bottom cannot be interested in it at all); but he makes it precisely as, under the presupposition of his own corporisation, is most in keeping with the interest of the species, to maintain the type of which as pure as possible is the secret task. The individual acts here, without knowing it, by order of something higher than itself, the species; hence the importance which it attaches to things which may and indeed must be, indifferent to itself as such. There is something quite peculiar in the profound unconscious seriousness with which two young persons of opposite sex who see each other for the first time regard each other, in the searching and penetrating glance they cast at one another, in the careful review which all the features and parts of their respective persons have to endure. This investigating and examining is the *meditation of the genius of the species* on the individual which is possible through these two and the combination of its qualities. According to the result of this meditation is the degree of their pleasure in each other and their yearning for each other. This yearning, even after it has attained a considerable degree, may be suddenly extinguished again by the discovery of something that had previously remained unobserved. In this way, then, the genius of the species meditates concerning the coming race in all who are capable of reproduction. The nature of this race is the great work with which Cupid is occupied, unceasingly active, speculating, and pondering. In comparison with the importance of his great affair, which concerns the species and all coming races, the affairs of individuals in their whole ephemeral totality are very trifling; therefore he is always ready to sacrifice these regardlessly. For he is related to them as an immortal to mortals, and his interests to theirs as infinite to finite. Thus, in the consciousness of managing affairs of a higher kind than all those which only concern individual weal or woe, he carries them on sublimely, undisturbed in the midst of the tumult of war, or in the bustle of business life, or during the raging of a plague, and pursues them even into the seclusion of the cloister.

We have seen in the above that the intensity of love increases with its individualisation, because we have shown that the physical qualities of two individuals can be such that, for the purpose of restoring as far as possible the type of the species, the one is quite specially and perfectly the completion or supplement of the other, which therefore desires it exclusively. Already in this case a considerable passion arises, which at once gains a nobler and more sublime appearance from the fact that it is directed to an individual object, and to it alone; thus, as it were, arises at the special order of the species. For the opposite reason, the mere sexual impulse is ignoble, because without individualisation it is directed to all, and strives to maintain the species only as regards quantity, with little respect to quality. But the individualising, and with it the intensity of the love, can reach so high a degree that without its satisfaction all the good things in the world, and even life itself, lose their value. It is then a wish which attains a vehemence that no other wish ever reaches, and therefore makes one ready for any sacrifice, and in case its fulfilment remains unalterably denied, may lead to madness or suicide. At the foundation of such an excessive passion there must lie, besides the considerations we have shown above, still others which we have not thus before our eyes. We must therefore assume that here not only the corporisation, but the *will* of the man and the *intellect* of the woman are specially suitable to each other, in consequence of which a perfectly definite individual can be produced by them alone, whose existence the genius of the species has here in view, for reasons which are inaccessible to us, since they lie in the nature of the thing in itself. Or, to speak more exactly, the will to live desires here to objectify itself in a perfectly definite individual, which can only be produced by this father with this mother. This metaphysical desire of the will in itself has primarily no other sphere of action in the series of existences than the hearts of the future parents, which accordingly are seized with this ardent longing, and now imagine themselves to desire on their own account what really for the present has only a purely metaphysical end, *i.e.*, an end which lies outside the series of actually existing things. Thus it is the ardent longing to enter existence of the future individual which has first become possible here, a longing which proceeds from the primary source of all being, and exhibits itself in the phenomenal world as the lofty passion of the future parents for each other, paying little regard to all that is outside itself; in fact, as an unparalleled illusion, on account of which such a lover would give up all the good things of this world to enjoy the possession of this woman, who yet can really give him nothing more than any other. That yet it is just this possession that is kept in view here is seen from the fact that even this lofty passion, like all others, is extinguished in its enjoyment—to the great astonishment of those who are possessed by it. It also becomes extinct when, through the woman turning out barren (which, according to Hufeland, may arise from nineteen accidental constitutional defects), the real metaphysical end is frustrated; just as daily happens in millions of germs trampled under foot, in which yet the same metaphysical life principle strives for existence; for which there is no other consolation than that an infinity of space, time, and matter, and consequently inexhaustible opportunity for return, stands open to the will to live.

The view which is here expounded must once have been present to the mind of Theophrastus Paracelsus, even if only in a fleeting form, though he has not handled this subject, and my whole system of thought was foreign to him; for, in quite a different context and in his desultory manner, he wrote the following remarkable words: *"Hi sunt, quos Deus copulavit, ut eam, quæ fuit Uriæ et David; quamvis ex diametro (sic enim sibi humana mens persuadebat) cum justo et legitimo matrimonio pugnaret hoc. . . . sed propter Salomonem,* QUI ALIUNDE NASCI NON POTUIT, *nisi ex Bathseba, conjuncto David semine, quamvis meretrice, conjunxit eos Deus"* (*De vita longa*, i. 5).

The longing of love, which the poets of all ages are unceasingly occupied with expressing in innumerable forms, and do not exhaust the subject, nay, cannot do it justice, this longing, which attaches the idea of endless happiness to the posses-

sion of a particular woman, and unutterable pain to the
thought that this possession cannot be attained,—this longing
and this pain cannot obtain their material from the wants of an
ephemeral individual; but they are the sighs of the spirit of
the species, which sees here, to be won or lost, a means for
the attainment of its ends which cannot be replaced, and therefore groans deeply. The species alone has infinite life, and
therefore is capable of infinite desires, infinite satisfaction, and
infinite pain. But these are here imprisoned in the narrow
breast of a mortal. No wonder, then, if such a breast seems
like to burst, and can find no expression for the intimations of
infinite rapture or infinite misery with which it is filled. This,
then, affords the materials for all erotic poetry of a sublime
kind, which accordingly rises into transcendent metaphors,
soaring above all that is earthly. This is the theme of Petrarch,
the material for the St. Preuxs, Werthers, and Jacopo Ortis,
who apart from it could not be understood nor explained. For
that infinite esteem for the loved one cannot rest upon some
spiritual excellences, or in general upon any objective, real
qualities of hers; for one thing, because she is often not sufficiently well known to the lover, as was the case with Petrarch.
The spirit of the species alone can see at one glance what
worth she has for *it*, for its ends. And great passions also arise,
as a rule, at the first glance:

> Who ever loved that loved not at first sight?
> —SHAKSPEARE, *As You Like It*, iii. 5.

In this regard a passage in the romance of *"Guzman de
Alfarache,"* by Mateo Aleman, which has been famous for 250
years, is remarkable: *"No es necessario, para que uno ame,
que pase distancia de tiempo, que siga discurso, ni haga elec-
cion, sino que con aquella primera y sola vista, concurran
juntamente cierta correspondencia ó consonancia, ó lo que
acó solemos vulgarmente decir, una confrontacion de sangre, ó
que por particular influxo suelen mover las estrellas."* (For one
to love it is not necessary that much time should pass, that he
should set about reflecting and make a choice; only that at
that first and only glance a certain correspondence and conso-
nance should be encountered on both sides, or that which in
common life we are wont to call a *sympathy of the blood,* and

to which a special influence of the stars generally impels), P. ii. lib. iii. c. 5. Accordingly the loss of the loved one, through a rival, or through death, is also for the passionate lover a pain that surpasses all others, just because it is of a transcendental kind, since it affects him not merely as an individual, but attacks him in his *essentia æterna*, in the life of the species into whose special will and service he was here called. Hence jealousy is such torment and so grim, and the surrender of the loved one is the greatest of all sacrifices. A hero is ashamed of all lamentations except the lamentation of love, because in this it is not he but the species that laments. In Calderon's "Zenobia the Great" there is in the first act a scene between Zenobia and Decius in which the latter says:

> *Cielos, luego tu me quieres?*
> *Perdiera cien mil victorias,*
> *Volviérame,* &c.

(Heaven! then thou lovest me? For this I would lose a thousand victories, would turn about, &c.)

Here, honour, which hitherto outweighed every interest, is beaten out of the field as soon as sexual love, *i.e.*, the interest of the species, comes into play, and sees before it a decided advantage; for this is infinitely superior to every interest of mere individuals, however important it may be. Therefore to this alone honour, duty, and fidelity yield after they have withstood every other temptation, including the threat of death. In the same way we find in private life that conscientiousness is in no point so rare as in this: it is here sometimes set aside even by persons who are otherwise honest and just, and adultery is recklessly committed when passionate love, *i.e.*, the interest of the species, has mastered them. It even seems as if in this they believed themselves to be conscious of a higher right than the interests of individuals can ever confer; just because they act in the interest of the species. In this reference Chamfort's remark is worth noticing: *"Quand un homme et une femme ont l'un pour l'autre une passion violente, il me semble toujours que quelque soient les obstacles qui les séparent, un mari, des parens, etc., les deux amans sont l'un a l'autre, de par la Nature, qu'ils s'appartiennent de droit divin, malgré les lois et les conventions humaines."* Whoever is in-

clined to be incensed at this should be referred to the remarkable indulgence which the Saviour shows in the Gospel to the
woman taken in adultery, in that He also assumes the same
guilt in the case of all present. From this point of view the
greater part of the "Decameron" appears as mere mocking and
jeering of the genius of the species at the rights and interests
of individuals which it tramples under foot. Differences of rank
and all similar circumstances, when they oppose the union of
passionate lovers, are set aside with the same ease and treated
as nothing by the genius of the species, which, persuing its
ends that concern innumerable generations, blows off as spray
such human laws and scruples. From the same deep-lying
grounds, when the ends of passionate love are concerned, every
danger is willingly encountered, and those who are otherwise
timorous here become courageous. In plays and novels also we
see, with ready sympathy, the young persons who are fighting
the battle of their love, *i.e.*, the interest of the species, gain
the victory over their elders, who are thinking only of the welfare of the individuals. For the efforts of the lovers appear to us
as much more important, sublime, and therefore right, than
anything that can be opposed to them, as the species is more
important than the individual. Accordingly the fundamental
theme of almost all comedies is the appearance of the genius
of the species with its aims, which are opposed to the personal
interest of the individuals presented, and therefore threaten to
undermine their happiness. As a rule it attains its end, which,
as in accordance with poetical justice, satisfies the spectator,
because he feels that the aims of the species are much to be
preferred to those of the individual. Therefore at the conclusion he leaves the victorious lovers quite confidently, because he shares with them the illusion that they have founded
their own happiness, while they have rather sacrificed it to
the choice of the species, against the will and foresight of their
elders. It has been attempted in single, abnormal comedies to
reverse the matter and bring about the happiness of the individuals at the cost of the aims of the species; but then the
spectator feels the pain which the genius of the species suffers,
and is not consoled by the advantages which are thereby assured to the individuals. As examples of this kind two very
well-known little pieces occur to me: *"La reine de* 16 *ans,"* and

"*Le marriage de raison.*" In tragedies containing love affairs, since the aims of the species are frustrated, the lovers who were its tools, generally perish also; for example, in "Romeo and Juliet," "Tancred," "Don Carlos," "Wallenstein," "The Bride of Messina," and many others.

The love of a man often affords comical, and sometimes also tragical phenomena; both because, taken possession of by the spirit of the species, he is now ruled by this, and no longer belongs to himself: his conduct thereby becomes unsuited to the individual. That which in the higher grades of love imparts such a tinge of poetry and sublimeness to his thoughts, which gives them even a transcendental and hyperphysical tendency, on account of which he seems to lose sight altogether of his real, very physical aim, is at bottom this, that he is now inspired by the spirit of the species whose affairs are infinitely more important than all those which concern mere individuals, in order to found under the special directions of this spirit the whole existence of an indefinitely long posterity with this individual and exactly determined nature, which it can receive only from him as father and the woman he loves as mother, and which otherwise could never, *as such,* attain to existence, while the objectification of the will to live expressly demands this existence. It is the feeling that he is acting in affairs of such transcendent importance which raises the lover so high above everything earthly, nay, even above himself, and gives such a hyperphysical clothing to his very physical desires, that love becomes a poetical episode even in the life of the most prosaic man; in which last case the matter sometimes assumes a comical aspect. That mandate of the will which objectifies itself in the species exhibits itself in the consciousness of the lover under the mask of the anticipation of an infinite blessedness which is to be found for him in the union with this female individual. Now, in the highest grades of love this chimera becomes so radiant that if it cannot be attained life itself loses all charm, and now appears so joyless, hollow, and insupportable that the disgust at it even overcomes the fear of death, so that it is then sometimes voluntarily cut short. The will of such a man has been caught in the vortex of the will of the species, or this has obtained such a great predominance over the individual will that if such a man cannot be effective in the first capacity, he disdains to be so in the last. The individual is here too weak a vessel to be capable of enduring the infinite longing of the will of the species concentrated upon a definite object. In this case, therefore, the issue is suicide, sometimes the double suicide of the two lovers; unless, to save life, nature allows madness to intervene, which then covers with its veil the consciousness of that hopeless state. No year passes without proving the reality of what has been expounded by several cases of all these kinds.

Not only, however, has the unsatisfied passion of love sometimes a tragic issue, but the satisfied passion also leads oftener to unhappiness than to happiness. For its demands often conflict so much with the personal welfare of him who is concerned that they undermine it, because they are incompatible with his other circumstances, and disturb the plan of life built upon them. Nay, not only with external circumstances is love often in contradiction, but even with the lover's own individuality, for it flings itself upon persons who, apart from the sexual relation, would be hateful, contemptible, and even abhorrent to the lover. But so much more powerful is the will of the species than that of the individual that the lover shuts his eyes to all those qualities which are repellent to him, overlooks all, ignores all, and binds himself for ever to the object of his passion—so entirely is he blinded by that illusion, which vanishes as soon as the will of the species is satisfied, and leaves behind a detested companion for life. Only from this can it be explained that we often see very reasonable and excellent men bound to termagants and she-devils, and cannot conceive how they could have made such a choice. On this account the ancients represented love as blind. Indeed, a lover may even know distinctly and feel bitterly the faults of temperament and character of his bride, which promise him a miserable life, and yet not be frightened away:—

> I ask not, I care not,
>   If guilt's in thy heart,
> I know that I love thee
>   Whatever thou art.

For ultimately he seeks not his own things, but those of a

third person, who has yet to come into being, although he is involved in the illusion that what he seeks is his own affair. But it is just this not seeking of one's own things which is everywhere the stamp of greatness, that gives to passionate love also a touch of sublimity, and makes it a worthy subject of poetry. Finally, sexual love is compatible even with the extremest hatred towards its object: therefore Plato has compared it to the love of the wolf for the sheep. This case appears when a passionate lover, in spite of all efforts and entreaties, cannot obtain a favourable hearing on any condition:—

> "I love and hate her."
> —SHAKSPEARE, *Cymb.*, iii. 5.

The hatred of the loved one which then is kindled sometimes goes so far that the lover murders her, and then himself. One or two examples of this generally happen every year; they will be found in the newspapers. Therefore Goethe's lines are quite correct:—

> By all despised love! By hellish element!
> Would that I knew a worse, that I might swear by!

It is really no hyperbole if a lover describes the coldness of his beloved and the delight of her vanity, which feeds on his sufferings, as cruelty; for he is under the influence of an impulse which, akin to the instinct of insects, compels him, in spite of all grounds of reason, to pursue his end unconditionally, and to undervalue everything else: he cannot give it up. Not one but many a Petrarch has there been who was compelled to drag through life the unsatisfied ardour of love, like a fetter, an iron weight at his foot, and breathe his sighs in lonely woods; but only in the one Petrarch dwelt also the gift of poetry; so that Goethe's beautiful lines hold good of him:—

> And when in misery the man was dumb
> A god gave me the power to tell my sorrow.

In fact, the genius of the species wages war throughout with the guardian geniuses of individuals, is their pursuer and enemy, always ready relentlessly to destroy personal happiness in order to carry out its ends; nay, the welfare of whole nations has sometimes been sacrificed to its humours. An example of this is given us by Shakspeare in "Henry VI.," pt. iii., act 3, sc. 2 and 3. All this depends upon the fact that the species, as that in which the root of our being lies, has a closer and earlier right to us than the individual; hence its affairs take precedence. From the feeling of this the ancients personified the genius of the species in Cupid, a malevolent, cruel, and therefore ill-reputed god, in spite of his childish appearance; a capricious, despotic demon, but yet lord of gods and men. A deadly shot, blindness, and wings are his attributes. The latter signify inconstancy; and this appears, as a rule, only with the disillusion which is the consequence of satisfaction.

Because the passion depended upon an illusion, which represented that which has only value for the species as valuable for the individual, the deception must vanish after the attainment of the end of the species. The spirit of the species which took possession of the individual sets it free again. Forsaken by this spirit, the individual falls back into its original limitation and narrowness, and sees with wonder that after such a high, heroic, and infinite effort nothing has resulted for its pleasure but what every sexual gratification affords. Contrary to expectation, it finds itself no happier than before. It observes that it has been the dupe of the will of the species. Therefore, as a rule, a Theseus who has been made happy will forsake his Ariadne. If Petrarch's passion had been satisfied, his song would have been silenced from that time forth, like that of the bird as soon as the eggs are laid.

Here let me remark in passing that however much my metaphysics of love will displease the very persons who are entangled in this passion, yet if rational considerations in general could avail anything against it, the fundamental truth disclosed by me would necessarily fit one more than anything else to subdue it. But the saying of the old comedian will, no doubt, remain true: *"Quæ res in se neque consilium, neque modum habet ullum, eam consilio regere non potes."*

Marriages from love are made in the interest of the species, not of the individuals. Certainly the persons concerned imagine they are advancing their own happiness; but their real end is one which is foreign to themselves, for it lies in the production of an individual which is only possible through them.

Brought together by this aim, they ought henceforth to try to get on together as well as possible. But very often the pair brought together by that instinctive illusion, which is the essence of passionate love, will, in other respects, be of very different natures. This comes to light when the illusion vanishes, as it necessarily must. Accordingly love marriages, as a rule, turn out unhappy; for through them the coming generation is cared for at the expense of the present. *"Quien se casa por amores, ha de vivir con dolores"* (Who marries from love must live in sorrow), says the Spanish proverb. The opposite is the case with marriages contracted for purposes of convenience, generally in accordance with the choice of the parents. The considerations prevailing here, of whatever kind they may be, are at least real, and cannot vanish of themselves. Through them, however, the happiness of the present generation is certainly cared for, to the disadvantage of the coming generation, and notwithstanding this it remains problematical. The man who in his marriage looks to money more than to the satisfaction of his inclination lives more in the individual than in the species; which is directly opposed to the truth; hence it appears unnatural, and excites a certain contempt. A girl who, against the advice of her parents, rejects the offer of a rich and not yet old man, in order, setting aside all considerations of convenience, to choose according to her instinctive inclination alone, sacrifices her individual welfare to the species. But just on this account one cannot withhold from her a certain approbation; for she has preferred what is of most importance, and has acted in the spirit of nature (more exactly, of the species), while the parents advised in the spirit of individual egoism. In accordance with all this, it appears as if in making a marriage either the individual or the interests of the species must come off a loser. And this is generally the case; for that convenience and passionate love should go hand in hand is the rarest of lucky accidents. The physical, moral, or intellectual deficiency of the nature of most men may to some extent have its ground in the fact that marriages are ordinarily entered into not from pure choice and inclination, but from all kinds of external considerations, and on account of accidental circumstances. If, however, besides convenience, inclination is also to a certain extent regarded, this is, as it were, an agreement with the genius of the species. Happy marriages are well known to be rare; just because it lies in the nature of marriage that its chief end is not the present but the coming generation. However, let me add, for the consolation of tender, loving natures, that sometimes passionate sexual love associates itself with a feeling of an entirely different origin—real friendship based upon agreement of disposition, which yet for the most part only appears when sexual love proper is extinguished in its satisfaction. This friendship will then generally spring from the fact that the supplementing and corresponding physical, moral, and intellectual qualities of the two individuals, from which sexual love arose, with reference to the child to be produced, are, with reference also to the individuals themselves, related to each other in a supplementary manner as opposite qualities of temperament and mental gifts, and thereby form the basis of a harmony of disposition.

The whole metaphysics of love here dealt with stands in close connection with my metaphysics in general, and the light which it throws upon this may be summed up as follows.

We have seen that the careful selection for the satisfaction of the sexual impulse, a selection which rises through innumerable degrees up to that of passionate love, depends upon the highly serious interest which man takes in the special personal constitution of the next generation. Now this exceedingly remarkable interest confirms two truths which have been set forth in the preceding chapters. (1.) The indestructibility of the true nature of man, which lives on in that coming generation. For that interest which is so lively and eager, and does not spring from reflection and intention, but from the inmost characteristics and tendencies of our nature, could not be so indelibly present and exercise such great power over man if he were absolutely perishable, and were merely followed in time by a race actually and entirely different from him. (2.) That his true nature lies more in the species than in the individual. For that interest in the special nature of the species, which is the root of all love, from the passing inclination to the serious passion, is for every one really the highest concern, the success or failure of which touches him most sensibly; therefore it is called *par excellence* the affair of the heart. Moreover, when this interest has expressed itself strongly and decidedly, everything which merely concerns one's own person is post-poned and necessarily sacrificed to it. Through this, then, man shows that the species lies closer to him than the individual, and he lives more immediately in the former than in the latter. Why does the lover hang with complete abandonment on the eyes of his chosen one, and is ready to make every sacrifice for her? Because it is his immortal part that longs after her; while it is only his mortal part that desires everything else. That vehement or intense longing directed to a particular woman is accordingly an immediate pledge of the indestructibility of the kernel of our being, and of its continued existence in the species. But to regard this continued existence as something trifling and insufficient is an error which arises from the fact that under the conception of the continued life of the species one thinks nothing more than the future existence of beings similar to us, but in no regard identical with us; and this again because, starting from knowledge directed towards without, one takes into consideration only the external form of the species as we apprehend it in perception, and not its inner nature. But it is just this inner nature which lies at the founda-tion of our own consciousness as its kernel, and hence indeed is more immediate than this itself, and, as thing in itself, free from the *principium individuationis*, is really the same and identical in all individuals, whether they exist together or after each other. Now this is the will to live, thus just that which desires life and continuance so vehemently. This accordingly is spared and unaffected by death. It can attain to no better state than its present one; and consequently for it, with life, the constant suffering and striving of the individuals is certain. To free it from this is reserved for the denial of the will to live, as the means by which the individual will breaks away from the stem of the species, and surrenders that existence in it. We lack conceptions for that which it now is; indeed all data for such conceptions are wanting. We can only describe it as that which is free to be will to live or not. Buddhism de-notes the latter case by the word Nirvana, the etymology of which was given in the note at the end of chapter 41. It is the point which remains for ever unattainable to all human knowledge, just as such.

If now, from the standpoint of this last consideration, we

contemplate the turmoil of life, we behold all occupied with its want and misery, straining all their powers to satisfy its infinite needs and to ward off its multifarious sorrows, yet without daring to hope anything else than simply the preservation of this tormented existence for a short span of time. In between, however, in the midst of the tumult, we see the glances of two lovers meet longingly: yet why so secretly, fearfully, and stealthily? Because these lovers are the traitors who seek to perpetuate the whole want and drudgery, which would otherwise speedily reach an end; this they wish to frustrate, as others like them have frustrated it before. This consideration already passes over into the subject of the following chapter.

VI

THE LIFE OF THE SPECIES

(CHAPTER XLII *from* SUPPLEMENTS TO THE FOURTH
BOOK OF THE WORLD AS WILL AND IDEA)

In the . . . [selection *On Death*] it was called to mind
that the (Platonic) Ideas of the different grades of beings,
which are the adequate objectification of the will to live, exhibit themselves in the knowledge of the individual, which is
bound to the form of time, as the *species, i.e.,* as the successive individuals of one kind connected by the bond of generation, and that therefore the species is the Idea broken up in
time. Accordingly the true nature of every living thing lies
primarily in its species: yet the species again has its existence
only in the individuals. Now, although the will only attains to
self-consciousness in the individual, thus knows itself immediately only as the individual, yet the deep-seated consciousness that it is really the species in which his true nature objectifies itself appears in the fact that for the individual the
concerns of the species as such, thus the relations of the sexes,
the production and nourishment of the offspring, are of incomparably greater importance and consequence than everything else. Hence, then, arises in the case of the brutes, heat
or rut (an excellent description of the vehemence of which
will be found in Burdach's "Physiology," vol. i. §§ 247, 257),
and, in the case of man, the careful and capricious selection
of the other individual for the satisfaction of the sexual impulse, which can rise to the height of passionate love, to the
fuller investigation of which I shall devote a special chapter:
hence also, finally the excessive love of parents for their offspring.

In the supplements to the second book the will was compared to the root and the intellect to the crown of the tree;
and this is the case inwardly or psychologically. But outwardly

or physiologically the genitals are the root and the head the
crown. The nourishing part is certainly not the genitals, but
the villi of the intestines: yet not the latter but the former
are the root; because through them the individual is connected
with the species in which it is rooted. For physically the individual is a production of the species, metaphysically a more
or less perfect picture of the Idea, which, in the form of time,
exhibits itself as species. In agreement with the relation expressed here, the greatest vitality, and also the decrepitude of
the brain and the genital organs, is simultaneous and stands
in connection. The sexual impulse is to be regarded as the
inner life of the tree (the species) upon which the life of the
individual grows, like a leaf that is nourished by the tree, and
assists in nourishing the tree; this is why that impulse is so
strong, and springs from the depths of our nature. To castrate
an individual means to cut him off from the tree of the species
upon which he grows, and thus severed, leave him to wither:
hence the degradation of his mental and physical powers. That
the service of the species, *i.e.*, fecundation, is followed in the
case of every animal individual by momentary exhaustion and
debility of all the powers, and in the case of most insects indeed by speedy death, on account of which Celsus said,
"*Seminis emissio est partis animæ jactura*"; that in the case
of man the extinction of the generative power shows that the
individual approaches death; that excessive use of this power
at every age shortens life, while, on the other hand, temperance
in this respect increases all the powers, and especially the muscular powers, on which account it was part of the training of
the Greek athletes; that the same restraint lengthens the life
of the insect even to the following spring; all this points to
the fact that the life of the individual is at bottom only borrowed from the species, and that all ·vital force is, as it were,
force of the species restricted by being dammed up. But this
is to be explained from the fact that the metaphysical substratum of life reveals itself directly in the species and only
by means of this in the individual. Accordingly the Lingam
with the Yoni, as the symbol of the species and its immortality,
is worshipped in India, and, as the counterpoise of death, is
ascribed as an attribute to the very divinity who presides over
death, Siva.

But without myth or symbol, the vehemence of the sexual impulse, the keen intentness and profound seriousness with which every animal, including man, pursues its concerns, shows that it is through the function which serves it that the animal belongs to that in which really and principally its true being lies, the *species;* while all other functions and organs directly serve only the individual, whose existence is at bottom merely secondary. In the vehemence of that impulse, which is the concentration of the whole animal nature, the consciousness further expresses itself that the individual does not endure, and therefore all must be staked on the maintenance of the species, in which its true existence lies.

To illustrate what has been said, let us now imagine a brute in rut, and in the act of generation. We see a seriousness and intentness never known in it at any other time. Now what goes on in it? Does it know that it must die, and that through its present occupation a new individual, which yet entirely resembles itself, will arise in order to take its place? Of all this it knows nothing, for it does not think. But it is as intently careful for the continuance of the species in time as if it knew all that. For it is conscious that it desires to live and exist, and it expresses the highest degree of this volition in the act of generation; this is all that then takes place in its consciousness. This is also quite sufficient for the permanence of the kind; just because the will is the radical and knowledge the adventitious. On this account the will does not require to be guided by knowledge throughout; but whenever in its primitive originality it has resolved, this volition will objectify itself of its own accord in the world of the idea. If now in this way it is that definite animal form which we have thought of that wills life and existence, it does not will life and existence in general, but in this particular form. Therefore it is the sight of its form in the female of its species that stimulates the will of the brute to the act of generation. This volition of the brute, when regarded from without and under the form of time, presents itself as such an animal form maintained through an infinite time by the constantly repeated replacement of one individual by another, thus by the alternation of death and reproduction, which so regarded appear only as the pulse-beats of that form which endures through all time. They may be compared to the forces of attraction and repulsion in which matter consists. That which is shown here in the brute holds good also of man; for although in him the act of generation is accompanied by complete knowledge of its final cause, yet it is not guided by this knowledge, but proceeds directly from the will to live as its concentration. It is accordingly to be reckoned among instinctive actions. For in reproduction the brute is just as little guided by knowledge of the end as in mechanical instincts; in these also the will manifests itself, in the main, without the mediation of knowledge, which here, as there, is only concerned with details. Reproduction is, to a certain extent, the most marvellous of all instincts, and its work the most astonishing.

These considerations explain why the sexual desire has a very different character from every other; it is not only the strongest, but even specifically of a more powerful kind than any other. It is everywhere tacitly assumed as necessary and inevitable, and is not, like other desires, a matter of taste and disposition. For it is the desire which even constitutes the nature of man. In conflict with it no motive is so strong that it would be certain of victory. It is so pre-eminently the chief concern that no other pleasures make up for the deprivation of its satisfaction; and, moreover, for its sake both brute and man undertake every danger and every conflict. A very naive expression of this disposition is the well-known inscription on the door of the *fornix* at Pompeii, decorated with the phallus: *"Heic habitat felicitas:"* this was for those going in naive, for those coming out ironical, and in itself humorous. On the other hand, the excessive power of the sexual passion is seriously and worthily expressed in the inscription which (according to Theon of Smyrna, *De Musica*, c. 47), Osiris had placed upon the column he erected to the eternal gods: "To Eros, the spirit, the heaven, the sun, the moon, the earth, the night, the day, and the father of all that is and that shall be"; also in the beautiful apostrophe with which Lucretius begins his work:

Æneadum genetrix, hominum divomque voluptas,
Alma Venus cet.

To all this corresponds the important *rôle* which the relation of the sexes plays in the world of men, where it is really the invisible central point of all action and conduct, and peeps out everywhere in spite of all veils thrown over it. It is the cause of war and the end of peace, the basis of what is serious, and the aim of the jest, the inexhaustible source of wit, the key to all allusions, and the meaning of all mysterious hints, of all unspoken offers and all stolen glances, the daily meditation of the young, and often also of the old, the hourly thought of the unchaste, and even against their will the constantly recurring imagination of the chaste, the ever ready material of a joke, just because the profoundest seriousness lies at its foundation. It is, however, the piquant element and the joke of life that the chief concern of all men is secretly pursued and ostensibly ignored as much as possible. But, in fact, we see it every moment seat itself, as the true and hereditary lord of the world, out of the fulness of its own strength, upon the ancestral throne, and looking down from thence with scornful glances, laugh at the preparations which have been made to bind it, imprison it, or at least to limit it and wherever it is possible to keep it concealed, or even so to master it that it shall only appear as a subordinate, secondary concern of life. But all this agrees with the fact that the sexual passion is the kernel of the will to live, and consequently the concentration of all desire; therefore in the text I have called the genital organs the focus of the will. Indeed, one may say man is concrete sexual desire; for his origin is an act of copulation and his wish of wishes is an act of copulation, and this tendency alone perpetuates and holds together his whole phenomenal existence. The will to live manifests itself indeed primarily as an effort to sustain the individual; yet this is only a step to the effort to sustain the species, and the latter endeavour must be more powerful in proportion as the life of the species surpasses that of the individual in duration, extension, and value. Therefore sexual passion is the most perfect manifestation of the will to live, its most distinctly expressed type; and the origin of the individual in it, and its primacy over all other desires of the natural man, are both in complete agreement with this.

One other remark of a physiological nature is in place here, a remark which throws light upon my fundamental doctrine expounded in the second book. As the sexual impulse is the most vehement of desires, the wish of wishes, the concentration of all our volition, and accordingly the satisfaction of it which exactly corresponds to the individual wish of any one, that is, the desire fixed upon a definite individual, is the summit and crown of his happiness, the ultimate goal of his natural endeavours, with the attainment of which everything seems to him to have been attained, and with the frustrating of which everything seems to him to have been lost:—so we find, as its physiological correlative, in the objectified will, thus in the human organism, the sperm or semen as the secretion of secretions, the quintessence of all animal fluids, the last result of all organic functions, and have in it a new proof of the fact that the body is only the objectivity of the will, *i.e.*, is the will itself under the form of the idea.

With reproduction is connected the maintenance of the offspring, and with the sexual impulse, parental love; and thus through these the life of the species is carried on. Accordingly the love of the brute for its young has, like the sexual impulse, a strength which far surpasses that of the efforts which merely concerns itself as an individual. This shows itself in the fact that even the mildest animals are ready to undertake for the sake of their young even the most unequal battle for life and death, and with almost all species of animals the mother encounters any danger for the protection of her young, nay, in many cases even faces certain death. In the case of man this instinctive parental love is guided and directed by reason, *i.e.*, by reflection. Sometimes, however, it is also in this way restricted, and with bad characters this may extend to the complete repudiation of it. Therefore we can observe its effects most purely in the lower animals. In itself, however, it is not less strong in man; here also, in particular cases, we see it entirely overcome self-love, and even extend to the sacrifice of life. Thus, for example, the French newspapers have just announced that at Cahors, in the department of Lot, a father has taken his own life in order that his son, who had been drawn for military service, should be the eldest son of a widow, and therefore exempt (*Galignani's Messenger* of 22d June 1843). Yet in the case of the lower animals, since they are capable of no reflection, the instinctive maternal affection (the male is generally ignorant of his paternity) shows itself directly and unsophisticated, and therefore with perfect distinctness

and in its whole strength. At bottom it is the expression of
the consciousness in the brute that its true being lies more
immediately in the species than in the individual, and therefore, when necessary, it sacrifices its life that the species may
be maintained in the young. Thus here, as also in the sexual
impulse, the will to live becomes to a certain extent transcendent, for its consciousness extends beyond the individual, in
which it is inherent, to the species. In order to avoid expressing
this second manifestation of the life of the species in a merely
abstract manner, and to present it to the reader in its magnitude and reality, I will give a few examples of the extraordinary strength of instinctive maternal affection.

The sea-otter, when pursued, seizes its young one and dives
with it; when it comes up again to take breath, it covers the
young one with its body, and receives the harpoon of the
hunter while the young one is escaping. A young whale is
killed merely to attract the mother, who hurries to it and seldom forsakes it so long as it still lives, even although she is
struck with several harpoons (Scoresby's "Journal of a Whaling
Voyage"; from the English of Kreis, p. 196). At Three Kings
Island, near New Zealand, there are colossal seals called sea-
elephants (*phoca proboscidea*). They swim round the island
in regular herds and feed upon fishes, but yet have certain
terrible enemies below water unknown to us, by whom they
are often severely wounded; hence their swimming together
requires special tactics. The females bring forth their young
upon the shore; while they are suckling them, which lasts from
seven to eight weeks, all the males form a circle round them
in order to prevent them, driven by hunger, from entering the
sea, and if this is attempted they prevent it by biting. Thus
they all fast together for between seven and eight weeks, and
all become very thin, simply in order that the young may not
enter the sea before they are able to swim well and observe
the necessary tactics which are then taught them with blows
and bites (Freycinet, *Voy. aux terres Australes*, 1826). We also
see here how parental affection, like every strong exertion of
the will (*cf.* chap. xix. 6), heightens the intelligence. Wild
ducks, white-throats, and many other birds, when the sportsman comes near their nest, fly in front of him with loud cries
and flap about as if their wings were injured, in order to attract

his attention from their young to themselves. The lark tries to entice the dog away from its nest by exposing itself. In the same way hinds and does induce the hunter to pursue them in order that their young may not be attacked. Swallows have flown into burning houses to rescue their young or perish with them. At Delfft, in a great fire, a stork allowed itself to be burnt in its nest rather than forsake its tender young, which could not yet fly (Hadr. Junius, *Descriptio Hollandiæ*). Mountain-cocks and woodcocks allow themselves to be taken upon the nest when brooding. *Muscicapa tyrannus* protects its nest with remarkable courage, and defends itself against eagles. An ant has been cut in two, and the fore half been seen to bring the pupæ to a place of safety. A bitch whose litter had been cut out of her belly crept up to them dying, caressed them, and began to whine violently only when they were taken from her (Burdach, *Physiologie als Erfahrungswissenschaft,* vol. ii. and iii.).

VII

ON THE ASSERTION OF THE
WILL TO LIVE[1]

(CHAPTER XLV *from* SUPPLEMENTS TO THE FOURTH
BOOK OF THE WORLD AS WILL AND IDEA)

If the will to live exhibited itself merely as an impulse to self-preservation, this would only be an assertion of the individual phenomenon for the span of time of its natural duration. The cares and troubles of such a life would not be great, and consequently existence would be easy and serene. Since, on the contrary, the will wills life absolutely and for all time, it exhibits itself also as sexual impulse, which has in view an endless series of generations. This impulse does away with that carelessness, serenity, and innocence which would accompany a merely individual existence, for it brings unrest and melancholy into the consciousness; misfortunes, cares, and misery into the course of life. If, on the other hand, it is voluntarily suppressed, as we see in rare exceptions, then this is the turning of the will, which changes its course. The will does not then transcend the individual, but is abolished in it. Yet this can only take place by means of the individual doing painful violence to itself. If, however, it does take place, then the freedom from care and the serenity of the purely individual existence is restored to the consciousness, and indeed in a higher degree. On the other hand, to the satisfaction of that most vehement of all impulses and desires is linked the origin of a new existence, thus carrying out of life anew, with all its burdens, cares, wants, and pains; certainly in another individual; yet if the two who are different in the phenomenon were so absolutely and in themselves, where would then be eternal justice? Life presents itself as a problem, a task to be worked out, and therefore, as a rule, as a constant conflict with neces-

[1] This selection is connected with § 60 of THE WORLD AS WILL AND IDEA, Dolphin Books, Doubleday & Company, Inc., 1961.

sity. Accordingly every one tries to get through with it and come off as well as he can. He performs life as a compulsory service which he owes. But who has contracted the debt?— His begetter, in the enjoyment of sensual pleasure. Thus, because the one has enjoyed this, the other must live, suffer, and die. However, we know and look back here to the fact that the difference of the similar is conditioned by space and time, which in this sense I have called the *principium individuationis*. Otherwise eternal justice could not be vindicated. Paternal love, on account of which the father is ready to do, to suffer, and to risk more for his child than for himself, and at the same time knows that he owes this, depends simply upon the fact that the begetter recognises himself in the begotten.

The life of a man, with its endless care, want, and suffering, is to be regarded as the explanation and paraphrase of the act of procreation, *i.e.*, the decided assertion of the will to live; and further, it is also due to this that he owes to nature the debt of death, and thinks with anxiety of this debt. Is this not evidence of the fact that our existence involves guilt? At any rate, we always exist, subject to the periodical payment of the toll, birth and death, and successively partake of all the sorrows and joys of life, so that none can escape us: this is just the fruit of the assertion of the will to live. Thus the fear of death, which in spite of all the miseries of life holds us firmly to it, is really illusory; but just as illusory is the impulse which has enticed us into it. This enticement itself may be seen objectively in the reciprocal longing glances of two lovers; 'they are the purest expression of the will to live, in its assertion. How soft and tender it is here! It wills well-being, and quiet pleasure, and mild joys for itself, for others, for all. It is the theme of Anacreon. Thus by allurements and flattery it makes its way into life. But when once it is there, misery introduces crime, and crime misery; horror and desolation fill the scene. It is the theme of Æschylus.

But now the act through which the will asserts itself and man arises is one of which all are, in their inmost being, ashamed, which they therefore carefully conceal; nay, if they are caught in it, are terrified as if they had been taken in a crime. It is an action of which in cold reflection one generally thinks with dislike, and in a lofty mood with loathing. Reflections which in this regard approach the matter more closely are offered by Montaigne in the fifth chapter of the third book, under the marginal heading: *"Ce que c'est que l'amour."* A peculiar sadness and repentance follows close upon it, is yet most perceptible after the first performance of the act, and in general is the more distinct the nobler is the character. Hence even Pliny, the pagan, says: *"Homini tantum primi coitus pœnitentia, augurium scilicet vitæ, a pœnitenda origine"* (*Hist. Nat.*, x. 83). And, on the other hand, in Goethe's "Faust," what do devil and witches practise and sing of on their Sabbath? Lewdness and obscenity. And in the same work (in the admirable "Paralipomena" to "Faust") what does incarnate Satan preach before the assembled multitude? Lewdness and obscenity. But simply and solely by means of the continual practice of such an act as this does the human race subsist. If now optimism were right, if our existence were to be thankfully recognised as the gift of the highest goodness guided by wisdom, and accordingly in itself praiseworthy, commendable, and agreeable, then certainly the act which perpetuates it would necessarily have borne quite another physiognomy. If, on the other hand, this existence is a kind of false step or error; if it is the work of an originally blind will, whose most fortunate development is that it comes to itself in order to abolish itself; then the act which perpetuates that existence must appear precisely as it does appear.

With reference to the first fundamental truth of my doctrine, the remark deserves a place here that the shame mentioned above which attaches to the act of generation extends even to the parts which are concerned in this, although, like all other parts, they are given us by nature. This is again a striking proof that not only the actions but even the body of man is to be regarded as the manifestation, the objectification, of his will, and as its work. For he could not be ashamed of a thing which existed without his will.

The act of generation is further related to the world, as the answer is related to the riddle. The world is wide in space and old in time, and of an inexhaustible multiplicity of forms. Yet all this is only the manifestation of the will to live; and the concentration, the focus of this will is the act of generation. Thus in this act the inner nature of the world expresses itself most distinctly. In this regard it is indeed worth noticing that this act itself is also distinctly called "the will" in the very significant German phrase, *"Er verlangte von ihr, sie sollte ihm zu Willen sein"* (He desired her to comply with his wishes). As the most distinct expression of the will, then, this act is the kernel, the compendium, the quintessence of the world. Therefore from it we obtain light as to the nature and tendency of the world: it is the answer to the riddle. Accordingly it is understood under "the tree of knowledge," for after acquaintance with it the eyes of every one are opened as to life, as Byron also says:

> The tree of knowledge has been plucked,—all's known.
> *—Don Juan*, i. 128.

It is not less in keeping with this quality that it is the open secret, which must never and nowhere be distinctly mentioned, but always and everywhere is understood as the principal matter, and is therefore constantly present to the thoughts of all, wherefore also the slightest allusion to it is instantly understood. The leading part which that act, and what is connected with it, plays in the world, because love intrigues are everywhere, on the one hand, pursued, and, on the other hand, assumed, is quite in keeping with the importance of this *punctum saliens* of the egg of the world. The source of the amusing is simply the constant concealment of the chief concern.

But see now how the young, innocent, human intellect, when that great secret of the world first becomes known to it, is startled at the enormity! The reason of this is that in the long course which the originally unconscious will had to traverse before it rose to intellect, especially to human, rational intellect, it became so strange to itself that it no longer knows its origin, that *pœnitenda origo,* and now, from the standpoint of pure, and therefore innocent, knowing, is horrified at it.

Since now the focus of the will, *i.e.,* its concentration and highest expression, is the sexual impulse and its satisfaction, this is very significantly and naïvely expressed in the symbolical language of nature through the fact that the individualised will, that is, the man and the brute, makes its entrance into the world through the door of the sexual organs.

The assertion of the will to live, which accordingly has its

centre in the act of generation, is in the case of the brute in-
fallible. For the will, which is the *natura naturans,* first arrives
at reflection in man. To arrive at reflection means, not merely
to know the momentary necessity of the individual will, how
to serve it in the pressing present—as is the case with the brute,
in proportion to its completeness and its necessities, which go
hand in hand—but to have attained a greater breadth of knowledge, by virtue of a distinct remembrance of the past, an ap-
proximate anticipation of the future, and thereby a general
survey of the individual life, both one's own life and that of
others, nay, of existence in general. Really the life of every
species of brute, through the thousands of years of its existence,
is to a certain extent like a single moment; for it is mere consciousness of the present, without that of the past and the
future, and consequently without that of death. In this sense
it is to be regarded as a permanent moment, a *Nunc stans.*
Here we see, in passing, most distinctly that in general the
form of life, or the manifestation of the will with consciousness, is primarily and immediately merely the present. Past
and future are added only in the case of man, and indeed
merely in conception, are known *in abstracto,* and perhaps illustrated by pictures of the imagination. Thus after the will
to live, *i.e.,* the inner being of nature, in the ceaseless striving
towards complete objectification and complete enjoyment, has
run through the whole series of the brutes,—which often occurs in the various periods of successive animal series each
arising anew on the same planet,—it arrives at last at reflection
in the being who is endowed with reason, man. Here now to
him the thing begins to be doubtful, the question forces itself
upon him whence and wherefore all this is, and chiefly whether
the care and misery of his life and effort is really repaid by the
gain? *"Le jeu vaut-il bien la chandelle?"* Accordingly here is
the point at which, in the light of distinct knowledge, he decides for the assertion or denial of the will to live; although
as a rule he can only bring the latter to consciousness in a
mythical form. We have consequently no ground for assuming that a still more highly developed objectification of the
will is ever reached, anywhere; for it has already reached its
turning-point here.

VIII

ON DEATH AND ITS RELATION TO THE INDESTRUCTIBILITY OF OUR TRUE NATURE[1]

(CHAPTER XLI *from* SUPPLEMENTS TO THE
FOURTH BOOK OF THE WORLD AS WILL AND IDEA)

Death is the true inspiring genius, or the muse of philosophy,
wherefore Socrates has defined the latter as *Meditatio Mortis.*
Indeed without death men would scarcely philosophise. Therefore it will be quite in order that a special consideration of
this should have its place here at the beginning of the last,
most serious, and most important of our books.

The brute lives without a proper knowledge of death; therefore the individual brute enjoys directly the absolute imperishableness of the species, for it is only conscious of itself as endless. In the case of men the terrifying certainty of death
necessarily entered with reason. But as everywhere in nature
with every evil a means of cure, or at least some compensation, is given, the same reflection which introduces the knowledge of death also assists us to *metaphysical* points of view,
which comfort us concerning it, and of which the brute has
no need and is incapable. All religious and philosophical systems are principally directed to this end, and are thus primarily
the antidote to the certainty of death, which the reflective reason produces out of its own means. Yet the degree in which
they attain this end is very different, and certainly *one* religion
or philosophy will, far more than the others, enable men to
look death in the face with a quiet glance. Brahmanism and
Buddhism, which teach man to regard himself as himself, the
original being, the Brahm, to which all coming into being and
passing away is essentially foreign, will achieve much more in
this respect than such as teach that man is made out of noth-

[1] This selection is connected with § 54 of THE WORLD AS WILL
AND IDEA, Dolphin Books, Doubleday & Company, Inc., 1961.

ing, and actually begins at birth his existence derived from
another. Answering to this we find in India a confidence and
a contempt for death of which one has no conception in Europe. It is, in fact, a hazardous thing to force upon a man,
by early imprinting them, weak and untenable conceptions in
this important regard, and thereby making him for ever incapable of taking up correct and stable ones. For example, to
teach him that he recently came out of nothing, and consequently through an eternity has been nothing, but yet for the
future will be imperishable, is just the same as to teach him
that although he is through and through the work of another,
yet he will be held responsible through all eternity for his actions. If, then, when the mind ripens and reflection appears,
the untenable nature of such doctrines forces itself upon him,
he has nothing better to put in its place, nay, is no longer
capable of understanding anything better, and thus loses the
comfort which nature had destined for him also, as a compensation for the certainty of death. In consequence of such a
process, we see even now in England (1844), among ruined
factory hands, the Socialists, and in Germany, among ruined
students, the young Hegelians, sink to the absolutely physical
point of view, which leads to the result: *edite, bibite, post
mortem nulla voluptas,* and so far may be defined as bestialism.

However, after all that has been taught concerning death,
it cannot be denied that, at least in Europe, the opinion of
men, nay, often even of the same individual, very frequently
vacillates between the conception of death as absolute annihilation and the assumption that we are, as it were, with skin
and hair, immortal. Both are equally false: but we have not
so much to find a correct mean as rather to gain the higher
point of view from which such notions disappear of themselves.

In these considerations I shall first of all start from the purely
empirical standpoint. Here there primarily lies before us the
undeniable fact that, according to the natural consciousness,
man not only fears death for his own person more than anything else, but also weeps violently over the death of those
that belong to him, and indeed clearly not egotistically, for
his own loss, but out of sympathy for the great misfortune
that has befallen them. Therefore he also censures those who
in such a case neither weep nor show sadness as hard-hearted

and unloving. It is parallel with this that revenge, in its highest degree, seeks the death of the adversary as the greatest evil that can be inflicted. Opinions change with time and place; but the voice of nature remains always and everywhere the same, and is therefore to be heeded before everything else. Now here it seems distinctly to say that death is a great evil. In the language of nature death means annihilation. And that death is a serious matter may be concluded from the fact that, as every one knows, life is no joke. We must indeed deserve nothing better than these two.

In fact, the fear of death is independent of all knowledge; for the brute has it, although it does not know death. Everything that is born brings it with it into the world. But this fear of death is _a priori_ only the reverse side of the will to live, which indeed we all are. Therefore in every brute the fear of its destruction is inborn, like the care for its maintenance. Thus it is the fear of death, and not the mere avoidance of pain, which shows itself in the anxious carefulness with which the brute seeks to protect itself, and still more its brood, from everything that might become dangerous. Why does the brute flee, trembling, and seek to conceal itself? Because it is simply the will to live, but, as such, is forfeited to death, and wishes to gain time. Such also, by nature, is man. The greatest evil, the worst that can anywhere threaten, is death; the greatest fear is the fear of death. Nothing excites us so irresistibly to the most lively interest as danger to the life of others; nothing is so shocking as an execution. Now the boundless attachment to life which appears here cannot have sprung from knowledge and reflection; to these it rather appears foolish, for the objective worth of life is very uncertain, and at least it remains doubtful whether it is preferable to not being, nay, if experience and reflection come to be expressed, not being must certainly win. If one knocked on the graves, and asked the dead whether they wished to rise again, they would shake their heads. Such is the opinion of Socrates in "Plato's Apology," and even the gay and amiable Voltaire cannot help saying, "_On aime la vie; mais le néant ne laisse pas d'avoir du bon;_" and again, "_Je ne sais pas ce que c'est que la vie éternelle, mais celle-ci est une mauvaise plaisanterie._" Besides, life must in any case soon end; so that the few years which perhaps one has yet to be vanish entirely before the endless time when one will be no more. Accordingly it appears to reflection even ludicrous to be so anxious about this span of time, to tremble so much if our own life or that of another is in danger, and to compose tragedies the horror of which has its strength in the fear of death. That powerful attachment to life is therefore irrational and blind; it can only be explained from the fact that our whole inner nature is itself will to live, to which, therefore, life must appear as the highest good, however embittered, short, and uncertain it may always be; and that that will, in itself and originally, is unconscious and blind. Knowledge, on the contrary, far from being the source of that attachment to life, even works against it, for it discloses the worthlessness of life, and thus combats the fear of death. When it conquers, and accordingly the man faces death courageously and composedly, this is honoured as great and noble, thus we hail then the triumph of knowledge over the blind will to live, which is yet the kernel of our own being. In the same way we despise him in whom knowledge is defeated in that conflict, and who therefore clings unconditionally to life, struggles to the utmost against approaching death, and receives it with despair; and yet in him it is only the most original being of ourselves and of nature that expresses itself. We may here ask, in passing, how could this boundless love of life and endeavour to maintain it in every way as long as possible be regarded as base, contemptible, and by the adherents of every religion as unworthy of this, if it were the gift of good gods, to be recognised with thankfulness? And how could it then seem great and noble to esteem it lightly? Meanwhile, what is confirmed by these considerations is—(1.) that the will to live is the inmost nature of man; (2.) that in itself it is unconscious and blind; (3.) that knowledge is an adventitious principle, which is originally foreign to the will; (4.) that knowledge conflicts with the will, and that our judgment applauds the victory of knowledge over the will.

If what makes death seem so terrible to us were the thought of not being, we would necessarily think with equal horror of the time when as yet we were not. For it is irrefutably certain that not being after death cannot be different from not being before birth, and consequently is also no more deplorable. A whole eternity has run its course while as yet we were not, but that by no means disturbs us. On the other hand, we find it hard, nay, unendurable, that after the momentary intermezzo of an ephemeral existence, a second eternity should follow in which we shall no longer be. Should, then, this thirst for existence have arisen because we have now tasted it and have found it so delightful? As was already briefly explained above, certainly not; far sooner could the experience gained have awakened an infinite longing for the lost paradise of non-existence. To the hope, also, of the immortality of the soul there is always added that of a "better world"—a sign that the present world is not much good. Notwithstanding all this, the question as to our state after death has certainly been discussed, in books and verbally, ten thousand times oftener than the question as to our state before birth. Yet theoretically the one is just as near at hand and as fair a problem as the other; and besides, whoever had answered the one would soon see to the bottom of the other. We have fine declamations about how shocking it would be to think that the mind of man, which embraces the world, and has so many very excellent thoughts, should sink with him into the grave; but we hear nothing about this mind having allowed a whole eternity to pass before it came into being with these its qualities, and how the world must have had to do without it all that time. Yet no question presents itself more naturally to knowledge, uncorrupted by the will, than this: An infinite time has passed before my birth; what was I during this time? Metaphysically, it might perhaps be answered, "I was always I; that is, all who during that time said I, were just I." But let us look away from this to our present entirely empirical point of view, and assume that I did not exist at all. Then I can console myself as to the infinite time after my death, when I shall not be, with the infinite time when I already was not, as a well-accustomed, and indeed very comfortable, state. For the eternity *a parte post* without me can be just as little fearful as the eternity *a parte ante* without me, since the two are distinguished by nothing except by the interposition of an ephemeral dream of life. All proofs, also, for continued existence after death may just as well be applied *in partem ante*, where they then demonstrate existence before life, in the assumption of which the Hindus and Buddhists therefore show themselves very consistent. Kant's ideality of time alone solves all these riddles. But we are not speaking of that now. This, however, results from what has been said, that to mourn for the time when one will be no more is just as absurd as it would be to mourn over the time when as yet one was not; for it is all the same whether the time which our existence does not fill is related to that which it does fill, as future or as past.

But, also, regarded entirely apart from these temporal considerations, it is in and for itself absurd to look upon not being as an evil; for every evil, as every good, presupposes existence, nay, even consciousness: but the latter ceases with life, as also in sleep and in a swoon; therefore the absence of it is well known to us, and trusted, as containing no evil at all: its entrance, however, is always an affair of a moment. From this point of view Epicurus considered death, and therefore quite rightly said "Death does not concern us"; with the explanation that when we are death is not, and when death is we are not (*Diog. Laert.*, x. 27). To have lost what cannot be missed is clearly no evil. Therefore ceasing to be ought to disturb us as little as not having been. Accordingly from the standpoint of knowledge there appears absolutely no reason to fear death. But consciousness consists in knowing; therefore, for consciousness death is no evil. Moreover, it is really not this *knowing* part of our *ego* that fears death, but the *fuga mortis* proceeds entirely and alone from the blind *will*, of which everything living is filled. To this, however, as was already mentioned above, it is essential, just because it is will to live, whose whole nature consists in the effort after life and existence, and which is not originally endowed with knowledge, but only in consequence of its objectification in animal individuals. If now the will, by means of knowledge, beholds death as the end of the phenomenon with which it has identified itself, and to which, therefore, it sees itself limited, its whole nature struggles against it with all its might. Whether now it has really something to fear from death we will investigate further on, and will then remember the real source of the fear of death, which has been shown here along with the requisite distinction of the willing and the knowing part of our nature.

Corresponding to this, then, what makes death so terrible

to us is not so much the end of life—for this can appear to no one specially worthy of regret—but rather the destruction of the organism; really because this is the will itself exhibiting itself as body. But we only really feel this destruction in the evils of disease or of old age; death itself, on the other hand, consists for the *subject* only in the moment when consciousness vanishes because the activity of the brain ceases. The extension of the stoppage to all the other parts of the organism which follows this is really already an event after death. Thus death, in a subjective regard, concerns the consciousness alone. Now what the vanishing of this may be every one can to a certain extent judge of from going to sleep; but it is still better known to whoever has really fainted, for in this the transition is not so gradual, nor accompanied by dreams, but first the power of sight leaves us, still fully conscious, and then immediately the most profound unconsciousness enters; the sensation that accompanies it, so far as it goes, is anything but disagreeable; and without doubt, as sleep is the brother of death, so the swoon is its twin-brother. Even violent death cannot be painful, for even severe wounds are not felt at all till some time afterwards, often not till the outward signs of them are observed. If they are rapidly mortal, consciousness will vanish before this discovery; if they result in death later, then it is the same as with other illnesses. All those also who have lost consciousness in water, or from charcoal fumes, or through hanging are well known to say that it happened without pain. And now, finally, the death which is properly in accordance with nature, death from old age, euthanasia, is a gradual vanishing and sinking out of existence in an imperceptible manner. Little by little in old age, the passions and desires, with the susceptibility for their objects, are extinguished; the emotions no longer find anything to excite them; for the power of presenting ideas to the mind always becomes weaker, its images fainter; the impressions no longer cleave to us, but pass over without leaving a trace, the days roll ever faster, events lose their significance, everything grows pale. The old man stricken in years totters about or rests in a corner now only a shadow, a ghost of his former self. What remains there for death to destroy? One day a sleep is his last, and his dreams are ————.

They are the dreams which Hamlet inquires after in the famous soliloquy. I believe we dream them even now.

I have here also to remark that the maintenance of the life process, although it has a metaphysical basis, does not go on without resistance, and consequently not without effort. It is this to which the organism yields every night, on account of which it then suspends the brain function and diminishes certain secretions, the respiration, the pulse, and the development of heat. From this we may conclude that the entire ceasing of the life process must be a wonderful relief to its motive force; perhaps this has some share in the expression of sweet contentment on the faces of most dead persons. In general the moment of death may be like the moment of awaking from a heavy dream that has oppressed us like a nightmare.

Up to this point the result we have arrived at is that death, however much it may be feared, can yet really be no evil. But often it even appears as a good thing, as something wished for, as a friend. All that have met with insuperable obstacles to their existence or their efforts, that suffer from incurable diseases or inconsolable griefs, have as a last refuge, which generally opens to them of its own accord, the return into the womb of nature, from which they arose for a short time, enticed by the hope of more favourable conditions of existence than have fallen to their lot, and the same path out of which constantly remains open. That return is the *cessio bonorum* of life. Yet even here it is only entered upon after a physical and moral conflict: so hard does one struggle against returning to the place from which one came out so lightly and readily, to an existence which has so much suffering and so little pleasure to offer. The Hindus give the god of death, Yama, two faces; one very fearful and terrible, and one very cheerful and benevolent. This partly explains itself from the reflections we have just made.

At the empirical point of view at which we still stand, the following consideration is one which presents itself of its own accord, and therefore deserves to be accurately defined by illustration, and thereby referred to its proper limits. The sight of a dead body shows me that sensibility, irritability, circulation of the blood, reproduction, &c., have here ceased. I conclude from this with certainty that what actuated these hitherto, which was yet always something unknown to me, now actuates them no longer, thus has departed from them. But if I should now wish to add that this must have been just what I have known only as consciousness, consequently as intelligence (soul), this would be not only an unjustified but clearly a false conclusion. For consciousness has always showed itself to me not as the cause, but as the product and result of the organised life, for it rose and sank in consequence of this in the different periods of life, in health and sickness, in sleep, in a swoon, in awaking, &c., thus always appeared as effect, never as cause of the organised life, always showed itself as something which arises and passes away, and again arises, so long as the conditions of this still exist, but not apart from them. Nay, I may also have seen that the complete derangement of consciousness, madness, far from dragging down with it and depressing the other forces, or indeed endangering life, heightens these very much, especially irritability or muscular force, and rather lengthens than shortens life, if other causes do not come in. Then, also: I knew individuality as a quality of everything organised, and therefore, if this is a self-conscious organism, also of consciousness. But there exists no occasion now to conclude that individuality was inherent in that vanished principle, which imparts life, and is completely unknown to me; all the less so as I see that everywhere in nature each particular phenomenon is the work of a general force which is active in thousands of similar phenomena. But, on the other hand, there is just as little occasion to conclude that because the organised life has ceased here that force which hitherto actuated it has also become nothing; as little as to infer the death of the spinner from the stopping of the spinning-wheel. If a pendulum, by finding its centre of gravity, at last comes to rest, and thus its individual apparent life has ceased, no one will imagine that gravitation is now annihilated; but every one comprehends that, after as before, it is active in innumerable phenomena. Certainly it might be urged against this comparison, that here also, in this pendulum, gravitation has not ceased to be active, but only to manifest its activity palpably; whoever insists on this may think, instead, of an electrical body, in which, after its discharge, electricity has actually ceased to be active. I only wished to show in this that we ourselves recog-

nise in the lowest forces of nature an eternity and ubiquity
with regard to which the transitory nature of their fleeting
phenomena never makes us err for a moment. So much the
less, then, should it come into our mind to regard the ceasing
of life as the annihilation of the living principle, and consequently death as the entire destruction of the man. Because
the strong arm which, three thousand years ago, bent the
bow of Ulysses is no more, no reflective and well-regulated
understanding will regard the force which acted so energeti-
cally in it as entirely annihilated, and therefore, upon further
reflection, will also not assume that the force which bends the
bow to-day first began with this arm. The thought lies far
nearer us, that the force which earlier actuated the life which
now has vanished is the same which is active in the life which
now flourishes: nay, this is almost inevitable. Certainly, however, we know that, as was explained in the second book,
only that is perishable which is involved in the causal series;
but only the states and forms are so involved. On the other
hand, untouched by the change of these which is introduced
by causes, there remain on the one side matter, and on the
other side natural forces; for both are the presupposition of
all these changes. But the principle of our life we must, primarily at least, conceive as a force of nature, until perhaps a
more profound investigation has brought us to know what it is
in itself. Thus, taken simply as a force of nature, the vital force
remains entirely undisturbed by the change of forms and
states, which the bond of cause and effect introduces and carries off again, and which alone are subject to the process of
coming into being and passing away, as it lies before us in
experience. Thus so far the imperishable nature of our true
being can be proved with certainty. But it is true this will not
satisfy the claims which are wont to be made upon proofs of
our continued existence after death, nor insure the consolation
which is expected from such proofs. However, it is always
something; and whoever fears death as an absolute annihilation cannot afford to despise the perfect certainty that the inmost principle of his life remains untouched by it. Nay, the
paradox might be set up, that that second thing also which,
just like the forces of nature, remains untouched by the continual change under the guidance of causality, thus matter,

by its absolute permanence, insures us indestructibility, by virtue of which whoever was incapable of comprehending any
other might yet confidently trust in a certain imperishableness. "What!" it will be said, "the permanence of the mere
dust, of the crude matter, is to be regarded as a continuance
of our being?" Oh! do you know this dust, then? Do you know
what it is and what it can do? Learn to know it before you
despise it. This matter which now lies there as dust and ashes
will soon, dissolved in water, form itself as a crystal, will shine
as metal, will then emit electric sparks, will by means of its
galvanic intensity manifest a force which, decomposing the
closest combinations, reduces earths to metals; nay, it will, of
its own accord, form itself into plants and animals, and from
its mysterious womb develop that life for the loss of which
you, in your narrowness, are so painfully anxious. Is it, then,
absolutely nothing to continue to exist as such matter? Nay,
I seriously assert that even this permanence of matter affords
evidence of the indestructibility of our true nature, though only
as in an image or simile, or, rather, only as in outline. To see
this we only need to call to mind the explanation of matter
given in chapter 24, from which it resulted that mere formless
matter—this basis of the world of experience which is never
perceived for itself alone, but assumed as constantly remaining—is the immediate reflection, the visibility in general, of
the thing in itself, thus of the will. Therefore, whatever absolutely pertains to the will as such holds good also of matter,
and it reflects the true eternal nature of the will under the
image of temporal imperishableness. Because, as has been said,
nature does not lie, no view which has sprung from a purely
objective comprehension of it, and been logically thought out,
can be absolutely false, but at the most only very one-sided
and imperfect. Such, however, is, indisputably, consistent
materialism; for instance, that of Epicurus, just as well as the
absolute idealism opposed to it, like that of Berkeley, and in
general every philosophical point of view which has proceeded
from a correct *apperçu,* and been honestly carried out. Only
they are all exceedingly one-sided comprehensions, and therefore, in spite of their opposition, they are all true, each from
a definite point of view; but as soon as one has risen above this
point of view, then they only appear as relatively and con-

ditionally true. The highest standpoint alone, from which one surveys them all and knows them in their relative truth, but also beyond this, in their falseness, can be that of absolute truth so far as this is in general attainable. Accordingly we see, as was shown above, that in the very crude, and therefore very old, point of view of materialism proper the indestructibility of our true nature in itself is represented, as by a mere shadow of it, the imperishableness of matter; as in the already higher naturalism of an absolute physics it is represented by the ubiquity and eternity of the natural forces, among which the vital force is at least to be counted. Thus even these crude points of view contain the assertion that the living being suffers no absolute annihilation through death, but continues to exist in and with the whole of nature.

The considerations which have brought us to this point, and to which the further explanations link themselves on, started from the remarkable fear of death which fills all living beings. But now we will change the standpoint and consider how, in contrast to the individual beings, the *whole* of nature bears itself with reference to death. In doing this, however, we still always remain upon the ground of experience.

Certainly we know no higher game of chance than that for death and life. Every decision about this we watch with the utmost excitement, interest, and fear; for in our eyes all in all is at stake. On the other hand, nature, which never lies, but is always straightforward and open, speaks quite differently upon this theme, speaks like Krishna in the Bhagavadgita. What it says is: The death or the life of the individual is of no significance. It expresses this by the fact that it exposes the life of every brute, and even of man, to the most insignificant accidents without coming to the rescue. Consider the insect on your path; a slight, unconscious turning of your step is decisive as to its life or death. Look at the wood-snail, without any means of flight, of defence, of deception, of concealment, a ready prey for all. Look at the fish carelessly playing in the still open net; the frog restrained by its laziness from the flight which might save it; the bird that does not know of the falcon that soars above it; the sheep which the wolf eyes and examines from the thicket. All these, provided with little foresight, go about guilelessly among the dangers that threaten their existence every moment. Since now nature exposes its organisms, constructed with such inimitable skill, not only to the predatory instincts of the stronger, but also to the blindest chance, to the humour of every fool, the mischievousness of every child without reserve, it declares that the annihilation of these individuals is indifferent to it, does it no harm, has no significance, and that in these cases the effect is of no more importance than the cause. It says this very distinctly, and it does not lie; only it makes no comments on its utterances, but rather expresses them in the laconic style of an oracle. If now the all-mother sends forth her children without protection to a thousand threatening dangers, this can only be because she knows that if they fall they fall back into her womb, where they are safe; therefore their fall is a mere jest. Nature does not act otherwise with man than with the brutes. Therefore its declaration extends also to man: the life and death of the individual are indifferent to it. Accordingly, in a certain sense, they ought also to be indifferent to us, for we ourselves are indeed nature. Certainly, if only we saw deep enough, we would agree with nature, and regard life and death as indifferently as it does. Meanwhile, by means of reflection, we must attribute that carelessness and indifference of nature towards the life of the individuals to the fact that the destruction of such a phenomenon does not in the least affect its true and proper nature.

If we further ponder the fact, that not only, as we have just seen, are life and death dependent upon the most trifling accidents, but that the existence of the organised being in general is an ephemeral one, that animal and plant arise to-day and pass away to-morrow, and birth and death follow in quick succession, while to the unorganised things which stand so much lower an incomparably longer duration is assured, and an infinite duration to the absolutely formless matter alone, to which, indeed, we attribute this *a priori*,—then, I think, the thought must follow of its own accord, even from the purely empirical, but objective and unprejudiced comprehension of such an order of things, that this is only a superficial phenomenon, that such a constant arising and passing away can by no means touch the root of things, but can only be relative, nay, only apparent, in which the true inner nature of that thing is not included, the nature which everywhere evades our glance and is thoroughly mysterious, but rather that this continues to exist undisturbed by it; although we can neither apprehend nor conceive the manner in which this happens, and must therefore think of it only generally as a kind of *tour de passe-passe* which took place there. For that, while what is most imperfect, the lowest, the unorganised, continues to exist unassailed, it is just the most perfect beings, the living creatures, with their infinitely complicated and inconceivably ingenious organisations, which constantly arise, new from the very foundation, and after a brief span of time absolutely pass into nothingness, to make room for other new ones like them coming into existence out of nothing—this is something so obviously absurd that it can never be the true order of things, but rather a mere veil which conceals this, or, more accurately, a phenomenon conditioned by the nature of our intellect. Nay, the whole being and not being itself of these individuals, in relation to which death and life are opposites, can only be relative. Thus the language of nature, in which it is given us as absolute, cannot be the true and ultimate expression of the nature of things and of the order of the world, but indeed only a *patois du pays, i.e.*, something merely relatively true, —something to be understood *cum grano salis*, or, to speak properly, something conditioned by our intellect; I say, an immediate, intuitive conviction of the kind which I have tried to describe in words will press itself upon every one; *i.e.*, certainly only upon every one whose mind is not of an utterly ordinary species, which is absolutely only capable of knowing the particular simply and solely as such, which is strictly limited to the knowledge of individuals, after the manner of the intellect of the brutes. Whoever, on the other hand, by means of a capacity of an only somewhat higher power, even just begins to see in the individual beings their universal, their Ideas, will also, to a certain extent, participate in that conviction, and that indeed as an immediate, and therefore certain, conviction. In fact, it is also only small, limited minds that fear death quite seriously as their annihilation, and persons of decidedly superior capacity are completely free from such terrors. Plato rightly bases the whole of philosophy upon the knowledge of the doctrine of Ideas, *i.e.*, upon the percep-

tion of the universal in the particular. But the conviction here
described, which proceeds directly from the comprehension of
nature, must have been exceedingly vivid in those sublime
authors of the Upanishads of the Vedas, who can scarcely be
thought of as mere men, for it speaks to us so forcibly out
of an innumerable number of their utterances that we must
ascribe this immediate illumination of their mind to the fact
that these wise men, standing nearer the origin of our race
in time, comprehended the nature of things more clearly and
profoundly than the already deteriorated race is able to do.
But certainly their comprehension is assisted by the natural
world of India, which is endowed with life in a very different
degree from our northern world. However, thorough reflection, as pursued by Kant's great mind, leads by another path
to the same result, for it teaches us that our intellect, in which
that phenomenal world which changes so fast exhibits itself,
does not comprehend the true ultimate nature of things, but
merely its phenomenal manifestation, and indeed, as I add,
because it is originally only destined to present the motives
to our will, *i.e.*, to be serviceable to it in the pursuit of its
paltry ends.

Let us, however, carry our objective and unprejudiced consideration of nature still further. If I kill a living creature,
whether a dog, a bird, a frog, or even only an insect, it is
really inconceivable that this being, or rather the original force
by virtue of which such a marvellous phenomenon exhibited
itself just the moment before, in its full energy and love of
life, should have been annihilated by my wicked or thoughtless
act. And again, on the other hand, the millions of animals
of every kind which come into existence every moment, in infinite variety, full of force and activity, can never, before the
act of their generation, have been nothing at all, and have
attained from nothing to an absolute beginning. If now in this
way I see one of these withdraw itself from my sight, without
me knowing where it goes, and another appear without me
knowing whence it comes; if, moreover, both have the same
form, the same nature, the same character, and only not the
same matter, which yet during their existence they continually
throw off and renew; then certainly the assumption, that that
which vanishes and that which appears in its place are one

and the same, which has only experienced a slight alteration, a renewal of the form of its existence, and that consequently death is for the species what sleep is for the individual; this assumption, I say, lies so close at hand that it is impossible not to light upon it, unless the mind, perverted in early youth by the imprinting of false views, hurries it out of the way, even from a distance, with superstitious fear. But the opposite assumption that the birth of an animal is an arising out of nothing, and accordingly that its death is its absolute annihilation, and this with the further addition that man, who has also originated out of nothing, has yet an individual, endless existence, and indeed a conscious existence, while the dog, the ape, the elephant, are annihilated by death, is really something against which the healthy mind revolts and which it must regard as absurd. If, as is sufficiently often repeated, the comparison of the results of a system with the utterances of the healthy mind is supposed to be a touchstone of its truth, I wish the adherents of the system which was handed down from Descartes to the pre-Kantian eclectics, nay, which even now is still the prevailing view of the great majority of cultured people in Europe, would apply this touchstone here.

Throughout and everywhere the true symbol of nature is the circle, because it is the schema or type of recurrence. This is, in fact, the most universal form in nature, which it carries out in everything, from the course of the stars down to the death and the genesis of organised beings, and by which alone, in the ceaseless stream of time, and its content, a permanent existence, *i.e.*, a nature, becomes possible.

If in autumn we consider the little world of insects, and see how one prepares its bed to sleep the long, rigid winter-sleep; another spins its coccoon to pass the winter as a chrysalis, and awake in spring rejuvenated and perfected; and, finally, how most of them, intending themselves to rest in the arms of death, merely arrange with care the suitable place for their egg, in order to issue forth again from it some day renewed;—this is nature's great doctrine of immortality, which seeks to teach us that there is no radical difference between sleep and death, but the one endangers existence just as little as the other. The care with which the insect prepares a cell, or hole, or nest, deposits its egg in it, together with food for the larva that will come out of it in the following spring, and then quietly dies, is just like the care with which in the evening a man lays ready his clothes and his breakfast for the next morning, and then quietly goes to sleep; and at bottom it could not take place at all if it were not that the insect which dies in autumn is in itself, and according to its true nature, just as much identical with the one which is hatched out in the spring as the man who lies down to sleep is identical with the man who rises from it.

If now, after these considerations, we return to ourselves and our own species, then cast our glance forward far into the future, and seek to present to our minds the future generations, with the millions of their individuals in the strange form of their customs and pursuits, and then interpose with the question: Whence will all these come? Where are they now? Where is the fertile womb of that nothing, pregnant with worlds, which still conceals the coming races? Would not the smiling and true answer to this be, Where else should they be than there where alone the real always was and will be, in the present and its content?—thus with thee, the foolish questioner, who in this mistaking of his own nature is like the leaf upon the tree, which, fading in autumn and about to fall, complains at its destruction, and will not be consoled by looking forward to the fresh green which will clothe the tree in spring, but says lamenting, "I am not these! These are quite different leaves!" Oh, foolish leaf! Whither wilt thou? And whence should others come? Where is the nothing whose abyss thou fearest? Know thine own nature, that which is so filled with thirst for existence; recognise it in the inner, mysterious, germinating force of the tree, which, constantly *one* and the same in all generations of leaves, remains untouched by all arising and passing away. Whether the fly which now buzzes round me goes to sleep in the evening, and buzzes again tomorrow, or dies in the evening, and in spring another fly buzzes which has sprung from its egg: that is in itself the same thing; but therefore the knowledge which exhibits this as two fundamentally different things is not unconditioned, but relative, a knowledge of the phenomenon, not of the thing in itself. In the morning the fly exists again; it also exists again

in the spring. What distinguishes for it the winter from the
night? In Burdach's "Physiology," vol. i. § 275, we read, "Till
ten o'clock in the morning no *Cercaria ephemera* (one of the
infusoria) is to be seen (in the infusion), and at twelve the
whole water swarms with them. In the evening they die, and
the next morning they again appear anew." So it was observed
by Nitzsch six days running.

So everything lingers but a moment, and hastens on to
death. The plant and the insect die at the end of the summer,
the brute and the man after a few years: death reaps unweariedly. Yet notwithstanding this, nay, as if this were not
so at all, everything is always there and in its place, just as
if everything were imperishable. The plant always thrives and
blooms, the insect hums, the brute and the man exist in un-
wasted youth, and the cherries that have already been enjoyed a thousand times we have again before us every summer. The nations also exist as immortal individuals, although
sometimes their names change; even their action, what they
do and suffer, is always the same; although history always
pretends to relate something different: for it is like the kaleido-
scope, which at every turn shows a new figure, while we really
always have the same thing before our eyes. What then
presses itself more irresistibly upon us than the thought that
that arising and passing away does not concern the real nature
of things, but this remains untouched by it, thus is imperishable, and therefore all and each that *wills* to exist actually exists continuously and without end. Accordingly at every given
point of time all species of animals, from the gnat to the elephant, exist together complete. They have already renewed
themselves many thousand times, and withal have remained
the same. They know nothing of others like them, who have
lived before them, or will live after them; it is the species which
always lives, and in the consciousness of the imperishable nature of the species and their identity with it the individuals
cheerfully exist. The will to live manifests itself in an endless
present, because this is the form of the life of the species,
which, therefore, never grows old, but remains always young.
Death is for it what sleep is for the individual, or what winking
is for the eye, by the absence of which the Indian gods are

known, if they appear in human form. As through the entrance of night the world vanishes, but yet does not for a moment cease to exist, so man and brute apparently pass away through death, and yet their true nature continues, just as undisturbed by it. Let us now think of that alternation of death and birth as infinitely rapid vibrations, and we have before us the enduring objectification of the will, the permanent Ideas of being, fixed like the rainbow on the waterfall. This is temporal immortality. In consequence of this, notwithstanding thousands of years of death and decay, nothing has been lost, not an atom of the matter, still less anything of the inner being, that exhibits itself as nature. Therefore every moment we can cheerfully cry, "In spite of time, death, and decay, we are still all together!"

Perhaps we would have to except whoever had once said from the bottom of his heart, with regard to this game, "I want no more." But this is not yet the place to speak of this.

But we have certainly to draw attention to the fact that the pain of birth and the bitterness of death are the two constant conditions under which the will to live maintains itself in its objectification, *i.e.*, our inner nature, untouched by the course of time and the death of races, exists in an everlasting present, and enjoys the fruit of the assertion of the will to live. This is analogous to the fact that we can only be awake during the day on condition that we sleep during the night; indeed the latter is the commentary which nature offers us for the understanding of that difficult passage.[2]

For the substratum, or the content, or the material of the *present,* is through all time really the same. The impossibility of knowing this identity directly is just *time,* a form and limitation of our intellect. That on account of it, for example, the future event is not yet, depends upon an illusion of which we become conscious when that event has come. That the essential form of our intellect introduces such an illusion explains and justifies itself from the fact that the intellect has come forth from the hands of nature by no means for the apprehension of the nature of things, but merely for the apprehen-

[2] The suspension of the *animal* functions is sleep, that of the *organic* functions is death.

sion of motives, thus for the service of an individual and temporal phenomenon of will.[3]

Whoever comprehends the reflections which here occupy
us will also understand the true meaning of the paradoxical
doctrine of the Eleatics, that there is no arising and passing
away, but the whole remains immovable. Light is also thrown
here upon the beautiful passage of Empedocles which Plutarch has preserved for us in the book, *"Adversus Coloten,"*
c. 12:—

> *Stulta, et prolixas non admittentia curas*
> *Pectora: qui sperant, existere posse, quod ante*
> *Non fuit, aut ullam rem pessum protinus ire;—*
> *Non animo prudens homo quod præsentiat ullus,*
> *Dum vivunt (namque hoc vitaï nomine signant),*
> *Sunt, et fortuna tum conflictantur utraque:*
> *Ante ortum nihil est homo, nec post funera quidquam.*

The very remarkable and, in its place, astonishing passage
in Diderot's *"Jacques le fataliste,"* deserves not less to be mentioned here: *"Un château immense, au frontispice duquel on
lisait: 'Je n'appartiens à personne, et j'appartiens à tout le
monde: vous y étiez avant que d'y entrer, vous y serez encore,
quand vous en sortirez.'"*

Certainly in the sense in which, when he is begotten, the
man arises out of nothing, he becomes nothing through death.
But really to learn to know this "nothing" would be very in-

---

[3] There is only *one present*, and this is always: for it is the sole
form of actual existence. One must attain to the insight that the
past is not *in itself* different from the present, but only in our apprehension, which has time as its form, on account of which alone
the present exhibits itself as different from the past. To assist this
insight, imagine all the events and scenes of human life, bad and
good, fortunate and unfortunate, pleasing and terrible as they successively present themselves in the course of time and difference
of places, in the most checkered multifariousness and variety, as
at once and together, and always present in the *Nunc stans,* while
it is only apparently that now this and now that is; then what the
objectification of the will to live really means will be understood.
Our pleasure also in *genre* painting depends principally upon the
fact that it fixes the fleeting scenes of life. The dogma of metempsychosis has proceeded from the feeling of the truth which has just
been expressed.

teresting; for it only requires moderate acuteness to see that this empirical nothing is by no means absolute, *i.e.*, such as would in every sense be nothing. We are already led to this insight by the observation that all qualities of the parents recur in the children, thus have overcome death. Of this, however, I will speak in a special chapter.

There is no greater contrast than that between the ceaseless flight of time, which carries its whole content with it, and the rigid immobility of what is actually present, which at all times is one and the same. And if from this point of view we watch in a purely objective manner the immediate events of life, the *Nunc stans* becomes clear and visible to us in the centre of the wheel of time. To the eye of a being of incomparably longer life, which at *one* glance comprehended the human race in its whole duration, the constant alternation of birth and death would present itself as a continuous vibration, and accordingly it would not occur to it at all to see in this an ever new arising out of nothing and passing into nothing; but just as to our sight the quickly revolving spark appears as a continuous circle, the rapidly vibrating spring as a permanent triangle, the vibrating cord as a spindle, so to this eye the species would appear as that which has being and permanence, death and life as vibrations.

We will have false conceptions of the indestructibility of our true nature by death, so long as we do not make up our minds to study it primarily in the brutes, but claim for ourselves alone a class apart from them, under the boastful name of immortality. But it is this pretension alone, and the narrowness of view from which it proceeds, on account of which most men struggle so obstinately against the recognition of the obvious truth that we are essentially, and in the chief respect, the same as the brutes; nay, that they recoil at every hint of our relationship with these. But it is this denial of the truth which more than anything else closes against them the path to real knowledge of the indestructibility of our nature. For if we seek anything upon a wrong path, we have just on that account forsaken the right path, and upon the path we follow we will never attain to anything in the end but late disillusion. Up, then, follow the truth, not according to preconceived notions, but as nature leads! First of all, learn to recognise in the aspect of every young animal the existence of the species that never grows old, which, as a reflection of its eternal youth, imparts to every individual a temporary youth, and lets it come forth as new and fresh as if the world were of to-day. Let one ask himself honestly whether the swallow of this year's spring is absolutely a different one from the swallow of the first spring, and whether really between the two the miracle of the creation out of nothing has repeated itself millions of times, in order to work just as often into the hands of absolute annihilation. I know well that if I seriously assured any one that the cat which now plays in the yard is still the same one which made the same springs and played the same tricks there three hundred years ago, he would think I was mad; but I also know that it is much madder to believe that the cat of to-day is through and through and in its whole nature quite a different one from the cat of three hundred years ago. One only requires truly and seriously to sink oneself in the contemplation of one of these higher vertebrates in order to become distinctly conscious that this unfathomable nature, taken as a whole, as it exists there, cannot possibly become nothing; and yet, on the other hand, one knows its transitoriness. This depends upon the fact that in this animal the infinite nature of its Idea (species) is imprinted in the finiteness of the individual. For in a certain sense it is of course true that in the individual we always have before us another being—in the sense which depends upon the principle of sufficient reason, in which are also included time and space, which constitute the *principium individuationis*. But in another sense it is not true—in the sense in which reality belongs to the permanent forms of things, the Ideas alone, and which was so clearly evident to Plato that it became his fundamental thought, the centre of his philosophy; and he made the comprehension of it the criterion of capacity for philosophising in general.

As the scattered drops of the roaring waterfall change with lightning rapidity, while the rainbow, whose supporter they are, remains immovably at rest, quite untouched by that ceaseless change, so every Idea, *i.e.*, every species of living creature remains quite untouched by the continual change of its individuals. But it is the Idea, or the species in which the will to live is really rooted, and manifests itself; and therefore also the will is only truly concerned in the continuance of the species. For example, the lions which are born and die are like the drops of the waterfall; but the *leonitas,* the Idea or form of the lion, is like the unshaken rainbow upon it. Therefore Plato attributed true being to the Ideas alone, *i.e.*, to the species; to the individuals only a ceaseless arising and passing away. From the profound consciousness of his imperishable nature really springs also the confidence and peace of mind with which every brute, and every human individual, moves unconcernedly along amid a host of chances, which may annihilate it any moment, and, moreover, moves straight on to death: out of its eyes, however, there shines the peace of the species, which that death does not affect, and does not concern. Even to man this peace could not be imparted by uncertain and changing dogmas. But, as was said, the contemplation of every animal teaches that death is no obstacle to the kernel of life, to the will in its manifestation. What an unfathomable mystery lies, then, in every animal! Look at the nearest one; look at your dog, how cheerfully and peacefully he lives! Many thousands of dogs have had to die before it came to this one's turn to live. But the death of these thousands has not affected the Idea of the dog; it has not been in the least disturbed by all that dying. Therefore the dog exists as fresh and endowed with primitive force as if this were its first day and none could ever be its last; and out of its eyes there shines the indestructible principle in it, the archæus. What, then, has died during those thousands of years? Not the dog—it stands unscathed before us; merely its shadow, its image in our form of knowledge, which is bound to time. Yet how can one even believe that that passes away which for ever and ever exists and fills all time? Certainly the matter can be explained empirically; in proportion as death destroyed the individuals, generation produced new ones. But this empirical explanation is only an apparent explanation: it puts one riddle in the place of the other. The metaphysical understanding of the matter, although not to be got so cheaply, is yet the only true and satisfying one.

Kant, in his subjective procedure, brought to light the truth that time cannot belong to the thing in itself, because it lies pre-formed in our apprehension. Now death is the temporal

end of the temporal phenomenon; but as soon as we abstract
time, there is no longer any end, and this word has lost all
significance. But I, here upon the objective path, am trying to
show the positive side of the matter, that the thing in itself
remains untouched by time, and by that which is only possible
through time, arising and passing away, and that the phenomena in time could not have even that ceaselessly fleeting
existence which stands next to nothingness, if there were not
in them a kernel of the infinite. Eternity is certainly a conception which has no perception as its foundation; accordingly
it has also a merely negative content; it signifies a timeless
existence. Time is yet merely an image of eternity, and in the
same way our temporal existence is a mere image of our true
nature. This must lie in eternity, just because time is only the
form of our knowledge; but on account of this alone do we
know our own existence, and that of all things as transitory,
finite, and subject to annihilation.

In the second book I have shown that the adequate objectivity of the will as the thing in itself, at each of its grades,
is the (Platonic) Idea; similarly in the third book that the
Ideas of things have the pure subject of knowledge as their
correlative; consequently the knowledge of them only appears
exceptionally and temporarily under specially favourable conditions. For individual knowledge, on the other hand, thus in
time, the *Idea* presents itself under the form of the *species,*
which is the Idea broken up through its entrance into time.
Therefore the species is the most immediate objectification of
the thing in itself, *i.e.,* of the will to live. The inmost nature
of every brute, and also of man, accordingly lies in the species;
thus the will to live, which is so powerfully active, is rooted
in this, not really in the individual. On the other hand, in the
individual alone lies the immediate consciousness: accordingly
it imagines itself different from the species, and therefore fears
death. The will to live manifests itself in relation to the individual as hunger and the fear of death: in relation to the
species as sexual instinct and passionate care for the offspring.
In agreement with this we find nature, which is free from that
delusion of the individual, as careful for the maintenance of
the species as it is indifferent to the destruction of the individuals: the latter are always only means, the former is the

end. Therefore a glaring contrast appears between its niggard-
liness in the endowment of the individuals and its prodigality
when the species is concerned. In the latter case from *one*
individual are often annually obtained a hundred thousand
germs, and more; for example, from trees, fishes, crabs, ter-
mites, and many others. In the former case, on the contrary,
only barely enough in the way of powers and organs is given
to each to enable it with ceaseless effort to maintain its life.
And, therefore, if an animal is injured or weakened it must,
as a rule, starve. And where an incidental saving was possible,
through the circumstance that one part could upon necessity
be dispensed with, it has been withheld, even out of order.
Hence, for example, many caterpillars are without eyes; the
poor creatures grope in the dark from leaf to leaf, which, since
they lack feelers, they do by moving three-fourths of their
body back and forward in the air, till they find some object.
Hence they often miss their food which is to be found close
by. But this happens in consequence of the *lex parsimoniæ
naturæ,* to the expression of which *natura nihil facit super-
vacaneum* one may add *et nihil largitur.* The same tendency
of nature shows itself also in the fact that the more fit the
individual is, on account of his age, for the propagation of
the species, the more powerfully does the *vis naturæ medi-
catrix* manifest itself in him, and therefore his wounds heal
easily, and he easily recovers from diseases. This diminishes
along with the power of generation, and sinks low after it is
extinct; for now in the eyes of nature the individual has become worthless.

If now we cast another glance at the scale of existences,
with the whole of their accompanying gradations of consciousness, from the polyp up to man, we see this wonderful pyra-
mid, kept in ceaseless oscillation certainly by the constant
death of the individuals, yet by means of the bond of generation, enduring in the species through the infinite course of
time. While, then, as was explained above, the *objective,* the
species, presents itself as indestructible, the *subjective,* which
consists merely in the self-consciousness of these beings, seems
to be of the shortest duration, and to be unceasingly destroyed,
in order, just as often, to come forth again from nothing in an
incomprehensible manner. But, indeed, one must be very

short-sighted to let oneself be deceived by this appearance, and not to comprehend that, although the form of temporal permanence only belongs to the objective, the subjective, *i.e.*, the will, which lives and manifests itself in all, and with it the subject of the *knowledge* in which all exhibits itself, must be not less indestructible; because the permanence of the objective, or external, can yet only be the phenomenal appearance of the indestructibility of the subjective or internal; for the former can possess nothing which it has not received on loan from the latter; and cannot be essentially and originally an objective, a phenomenon, and then secondarily and accidentally a subjective, a thing in itself, a self-consciousness. For clearly the former as a manifestation presupposes something which manifests itself, as being for other presupposes a being for self, and as object presupposes a subject; and not conversely: because everywhere the root of things must lie in that which they are for themselves, thus in the subjective, not in the objective, *i.e.*, in that which they are only for others, in a foreign consciousness. Accordingly we found in the first book that the right starting-point for philosophy is essentially and necessarily the subjective, *i.e.*, the idealistic starting-point; and also that the opposite starting-point, that which proceeds from the objective, leads to materialism. At bottom, however, we are far more one with the world than we commonly suppose: its inner nature is our will, its phenomenal appearance is our idea. For any one who could bring this unity of being to distinct consciousness, the difference between the continuance of the external world after his death and his own continuance after death would vanish. The two would present themselves to him as one and the same; nay, he would laugh at the delusion that could separate them. For the understanding of the indestructibility of our nature coincides with that of the identity of the macrocosm and the microcosm. Meanwhile one may obtain light upon what is said here by a peculiar experiment, performed by means of the imagination, an experiment which might be called metaphysical. Let any one try to present vividly to his mind the time, in any case not far distant, when he will be dead. Then he thinks himself away and lets the world go on existing; but soon, to his own astonishment, he will discover that he was nevertheless still there. For he intended to present the world to his mind without himself; but the ego is the immediate element in consciousness, through which alone the world is brought about, and for which alone it exists. This centre of all existence, this kernel of all reality, is to be abolished, and yet the world is to go on existing; it is a thought which can be conceived in the abstract, but not realised. The endeavour to accomplish this, the attempt to think the secondary without the primary, the conditioned without the condition, that which is supported without the supporter, always fails, much in the same way as the attempt to think an equilateral, right-angled triangle, or a destruction or origination of matter, and similar impossibilities. Instead of what was intended, the feeling here presses upon us that the world is not less in us than we in it, and that the source of all reality lies within us. The result is really this: the time when I shall not be will objectively come; but subjectively it can never come. It might therefore, indeed, be asked, how far every one, in his heart, actually believes in a thing which he really cannot conceive at all; or whether, since the profound consciousness of the indestructibleness of our true nature associates itself with that merely intellectual experiment, which, however, has already been made more or less distinctly by every one, whether, I say, our own death is not perhaps for us at bottom the most incredible thing in the world.

The deep conviction of the indestructibleness of our nature through death, which, as is also shown by the inevitable qualms of conscience at its approach, every one carries at the bottom of his heart, depends altogether upon the consciousness of the original and eternal nature of our being: therefore Spinoza expresses it thus: "*Sentimus, experimurque, nos æternos esse.*" For a reasonable man can only think of himself as imperishable, because he thinks of himself as without beginning, as eternal, in fact as timeless. Whoever, on the other hand, regards himself as having become out of nothing must also think that he will again become nothing; for that an eternity had passed before he was, and than a second eternity had begun, through which he will never cease to be, is a monstrous thought. Really the most solid ground for our immortality is the old principle: "*Ex nihilo nihil fit, et in nihilum nihil potest reverti.*" Theophrastus Paracelsus very happily says

(Works, Strasburg, 1603, vol. ii. p. 6): "The soul in me has arisen out of something; therefore it does not come to nothing; for it comes out of something." He gives the true reason. But whoever regards the birth of the man as his absolute beginning must regard death as his absolute end. For both are what they are in the same sense; consequently every one can only think of himself as *immortal* so far as he also thinks of himself as *unborn*, and in the same sense. What birth is, that also is death, according to its nature and significance: it is the same line drawn in two directions. If the former is an actual arising out of nothing, then the latter is also an actual annihilation. But in truth it is only by means of the *eternity* of our real being that we can conceive it as imperishable, and consequently this imperishableness is not temporal. The assumption that man is made out of nothing leads necessarily to the assumption that death is his absolute end. Thus in this the Old Testament is perfectly consistent; for no doctrine of immortality is suitable to a creation out of nothing. New Testament Christianity has such a doctrine because it is Indian in spirit, and therefore more than probably also of Indian origin, although only indirectly, through Egypt. But to the Jewish stem, upon which that Indian wisdom had to be grafted in the Holy Land, such a doctrine is as little suited as the freedom of the will to its determinism, or as

> *Humano capiti cervicem pictor equinam*
> *Jungere si velit.*

It is always bad if one cannot be thoroughly original, and dare not carve out of the whole wood. Brahmanism and Buddhism, on the other hand, have quite consistently, besides the continued existence after death, an existence before birth to expiate the guilt of which we have this life. Moreover, how distinctly conscious they were of the necessary consistency in this is shown by the following passage from Colebrooke's "History of the Indian Philosophy" in the "Transac. of the Asiatic London Society," vol. i. p. 577: "Against the system of the Bhagavatas which is but partially heretical, the objection upon which the chief stress is laid by Vyaso is, that the soul would not be eternal if it were a production, and consequently had a beginning." Further, in Upham's "Doctrine of Buddhism,"

p. 110, it is said: "The lot in hell of impious persons called Deitty is the most severe: these are they who, discrediting the evidence of Buddha, adhere to the heretical doctrine that all living beings had their beginning in the mother's womb, and will have their end in death."

Whoever conceives his existence as merely accidental must certainly fear that he will lose it by death. On the other hand, whoever sees, even only in general, that his existence rests upon some kind of original necessity will not believe that this which has produced so wonderful a thing is limited to such a brief span of time, but that it is active in every one. But he will recognise his existence as necessary who reflects that up till now, when he exists, already an infinite time, thus also an infinity of changes, has run its course, but in spite of this he yet exists; thus the whole range of all possible states has already exhausted itself without being able to destroy his existence. *If he could ever not be, he would already not be now.* For the infinity of the time that has already elapsed, with the exhausted possibility of the events in it, guarantees that *what exists, exists necessarily.* Therefore every one must conceive himself as a necessary being, *i.e.,* as a being whose existence would follow from its true and exhaustive definition if one only had it. In this line of thought, then, really lies the only immanent proof of the imperishableness of our nature, *i.e.,* the only proof of this that holds good within the sphere of empirical data. In this nature existence must inhere, because it shows itself as independent of all states which can possibly be introduced through the chain of causes; for these states have already done what they could, and yet our existence has remained unshaken by it, as the ray of light by the storm wind which it cuts through. If time, of its own resources, could bring us to a happy state, then we would already have been there long ago; for an infinite time lies behind us. But also: if it could lead us to destruction, we would already have long been no more. From the fact that we now exist, it follows, if well considered, that we must at all times exist. For we are ourselves the nature which time has taken up into itself in order to fill its void; consequently it fills the whole of time, present, past, and future, in the same way, and it is just as impossible for us to fall out of existence as to fall out of space. Carefully considered, it is inconceivable that what once exists in all the strength of reality should ever become nothing, and then not be, through an infinite time. Hence has arisen the Christian doctrine of the restoration of all things, that of the Hindus of the constantly repeated creation of the world by Brahma, together with similar dogmas of the Greek philosophers. The great mystery of our being and not being, to explain which these and all kindred dogmas have been devised, ultimately rests upon the fact that the same thing which objectively constitutes an infinite course of time is subjectively an indivisible, ever present present: but who comprehends it? It has been most distinctly set forth by Kant in his immortal doctrine of the ideality of time and the sole reality of the thing in itself. For it results from this that the really essential part of things, of man, of the world, lies permanently and enduringly in the *Nunc stans,* firm and immovable; and that the change of the phenomena and events is a mere consequence of our apprehension of them by means of our form of perception, which is time. Accordingly, instead of saying to men, "Ye have arisen through birth, but are immortal," one ought to say to them, "Ye are not nothing." If, however, this does not succeed, but the anxious heart raises its old lament, "I see all beings arise through birth out of nothing, and after a brief term again return to this; my existence also, now in the present, will soon lie in the distant past, and I will be nothing!"—the right answer is, "Dost thou not exist? Hast thou not within thee the valuable present, after which ye children of time so eagerly strive, now within, actually within? And dost thou understand how thou hast attained to it? Knowest thou the paths which have led thee to it, that thou canst know they will be shut against thee by death? An existence of thyself after the destruction of thy body is not conceivable by thee as possible; but can it be more inconceivable to thee than thy present existence, and how thou hast attained to it? Why shouldst thou doubt but that the secret paths to this present, which stood open to thee, will also stand open to every future present?"

If, then, considerations of this kind are at any rate adapted to awaken the conviction that there is something in us which death cannot destroy, this yet only takes place by raising us to a point of view from which birth is not the beginning of our existence. But from this it follows that what is proved to be indestructible by death is not properly the individual, which, moreover, as having arisen through generation, and having in itself the qualities of the father and mother, presents itself as a mere difference of the species, but as such can only be finite. As, in accordance with this, the individual has no recollection of its existence before its birth, so it can have no remembrance of its present existence after death. But every one places his ego in *consciousness;* this seems to him therefore to be bound to individuality, with which, besides, everything disappears which is peculiar to him, as to this, and distinguishes him from others. His continued existence without individuality becomes to him therefore indistinguishable from the continuance of other beings, and he sees his ego sink. But whoever thus links his existence to the identity of consciousness, and therefore desires an endless existence after death for this, ought to reflect that he can certainly only attain this at the price of just as endless a past before birth. For since he has no remembrance of an existence before birth, thus his consciousness begins with birth, he must accept his birth as an origination of his existence out of nothing. But then he purchases the endless time of his existence after death for just as long a time before birth; thus the account balances without any profit for him. If, on the other hand, the existence which death leaves untouched is different from that of the individual consciousness, then it must be independent of birth, just as of death; and therefore, with regard to it, it must be equally true to say, "I will always be," and "I have always been"; which then gives two infinities for one. But the great equivocation really lies in the word "I," as any one will see at once who remembers the contents of our second book, and the separation which is made there of the willing from the knowing part of our nature. According as I understand this word I can say, "Death is my complete end"; or, "This my personal phenomenal existence is just as infinitely small a part of my true nature as I am of the world." But the "I" is the dark point in consciousness, as on the retina the exact point at which the nerve of sight enters is blind, as the brain itself is entirely without sensation, the body of the sun is dark, and the eye sees all except itself. Our faculty

of knowledge is directed entirely towards without, in accordance with the fact that it is the product of a brain function,
which has arisen for the purpose of mere self-maintenance,
thus of the search for nourishment and the capture of prey.
Therefore every one knows himself only as this individual as it
presents itself in external perception. If, on the other hand, he
could bring to consciousness what he is besides and beyond
this, then he would willingly give up his individuality, smile
at the tenacity of his attachment to it, and say, "What is the
loss of this individuality to me, who bear in myself the possibility of innumerable individualities?" He would see that even
if a continued existence of his individuality does not lie before him, it is yet quite as good as if he had such an existence,
because he carries in himself complete compensation for it.
Besides, however, it may further be taken into consideration
that the individuality of most men is so miserable and worthless that with it they truly lose nothing, and that that in them
which may still have some worth is the universal human element; but to this imperishableness can be promised. Indeed,
even the rigid unalterableness and essential limitation of every individual would, in the case of an endless duration of it,
necessarily at last produce such great weariness by its monot-
ony that only to be relieved of this one would prefer to become nothing. To desire that the individuality should be immortal really means to wish to perpetuate an error infinitely.
For at bottom every individuality is really only a special error,
a false step, something that had better not be; nay, something which it is the real end of life to bring us back from.
This also finds confirmation in the fact that the great majority,
indeed really all men, are so constituted that they could not
be happy in whatever kind of world they might be placed.
In proportion as such a world excluded want and hardship,
they would become a prey to ennui, and in proportion as this
was prevented, they would fall into want, misery, and suffering. Thus for a blessed condition of man it would be by no
means sufficient that he should be transferred to a "better
world," but it would also be necessary that a complete change
should take place in himself; that thus he should no longer
be what he is, and, on the contrary, should become what he is
not. But for this he must first of all cease to be what he is:

this desideratum is, as a preliminary, supplied by death, the moral necessity of which can already be seen from this point of view. To be transferred to another world and to have his whole nature changed are, at bottom, one and the same. Upon this also ultimately rests that dependence of the objective upon the subjective which the idealism of our first book shows. Accordingly here lies the point at which the transcendent philosophy links itself on to ethics. If one considers this one will find that the awaking from the dream of life is only possible through the disappearance along with it of its whole ground-warp also. But this is its organ itself, the intellect together with its forms, with which the dream would spin itself out without end, so firmly is it incorporated with it. That which really dreamt this dream is yet different from it, and alone remains over. On the other hand, the fear that with death all will be over may be compared to the case of one who imagines in a dream that there are only dreams without a dreamer. But now, after an individual consciousness has once been ended by death, would it even be desirable that it should be kindled again in order to continue for ever? The greater part of its content, nay, generally its whole content, is nothing but a stream of small, earthly, paltry thoughts and endless cares. Let them, then, at last be stilled! Therefore with a true instinct, the ancients inscribed upon their gravestones: *Securitati perpetuæ;—*or *Bonæ quieti.* But if here, as so often has happened, a continued existence of the individual consciousness should be desired, in order to connect with it a future reward or punishment, what would really be aimed at in this would simply be the compatibility of virtue and egoism. But these two will never embrace: they are fundamentally opposed. On the other hand, the conviction is well founded, which the sight of noble conduct calls forth, that the spirit of love, which enjoins one man to spare his enemy, and another to protect at the risk of his life some one whom he has never seen before, can never pass away and become nothing.

The most thorough answer to the question as to the continued existence of the individual after death lies in Kant's great doctrine of the *ideality of time,* which just here shows itself specially fruitful and rich in consequences, for it substitutes a purely theoretical but well-proved insight for dogmas which upon one path as upon the other lead to the absurd, and thus settles at once the most exciting of all metaphysical questions. Beginning, ending, and continuing are conceptions which derive their significance simply and solely from time, and are therefore valid only under the presupposition of this. But time has no absolute existence; it is not the manner of being of the thing in itself, but merely the form of our *knowledge* of our existence and nature, and that of all things, which is just on this account very imperfect, and is limited to mere phenomena. Thus with reference to this knowledge alone do the conceptions of ceasing and continuing find application, not with reference to that which exhibits itself in these, the inner being of things in relation to which these conceptions have therefore no longer any meaning. For this shows itself also in the fact that an answer to the question which arises from those time-conceptions is impossible, and every assertion of such an answer, whether upon one side or the other, is open to convincing objections. One might indeed assert that our true being continues after death because it is false that it is destroyed; but one might just as well assert that it is destroyed because it is false that it continues: at bottom the one is as true as the other. Accordingly something like an antinomy might certainly be set up here. But it would rest upon mere negations. In it one would deny two contradictorily opposite predicates of the subject of the judgment, but only because the whole category of these predicates would be inapplicable to that subject. But if now one denies these two predicates, not together, but separately, it appears as if the contradictory opposite of the predicate which in each case is denied were proved of the subject of the judgment. This, however, depends upon the fact that here incommensurable quantities are compared, for the problem removes us to a scene where time is abolished, and yet asks about temporal properties which it is consequently equally false to attribute to, or to deny of the subject. This just means: the problem is transcendent. In this sense death remains a mystery.

On the other hand, adhering to that distinction between phenomenon and thing in itself, we can make the assertion that, as phenomenon, man is certainly perishable, but yet his true being will not be involved in this. Thus this true being is indestructible, although, on account of the elimination of time-conceptions which is connected with it, we cannot attribute to it continuance. Accordingly we would be led here to the conception of an indestructibility which would yet be no continuance. Now this is a conception which, having been obtained on the path of abstraction, can certainly also be thought in the abstract, but yet cannot be supported by any perception, and consequently cannot really become distinct; yet, on the other hand, we must here keep in mind that we have not, like Kant, absolutely given up the knowledge of the thing in itself, but know that it is to be sought for in the will. It is true that we have never asserted an absolute and exhaustive knowledge of the thing in itself, but rather have seen very well that it is impossible to know anything as it is absolutely and in itself. For as soon as I *know,* I have an idea; but this idea, just because it is *my* idea, cannot be identical with what is known, but repeats it in an entirely different form, for it makes a being for other out of a being for self, and is thus always to be regarded as a phenomenal appearance of the thing in itself. Therefore for a *knowing* consciousness, however it may be constituted, there can be always only phenomena. This is not entirely obviated even by the fact that it is my own nature which is known; for, since it falls within my *knowing* consciousness, it is already a reflex of my nature, something different from this itself, thus already in a certain degree phenomenon. So far, then, as I am a knowing being, I have even in my own nature really only a phenomenon; so far, on the other hand, as I am directly this nature itself, I am not a *knowing* being. For it is sufficiently proved in the second book that knowledge is only a secondary property of our being, and introduced by its animal nature. Strictly speaking, then, we know even our own will always merely as phenomenon, and not as it may be absolutely in and for itself. But in that second book, and also in my work upon the will in nature, it is fully explained and proved that if, in order to penetrate into the inner nature of things, leaving what is given merely indirectly and from without, we stick to the only phenomenon into the nature of which an immediate insight from within is attainable, we find in this quite definitely, as the ultimate kernel of reality, the will, in which therefore we recognise the thing in itself in so far as it has here no longer space, although it still has time, for its form consequently really only in its most immediate manifestation, and with the reservation that this knowledge of it is still not exhaustive and entirely adequate. Thus in this sense we retain here also the conception of will as that of the thing in itself.

The conception of ceasing to be is certainly applicable to man as a phenomenon in time, and empirical knowledge plainly presents death as the end of this temporal existence. The end of the person is just as real as was its beginning, and in the same sense as before birth we were not, after death we shall be no more. Yet no more can be destroyed by death than was produced by birth; thus not that through which birth first became possible. In this sense *natus et denatus* is a beautiful expression. But now the whole of empirical knowledge affords us merely phenomena; therefore only phenomena are involved in the temporal processes of coming into being and passing away, and not that which manifests itself in the phenomena, the thing in itself. For this the opposition of coming into being and passing away conditioned by the brain, does not exist at all, but has here lost meaning and significance. It thus remains untouched by the temporal end of a temporal phenomenon, and constantly retains that existence to which the conceptions of beginning, end, and continuance are not applicable. But the thing in itself, so far as we can follow it, is in every phenomenal being the will of this being: so also in man. Consciousness, on the other hand, consists in knowledge. But knowledge, as activity of the brain, and consequently as function of the organism, belongs, as has been sufficiently proved, to the mere phenomenon, and therefore ends with this. The will alone, whose work, or rather whose image was the body, is that which is indestructible. The sharp distinction of will from knowledge, together with the primacy of the former, which constitutes the fundamental characteristic of my philosophy, is therefore the only key to the contradiction which presents itself in so many ways, and arises ever anew in every consciousness, even the most crude, that death is our end, and that yet we must be eternal and indestructible, thus the *sentimus, experimurque nos æternos esse* of Spinoza. All philosophers have erred in this: they place the metaphysical, the indestructible, the eternal element in man in the *intellect*. It lies exclusively in the *will*, which is entirely different from the intellect, and alone is original. The intellect, as was most fully shown in the second book, is a secondary phenomenon, and conditioned by the brain, therefore beginning and ending with this. The will alone is that which conditions, the kernel of the whole phenomenon, consequently free from the forms of the phenomenon to which time belongs, thus also indestructible. Accordingly with death consciousness is certainly lost, but not that which produced and sustained consciousness; life is extinguished, but not the principle of life also, which manifested itself in it. Therefore a sure feeling informs every one that there is something in him which is absolutely imperishable and indestructible. Indeed the freshness and vividness of memories of the most distant time, of earliest childhood, bears witness to the fact that something in us does not pass away with time, does not grow old, but endures unchanged. But what this imperishable element is one could not make clear to oneself. It is not consciousness any more than it is the body upon which clearly consciousness depends. But it is just that which, when it appears in consciousness, presents itself as *will*. Beyond this immediate manifestation of it we certainly cannot go; because we cannot go beyond consciousness; therefore the question what that may be when it does not come within consciousness, *i.e.*, what it is absolutely in itself, remains unanswerable.

In the phenomenon, and by means of its forms, time and space, as *principium individuationis*, what presents itself is that the human individual perishes, while the human race, on the contrary, always remains and lives. But in the true being of things, which is free from these forms, this whole distinction between the individual and the race also disappears, and the two are immediately one. The whole will to live is in the individual, as it is in the race, and therefore the continuance of the species is merely the image of the indestructibility of the individual.

Since, then, the infinitely important understanding of the indestructibility of our true nature by death depends entirely upon the distinction between phenomenon and thing in itself, I wish now to bring this difference into the clearest light by explaining it in the opposite of death, thus in the origin of the animal existence, *i.e.*, generation. For this process, which is just as mysterious as death, presents to us most directly the fundamental opposition between the phenomenal appearance and the true being of things, *i.e.*, between the world as idea and the world as will, and also the entire heterogeneity of the laws of these two. The act of procreation presents itself to us in a twofold manner: first, for self-consciousness, whose only object, as I have often shown, is the will, with all its affections; and then for the consciousness of other things, *i.e.*, the world of idea, or the empirical reality of things. Now, from the side of the will, thus inwardly, subjectively, for self-consciousness, that act presents itself as the most immediate and complete satisfaction of the will, *i.e.*, as sensual pleasure. From the side of the idea, on the other hand, thus externally, objectively, for the consciousness of other things, this act is just the woof of the most cunning of webs, the foundation of the inexpressibly complicated animal organism, which then only requires to be developed to become visible to our astonished eyes. This organism, whose infinite complication and perfection is only known to him who has studied anatomy, cannot, from the side of the idea, be otherwise conceived and thought of than as a system devised with the most ingenious forethought and carried out with the most consummate skill and exactness, as the most arduous work of profound reflection. But from the side of the will we know, through self-consciousness, the production of this organism as the work of an act which is exactly the opposite of all reflection, an impetuous, blind impulse, an exceedingly pleasurable sensation. This opposition is closely related to the infinite contrast, which is shown above, between the absolute facility with which nature produces its works, together with the correspondingly boundless carelessness with which it abandons them to destruction, and the incalculably ingenious and studied construction of these very works, judging from which they must have been infinitely difficult to make, and their maintenance should have been provided for with all conceivable care; while we have the opposite before our eyes. If now by this certainly very unusual consideration, we have brought together in the boldest manner the two heterogeneous sides of the world, and, as it were, grasped them with one hand, we must now hold them fast in order to convince ourselves of the entire invalidity of the laws of the phenomenon, or the world as idea, for that of will, or the thing in itself. Then it will become more comprehensible to us that while on the side of the idea, that is, in the phenomenal world, there exhibits itself to us now an arising out of nothing, and now an entire annihilation of what has arisen, from that other side, or in itself, a nature lies before us with reference to which the conceptions of arising and passing away have no significance. For, by going back to the root, where, by means of self-consciousness, the phenomenon and the thing in itself meet, we have just, as it were, palpably apprehended that the two are absolutely incommensurable, and the whole manner of being of the one, together with all the fundamental laws of its being, signify nothing, and less than nothing, in the other. I believe that this last consideration will only be rightly understood by a few, and that it will be displeasing and even offensive to all who do not understand it, but I shall never on this account omit anything that can serve to illustrate my fundamental thought.

At the beginning of this chapter I have explained that the great clinging to life, or rather fear of death, by no means springs from knowledge, in which case it would be the result of the known value of life; but that that fear of death has its root directly in the *will*, out of the original nature of which it proceeds, in which it is entirely without knowledge, and therefore blind will to live. As we are allured into life by the wholly illusory inclination to sensual pleasure, so we are retained in it by the fear of death, which is certainly just as illusory. Both spring directly from the will, which in itself is unconscious. If, on the contrary, man were merely a *knowing* being, then death would necessarily be to him not only indifferent, but even welcome. The reflection to which we have here attained now teaches that what is affected by death is merely the *knowing* consciousness, and the will, on the other hand, because it is the thing in itself, which lies at the foundation of every phenomenon, is free from all that depends upon temporal determinations, thus is also imperishable. Its striving towards existence and manifestation, from which the world results, is constantly satisfied, for this accompanies it as the

shadow accompanies the body, for it is merely the visibility
of its nature. That yet in us it fears death results from the fact
that here knowledge presents its existence to it as merely in
the individual phenomenon, whence the illusion arises that it
will perish with this, as my image in a mirror seems to be
destroyed along with it if the mirror is broken; this then, as
contrary to its original nature, which is a blind striving towards
existence, fills it with horror. From this now it follows that that
in us which alone is capable of fearing death, and also alone
fears it, the *will*, is not affected by it; and that, on the other
hand, what is affected by it and really perishes is that which
from its nature is capable of no fear, and in general of no desire or emotion, and is therefore indifferent to being and not
being, the mere subject of knowledge, the intellect, whose existence consists in its relation to the world of idea, *i.e.*, the
objective world, whose correlative it is, and with whose existence its own is ultimately one. Thus, although the individual
consciousness does not survive death, yet that survives it which
alone struggles against it—the will. This also explains the contradiction that from the standpoint of knowledge philosophers
have always proved with cogent reasons that death is no evil;
yet the fear of death remains inevitable for all, because it is
rooted, not in knowledge, but in the will. It is also a result
of the fact that only the will, and not the intellect, is indestructible, that all religions and philosophies promise a reward
in eternity only to the virtues of the will, or heart, not to those
of the intellect, or head.

The following may also serve to illustrate this consideration.
The will, which constitutes our true being, is of a simple nature; it merely wills, and does not know. The subject of knowledge, on the other hand, is a secondary phenomenon, arising
from the objectification of the will; it is the point of unity of
the sensibility of the nervous system, as it were the focus in
which the rays of the activity of all the parts of the brain unite.
With this, then, it must perish. In self-consciousness, as that
which alone knows, it stands over against the will as its spectator, and, although sprung from it, knows it as something different from itself, something foreign to it, and consequently
also only empirically, in time, by degrees, in its successive ex-
citements and acts, and also learns its decisions only *a pos-*

teriori, and often very indirectly. This explains the fact that our own nature is a riddle to us, *i.e.,* to our intellect, and that the individual regards itself as having newly arisen and as perishable; although its true nature is independent of time, thus is eternal. As now the *will* does not *know,* so conversely the intellect, or the subject of knowledge, is simply and solely *knowing,* without ever *willing.* This can be proved even physically in the fact that, as was already mentioned in the second book, according to Bichat, the various emotions directly affect all parts of the organism and disturb their functions, with the exception of the brain, which can only be affected by them very indirectly, *i.e.,* just in consequence of those disturbances (*De la vie et de la mort,* art. 6, § 2). But from this it follows that the subject of knowledge, for itself and as such, cannot take part or interest in anything, but for it the being or not being of everything, nay, even of its own self, is a matter of indifference. Now why should this purely neutral being be immortal? It ends with the temporal manifestation of the will, *i.e.,* the individual, as it arose with it. It is the lantern which is extinguished when it has served its end. The intellect, like the perceptible world which exists only in it, is a mere phenomenon; but the finiteness of both does not affect that of which they are the phenomenal appearance. The intellect is the function of the cerebral nervous system; but the latter, like the rest of the body, is the objectivity of the *will.* Therefore the intellect depends upon the somatic life of the organism; but this itself depends upon the will. The organised body may thus, in a certain sense, be regarded as the link between the will and the intellect; although really it is only the will itself exhibiting itself spatially in the perception of the intellect. Death and birth are the constant renewal of the consciousness of the will, in itself without end and without beginning, which alone is, as it were, the substance of existence (but each such renewal brings a new possibility of the denial of the will to live). Consciousness is the life of the subject of knowledge, or the brain, and death is its end. And therefore, finally, consciousness is always new, in each case beginning at the beginning. The will alone is permanent; and, moreover, it is it alone that permanence concerns; for it is the will to live. The knowing subject for itself is not concerned about anything. In the ego, however, the two are bound up together. In every animal existence the will has achieved an intellect which is the light by which it here pursues its ends. It may be remarked by the way that the fear of death may also partly depend upon the fact that the individual will is so loath to separate from the intellect which has fallen to its lot through the course of nature, its guide and guard, without which it knows that it is helpless and blind.

Finally, this explanation also agrees with the commonplace moral experience which teaches us that the will alone is real, while its objects, on the other hand, as conditioned by knowledge, are only phenomena, are only froth and vapour, like the wine which Mephistopheles provided in Auerbach's cellar: after every sensuous pleasure we also say, "And yet it seemed as I were drinking wine."

The terrors of death depend for the most part upon the false illusion that now the ego vanishes and the world remains. But rather is the opposite the case; the world vanishes, but the inmost kernel of the ego, the supporter and producer of that subject, in whose idea alone the world has its existence, remains. With the brain the intellect perishes, and with the intellect the objective world, its mere idea. That in other brains, afterwards as before, a similar world lives and moves is, with reference to the intellect which perishes, a matter of indifference. If, therefore, reality proper did not lie in the *will*, and if the moral existence were not that which extends beyond death, then, since the intellect, and with it its world, is extinguished, the true nature of things in general would be no more than an endless succession of short and troubled dreams, without connection among themselves; for the permanence of unconscious nature consists merely in the idea of time of conscious nature. Thus a world-spirit dreaming without end or aim, dreams which for the most part are very troubled and heavy, would then be all in all.

When, now, an individual experiences the fear of death, we have really before us the extraordinary, nay, absurd, spectacle of the lord of the worlds, who fills all with his being, and through whom alone everything that is has its existence, desponding and afraid of perishing, of sinking into the abyss of eternal nothingness;—while, in truth, all is full of him, and there is no place where he is not, no being in which he does not live; for it is not existence that supports him, but he that supports existence. Yet it is he who desponds in the individual who suffers from the fear of death, for he is exposed to the illusion produced by the *principium individuationis* that his existence is limited to the nature which is now dying. This illusion belongs to the heavy dream into which, as the will to live, he has fallen. But one might say to the dying individual: "Thou ceasest to be something which thou hadst done better never to become."

So long as no denial of the will takes place, what death leaves untouched is the germ and kernel of quite another existence, in which a new individual finds itself again, so fresh and original that it broods over itself in astonishment. What sleep is for the individual, death is for the will as thing in itself. It would not endure to continue the same actions and sufferings throughout an eternity without true gain, if memory and individuality remained to it. It flings them off, and this is lethe; and through this sleep of death it reappears refreshed and fitted out with another intellect, as a new being—"a new day tempts to new shores."

As the self-asserting will to live man has the root of his existence in the species. Accordingly death is the loss of one individuality and the assumption of another, consequently a change of individuality under the exclusive guidance of one's own will. For in this alone lies the eternal power which could produce its existence with its ego, yet, on account of its nature, was not able to maintain it in existence. For death is the *démenti* which the essence (*essentia*) of every one receives in its claim to existence (*existentia*), the appearance of a contradiction which lies in every individual existence:

> For all that arises
> Is worthy of being destroyed.

But an infinite number of such existences, each with its ego, stands within reach of this power, thus of the will, which, however, will again prove just as transitory and perishable. Since now every ego has its separate consciousness, that infinite number of them is, with reference to such an ego, not different from a single one. From this point of view it appears to me not accidental that *ævum* signifies both the individual term of life and infinite time. Indeed from this point of view it may be seen, although indistinctly, that ultimately and in themselves both are the same; and according to this there would really be no difference whether I existed only through my term of life or for an infinite time.

Certainly, however, we cannot obtain an idea of all that is said above entirely without time-concepts; yet when we are dealing with the thing in itself these ought to be excluded. But it belongs to the unalterable limitations of our intellect that it can never entirely cast off this first and most immediate form of all its ideas, in order to operate without it. Therefore we certainly come here upon a kind of metempsychosis, although with the important difference that it does not concern the whole *psyche*, not the *knowing* being, but the *will* alone; and thus, with the consciousness that the form of time only enters here as an unavoidable concession to the limitation of our intellect, so many absurdities which accompany the doctrine of metempsychosis disappear. If, indeed, we now call in the assistance of the fact, to be explained in chapter 43, that the character, *i.e.*, the will, is inherited from the father, and the intellect, on the other hand, from the mother, it agrees very well with our view that the will of a man, in itself individual, separated itself in death from the intellect received from the mother in generation, and in accordance with its now modified nature, under the guidance of the absolutely necessary course of the world harmonising with this, received through a new generation a new intellect, with which it became a new being, which had no recollection of an earlier existence; for the intellect, which alone has the faculty of memory, is the mortal part or the form, while the will is the eternal part, the substance. In accordance with this, this doctrine is more correctly denoted by the word palingenesis than by metempsychosis. These constant new births, then, constitute the succession of the life-dreams of a will which in itself is indestructible, until, instructed and improved by so much and such various successive knowledge in a constantly new form, it abolishes or abrogates itself.

The true and, so to speak, esoteric doctrine of Buddhism, as we have come to know it through the latest investigations, also agrees with this view, for it teaches not metempsychosis, but a peculiar palingenesis, resting upon a moral basis which it works out and explains with great profundity. This may be seen from the exposition of the subject, well worth reading and pondering, which is given is Spence Hardy's "Manual of Buddhism," pp. 394–96 (with which compare pp. 429, 440, and 445 of the same book), the confirmation of which is to be found in Taylor's *"Prabodh Chandro Daya,"* London, 1812, p. 35; also in Sangermano's "Burmese Empire," p. 6, and in the "Asiatic Researches," vol. vi. p. 179, and vol. ix. p. 256. The very useful German compendium of Buddhism by Köppen is also right upon this point. Yet for the great mass of Buddhists this doctrine is too subtle; therefore to them simple metempsychosis is preached as a comprehensible substitute.

Besides, it must not be neglected that even empirical grounds support a palingenesis of this kind. As a matter of fact there does exist a connection between the birth of the newly appearing beings and the death of those that are worn out. It shows itself in the great fruitfulness of the human race which appears as a consequence of devastating diseases. When in the fourteenth century the black death had for the most part depopulated the old world, a quite abnormal fruitfulness appeared among the human race, and twin-births were very frequent. The circumstance was also very remarkable that none of the children born at this time obtained their full number of teeth; thus nature, exerting itself to the utmost, was niggardly in details. This is related by F. Schnurrer, *"Chronik der Seuchen,"* 1825. Casper also, *"Ueber die wahrscheinliche Lebensdauer des Menschen,"* 1835, confirms the principle that the number of births in a given population has the most decided influence upon the length of life and mortality in it, as this always keeps pace with the mortality: so that always and everywhere the deaths and the births increase and decrease in like proportion; which he places beyond doubt by an accumulation of evidence collected from many lands and their various provinces. And yet it is impossible that there can be a *physical* causal connection between my early death and the fruitfulness of a marriage with which I have nothing to do, or conversely. Thus here the metaphysical appears undeniably and in a stupendous manner as the immediate ground of explanation of the physical. Every new-born being indeed comes fresh and blithe into the new existence, and enjoys it as a free gift: but there is, and can be, nothing freely given. Its fresh existence is paid for by the old age and death of a worn-out existence which has perished, but which contained the indestructible seed out of which this new existence has arisen: they are *one* being. To show the bridge between the two would certainly be the solution of a great riddle.

The great truth which is expressed here has never been entirely unacknowledged, although it could not be reduced to its exact and correct meaning, which is only possible through the doctrine of the primacy and metaphysical nature of the will and the secondary, merely organic nature of the intellect. We find the doctrine of metempsychosis, springing from the earliest and noblest ages of the human race, always spread abroad in the earth as the belief of the great majority of mankind, nay, really as the teaching of all religions, with the exception of that of the Jews and the two which have proceeded from it: in the most subtle form, however, and coming nearest to the truth, as has already been mentioned, in Buddhism. Accordingly, while Christians console themselves with the thought of meeting again in another world, in which one regains one's complete personality and knows oneself at once, in those other religions the meeting again is already going on now, only incognito. In the succession of births, and by virtue of metempsychosis or palingenesis, the persons who now stand in close connection or contact with us will also be born along with us at the next birth, and will have the same or analogous relations and sentiments towards us as now, whether these are of a friendly or a hostile description. (*Cf.*, for example, Spence Hardy's "Manual of Buddhism," p. 162.) Recognition is certainly here limited to an obscure intimation, a reminiscence which cannot be brought to distinct consciousness, and refers to an infinitely distant time;—with the exception, however, of Buddha himself, who has the prerogative of distinctly knowing his own earlier births and those of others;—as this is described in the "Jâtaka." But, in fact, if at favourable moment one contemplates, in a purely objective manner, the action of men in reality; the intuitive conviction is forced upon one that it not only is and remains constantly the same, according to the

(Platonic) Idea, but also that the present generation, in its true inner nature, is precisely and substantially identical with every generation that has been before it. The question simply is in what this true being consists. The answer which my doctrine gives to this question is well known. The intuitive conviction referred to may be conceived as arising from the fact that the multiplying-glasses, time and space, lose for a moment their effect. With reference to the universality of the belief in metempsychosis, Obry says rightly, in his excellent book, *"Du Nirvana Indien,"* p. 13: *"Cette vieille croyance a fait le tour du monde, et était tellement répandue dans la haute antiquité, qu'un docte Anglican l'avait jugée sans père, sans mère, et sans généalogie"* (*Ths. Burnet, dans Beausobre, Hist. du Manichéisme,* ii. p. 391). Taught already in the "Vedas," as in all the sacred books of India, metempsychosis is well known to be the kernel of Brahmanism and Buddhism. It accordingly prevails at the present day in the whole of non-Mohammedan Asia, thus among more than half of the whole human race, as the firmest conviction, and with an incredibly strong practical influence. It was also the belief of the Egyptians (Herod., ii. 123), from whom it was received with enthusiasm by Orpheus. Pythagoras, and Plato: the Pythagoreans, however, specially retained it. That it was also taught in the mysteries of the Greeks undeniably follows from the ninth book of Plato's "Laws" (pp. 38 and 42, ed. Bip.). The "Edda" also, especially in the "Völuspá," teaches metempsychosis. Not less was it the foundation of the religion of the Druids (*Cæs. de bello Gall.,* vi.; *A. Pictet, Le mystère des Bardes de l'ile de Bretagne,* 1856). Even a Mohammedan sect in Hindostan, the Bohrahs, of which Colebrooke gives a full account in the "Asiatic Researches," vol. vii. p. 336 *sqq.,* believes in metempsychosis, and accordingly refrains from all animal food. Also among American Indians and negro tribes, nay, even among the natives of Australia, traces of this belief are found, as appears from a minute description given in the *Times* of 29th January 1841 of the execution of two Australian savages for arson and murder. It is said there: "The younger of the two prisoners met his end with a dogged and a determined spirit, as it appeared, of revenge; the only intelligible expressions made use of conveyed an impression that he would rise up a

'white fellow,' which it was considered strengthened his resolution." Also in a book by Ungewitter, *"Der Welttheil Austra-
lien,"* it is related that the Papuas in Australia regarded the
whites as their own relations who had returned to the world.
According to all this, the belief in metempsychosis presents
itself as the natural conviction of man, whenever he reflects at
all in an unprejudiced manner. It would really be that which
Kant falsely asserts of his three pretended Ideas of the reason,
a philosopheme natural to human reason, which proceeds from
its forms; and when it is not found it must have been displaced by positive religious doctrines coming from a different
source. I have also remarked that it is at once obvious to every
one who hears of it for the first time. Let any one only observe
how earnestly Lessing defends it in the last seven paragraphs
of his *"Erziehung des Menschengeschlechts."* Lichtenberg
also says in his *"Selbstcharacteristik:"* "I cannot get rid of the
thought that I died before I was born." Even the excessively
empirical Hume says in his sceptical essay on immortality,
p. 23: "The metempsychosis is therefore the only system of
this kind that philosophy can hearken to."[4] What resists this
belief, which is spread over the whole human race and com-
mends itself alike to the wise and to the vulgar, is Judaism,
together with the two religions which have sprung from it,
because they teach the creation of man out of nothing, and
he has then the hard task of linking on to this the belief in an
endless existence *a parte post.* They certainly have succeeded,
with fire and sword, in driving out of Europe and part of
Asia that consoling primitive belief of mankind; it is still doubtful for how long. Yet how difficult this was is shown by the
oldest Church histories. Most of the heretics were attached to
this primitive belief; for example, Simonists, Basilidians, Val-

[4] This posthumous essay is to be found in the "Essays on Suicide
and the Immortality of the Soul" by the late David Hume, Basil,
1799, sold by James Decker. By this reprint at Bâle these two
works of one of the greatest thinkers and writers of England were
rescued from destruction, when in their own land, in consequence
of the stupid and utterly contemptible bigotry which prevailed,
they had been suppressed through the influence of a powerful and
insolent priesthood, to the lasting shame of England. They are entirely passionless, coldly rational investigations of the two subjects
named.

entinians, Marcionists, Gnostics, and Manichæans. The Jews themselves have in part fallen into it, as Tertullian and Justinus (in his dialogues) inform us. In the Talmud it is related that Abel's soul passed into the body of Seth, and then into that of Moses. Even the passage of the Bible, Matt. xvi. 13–15, only obtains a rational meaning if we understand it as spoken under the assumption of the dogma of metempsychosis. Luke, it is true, who also has the passage (ix. 18–20), attributes to the Jews the assumption that such an ancient prophet can rise again body and all, which, since they know that he has already lain between six and seven hundred years in his grave, and consequently has long since turned to dust, would be a palpable absurdity. In Christianity, however, the doctrine of original sin, *i.e.*, the doctrine of punishment for the sins of another individual, has taken the place of the transmigration of souls and the expiation in this way of all the sins committed in an earlier life. Both identify, and that with a moral tendency, the existing man with one who has existed before; the transmigration of souls does so directly, original sin indirectly.

Death is the great reprimand which the will to live, or more especially the egoism, which is essential to this, receives through the course of nature; and it may be conceived as a punishment for our existence.[5] It is the painful loosing of the knot which the act of generation had tied with sensual pleasure, the violent destruction coming from without of the fundamental error of our nature: the great disillusion. We are at bottom something that ought not to be: therefore we cease to be. Egoism consists really in the fact that man limits all reality to his own person, in that he imagines that he lives in this alone and not in others. Death teaches him better, for it destroys this person, so that the true nature of man, which is his will, will henceforth live only in other individuals; while his intellect, which itself belonged only to the phenomenon, *i.e.*, to the world as idea, and was merely the form of the external world, also continues to exist in the condition of being idea, *i.e.*, in the *objective* being of things as such, thus also only in the existence of what was hitherto the external world. His whole ego thus lives from this time forth only in that which

[5] Death says: Thou art the product of an act which should not have been; therefore to expiate it thou must die.

he had hitherto regarded as non-ego: for the difference between external and internal ceases. We call to mind here that
the better man is he who makes the least difference between
himself and others, does not regard them as absolute non-ego,
while for the bad man this difference is great, nay, absolute.
I have worked this out in my prize essay on the foundation of
morals. According to what was said above, the degree in which
death can be regarded as the annihilation of the man is in
proportion to this difference. But if we start from the fact that
the distinction of outside me and in me, as a spatial distinction,
is only founded in the phenomenon, not in the thing in itself,
thus is no absolutely real distinction, then we shall see in the
losing of our own individuality only the loss of a phenomenon,
thus only an apparent loss. However much reality that distinction has in the empirical consciousness, yet from the metaphysical standpoint the propositions, "I perish, but the world
endures," and "The world perishes but I endure," are at bottom not really different.

But, besides all this, death is the great opportunity no longer
to be I;—to him who uses it. During life the will of man is
without freedom: his action takes place with necessity upon
the basis of his unalterable character in the chain of motives.
But every one remembers much that he has done, and on
account of which he is by no means satisfied with himself. If
now he were to go on living, he would go on acting in the
same way, on account of the unalterable nature of his character. Accordingly he must cease to be what he is in order to
be able to arise out of the germ of his nature as a new and
different being. Therefore death looses these bonds; the will
again becomes free; for freedom lies in the *Esse*, not in the
Operari. "*Finditur nodus cordis, dissolvuntur omnes dubitationes, ejusque opera evanescunt*," is a very celebrated saying
of the Vedas, which all Vedantic writers frequently repeat.[6]
Death is the moment of that deliverance from the onesidedness
of an individuality which does not constitute the inmost kernel
of our being, but is rather to be thought of as a kind of aberration of it. The true original freedom re-enters at this moment,

[6] *Sancara, s. de theologumenis Vedanticorum*, ed. F. H. H. Win-
dischmann, p. 37; "*Oupnekhat*," vol. i. p. 387 *et* p. 78; Colebrooke's
"Miscellaneous Essays," vol. i. p. 363.

which, in the sense indicated, may be regarded as a *restitutio in integrum*. The peace and quietness upon the countenance of most dead persons seems to have its origin in this. Quiet and easy is, as a rule, the death of every good man: but to die willingly, to die gladly, to die joyfully, is the prerogative of the resigned, of him who surrenders and denies the will to live. For only he wills to die *really*, and not merely *apparently*, and consequently he needs and desires no continuance of his person. The existence which we know he willingly gives up: what he gets instead of it is in our eyes *nothing*, because our existence is, with reference to that, *nothing*. The Buddhist faith calls it Nirvana[7] *i.e.*, extinction.

[7] The etymology of the word Nirvana is variously given. According to Colebrooke ("Transact. of the Royal Asiat. Soc.," vol. i. p. 566) it comes from *va*, "to blow," like the wind, and the prefixed negative *nir*, and thus signifies a calm, but as an adjective "extinguished." Obry, also, *Du Nirvana Indien*, p. 3, says: *"Nirvanam en sanscrit signifie à la lettre extinction, telle que celle d'un feu."* According to the "Asiatic Journal," vol. xxiv. p. 735, the word is really Neravana, from *nera*, "without," and *vana*, "life," and the meaning would be *annihilatio*. In "Eastern Monachism," by Spence Hardy, p. 295, Nirvana is derived from *vana*, "sinful desires," with the negative *nir*. J. J. Schmidt, in his translation of the history of the Eastern Mongolians, says that the Sanscrit word Nirvana is translated into Mongolian by a phrase which signifies "departed from misery," "escaped from misery." According to the learned lectures of the same in the St. Petersburg Academy, Nirvana is the opposite of Sanfara, which is the world of constant re-birth, of longings and desires, of illusion of the senses and changing forms, of being born, growing old, becoming sick, and dying. In the Burmese language the word Nirvana, according to the analogy of other Sanscrit words, becomes transformed into Nieban, and is translated by "complete vanishing." See Sangermano's "Description of the Burmese Empire," translated by Tandy, Rome, 1833, § 27. In the first edition of 1819 I also wrote Nieban, because we then knew Buddhism only from meagre accounts of the Burmese.

IX

COMPARATIVE ANATOMY

(*from* ON THE WILL IN NATURE)

Now, from my proposition: that the Will is what Kant calls
the "thing in itself" or the ultimate substratum of every phenomenon, I had however not only deduced that the will is the
agent in all inner, unconscious functions of the body, but also
that the organism itself is nothing but the will which has entered the region of representation, the will itself, perceived
in the cognitive form of Space. I had accordingly said that,
just as each single momentary act of willing presents itself at
once directly and infallibly in the outer perception of the body
as one of its actions, so also must the collective volition of each
animal, the totality of its efforts, be faithfully portrayed in its
whole body, in the constitution of its organism; and that the
means supplied by its organisation for attaining the aims of
its will must as a whole exactly correspond to those aims—in
short, that the same relation must exist between the whole
character of its volition and the shape and nature of its body,
as between each single act of its will and the single bodily
action which carries it out. Even this too has recently been
recognised as a fact, and accordingly been confirmed *a posteriori,* by thoughtful zootomists and physiologists from their
own point of view and independently of my doctrine: their
judgments on this point make Nature testify even here to the
truth of my theory.

In Pander and d'Alton's admirable illustrated work[1] we
find: "Just as all that is characteristic in the formation of bones
springs from the *character* of the animals, so does that character, on the other hand, develop out of their *tendencies and
desires.* These *tendencies and desires* of animals, which are

[1] Pander and d'Alton, "Ueber die Skelette der Raubthiere," 1822,
p. 7.

so vividly expressed in their whole organisation and of which
that organisation only appears to be the medium, cannot be
explained by special primary forces, since we can only deduce
their inner reason from the general life of Nature." By this
last turn the author shows indeed that he has arrived at the
point where, like all other investigators of Nature, he is brought
to a standstill by the metaphysical; but he also shows, that up
to this point beyond which Nature eludes investigation, *tendencies and desires* (*i.e.* will) were the utmost thing knowable.
The shortest expression for his last conclusion about animals
would be "As they will, so they are."

The learned and thoughtful Burdach,[2] when treating of the
ultimate reason of the genesis of the embryo in his great work
on Physiology, bears witness no less explicitly to the truth of
my view. I must not, unfortunately, conceal the fact that in a
weak moment, misled Heaven knows by what or how, this
otherwise excellent man brings in just here a few sentences
taken from that utterly worthless, tyrannically imposed
pseudo-philosophy, about 'thought' being what is primary (it
is just what is last and most conditioned of all) yet 'no representation' (that is to say, a wooden iron). Immediately after
however, under the returning influence of his own better self,
he proclaims the real truth (p. 710): "The brain curves itself
outwards to the retina, because the central part of the embryo
desires to take in the impressions of the activity of the world;
the mucous membrane of the intestinal canal develops into the
lung, because the organic body *desires* to enter into relation
with the elementary substances of the universe; organs of generation spring from the vascular system, because the individual
only lives in the species, and because the life which has commenced in the individual *desires* to multiply." This assertion of
Burdach's, which so entirely agrees with my doctrine, reminds
me of a passage in the ancient Mahabharata, which it is really
difficult not to regard as a mythical version of the same truth.
It is in the third Canto of "Sundas and Upasunda" in Bopp's
"Ardschuna's Reise zu Indra's Himmel"[3] (1824); Brahma has

[2] Burdach, "Physiologie," vol. 2, § 474.
[3] Bopp, "Ardschuna's Reise zu Indra's Himmel, nebst anderen
Episoden des Mahabharata" (Ardshuna's Journey to Indra's Heaven,
together with other episodes from the Mahabharata), 1824.

just created Tilottama, the fairest of women, who is walking round the circle of the assembled gods. Shiva conceives so violent a longing to gaze at her as she turns successively round the circle, that four faces arise in him according to her different positions, that is, according to the four cardinal points. This may account for Shiva being represented with five heads, as Pansh Mukhti Shiva. Countless eyes arise on every part of Indra's body likewise on the same occasion. In fact, every organ must be looked upon as the expression of a universal manifestation of the will, *i.e.* of one made once for all, of a fixed longing, of an act of volition proceeding, not from the individual, but from the species. Every animal form is a longing of the will to live which is roused by circumstances; for instance, the will is seized with a longing to live on trees, to hang on their branches, to devour their leaves, without contention with other animals and without ever touching the ground: this longing presents itself throughout endless time in the form (or Platonic Idea) of the sloth. It can hardly walk at all, being only adapted for climbing; helpless on the ground, it is agile on trees and looks itself like a moss-clad bough in order to escape the notice of its pursuers. But now let us consider the matter from a somewhat more methodical and less poetical point of view.

The manifest adaptation of each animal for its mode of life and outward means of subsistence, even down to the smallest detail, together with the exceeding perfection of its organisation, form abundant material for teleological contemplation, which has always been a favourite occupation of the human mind, and which, extended even to inanimate Nature, has become the argument of the Physico-theological Proof. The universal fitness for their ends, the obviously intentional design in all the parts of the organism of the lower animals without exception, proclaim too distinctly for it ever to have been seriously questioned, that here no forces of Nature acting by chance and without plan have been at work, but a will. Now, that a will should act otherwise than under the guidance of knowledge was inconceivable, according to empirical science and views. For, up to my time, *will* and *intellect* had been regarded as absolutely inseparable, nay, the will was looked upon as a mere operation of the intellect, that presumptive basis of all that is spiritual. Accordingly wherever the will acted, knowledge must have been its guide; consequently it must have been its guide here also. But the mediation of knowledge, which, as such, is exclusively directed towards the outside, brings with it, that a will acting by means of it, can only act outwardly, that is, only from *one* being upon *another*. Therefore the will, of which unmistakable traces had been found, was not sought for where these were discovered, but was removed to the outside, and the animal became the product of a will foreign to it, guided by knowledge, which must have been very clear knowledge indeed, nay, the deeply excogitated conception of a purpose; and this purpose must have preceded the animal's existence, and, together with the will, whose product the animal is, have lain outside that animal. According to this, the animal would have existed in representation before existing in reality. This is the basis of the train of thought on which the Physico-theological Proof is founded. But this proof is no mere scholastic sophism, like the Ontological Proof: nor does it contain an untiring natural opponent within itself, like the Cosmological Proof, in that very same law of causality to which it owes its existence. On the contrary, it is, in reality, for the educated, what the Keraunological Proof is for the vulgar, and its plausibility is so great, so potent, that the most eminent and at the same time least prejudiced minds have been deeply entangled in it. Voltaire, for instance, who, after all sorts of other doubts, always comes back to it, sees no possibility of getting over it and even places its evidence almost on a level with that of a mathematical demonstration. Even Priestley too declares it to be irrefutable.[4] Hume's reflection and acumen alone stood the test, even in this case; in his "Dialogues on Natural Religion,"[5] which are so well worth reading, this true precursor of Kant calls attention to the fact, that there is no resemblance at all between the works of Nature and those of an Art which proceeds according to a design. Now it is precisely where he cuts asunder the *nervus probandi* of this extremely insidious proof, as well as that of the two others—in his "Critique of Judgment" and in his "Critique of Pure Reason"—that Kant's merit shines

---

[4] Priestley, "Disqu. on Matter and Spirit," sect. 16, p. 188.

[5] Part 7, and in other places.

most brilliantly. A very brief summary of this Kantian refutation of the Physico-theological Proof may be found in my chief work.[6] Kant has earned for himself great merit by it; for nothing stands so much in the way of a correct insight into Nature and into the essence of things as this view, by which they are looked upon as having been made according to a preconceived plan. Therefore, if a Duke of Bridgewater offers a prize of high value for the confirmation and perpetuation of such fundamental errors, let it be our task, following in the footsteps of Hume and Kant, to work undauntedly at their destruction, without any other reward than truth. Truth deserves respect: not what is opposed to it. Nevertheless here, as elsewhere, Kant has confined himself to negation; but a negation only takes full effect when it has been completed by a correct affirmation, this alone giving entire satisfaction and in itself dislodging and superseding error, according to the words of Spinoza: *Sicut lux se ipsa et tenebras manifestat, sic veritas norma sui et falsi est.* First of all therefore we say: the world is not made with the help of knowledge, consequently also not from the outside, but from the inside; and next we endeavour to point out the *punctum saliens* of the world-egg. The physico-theological thought, that Nature must have been regulated and fashioned by an intellect, however well it may suit the untutored mind, is nevertheless fundamentally wrong. For the intellect is only known to us in animal nature, consequently as an absolutely secondary and subordinate principle in the world, a product of the latest origin; it can never therefore have been the condition of the existence of that world. Now the will on the contrary, being that which fills every thing and manifests itself immediately in each—thus showing each thing to be its phenomenon—appears everywhere as that which is primary. It is just for this reason, that the explanation of all teleological facts is to be found in the will of the being itself in which they are observed.

Besides, the Physico-theological Proof may be simply invalidated by the empirical observation, that works produced by animal instinct, such as the spider's web, the bee's honeycomb and its cells, the white ant's constructions, &c. &c., are

[6] See THE WORLD AS WILL AND IDEA, Dolphin Books, Doubleday & Company, Inc., 1961.

throughout constituted as if they were the result of an intentional conception, of a wide-reaching providence and of rational deliberation; whereas they are evidently the work of a blind impulse, *i.e.*, of a will not guided by knowledge. From this it follows, that the conclusion from such and such a nature to such and such a mode of coming into being, has not the same certainty as the conclusion from a consequent to its reason, which is in all cases a sure one. I have devoted the twenty-seventh chapter of the second volume of my chief work to a detailed consideration of the mechanical instincts of animals, which may be used, together with the preceding one on Teleology, to complete the whole examination of this subject in the present chapter.

Now, if we enter more closely into the above-mentioned fitness of every animal's organisation for its mode of life and means of subsistence, the question that first presents itself is, whether that mode of life has been adapted to the organisation, or *vice versa*. At first sight, the former assumption would seem to be the more correct one; since, in Time, the organisation precedes the mode of life, and the animal is thought to have adopted the mode of existence for which its structure was best suited, making the best use of the organs it found within itself: thus, for instance, we think that the bird flies because it has wings, and that the ox butts because it has horns; not conversely. This view is shared by Lucretius (always an ominous sign for an opinion):

> *Nil ideo quoniam natum est in corpore, ut uti*
> *Possemus; sed, quod natum est, id procreat usum.*

Only this assumption does not explain how, collectively, the quite different parts of an animal's organism so exactly correspond to its way of life; how no organ interferes with another, each rather assisting the others and none remaining unemployed; also that no subordinate organ would be better suited to another mode of existence, while the life which the animal really leads is determined by the principal organs alone, but, on the contrary, each part of the animal not only corresponds to every other part, but also to its mode of life: its claws, for instance, are invariably adapted for seizing the prey which its teeth are suited to tear and break, and its intestinal canal to digest: its limbs are constructed to convey it where that prey is to be found, and no organ ever remains unemployed. The ant-bear, for instance, is not only armed with long claws on its fore-feet, in order to break into the nests of the white ant, but also with a prolonged cylindrical muzzle, in order to penetrate into them, with a small mouth and a long, threadlike tongue, covered with a glutinous slime, which it inserts into the white ants' nests and then withdraws covered with the insects that adhere to it: on the other hand it has no teeth, because it does not want them. Who can fail to see that the ant-bear's form stands in the same relation to the white ants, as an act of the will to its motive? The contradiction between the powerful fore-feet and long, strong, curved claws of the ant-bear and its complete lack of teeth, is at the same time so extraordinary, that if the earth ever undergoes a fresh transformation, the newly arising race of rational beings will find it an insoluble enigma, if white ants are unknown to them. The necks of birds, as of quadrupeds, are generally as long as their legs, to enable them to reach down to the ground where they pick up their food; but those of aquatic birds are often a good deal longer, because they have to fetch up their nourishment from under the water while swimming.[7] Moor-fowl have exceedingly long legs, to enable them to wade without drowning or wetting their bodies, and a correspondingly long neck and beak, this last being more or less strong, according to the things (reptiles, fishes or worms) which have to be crushed; and the intestines of these animals are invariably adapted likewise to this end. On the other hand, moor-fowl are provided neither with talons, like birds of prey, nor with web-feet, like ducks: for the *lex parsimoniæ naturæ* admits of no superfluous organ. Now, it is precisely this very law, added to the circumstance, that no organ required for its mode of life is ever wanting in any animal, and that all, even the most heterogeneous, harmonize together and are, as it were, cal-

---

[7] I have seen (Zooplast. Cab. 1860) a humming-bird (*colibri*) with a beak as long as the whole bird, head and tail included. This bird must certainly have had to fetch out its food from a considerable depth, were it only from the calyx of a flower (Cuvier, "Anat. Comp." vol. iv. p. 374); otherwise it would not have given itself the luxury, or submitted to the encumbrance, of such a beak.

culated for a quite specially determined way of life, for the element in which the prey dwells, for the pursuit, the overcoming, the crushing and digesting of that prey,—all this, we say, proves, that the animal's structure has been determined by the mode of life by which the animal desired to find its sustenance, and not *vice versa*. It also proves, that the result is exactly the same as if a knowledge of that mode of life and of its outward conditions had preceded the structure, and as if therefore each animal had chosen its equipment before it assumed a body; just as a sportsman before starting chooses his whole equipment, gun, powder, shot, pouch, hunting-knife and dress, according to the game he intends chasing. The latter does not take aim at the wild boar because he happens to have a rifle: he took the rifle with him and not a fowling-piece, because he intended to hunt the wild boar; and the ox does not butt because it happens to have horns: it has horns because it intends to butt. Now, to render this proof complete, we have the additional circumstance, that in many animals, during the time they are growing, the effort of the will to which a limb is destined to minister, manifests itself before the existence of the limb itself, its employment thus anticipating its existence. Young he-goats, rams, calves, for instance, butt with their bare polls before they have any horns; the young boar tries to gore on either side, before its tusks are fully developed which would respond to the intended effect, while on the other hand, it neglects to use the smaller teeth it already has in its mouth and with which it might really bite. Thus its mode of defending itself does not adapt itself to the existing weapons, but *vice versa*. This had already been noticed by Galenus[8] and by Lucretius[9] before him. All these circumstances give us complete certainty, that the will does not, as a supplementary thing proceeding from the intellect, employ those instruments which it may happen to find, or use the parts because just they and no others chance to be there; but that what is primary and original, is the endeavour to live in this particular way, to contend in this manner, an endeavour which manifests itself not only in the employment, but even in the existence of the weapon: so much so indeed, that the

[8] Galenus, "De Usu Partium Anim.," i. 1.
[9] Lucretius, v. pp. 1032–1039.

use of the weapon frequently precedes its existence, thus denoting that it is the weapon which arises out of the existence
of the endeavour, not, conversely, the desire to use it out of the
existence of the weapon. From which it follows, that the structure of each animal is adapted to its will.

This truth forces itself upon thoughtful zoologists and
zootomists with such cogency, that unless their mind is at the
same time purified by a deeper philosophy, it may lead them
into strange errors. Now this actually happened to a very eminent zoologist, the immortal De Lamarck, who has acquired
everlasting fame by his discovery of the classification of animals in *vertebrata* and *non-vertebrata*, so admirable in depth
of view. For he quite seriously maintains and tries to prove [10]
at length, that the shape of each animal species, the weapons
peculiar to it, and its organs of every sort destined for outward
use, were by no means present at the origin of that species, but
have on the contrary *come into being* gradually *in the course of
time* and through continued generation, in consequence of the
exertions of the animal's will, evoked by the nature of its position and surroundings, through its own repeated efforts and
the habits to which these gave rise. Aquatic birds and mam-
malia that swim, he says, have only become web-footed
through stretching their toes asunder in swimming; moor-fowl
acquired their long legs and necks by wading; horned cattle
only gradually acquired horns because as they had no proper
teeth for combating, they fought with their heads, and this
combative propensity in course of time produced horns or
antlers; the snail was originally, like other *mollusca*, without
feelers; but out of the desire to feel the objects lying before it,
these gradually arose; the whole feline species acquired claws
only in course of time, from their desire to tear the flesh of
their prey, and the movable coverings of those claws, from the
necessity of protecting them in walking without being prevented from using them when they wished; the giraffe, in the
barren, grassless African deserts, being reduced for its food
to the leaves of lofty trees, stretched out its neck and forelegs
until at last it acquired its singular shape, with a height in

[10] De Lamarck, "Philosophie Zoologique," vol. i. c. 7, and "His-
toire Naturelle des Animaux sans Vertèbres," vol. i. Introd. pp.
180–212.

front of twenty feet, and thus De Lamarck goes on describing a multitude of animal species as arising according to the same principle, in doing which he overlooks the obvious objection which may be made, that long before the organs necessary for its preservation could have been produced by means of such endeavours as these through countless generations, the whole species must have died out from the want of them. To such a degree may we be blinded by a hypothesis which has once laid hold of us! Nevertheless in this instance the hypothesis arose out of a very correct and profound view of Nature: it is an error of genius, which in spite of all the absurdity it contains, still does honour to its originator. The true part of it belongs to De Lamarck, as an investigator of Nature; he saw rightly that the primary element which has determined the animal's organisation, is the will of that animal itself. The false part must be laid to the account of the backward state of Metaphysics in France, where the views of Locke and of his feeble follower, Condillac, in fact still hold their ground and therefore bodies are held to be things in themselves, Time and Space qualities of things in themselves; and where the great doctrine of the Ideal nature of Space and of Time and of all that is represented in them, which has been so extremely fertile in its results, has not yet penetrated. De Lamarck therefore could not conceive his construction of living beings otherwise than in Time, through succession. Errors of this sort, as well as the gross, absurd, atomic theory of the French and the edifying physico-theological considerations of the English, have been banished for ever from Germany by Kant's profound influence. So salutary was the effect produced by this great mind, even upon a nation capable of subsequently forsaking him to run after charlatanism and empty bombast. But the thought could never enter into De Lamarck's head, that the animal's will, as a thing in itself, might lie outside Time, and in this sense be prior to the animal itself. Therefore he assumes the animal to have first been without any clearly defined organs, but also without any clearly defined tendencies, and to have been equipped only with perception. Through this it learns to know the circumstances in which it has to live and from that knowledge arise its desires, i.e., its will, from which again spring its organs or definite embodiment; this last indeed with the help of generation and therefore in boundless Time. If De Lamarck had had the courage to carry out his theory fully, he ought to have assumed a primary animal which, to be consistent, must have originally had neither shape nor organs, and then proceeded to transform itself according to climate and local conditions into myriads of animal shapes of all sorts, from the gnat to the elephant.—But this primary animal is in truth the *will to live;* as such however, it is metaphysical, not physical. Most certainly the shape and organisation of each animal species has been determined by its own will according to the circumstances in which it wished to live; not however as a thing physical in Time, but on the contrary as a thing metaphysical outside Time. The will did not proceed from the intellect, nor did the intellect exist, together with the animal, before the will made its appearance as a mere accident, a secondary, or rather tertiary, thing. It is on the contrary the will which is the *prius,* the thing in itself: its phenomenon (mere representation in the cognitive intellect and its forms of Space and Time) is the animal, fully equipped with all its organs which represent the will to live in those particular circumstances. Among these organs is the intellect also—knowledge itself—which, like the rest of those organs, is exactly adapted to the mode of life of each animal; whereas, according to De Lamarck, it is the will which arises out of knowledge. Behold the countless varieties of animal shapes; how entirely is each of them the mere image of its volition, the evident expression of the strivings of the will which constitute its character! Their difference in shape is only the portrait of their difference in character. Ferocious animals, destined for combat and rapine, appear armed with formidable teeth and claws and strong muscles; their sight is adapted for great distances, especially when they have to mark their prey from a dizzy height, as is the case with eagles and condors. Timid animals, whose will it is to seek their safety in flight instead of contest, present themselves with light, nimble legs and sharp hearing in lieu of all weapons; a circumstance which has even necessitated a striking prolongation of the outer ear in the most timid of them all, the hare. The interior corresponds to the exterior: carnivorous animals have short intestines; herbivorous animals long ones, suited to a protracted assimilation. Vigorous respiration and rapid circulation of the blood, represented by appropriate organs, always accompany great muscular strength and irritability as their necessary conditions, and nowhere is contradiction possible. Each particular striving of the will presents itself in a particular modification of shape. The abode of the prey therefore has determined the shape of its pursuer: if that prey takes refuge in regions difficult of access, in remote hiding places, in night or darkness, the pursuer assumes the form best suited to those circumstances, and no shape is rejected as too grotesque by the will to live, in order to attain its ends. The cross-bill (*loxia curvirostra*) presents itself with this abnormal form of its organ of nutrition, in order to be able to extract the seeds out of the scales of the fir-cone. Moor-fowls appear equipped with extra long legs, extra long necks and extra long beaks, in short, the strangest shapes, in order to seek out reptiles in their marshes. Then we have the ant-bear with its body four feet long, its short legs, its strong claws, and its long, narrow, toothless muzzle provided with a threadlike, glutinous tongue for the purpose of digging out the white ants from their nests. The pelican goes fishing with a huge pouch under its beak in which to pack its fish, when caught. In order to surprise their prey while asleep in the night, owls fly out provided with enormous pupils which enable them to see in the dark, and with very soft feathers to make their flight noiseless and thus permit them to fall unawares upon their sleeping prey without awakening it by their movements. *Silurus, gymnotus* and *torpedo* bring a complete electric apparatus into the world with them, in order to stun their prey before they can reach it; and also as a defence against *their own* pursuers. For wherever anything living breathed, there immediately came another to devour it, and every animal is in a way designed and calculated throughout, down to the minutest detail, for the purpose of destroying some other animal. Ichneumons, for instance, among insects, lay their eggs in the bodies of certain caterpillars and similar *larvæ*, in which they bore holes with their stings, in order to ensure nourishment for their future brood. Now those kinds which feed on *larvæ* that crawl about freely, have short stings not more than about one-third of an inch long, whereas *pimpla manifestator*, which feeds upon *chelostoma maxillosa*, whose *larvæ* lie hidden in old trees at great depth and are not accessible to it, has a sting two inches long; and the sting of the *ichneumon strobillæ* which lays its eggs in *larvæ* dwelling in fir-cones, is nearly as long. With these stings they penetrate to the *larva* in which they bore a hole and deposit one egg, whose product subsequently devours this *larva*. Just as clearly does the will to escape their enemies manifest itself in the defensive equipment of animals that are the objects of pursuit. Hedgehogs and porcupines raise up a forest of spears; armadillos, scaly ant-eaters and tortoises appear cased from head to foot in armour which is inaccessible to tooth, beak or claw; and so it is, on a smaller scale, with the whole class of *crustacea*. Others again seek protection by deceiving their pursuers rather than by resisting them physically: thus the sepia has provided itself with materials for surrounding itself with a dark cloud on the approach of danger. The sloth is deceptively like its moss-clad bough, and the frog its leaf; and many insects resemble their dwelling-places. The negro's louse is black;[11] so, to be sure, is our flea also; but the latter, in providing itself with an extremely powerful apparatus for making irregular jumps to a considerable distance, trusted to these for protection.—We can however make the anticipation in all these arrangements more intelligible to ourselves by the same anticipation which shows itself in the mechanical instincts of animals. Neither the young spider nor the ant-lion know the prey for which they lay traps, when they do it for the first time. And it is the same when they are on the defensive. According to Latreille, the insect *bombex* kills the *parnope* with its sting, although it neither eats it nor is attacked by it, simply because the *parnope* will lay its eggs in the *bombex's* nest, and by doing this will interfere with the development of its eggs; yet it does not know this. Anticipations of this kind once more confirm the ideal nature of Time, which indeed always becomes manifest as soon as the will as thing in itself is in question. Not only with respect to the points here mentioned, but to many others besides, the mechanical instincts and physiological functions of animals serve to explain each other mutually, because the will without knowledge is the agent in both.

[11] Blumenbach, "De hum. gen. variet. nat." p. 50. Sömmering, "On the Negro," p. 8.

As the will has equipped itself with every organ and every weapon, offensive as well as defensive, so has it likewise provided itself in every animal shape with an *intellect*, as a means of preservation for the individual and the species. It was precisely in this account that the ancients called the intellect the guide and leader. Accordingly the intellect, being exclusively destined to serve the will, always exactly corresponds to it. Beasts of prey stood in greater need of intellect, and in fact have more intelligence, than herbivorous animals. The elephant certainly forms an exception, and so does even the horse to a certain extent; but the admirable intelligence of the elephant was necessary on account of the length of its life (200 years) and of the scantiness of its progeny, which obliged it to provide for a longer and surer preservation of the individual: and this moreover in countries teeming with the most rapacious, the strongest and the nimblest beasts of prey. The horse too has a longer life and a scantier progeny than the ruminants, and as it has neither horns, tusks, trunk, nor indeed any weapon save perhaps its hoofs, it needed greater intelligence and swiftness in order to elude pursuit. Monkeys needed their extraordinary intelligence, partly because of the length of their life, which even in the moderate-sized animal extends to fifty years; partly also because of their scanty progeny, which is limited to one at a time, but especially because of their *hands*, which, to be properly used, required the direction of an understanding. For monkeys depend upon their hands, not only for their defence by means of outer weapons such as sticks and stones, but also for their nourishment, this last necessitating a variety of artificial means and a social and artificial system of rapine in general, the passing from hand to hand of stolen fruit, the placing of sentinels, &c. &c. Add to this, that it is especially in their youth, before they have attained their full muscular development, that this intelligence is most prominent. In the *pongo* or ourang-outang for instance, the brain plays a far more important part and the understanding is much greater during its youth than at its maturity, when the muscular powers having attained full development, they take the place of the proportionately declining intellect. This holds good of all sorts of monkeys, so that here therefore the intellect acts for a time vicariously for the yet undeveloped muscular strength. We find this process discussed at length in the "Résumé des Observations de Fr. Cuvier sur l'instinct et l'intelligence des animaux," par Flourens (1841), from which I have quoted the whole passage referring to this question in the second volume of my chief work, at the end of the thirty-first chapter, and this is my only reason for not repeating it here. On the whole, intelligence gradually increases from the rodents[12] to the ruminants, from the ruminants to the pachyderms, and from these again to the beasts of prey and finally to the *quadrumana,* and anatomy shows a gradual development of the brain in similar order which corresponds to this result of external observation. (According to Flourens and Fr. Cuvier.) Among the reptiles, serpents are the most intelligent, for they may even be trained; this is so, because they are beasts of prey and propagate more slowly than the rest—especially the venomous ones. And here also, as with the physical weapons, we find the will everywhere as the *prius;* its equipment, the intellect, as the *posterius.* Beasts of prey do not hunt, nor do foxes thieve, because they have more intelligence; on the contrary, they have more intelligence, just as they have stronger teeth and claws too, because they wished to live by hunting and thieving. The fox even made up at once for his inferiority in muscular power and strength of teeth by the extraordinary subtility of his understanding. Our thesis is singularly illustrated by the case of the bird *dodo* or *dronte* (*didus ineptus*) on the island of Mauritius, whose species, it is well known, has died out, and which, as its Latin name denotes, was exceedingly stupid, and this explains its disappearance; so that here it seems indeed as if Nature had for

12 That the lowest place should be given to the rodents, seems however to proceed from *a priori* rather than from *a posteriori* considerations: that is to say, from the circumstance, that their brain has extremely faint or small convolutions; so that too much weight may have been given to this point. In sheep and calves the convolutions are numerous and deep, yet how is it with their intelligence? The mechanical instincts of the beaver are again greatly assisted by its understanding, and even rabbits show remarkable intelligence (see Leroy's beautiful work: "Letters Philosophiques sur l'Intelligence des Animaux," lettre 3, p. 149). Even rats give proof of quite uncommon intelligence, of which some remarkable instances may be found in the "Quarterly Review," No. 201, Jan.–March, 1857, in a special article entitled "Rats."

once gone too far in her *lex parsimoniæ* and thereby in a sense brought forth an abortion in the species, as she so often does in the individual, which was unable to subsist, precisely because it was an abortion. If, on this occasion, anyone were to raise the question as to whether Nature ought not to have provided insects with at least sufficient intelligence to prevent them from flying into the flame of a candle, our answer would be: most certainly; only she did not know that men would make candles and light them, and *natura nihil agit frustra*. Insect intelligence is therefore only insufficient where the surroundings are artificial.

Everywhere indeed intelligence depends in the first instance upon the cerebral system, and this stands in a necessary relation to the rest of the organism; therefore cold-blooded animals are greatly inferior to warm-blooded ones, and invertebrate animals to *vertebrata*. But the organism is precisely nothing but the will become visible, to which, as that which is absolutely *prius*, everything constantly refers. The needs and aims of that will give in each phenomenon the rule for the means to be employed, and these means must harmonize with one another. Plants have no self-consciousness because they have no power of locomotion; for of what use would self-consciousness be to them unless it enabled them to seek what was salutary and flee what was noxious to them? And conversely, of what use could power of locomotion be to them, as they have no self-consciousness with which to guide it. The inseparable duality of Sensibility and Irritability does not yet appear therefore in the plant; they continue slumbering in the reproductive force which is their fundament, and in which alone the will here objectifies itself. The sun-flower, and every other plant, wills for light; but as yet their movement towards light is not separate from their apprehension of it, and both coincide with their growth.—Human understanding, which is so superior to that of all other beings, and is assisted by Reason (the faculty for non-perceptible representations, *i.e.*, for conceptions; reflection, thinking faculty), is nevertheless only just proportionate, partly to Man's requirements, which greatly surpass those of animals and multiply to infinity; partly to his entire lack of all natural weapons and covering, and to his relatively weaker muscular strength, which is greatly inferior to that of monkeys of his own size; lastly also, to the slowness with which his race multiplies and the length of his childhood and life, which demand secure preservation of the individual. All these great requirements had to be satisfied by means of intellectual powers, which, for this reason, predominate in him. But we find the intellect secondary and subordinate everywhere, and destined exclusively to serve the purposes of the will. As a rule too, it always remains true to its destiny and subservient to the will. How nevertheless, it frees itself in particular instances from this bondage through an abnormal preponderance of cerebral life, whereby purely objective cognition becomes possible which may be enhanced to genius, I have shown at length in the æsthetic part of my chief work.

Now, after all these reflections upon the precise agreement between the will and the organisation of each animal, if we inspect a well-arranged osteological collection from this point of view, it will certainly seem to us as if we saw one and the same being (De Lamarck's primary animal, or, more properly, *the will to live*) changing its shape according to circumstances, and thus producing all this multiplicity of forms out of the same number and arrangement of its bones, by prolonging and curtailing, strengthening and weakening them. This number and arrangement of the bones, which Geoffroy de St. Hilaire[13] called the anatomical element, continues, as he has thoroughly shown, in all essential points unchanged: it is a constant magnitude, something which is absolutely given beforehand, irrevocably fixed by an unfathomable necessity—an immutability which I should compare with the permanence of matter in all physical and chemical changes: but to this I shall soon return. Conjointly with this immutability of the anatomical element, we have the greatest susceptibility to modification, the greatest plasticity and flexibility of these same bones with reference to size, shape and adaptation to different purposes, all which we see determined by the will with primary strength and freedom according to the aims prescribed to it by external circumstances: it makes out of these materials whatever its necessity for the time being requires. If it desires

[13] "Principes de Philosophie Zoologique," 1830.

to climb about in trees, it catches at the boughs at once with four hands, while it stretches the *ulna* and *radius* to an excessive length and immediately prolongs the *os coccygis* to a curly tail, a yard long, in order to hang by it to the boughs and swing itself from one branch to another. If, on the other hand, it desires to crawl in the mud as a crocodile, to swim as a seal, or to burrow as a mole, these same arm-bones are shortened till they are no longer recognisable; in the last case the *metacarpus* and *phalanges* are enlarged to disproportionately large shovel-paws, to the prejudice of the other bones. But if it wishes to fly through the air as a bat, not only are the *os humeri, radius* and *alnus* prolonged in an incredible manner, but the usually small and subordinate *carpus, metacarpus* and *phalanges digitorum* expand to an immense length, as in St. Anthony's vision, outmeasuring the length of the animal's body, in order to spread out the wing-membrane. If, in order to browse upon the tops of very tall African trees, it has, as a giraffe, placed itself upon extraordinarily high fore-legs, the same seven *vertebræ* of the neck, which never vary as to number and which, in the mole, were contracted so as to be no longer recognisable, are now prolonged to such a degree, that here, as everywhere else, the neck acquires the same length as the fore-legs, in order to enable the head to reach down to drinking-water. But where, as is the case when it appears as the elephant, a long neck could not have borne the weight of the enormous, unwieldy head—a weight increased moreover by tusks a yard long—the neck remains short, as an exception, and a trunk is let down as an expedient, to lift up food and draw water from below and also to reach up to the tops of trees. In accordance with these transformations, we see in all of them the skull, the receptacle containing the understanding, at the same time proportionately expand, develop, curve itself, as the mode of procuring nourishment becomes more or less difficult and requires more or less intelligence; and the different degrees of the understanding manifest themselves clearly to the practised eye in the curves of the skull.

Now, in all this, that *anatomical element* we have mentioned above as fixed and invariable, certainly remains in so far an enigma, as it does not come within the teleological explanation, which only begins after the assumption of that element; since the intended organ might in many cases have been rendered equally suitable for its purpose even with a different number and disposition of bones. It is easy to understand, for instance, why the human skull should be formed out of eight bones: that is, to enable them to be drawn together by the fontanels during birth; but we do not see why a chicken which breaks through its egg-shell should necessarily have the same number of skull-bones. We must therefore assume this anatomical element to be based, partly on the unity and identity of the will to live in general, partly on the circumstance, that the archetypal forms of animals have proceeded one from the other,[14] wherefore the fundamental type of the whole race was preserved.

No other explanation or assumption enables us nearly as well to understand either the complete suitableness to purpose and to the external conditions of existence I have here shown in the skeleton, or the admirable harmony and fitness of internal mechanism in the structure of each animal, as the truth I have elsewhere firmly established: that the body of an animal is precisely nothing but the *will itself* of that animal brought to cerebral perception as representation—through the forms of Space, Time and Causality—in other words, the mere visibility, objectivity of the Will. For, if this is once pre-supposed, everything in and belonging to that body must conspire towards the final end: the life of this animal. Nothing superfluous, nothing deficient, nothing inappropriate, nothing insufficient or incomplete of its kind, can therefore be found in it; on the contrary, all that is required must be there, and just in the proportion needed, never more. For here artist, work and materials are one and the same. Each organism is therefore a consummate master-piece of exceeding perfection. Here the will did not first cherish the intention, first recognise the end and then adapt the means to it and conquer the material; its willing was rather immediately the aim and immediately the attainment of that aim; no foreign appliances needing to be overcome were wanted—willing, doing and attaining were here one and the same. Thus the organism presents itself as a mir-

14 "Parerga," vol. ii. § 91; § 93 of the 2nd edition.

acle which admits of no comparison with any work of human artifice wrought by the lamplight of knowledge.[15]

Our admiration for the consummate perfection and fitness for their ends in all the works of Nature, is at the bottom based upon our viewing them in the same light as we do our own works. In these, in the first place, the will to do the work and the work are two different things; then again two other things lie between these two: firstly, the medium of representation, which, taken by itself, is foreign to the will, through which the will must pass before it realizes itself here; and secondly the material foreign to the will here at work, on which a form foreign to it has to be forced, which it resists, because the material already belongs to another will, that is to say, to its own nature, its *forma substantialis*, the (Platonic) Idea, expressed by it: therefore this material has first to be overcome, and however deeply the artificial form may have penetrated, will always continue inwardly resisting. It is quite a different thing with Nature's works, which are not, like our own, indirect, but on the contrary, direct manifestations of the will. Here the will acts in its primordial nature, that is, unconsciously. No mediating representation here separates the will and the work: they are one. And even the material is one with them: for matter is the mere visibility of the will. There-

[15] The appearance of every animal therefore presents a totality, a unity, a perfection and a rigidly carried out harmony in all its parts which is so entirely based upon a single fundamental thought, that even the strangest animal shape seems to the attentive observer as if it were the only right, nay, only possible form of existence, and as if there could be no other than just this very one. The expression "natural" used to denote that a thing is a matter of course, and that it cannot be otherwise, is in its deepest foundation based upon this. Göthe himself was struck by this unity when contemplating whelks and crabs at Venice, and it caused him to exclaim: "How delightful, how glorious is a living thing! how well adapted for its condition; how true, how real!" ("Life," vol. iv. p. 223). No artist therefore, who has not made it his business to study such forms for years and to penetrate into their meaning and comprehension, can rightly imitate them. Without this study his work will seem as if it were pasted together: the parts no doubt will be there, but the bond which unites them and gives them cohesion, the spirit, the idea, which is the objectivity of the primary act of the will presenting itself as this or that particular species, will be wanting. [Add. to 3rd ed.]

fore here we find Matter completely permeated by Form; or, better still, they are of quite the same origin, only existing mutually one for the other; and in so far they are one. That we separate them in works of Nature as well as in works of Art, is a mere abstraction. Pure Matter, absolutely without Form or quality, which we think as the material of a product of Nature, is merely an *ens rationis* and cannot enter into any experience; whereas the material of a work of Art is empirical Matter, consequently already has a Form. The [distinctive] character of Nature's products is the identity of form and substance; that of products of Art the diversity of these two. It is because Matter is the mere visibility of Form in Nature's products, that, even empirically, we see Form appear as a mere production of Matter, bursting forth from its inside in crystallisation, in vegetable and animal *generatio æquivoca*, which last cannot be doubted, at any rate in the *epizoa*.—For this reason we may even assume that nowhere, either on any planet or satellite, will Matter come to a state of endless repose, but rather that its inherent forces (*i.e.*, the will, whose mere visibility it is) will always put an end again to the repose which has commenced, always awaking again from their sleep, to resume their activity as mechanical, physical, chemical, organic forces; since at all times they only wait for the opportunity to do so.

But if we want to understand Nature's proceeding, we must not try to do it by comparing her works with our own. The real essence of every animal form, is an act of the will outside representation, consequently outside its forms of Space and Time also; which act, just on that account, knows neither sequence nor juxtaposition, but has, on the contrary, the most indivisible unity. But when our cerebral perception comprehends that form, and still more when its inside is dissected by the anatomical knife, then that which originally and in itself was foreign to knowledge and its laws, is brought under the light of knowledge; but then also, it has to present itself in conformity with the laws and forms of knowledge. The original unity and indivisibility of that act of the will, of that truly metaphysical being, then appears divided into parts lying side by side and functions following one upon another, which all nevertheless present themselves as connected together in closest relationship one to another for mutual help and support, as means and ends one to the other. The understanding, in thus apprehending these things, now perceives the original unity re-establishing itself out of a multiplicity which its own form of knowledge had first brought about, and involuntarily taking for granted that its own way of perceiving this is the way in which this animal form comes into being, it is now struck with admiration for the profound wisdom with which those parts are arranged, those functions combined. This is the meaning of Kant's great doctrine, that Teleology is brought into Nature by our own understanding, which accordingly wonders at a miracle of its own creation. If I may use a trivial simile to elucidate so sublime a matter, this astonishment very much resembles that of our understanding when it discovers that all multiples of 9, when their single figures are added together, give as their product either the number 9 or one whose single figures again make 9; yet it is that very understanding itself which has prepared for itself this surprise in the decimal system. According to the Physico-theological argument, the actual existence of the world has been preceded by its existence in an intellect: if the world is designed for an end, it must have existed as representation before it came into being. Now I say, on the contrary, in Kant's sense: if the world is to be representation, it must present itself as designed for an end; and this only takes place in an intellect.

It undoubtedly follows from my doctrine, that every being is its own work. Nature, which is incapable of falsehood and is as *naïve* as genius, asserts the same thing downright; since each being merely kindles the spark of life at another exactly similar being, and then makes itself before our eyes, taking the materials for this from outside, form and movement from its own self: this process we call growth and development. Thus, even empirically, each being stands before us as its own work. But Nature's language is not understood because it is too simple.

X

ON THE SENSES

(CHAPTER III *from* SUPPLEMENTS TO THE FIRST BOOK OF THE WORLD AS WILL AND IDEA)

It is not the object of my writings to repeat what has been said by others, and therefore I only make here some special remarks of my own on the subject of the senses.

The senses are merely the channels through which the brain receives from without (in the form of sensations) the materials which it works up into ideas of perception. Those sensations which principally serve for the objective comprehension of the external world must in themselves be neither agreeable nor disagreeable. This really means that they must leave the will entirely unaffected. Otherwise the sensation *itself* would attract our attention, and we would remain at the *effect* instead of passing to the *cause*, which is what is aimed at here. For it would bring with it that marked superiority, as regards our consideration, which the will always has over the mere idea, to which we only turn when the will is silent. Therefore colours and sounds are in themselves, and so long as their impression does not pass the normal degree, neither painful nor pleasurable sensations, but appear with the indifference that fits them to be the material of pure objective perception. This is as far the case as was possible in a body which is in itself through and through will; and just in this respect it is worthy of admiration. Physiologically it rests upon the fact that in the organs of the nobler senses, thus in sight and hearing, the nerves which have to receive the specific outward impression are quite insusceptible to any sensation of pain, and know no other sensation than that which is specifically peculiar to them, and which serves the purpose of mere apprehension. Thus the retina, as also the optic nerve, is insensible to every injury; and this is also the case with the nerve of hearing. In both organs pain is only felt in their other parts, the surroundings of the nerve of sense which is peculiar to them, never in this nerve itself. In the case of the eye such pain is felt principally in the *conjunctiva;* in the case of the ear, in the *meatus auditorius.* Even with the brain this is the case, for if it is cut into directly, thus from above, it has no feeling. Thus only on account of this indifference with regard to the will which is peculiar to them are the sensations of the eye capable of supplying the understanding with such multifarious and finely distinguished data, out of which it constructs in our head the marvellous objective world, by the application of the law of causality upon the foundation of the pure perceptions of space and time. Just that freedom from affecting the will which is characteristic of sensations of colour enables them, when their energy is heightened by transparency, as in the glow of an evening sky, in painted glass, and the like, to raise us very easily into the state of pure objective will-less perception, which, as I have shown in my third book, is one of the chief constituent elements of the æsthetic impression. Just this indifference with regard to the will fits sounds to supply the material for denoting the infinite multiplicity of the conceptions of the reason.

Outer sense, that is, receptivity for external impressions as pure data for the understanding, is divided into *five senses,* and these accommodate themselves to the four elements, *i.e.,* the four states of aggregation, together with that of imponderability. Thus the sense for what is firm (earth) is touch; for what is fluid (water), taste; for what is in the form of vapour, *i.e.,* volatile (vapour, exhalation), smell; for what is permanently elastic (air), hearing; for what is imponderable (fire, light), sight. The second imponderable, heat, is not properly an object of the senses, but of general feeling, and therefore always affects the *will* directly, as agreeable or disagreeable. From this classification there also follows the relative dignity of the senses. Sight has the highest rank, because its sphere is the widest and its susceptibility the finest. This rests upon the fact that what affects it is an imponderable, that is, something which is scarcely corporeal, but is *quasi* spiritual. Hearing has the second place, corresponding to air. However, touch is a more thorough and well-informed sense.

For while each of the other senses gives us only an entirely one-sided relation to the object, as its sound, or its relation to light, touch, which is closely bound up with general feeling and muscular power, supplies the understanding with the data at once for the form, magnitude, hardness, softness, texture, firmness, temperature, and weight of bodies, and all this with the least possibility of illusion and deception, to which all the other senses are far more subject. The two lowest senses, smell and taste, are no longer free from a direct affection of the will, that is, they are always agreeably or disagreeably affected, and are therefore more subjective than objective.

Sensations of hearing are exclusively in *time*, and therefore the whole nature of music consists in degrees of time, upon which depends both the quality or pitch of tones, by means of vibrations, and also their quantity or duration, by means of time. The sensations of sight, on the other hand, are primarily and principally in *space;* but secondarily, by reason of their duration, they are also in time.

Sight is the sense of the understanding which perceives; hearing is the sense of the reason which thinks and apprehends. Words are only imperfectly represented by visible signs; and therefore I doubt whether a deaf and dumb man, who can read, but has no idea of the sound of the words, works as quickly in thinking with the mere visible signs of conceptions as we do with the real, *i.e.,* the audible words. If he cannot read, it is well known that he is almost like an irrational animal, while the man born blind is from the first a thoroughly rational being.

Sight is an *active*, hearing a *passive* sense. Therefore sounds affect our mind in a disturbing and hostile manner, and indeed they do so the more in proportion as the mind is active and developed; they distract all thoughts and instantly destroy the power of thinking. On the other hand, there is no analogous disturbance through the eye, no direct effect of what is seen, *as such,* upon the activity of thought (for naturally we are not speaking here of the influence which the objects looked at have upon the will); but the most varied multitude of things before our eyes admits of entirely unhindered and quiet thought. Therefore the thinking mind lives at peace with the eye, but is always at war with the ear. This opposition of the two senses is also confirmed by the fact that if deaf and dumb persons are cured by galvanism they become deadly pale with terror at the first sounds they hear (Gilbert's *"Annalen der Physik,"* vol. x. p. 382), while blind persons, on the contrary, who have been operated upon, behold with ecstasy the first light, and unwillingly allow the bandages to be put over their eyes again. All that has been said, however, can be explained from the fact that hearing takes place by means of a mechanical vibration of the nerve of hearing which is at once transmitted to the brain, while seeing, on the other hand, is a real *action* of the retina which is merely stimulated and called forth by light and its modifications; as I have shown at length in my physiological theory of colours. But this whole opposition stands in direct conflict with that coloured-ether, drumbeating theory which is now everywhere unblushingly served up, and which seeks to degrade the eye's sensation of light to a mechanical vibration, such as primarily that of hearing actually is, while nothing can be more different than the still, gentle effect of light and the alarm-drum of hearing. If we add to this the remarkable circumstance that although we hear with two ears, the sensibility of which is often very different, yet we never hear a sound double, as we often see things double with our two eyes, we are led to the conjecture that the sensation of hearing does not arise in the labyrinth or in the cochlea, but deep in the brain where the two nerves of hearing meet, and thus the impression becomes simple. But this is where the *pons Varolii* encloses the *medulla oblongata,* thus at the absolutely lethal spot, by the injury of which every animal is instantly killed, and from which the nerve of hearing has only a short course to the labyrinth, the seat of acoustic vibration. Now it is just because its source is here, in this dangerous place, in which also all movement of the limbs originates, that we start at a sudden noise; which does not occur in the least degree when we suddenly see a light; for example, a flash of lightning. The optic nerve, on the contrary, proceeds from its *thalami* much further forward (though perhaps its source lies behind them), and throughout its course is covered by the anterior lobes of the brain, although always separated from them till, having extended quite out of the brain, it is spread out in the retina, upon which, on stimulation by light, the sensation first arises, and where it is really localised. This is shown in my essay upon sight and colour. This origin of the auditory nerve explains, then, the great disturbance which the power of thinking suffers from sound, on account of which thinking men, and in general all people of much intellect, are without exception absolutely incapable of enduring any noise. For it disturbs the constant stream of their thoughts, interrupts and paralyses their thinking, just because the vibration of the auditory nerve extends so deep into the brain, the whole mass of which feels the oscillations set up through this nerve, and vibrates along with them, and because the brains of such persons are more easily moved than those of ordinary men. On the same readiness to be set in motion, and capacity for transmission, which characterises their brains depends the fact that in the case of persons like these every thought calls forth so readily all those analogous or related to it whereby the similarities, analogies, and relations of things in general come so quickly and easily into their minds; that the same occasion which millions of ordinary minds have experienced before brings them to *the* thought, to *the* discovery, that other people are subsequently surprised they did not reach themselves, for they certainly can think afterwards, but they cannot think before. Thus the sun shone on all statues, but only the statue of Memnon gave forth a sound. For this reason Kant, Goethe, and Jean Paul were highly sensitive to every noise, as their biographers bear witness.[1] Goethe in his last years bought a house which had fallen into disrepair close to his own, simply in order that he might not have to endure the noise that would be made in repairing it. Thus it was in vain that in his youth he followed the drum in order to harden himself against noise. It is not a matter of custom. On the other hand, the truly stoical indifference to noise of ordinary minds is astonishing. No noise disturbs them in their thinking, reading, writing, or other occupations, while the finer mind is rendered quite incapable by it. But just that which makes

[1] Lichtenberg says in his *"Nachrichten und Bemerkungen von und über sich selbst"* (*Vermischte Schriften, Göttingen,* 1800, vol. i. p. 43): "I am extremely sensitive to all noise, but it entirely loses its disagreeable character as soon as it is associated with a rational purpose."

them so insensible to noise of every kind makes them also insensible to the beautiful in plastic art, and to deep thought or fine expression in literary art; in short, to all that does not touch their personal interests. The following remark of Lichtenberg's applies to the paralysing effect which noise has upon highly intellectual persons: "It is always a good sign when an artist can be hindered by trifles from exercising his art. F—— used to stick his fingers into sulphur if he wished to play the piano. . . . Such things do not interfere with the average mind; . . . it acts like a coarse sieve" (*Vermischte Schriften*, vol. i. p. 398). I have long really held the opinion that the amount of noise which any one can bear undisturbed stands in inverse proportion to his mental capacity, and therefore may be regarded as a pretty fair measure of it. Therefore, if I hear the dogs barking for hours together in the court of a house without being stopped, I know what to think of the intellectual capacity of the inhabitants. The man who habitually slams the door of a room, instead of shutting it with his hand, or allows this to go on in his house, is not only ill-bred, but is also a coarse and dull-minded fellow. That in English "sensible" also means gifted with understanding is based upon accurate and fine observation. We shall only become quite civilised when the ears are no longer unprotected, and when it shall no longer be the right of everybody to sever the consciousness of each thinking being, in its course of a thousand steps, with whistling, howling, bellowing, hammering, whip-cracking, barking, &c. &c. The Sybarites banished all noisy trades without the town; the honourable sect of the Shakers in North America permit no unnecessary noise in their villages, and the Moravians have a similar rule. Something more is said upon this subject in the thirtieth chapter of the second volume of the "Parerga."

The effect of music upon the mind, so penetrating, so direct, so unfailing, may be explained from the *passive* nature of hearing which has been discussed; also the after effect which sometimes follows it, and which consists in a specially elevated frame of mind. The vibrations of the tones following in rationally combined numerical relations set the fibre of the brain itself in similar vibration. On the other hand, the *active* nature of sight, opposed as it is to the passive nature of hearing, makes it intelligible why there can be nothing analogous to music for the eye, and the piano of colours was an absurd mistake. Further, it is just on account of the active nature of the sense of sight that it is remarkably acute in the case of beasts that hunt, *i.e.*, beasts of prey, while conversely the *passive* sense of hearing is specially acute in those beasts that are hunted, that flee, and are timid, so that it may give them timely warning of the pursuer that is rushing or creeping upon them.

Just as we have recognised in sight the sense of the understanding, and in hearing the sense of the reason, so we might call smell the sense of the memory, because it recalls to us more directly than any other the specific impression of an event or a scene even from the most distant past.

XI

ON THE VANITY AND SUFFERING
OF LIFE[1]

(from SUPPLEMENTS TO THE FOURTH
BOOK OF THE WORLD AS WILL AND IDEA)

Awakened to life out of the night of unconsciousness, the will finds itself an individual, in an endless and boundless world, among innumerable individuals, all striving, suffering, erring; and as if through a troubled dream it hurries back to its old unconsciousness. Yet till then its desires are limitless, its claims inexhaustible, and every satisfied desire gives rise to a new one. No possible satisfaction in the world could suffice to still its longings, set a goal to its infinite cravings, and fill the bottomless abyss of its heart. Then let one consider what as a rule are the satisfactions of any kind that a man obtains. For the most part, nothing more than the bare maintenance of this existence itself, extorted day by day with unceasing trouble and constant care in the conflict with want, and with death in prospect. Everything in life shows that earthly happiness is destined to be frustrated or recognized as an illusion. The grounds of this lie deep in the nature of things. Accordingly the life of most men is troubled and short. Those who are comparatively happy are so, for the most part, only apparently, or else, like men of long life, they are rare exceptions, a possibility of which there had to be,—as decoy-birds. Life presents itself as a continual deception in small things as in great. If it has promised, it does not keep its word, unless to show how little worth desiring were the things desired: thus we are deluded now by hope, now by what was hoped for. If it has given, it did so in order to take. The enchantment of distance shows us paradises which vanish like optical illusions when we have allowed ourselves to be mocked by them. Happiness

[1] This chapter is connected with §§ 56–59 of THE WORLD AS WILL AND IDEA, Dolphin Books, Doubleday & Company, Inc., 1961.

accordingly always lies in the future, or else in the past, and the present may be compared to a small dark cloud which the wind drives over the sunny plain: before and behind it all is bright, only it itself always casts a shadow. The present is therefore always insufficient; but the future is uncertain, and the past irrevocable. Life with its hourly, daily, weekly, yearly, little, greater, and great misfortunes, with its deluded hopes and its accidents destroying all our calculations, bears so distinctly the impression of something with which we must become disgusted, that it is hard to conceive how one has been able to mistake this and allow oneself to be persuaded that life is there in order to be thankfully enjoyed, and that man exists in order to be happy. Rather that continual illusion and disillusion, and also the nature of life throughout, presents itself to us as intended and calculated to awaken the conviction that nothing at all is worth our striving, our efforts and struggles, that all good things are vanity, the world in all its ends bankrupt, and life a business which does not cover its expenses;—so that our will may turn away from it.

The way in which this vanity of all objects of the will makes itself known and comprehensible to the intellect which is rooted in the individual, is primarily *time*. It is the form by means of which that vanity of things appears as their perishableness; for on account of this all our pleasures and joys disappear in our hands, and we afterwards ask astonished where they have remained. That nothingness itself is therefore the only *objective* element in time, *i.e.*, that which corresponds to it in the inner nature of things, thus that of which it is the expression. Just on this account time is the *a priori* necessary form of all our perceptions; in it everything must present itself, even we ourselves. Accordingly, first of all, our life is like a payment which one receives in nothing but copper pence, and yet must then give a discharge for: the copper pence are the days; the discharge is death. For at last time makes known the judgment of nature concerning the work of all the beings which appear in it, in that it destroys them:—

> And rightly so, for all that arises
> Is worthy only of being destroyed.
> Hence were it better that nothing arose.

Thus old age and death, to which every life necessarily hurries on, are the sentence of condemnation on the will to live, coming from the hands of nature itself, and which declares that this will is an effort which frustrates itself. "What thou hast wished," it says, "ends thus: desire something better." Hence the instruction which his life affords to every one consists, as a whole, in this, that the objects of his desires continually delude, waver, and fall, and accordingly bring more misery than joy, till at last the whole foundation upon which they all stand gives way, in that his life itself is destroyed and so he receives the last proof that all his striving and wishing was a perversity, a false path:—

> Then old age and experience, hand in hand,
> Lead him to death, and make him understand,
> After a search so painful and so long,
> That all his life he has been in the wrong.

We shall, however, enter into the details of the matter, for it is in these views that I have met with most contradiction. First of all, I have to confirm by the following remarks the proof given in the text of the negative nature of all satisfaction, thus of all pleasure and all happiness, in opposition to the positive nature of pain.

We feel pain, but not painlessness; we feel care, but not the absence of care; fear, but not security. We feel the wish as we feel hunger and thirst; but as soon as it has been fulfiled, it is like the mouthful that has been taken, which ceases to exist for our feeling the moment it is swallowed. Pleasures and joys we miss painfully whenever they are wanting; but pains, even when they cease after having long been present, are not directly missed, but at the most are intentionally thought of by means of reflection. For only pain and want can be felt positively, and therefore announce themselves; well-being, on the other hand, is merely negative. Therefore we do not become conscious of the three greatest blessings of life, health, youth, and freedom, so long as we possess them, but only after we have lost them; for they also are negations. We only observe that days of our life were happy after they have given place to unhappy ones. In proportion as pleasures increase, the susceptibility for them decreases: what is cus-

tomary is no longer felt as a pleasure. Just in this way, however, is the susceptibility for suffering increased, for the loss
of what we are accustomed to is painfully felt. Thus the measure of what is necessary increases through possession, and
thereby the capacity for feeling pain. The hours pass the
quicker the more agreeably they are spent, and the slower
the more painfully they are spent; because pain, not pleasure,
is the positive, the presence of which makes itself felt. In the
same way we become conscious of time when we are bored,
not when we are diverted. Both these cases prove that our
existence is most happy when we perceive it least, from which
it follows that it would be better not to have it. Great and
lively joy can only be conceived as the consequence of great
misery, which has preceded it; for nothing can be added to a
state of permanent satisfaction but some amusement, or the
satisfaction of vanity. Hence all poets are obliged to bring their
heroes into anxious and painful situations, so that they may
be able to free them from them. Dramas and Epics accordingly
always describe only fighting, suffering, tormented men; and
every romance is a rareeshow in which we observe the spasms
and convulsions of the agonised human heart. Walter Scott
has naïvely expressed this æsthetic necessity in the conclusion
to his novel, "Old Mortality." Voltaire, who was so highly favoured both by nature and fortune, says, in entire agreement
with the truth proved by me: *"Le bonheur n'est qu'un rève, et
la douleur est réelle."* And he adds: *"Il y a quatre-vingts ans
que je l'éprouve. Je n'y sais autre chose que me résigner, et
me dire que les mouches sont nées pour être mangées par les
araignées, et les hommes pour être dévorés par les chagrins."*

Before so confidently affirming that life is a blessing worth
desiring or giving thanks for, let one compare calmly the sum
of the possible pleasures which a man can enjoy in his life
with the sum of the possible sorrows which may come to him
in his life. I believe the balance will not be hard to strike. At
bottom, however, it is quite superfluous to dispute whether
there is more good or evil in the world: for the mere existence
of evil decides the matter. For the evil can never be annulled,
and consequently can never be balanced by the good which
may exist along with it or after it.

Mille piacer' non vagliono un tormento.—Petrarch
(A thousand pleasures are not worth one torment.)

For that a thousand had lived in happiness and pleasure would never do away with the anguish and death-agony of a single one; and just as little does my present well-being undo my past suffering. If, therefore, the evils in the world were a hundred times less than is the case, yet their mere existence would be sufficient to establish a truth which may be expressed in different ways, though always somewhat indirectly, the truth that we have not to rejoice but rather to mourn at the existence of the world;—that its non-existence would be preferable to its existence;—that it is something which at bottom ought not to be, &c., &c. Very beautiful is Byron's expression of this truth:—

Our life is a false nature,—'tis not in
The harmony of things, this hard decree,
This uneradicable taint of sin,
This boundless Upas, this all-blasting tree
Whose root is earth, whose leaves and branches be
The skies, which rain their plagues on men like dew—
Disease, death, bondage—all the woes we see—
And worse, the woes we see not—which throb through
The immedicable soul, with heart-aches ever new.

If the world and life were an end in themselves, and accordingly required theoretically no justification and practically no indemnification or compensation, but existed, for instance, as Spinoza and the Spinozists of the present day represent it, as the single manifestation of a God, who, *animi causa,* or else in order to mirror himself, undertook such an evolution of himself; and hence its existence neither required to be justified by reasons nor redeemed by results;—then the sufferings and miseries of life would not indeed have to be fully equalled by the pleasures and well-being in it; for this, as has been said, is impossible, because my present pain is never abolished by future joys, for the latter fill their time as the former fills its time: but there would have to be absolutely no suffering, and death also would either have not to be, or else to have no terrors for us. Only thus would life pay for itself.

But since now our state is rather something which had better not be, everything about us bears the trace of this,—just as in hell everything smells of sulphur—for everything is always imperfect and illusory, everything agreeable is displaced by something disagreeable, every enjoyment is only a half one, every pleasure introduces its own disturbance, every relief new difficulties, every aid of our daily and hourly need leaves us each moment in the lurch and denies its service, the step upon which we place our foot so often gives way under us, nay, misfortunes great and small are the element of our life; and, in a word, we are like Phineus, whose food was all tainted and made uneatable by the harpies.[2] Two remedies for this are tried: first, prudence, foresight, cunning; it does not fully instruct us, is insufficient, and leads to defeat. Secondly, the stoical equanimity which seeks to arm us against all misfortunes by preparedness for everything and contempt of all: practically it becomes cynical renunciation, which prefers once for all to reject all means of relief and all alleviations—it reduces us to the position of dogs, like Diogenes in his tub. The truth is, we ought to be wretched, and we are so. The chief source of the serious evils which affect men is man himself: *homo homini lupus*. Whoever keeps this last fact clearly in view beholds the world as a hell, which surpasses that of Dante in this respect, that one man must be the devil of another. For this, one is certainly more fitted than another; an arch-fiend, indeed, more fitted than all others, appearing in the form of a conqueror, who places several hundred thousand men opposite each other, and says to them: "To suffer and die is your destiny; now shoot each other with guns and cannons," and they do so.

In general, however, the conduct of men towards each other is characterised as a rule by injustice, extreme unfairness, hardness, nay, cruelty: an opposite course of conduct appears only as an exception. Upon this depends the necessity of the State and legislation, and upon none of your false pretences. But in all cases which do not lie within the reach of the law, that regardlessness of his like, peculiar to man, shows itself at once; a regardlessness which springs from his boundless

[2] All that we lay hold of resists us because it has its own will, which must be overcome.

egoism, and sometimes also from wickedness. How man deals with man is shown, for example, by negro slavery, the final end of which is sugar and coffee. But we do not need to go so far: at the age of five years to enter a cotton-spinning or other factory, and from that time forth to sit there daily, first ten, then twelve, and ultimately fourteen hours, performing the same mechanical labour, is to purchase dearly the satisfaction of drawing breath. But this is the fate of millions, and that of millions more is analogous to it.

We others, however, can be made perfectly miserable by trifling misfortunes; perfectly happy, not by the world. Whatever one may say, the happiest moment of the happy man is the moment of his falling asleep, and the unhappiest moment of the unhappy that of his awaking. An indirect but certain proof of the fact that men feel themselves unhappy, and consequently are so, is also abundantly afforded by the fearful envy which dwells in us all, and which in all relations of life, on the occasion of any superiority, of whatever kind it may be, is excited, and cannot contain its poison. Because they feel themselves unhappy, men cannot endure the sight of one whom they imagine happy; he who for the moment feels himself happy would like to make all around him happy also, and says:

Que tout le monde ici soit heureux de ma joie.

If life were in itself a blessing to be prized, and decidedly to be preferred to non-existence, the exit from it would not need to be guarded by such fearful sentinels as death and its terrors. But who would continue in life as it is if death were less terrible? And again, who could even endure the thought of death if life were a pleasure! But thus the former has still always this good, that it is the end of life, and we console ourselves with regard to the suffering of life with death, and with regard to death with the suffering of life. The truth is, that the two inseparably belong to each other, for together they constitute a deviation from the right path, to return to which is as difficult as it is desirable.

If the world were not something which, expressed *practically*, ought not to be, it would also not be *theoretically* a problem; but its existence would either require no explanation, inasmuch as it would be so entirely self-evident that wonder concerning it or a question about it could arise in no mind, or its end would present itself unmistakably. Instead of this, however, it is indeed an insoluble problem; for even the most perfect philosophy will yet always contain an unexplained element, like an insoluble deposit or the remainder which the irrational relation of two quantities always leaves over. Therefore if one ventures to raise the question why there is not rather nothing than this world, the world cannot be justified from itself, no ground, no final cause of its existence can be found in itself, it cannot be shown that it exists for its own sake, *i.e.*, for its own advantage. In accordance with my teaching, this can certainly be explained from the fact that the principle of its existence is expressly one which is without ground, a blind will to live, which as thing in itself cannot be made subject to the principle of sufficient reason, which is merely the form of the phenomenon, and through which alone every why is justified. But this also agrees with the nature of the world, for only a blind will, no seeing will, could place itself in the position in which we behold ourselves. A seeing will would rather have soon made the calculation that the business did not cover the cost, for such a mighty effort and struggle with the straining of all the powers, under constant care, anxiety, and want, and with the inevitable destruction of every individual life, finds no compensation in the ephemeral existence itself, which is so obtained, and which passes into nothing in our hands. Hence, then, the explanation of the world from the Anaxagorean νους, *i.e.*, from a will accompanied by *knowledge,* necessarily demands optimism to excuse it, which accordingly is set up and maintained in spite of the loudly crying evidence of a whole world full of misery. Life is there given out to be a gift, while it is evident that every one would have declined such a gift if he could have seen it and tested it beforehand; just as Lessing admired the understanding of his son, who, because he had absolutely declined to enter life, had to be forcibly brought into it with the forceps, but was scarcely there when he hurried away from it again. On the other hand, it is then well said that life should be, from one end to the other, only a lesson; to which, however, any one might reply: "For this very reason I wish I had been left in the peace of the all-sufficient nothing, where I would have had no need of lessons or of anything else." If indeed it should now be added that he must one day give an account of every hour of his life, he would be more justified in himself demanding an account of why he had been transferred from that rest into such a questionable, dark, anxious, and painful situation. To this, then, we are led by false views. For human existence, far from bearing the character of a *gift*, has entirely the character of a *debt* that has been contracted. The calling in of this debt appears in the form of the pressing wants, tormenting desires, and endless misery established through this existence. As a rule, the whole lifetime is devoted to the paying off of this debt; but this only meets the interest. The payment of the capital takes place through death. And when was this debt contracted? At the begetting.

Accordingly, if we regard man as a being whose existence is a punishment and an expiation, we then view him in a right light. The myth of the fall (although probably, like the whole of Judaism, borrowed from the Zend-Avesta: Bundahish, 15), is the only point in the Old Testament to which I can ascribe metaphysical, although only allegorical, truth; indeed it is this alone that reconciles me to the Old Testament. Our existence resembles nothing so much as the consequence of a false step and a guilty desire. New Testament Christianity, the ethical spirit of which is that of Brahmanism and Buddhism, and is therefore very foreign to the otherwise optimistic spirit of the Old Testament, has also, very wisely, linked itself on precisely to that myth: indeed, without this it would have found no point of connection with Judaism at all. If any one desires to measure the degree of guilt with which our existence is tainted, then let him look at the suffering that is connected with it. Every great pain, whether bodily or mental, declares what we deserve: for it could not come to us if we did not deserve it. That Christianity also regards our existence in this light is shown by a passage in Luther's Commentary on Galatians, chap. 3, which I only have beside me in Latin: "*Sumus autem nos omnes corporibus et rebus subjecti Diabolo, et hospites sumus in mundo, cujus ipse princeps et Deus est. Ideo panis, quem edimus, potus, quem bibimus, vestes, quibus utimur, imo aër et totum quo vivimus in carne, sub ipsius imperio est.*"

An outcry has been made about the melancholy and discon-
solate nature of my philosophy; yet it lies merely in the fact
that instead of inventing a future hell as the equivalent of sin,
I show that where guilt lies in the world there is also already
something akin to hell; but whoever is inclined to deny this
can easily experience it.

And to this world, to this scene of tormented and agonised
beings, who only continue to exist by devouring each other,
in which, therefore, every ravenous beast is the living grave
of thousands of others, and its self-maintenance is a chain of
painful deaths; and in which the capacity for feeling pain increases with knowledge, and therefore reaches its highest degree in man, a degree which is the higher the more intelligent
the man is; to this world it has been sought to apply the system
of optimism, and demonstrate to us that it is the best of all
possible worlds. The absurdity is glaring. But an optimist bids
me open my eyes and look at the world, how beautiful it is in
the sunshine, with its mountains and valleys, streams, plants,
animals, &c. &c. Is the world, then, a rareeshow? These things
are certainly beautiful to *look at*, but to *be* them is something
quite different. Then comes a teleologist, and praises to me
the wise arrangement by virtue of which it is taken care that
the planets do not run their heads together, that land and sea
do not get mixed into a pulp, but are held so beautifully apart,
also that everything is neither rigid with continual frost nor
roasted with heat; in the same way, that in consequence of
the obliquity of the ecliptic there is no eternal spring, in which
nothing could attain to ripeness, &c. &c. But this and all like
it are mere *conditiones sine quibus non*. If in general there is
to be a world at all, if its planets are to exist at least as long
as the light of a distant fixed star requires to reach them, and
are not, like Lessing's son, to depart again immediately after
birth, then certainly it must not be so clumsily constructed
that its very framework threatens to fall to pieces. But if one
goes on to the results of this applauded work, considers the
players who act upon the stage which is so durably constructed, and now sees how with sensibility pain appears, and
increases in proportion as the sensibility develops to intelligence, and then how, keeping pace with this, desire and suffering come out ever more strongly, and increase till at last

human life affords no other material than this for tragedies
and comedies, then whoever is honest will scarcely be disposed
to set up hallelujahs. David Hume, in his "Natural History of
Religion," §§ 6, 7, 8, and 13, has also exposed, mercilessly but
with convincing truth, the real though concealed source of
these last. He also explains clearly in the tenth and eleventh
books of his "Dialogues on Natural Religion," with very perti-
nent arguments, which are yet of quite a different kind from
mine, the miserable nature of this world and the untenableness
of all optimism; in doing which he attacks this in its origin.
Both works of Hume's are as well worth reading as they are
unknown at the present day in Germany, where, on the other
hand, incredible pleasure is found, patriotically, in the most
disgusting nonsense of home-bred boastful mediocrities, who
are proclaimed great men. Hamann, however, translated these
dialogues; Kant went through the translation, and late in life
wished to induce Hamann's son to publish them because the
translation of Platner did not satisfy him (see Kant's biography
by F. W. Schubert, pp. 81 and 165). From every page of
David Hume there is more to be learned than from the collected philosophical works of Hegel, Herbart, and Schleier-
macher together.

The founder of systematic optimism, again, is Leibnitz
whose philosophical merit I have no intention of denying although I have never succeeded in thinking myself into the
monadology, pre-established harmony, and *identitas indis-*
cernibilium. His *"Nouveaux essays sur l'entendement"* are,
however, merely an excerpt, with a full yet weak criticism,
with a view to correction, of Locke's work which is justly of
world-wide reputation. He here opposes Locke with just as
little success as he opposes Newton in the *"Tentamen de*
motuum cœlestium causis," directed against the system of
gravitation. The "Critique of Pure Reason" is specially directed
against this Leibnitz-Wolfian philosophy, and has a polemical,
nay, a destructive relation to it, just as it is related to Locke
and Hume as a continuation and further construction. That
at the present day the professors of philosophy are on all sides
engaged in setting Leibnitz, with his juggling, upon his legs
again, nay, in glorifying him, and, on the other hand, in de-
preciating and setting aside Kant as much as possible, has its

sufficient reason in the *primum vivere;* the "Critique of Pure Reason" does not admit of one giving out Judaistic mythology as philosophy, nor of one speaking, without ceremony, of the "soul" as a given reality, a well-known and well-accredited person, without giving account of how one arrived at this conception, and what justification one has for using it scientifically. But *primum vivere, deinde philosophari!* Down with Kant, *vivat* our Leibnitz! To return, then, to Leibnitz, I cannot ascribe to the Théodicée, as a methodical and broad unfolding of optimism, any other merit than this, that it gave occasion later for the immortal *"Candide"* of the great Voltaire; whereby certainly Leibnitz's often-repeated and lame excuse for the evil of the world, that the bad sometimes brings about the good, received a confirmation which was unexpected by him. Even by the name of his hero Voltaire indicates that it only requires sincerity to recognise the opposite of optimism. Really upon this scene of sin, suffering, and death optimism makes such an extraordinary figure that one would be forced to regard it as irony if one had not a sufficient explanation of its origin in the secret source of it (insincere flattery, with insulting confidence in its success), which, as was mentioned above, is so delightfully disclosed by Hume.

But indeed to the palpably sophistical proofs of Leibnitz that this is the best of all possible worlds, we may seriously and honestly oppose the proof that it is the worst of all possible worlds. For possible means, not what one may construct in imagination, but what can actually exist and continue. Now this world is so arranged as to be able to maintain itself with great difficulty; but if it were a little worse, it could no longer maintain itself. Consequently a worse world, since it could not continue to exist, is absolutely impossible: thus this world itself is the worst of all possible worlds. For not only if the planets were to run their heads together, but even if any one of the actually appearing perturbations of their course, instead of being gradually balanced by others, continued to increase, the world would soon reach its end. Astronomers know upon what accidental circumstances—principally the irrational relation to each other of the periods of revolution—this depends, and have carefully calculated that it will always go on well; consequently the world also can continue and go on. We will hope that, although Newton was of an opposite opinion, they have not miscalculated, and consequently that the mechanical perpetual motion realised in such a planetary system will not also, like the rest, ultimately come to a standstill. Again, under the firm crust of the planet dwell the powerful forces of nature which, as soon as some accident affords them free play, must necessarily destroy that crust, with everything living upon it, as has already taken place at least three times upon our planet, and will probably take place oftener still. The earthquake of Lisbon, the earthquake of Haiti, the destruction of Pompeii, are only small, playful hints of what is possible. A small alteration of the atmosphere, which cannot even be chemically proved, causes cholera, yellow fever, black death, &c., which carry off millions of men; a somewhat greater alteration would extinguish all life. A very moderate increase of heat would dry up all the rivers and springs. The brutes have received just barely so much in the way of organs and powers as enables them to procure with the greatest exertion sustenance for their own lives and food for their offspring; therefore if a brute loses a limb, or even the full use of one, it must generally perish. Even of the human race, powerful as are the weapons it possesses in understanding and reason, nine-tenths live in constant conflict with want, always balancing themselves with difficulty and effort upon the brink of destruction. Thus throughout, as for the continuance of the whole, so also for that of each individual being the conditions are barely and scantily given, but nothing over. The individual life is a ceaseless battle for existence itself; while at every step destruction threatens it. Just because this threat is so often fulfilled provision had to be made, by means of the enormous excess of the germs, that the destruction of the individuals should not involve that of the species, for which alone nature really cares. The world is therefore as bad as it possibly can be if it is to continue to be at all. *Q. E. D.* The fossils of the entirely different kinds of animal species which formerly inhabited the planet afford us, as a proof of our calculation, the records of worlds the continuance of which was no longer possible, and which consequently were somewhat worse than the worst of possible worlds.

Optimism is at bottom the unmerited self-praise of the real

originator of the world, the will to live, which views itself complacently in its works; and accordingly it is not only a false, but also a pernicious doctrine. For it presents life to us as a desirable condition, and the happiness of man as the end of it. Starting from this, every one then believes that he has the most just claim to happiness and pleasure; and if, as is wont to happen, these do not fall to his lot, then he believes that he is wronged, nay, that he loses the end of his existence; while it is far more correct to regard work, privation, misery, and suffering, crowned by death, as the end of our life (as Brahmanism and Buddhism, and also genuine Christianity do); for it is these which lead to the denial of the will to live. In the New Testament the world is represented as a valley of tears, life as a process of purifying or refining, and the symbol of Christianity is an instrument of torture. Therefore, when Leibnitz, Shaftesbury, Bolingbroke, and Pope brought forward optimism, the general offence which it gave depended principally upon the fact that optimism is irreconcilable with Christianity; as Voltaire states and explains in the preface to his excellent poem, *"Le désastre de Lisbonne,"* which is also expressly directed against optimism. This great man, whom I so gladly praise, in opposition to the abuse of venal German ink-slingers, is placed decidedly higher than Rousseau by the insight to which he attained in three respects, and which prove the greater depth of his thinking: (1) the recognition of the preponderating magnitude of the evil and misery of existence with which he is deeply penetrated; (2) that of the strict necessity of the acts of will; (3) that of the truth of Locke's principle, that what thinks may also be material: while Rousseau opposes all this with declamations in his *"Profession de foi du vicaire Savoyard,"* a superficial Protestant pastor's philosophy; as he also in the same spirit attacks the beautiful poem of Voltaire which has just been referred to with ill-founded, shallow, and logically false reasoning, in the interests of optimism, in his long letter to Voltaire of 18th August 1756, which is devoted simply to this purpose. Indeed, the fundamental characteristic of Rousseau's whole philosophy is this, that in the place of the Christian doctrine of original sin, and the original depravity of the human race, he puts an original goodness and unlimited perfectibility of it, which has only been led astray by civilisation and its consequences, and then founds upon this his optimism and humanism.

As in *"Candide"* Voltaire wages war in his facetious manner against optimism, Byron has also done so in his serious and tragic style, in his immortal masterpiece, "Cain," on account of which he also has been honoured with the invectives of the obscurantist, Friedrich Schlegel. If now, in conclusion, to confirm my view, I were to give what has been said by great men of all ages in this anti-optimistic spirit, there would be no end to the quotations, for almost every one of them has expressed in strong language his knowledge of the misery of this world. Thus, not to confirm, but merely to embellish this chapter, a few quotations of this kind may be given at the end of it.

First of all, let me mention here that the Greeks, far as they were from the Christian and lofty Asiatic conception of the world, and although they decidedly stood at the point of view of the assertion of the will, were yet deeply affected by the wretchedness of existence. This is shown even by the invention of tragedy, which belongs to them. Another proof of it is afforded us by the custom of the Thracians, which is first mentioned by Herodotus, though often referred to afterwards—the custom of welcoming the new-born child with lamentations, and recounting all the evils which now lie before it; and, on the other hand, burying the dead with mirth and jesting, because they are no longer exposed to so many and great sufferings.

It is not to be attributed to historical relationship, but to the moral identity of the matter, that the Mexicans welcomed the new-born child with the words, "My child, thou art born to endure; therefore endure, suffer, and keep silence." And, following the same feeling, Swift (as Walter Scott relates in his Life of Swift) early adopted the custom of keeping his birthday not as a time of joy but of sadness, and of reading on that day the passage of the Bible in which Job laments and curses the day on which it was said in the house of his father a man-child is born.

Well known and too long for quotation is the passage in the "Apology of Socrates," in which Plato makes this wisest of mortals say that death, even if it deprives us of consciousness for ever, would be a wonderful gain, for a deep, dreamless sleep every day is to be preferred even to the happiest life.

Even Pliny says: *"Quapropter hoc primum quisque in remediis animi sui habeat, ex omnibus bonis, quæ homini natura tribuit, nullum melius esse tempestiva morte"* (*Hist. Nat.* 28, 2).

Shakspeare puts the words in the mouth of the old king Henry IV.:—

> O heaven! that one might read the book of fate,
> And see the revolution of the times,
> .   .   .   .   .   how chances mock,
> And changes fill the cup of alteration
> With divers liquors! O, if this were seen,
> The happiest youth,—viewing his progress through,
> What perils past, what crosses to ensue,—
> Would shut the book, and sit him down and die.

Finally, Byron:—

> Count o'er the joys thine hours have seen,
>   Count o'er thy days from anguish free,
> And know, whatever thou hast been,
>   'Tis something better not to be.

Baltazar Gracian also brings the misery of our existence before our eyes in the darkest colours in the "Criticon," Parte i., Crisi 5, just at the beginning, and Crisi 7 at the end, where he explicitly represents life as a tragic farce.

Yet no one has so thoroughly and exhaustively handled this subject as, in our own day, Leopardi. He is entirely filled and penetrated by it: his theme is everywhere the mockery and wretchedness of this existence; he presents it upon every page of his works, yet in such a multiplicity of forms and applications, with such wealth of imagery that he never wearies us, but, on the contrary, is throughout entertaining and exciting.

XII

ON THE SUFFERINGS OF THE WORLD

(from PARERGA*)*

Unless *suffering* is the direct and immediate object of life, our existence must entirely fail of its aim. It is absurd to look upon the enormous amount of pain that abounds everywhere in the world, and originates in needs and necessities inseparable from life itself, as serving no purpose at all and the result of mere chance. Each separate misfortune, as it comes, seems, no doubt, to be something exceptional; but misfortune in general is the rule.

I know of no greater absurdity than that propounded by most systems of philosophy in declaring evil to be negative in its character. Evil is just what is positive; it makes its own existence felt. Leibnitz is particularly concerned to defend this absurdity; and he seeks to strengthen his position by using a palpable and paltry sophism. It is the good which is negative; in other words, happiness and satisfaction always imply some desire fulfilled, some state of pain brought to an end.

This explains the fact that we generally find pleasure to be not nearly so pleasant as we expected, and pain very much more painful.

The pleasure in this world, it has been said, outweighs the pain; or, at any rate, there is an even balance between the two. If the reader wishes to see shortly whether this statement is true, let him compare the respective feelings of two animals, one of which is engaged in eating the other.

The best consolation in misfortune or affliction of any kind will be the thought of other people who are in a still worse plight than yourself; and this is a form of consolation open to every one. But what an awful fate this means for mankind as a whole!

We are like lambs in a field, disporting themselves under the eye of the butcher, who chooses out first one and then another for his prey. So it is that in our good days we are all unconscious of the evil Fate may have presently in store for us—sickness, poverty, mutilation, loss of sight or reason.

No little part of the torment of existence lies in this, that Time is continually pressing upon us, never letting us take breath, but always coming after us, like a taskmaster with a whip. If at any moment Time stays his hand, it is only when we are delivered over to the misery of boredom.

But misfortune has its uses; for, as our bodily frame would burst asunder if the pressure of the atmosphere was removed, so, if the lives of men were relieved of all need, hardship and adversity; if everything they took in hand were successful, they would be so swollen with arrogance that, though they might not burst, they would present the spectacle of un-bridled folly—nay, they would go mad. And I may say, fur-ther, that a certain amount of care or pain or trouble is neces-sary for every man at all times. A ship without ballast is un-stable and will not go straight.

Certain it is that *work, worry, labor* and *trouble*, form the lot of almost all men their whole life long. But if all wishes were fulfilled as soon as they arose, how would men occupy their lives? what would they do with their time? If the world were a paradise of luxury and ease, a land flowing with milk and honey, where every Jack obtained his Jill at once and without any difficulty, men would either die of boredom or hang themselves; or there would be wars, massacres, and mur-ders; so that in the end mankind would inflict more suffering on itself than it has now to accept at the hands of Nature.

In early youth, as we contemplate our coming life, we are like children in a theatre before the curtain is raised, sitting there in high spirits and eagerly waiting for the play to begin. It is a blessing that we do not know what is really going to happen. Could we foresee it, there are times when children might seem like innocent prisoners, condemned, not to death, but to life, and as yet all unconscious of what their sentence means. Nevertheless, every man desires to reach old age; in other words, a state of life of which it may be said: "It is bad to-day, and it will be worse to-morrow; and so on till the worst of all."

If you try to imagine, as nearly as you can, what an amount of misery, pain and suffering of every kind the sun shines upon in its course, you will admit that it would be much better if, on the earth as little as on the moon, the sun were able to call forth the phenomena of life; and if, here as there, the surface were still in a crystalline state.

Again, you may look upon life as an unprofitable episode, disturbing the blessed calm of non-existence. And, in any case, even though things have gone with you tolerably well, the longer you live the more clearly you will feel that, on the whole, life is *a disappointment, nay, a cheat.*

If two men who were friends in their youth meet again when they are old, after being separated for a life-time, the chief feeling they will have at the sight of each other will be one of complete disappointment at life as a whole; because their thoughts will be carried back to that earlier time when life seemed so fair as it lay spread out before them in the rosy light of dawn, promised so much—and then performed so little. This feeling will so completely predominate over every other that they will not even consider it necessary to give it words; but on either side it will be silently assumed, and form the ground-work of all they have to talk about.

He who lives to see two or three generations is like a man who sits some time in the conjurer's booth at a fair, and witnesses the performance twice or thrice in succession. The tricks were meant to be seen only once; and when they are no longer a novelty and cease to deceive, their effect is gone.

While no man is much to be envied for his lot, there are countless numbers whose fate is to be deplored.

Life is a task to be done. It is a fine thing to say *defunctus est;* it means that the man has done his task.

If children were brought into the world by an act of pure reason alone, would the human race continue to exist? Would not a man rather have so much sympathy with the coming generation as to spare it the burden of existence? or at any rate not take it upon himself to impose that burden upon it in cold blood.

I shall be told, I suppose, that my philosophy is comfortless

—because I speak the truth; and people prefer to be assured
that everything the Lord has made is good. Go to the priests,
then, and leave philosophers in peace! At any rate, do not
ask us to accommodate our doctrines to the lessons you have
been taught. That is what those rascals of sham philosophers
will do for you. Ask them for any doctrine you please, and
you will get it. Your University professors are bound to preach
optimism; and it is an easy and agreeable task to upset their
theories.

I have reminded the reader that every state of welfare, every feeling of satisfaction, is negative in its character; that is
to say, it consists in freedom from pain, which is the positive
element of existence. It follows, therefore, that the happiness
of any given life is to be measured, not by its joys and pleasures, but by the extent to which it has been free from suffering—from positive evil. If this is the true standpoint, the lower
animals appear to enjoy a happier destiny than man. Let us
examine the matter a little more closely.

However varied the forms that human happiness and misery may take, leading a man to seek the one and shun the
other, the material basis of it all is bodily pleasure or bodily
pain. This basis is very restricted: it is simply health, food,
protection from wet and cold, the satisfaction of the sexual
instinct; or else the absence of these things. Consequently, as
far as real physical pleasure is concerned, the man is not better off than the brute, except in so far as the higher possibilities
of his nervous system make him more sensitive to every kind
of pleasure, but also, it must be remembered, to every kind
of pain. But then compared with the brute, how much stronger
are the passions aroused in him! what an immeasurable difference there is in the depth and vehemence of his emotions!
—and yet, in the one case, as in the other, all to produce the
same result in the end: namely, health, food, clothing, and
so on.

The chief source of all this passion is that thought for what
is absent and future, which, with man, exercises such a powerful influence upon all he does. It is this that is the real origin
of his cares, his hopes, his fears—emotions which affect him
much more deeply than could ever be the case with those
present joys and sufferings to which the brute is confined. In

his powers of reflection, memory and foresight, man possesses, as it were, a machine for condensing and storing up his pleasures and his sorrows. But the brute has nothing of the kind; whenever it is in pain, it is as though it were suffering for the first time, even though the same thing should have previously happened to it times out of number. It has no power of summing up its feelings. Hence its careless and placid temper: how much it is to be envied! But in man reflection comes in, with all the emotions to which it gives rise; and taking up the same elements of pleasure and pain which are common to him and the brute, it develops his susceptibility to happiness and misery to such a degree that, at one moment the man is brought in an instant to a state of delight that may even prove fatal, at another to the depths of despair and suicide.

If we carry our analysis a step farther, we shall find that, in order to increase his pleasures, man has intentionally added to the number and pressure of his needs, which in their orginal state were not much more difficult to satisfy than those of the brute. Hence luxury in all its forms; delicate food, the use of tobacco and opium, spirituous liquors, fine clothes, and the thousand and one things that he considers necessary to his existence.

And above and beyond all this, there is a separate and peculiar source of pleasure, and consequently of pain, which man has established for himself, also as the result of using his powers of reflection; and this occupies him out of all proportion to its value, nay, almost more than all his other interests put together—I mean ambition and the feeling of honor and shame; in plain words, what he thinks about the opinion other people have of him. Taking a thousand forms, often very strange ones, this becomes the goal of almost all the efforts he makes that are not rooted in physical pleasure or pain. It is true that besides the sources of pleasure which he has in common with the brute, man has the pleasures of the mind as well. These admit of many gradations, from the most innocent trifling or the merest talk up to the highest intellectual achievements; but there is the accompanying boredom to be set against them on the side of suffering. Boredom is a form of suffering unknown to brutes, at any rate in their natural state; it is only the very cleverest of them who show faint traces of it when they are domesticated; whereas in the case of man it has become a downright scourge. The crowd of miserable wretches whose one aim in life is to fill their purses but never to put anything into their heads, offers a singular instance of this torment of boredom. Their wealth becomes a punishment by delivering them up to misery of having nothing to do; for, to escape it, they will rush about in all directions, traveling here, there and everywhere. No sooner do they arrive in a place than they are anxious to know what amusements it affords; just as though they were beggars asking where they could receive a dole! Of a truth, need and boredom are the two poles of human life. Finally, I may mention that as regards the sexual relation, a man is committed to a peculiar arrangement which drives him obstinately to choose one person. This feeling grows, now and then, into a more or less passionate love,[1] which is the source of little pleasure and much suffering.

It is, however, a wonderful thing that the mere addition of thought should serve to raise such a vast and lofty structure of human happiness and misery; resting, too, on the same narrow basis of joy and sorrow as man holds in common with the brute, and exposing him to such violent emotions, to so many storms of passion, so much convulsion of feeling, that what he has suffered stands written and may be read in the lines on his face. And yet, when all is told, he has been struggling ultimately for the very same things as the brute has attained, and with an incomparably smaller expenditure of passion and pain.

But all this contributes to increase the measures of suffering in human life out of all proportion to its pleasures; and the pains of life are made much worse for man by the fact that death is something very real to him. The brute flies from death instinctively without really knowing what it is, and therefore without ever contemplating it in the way natural to a man, who has this prospect always before his eyes. So that even if only a few brutes die a natural death, and most of them live only just long enough to transmit their species, and then, if not earlier, become the prey of some other animal,—whilst

[1] I have treated this subject at length in "The Metaphysics of the Love of the Sexes," p. 69.

man, on the other hand, manages to make so-called natural death the rule, to which, however, there are a good many exceptions,—the advantage is on the side of the brute, for the reason stated above. But the fact is that man attains the natural term of years just as seldom as the brute; because the unnatural way in which he lives, and the strain of work and emotion, lead to a degeneration of the race; and so his goal is not often reached.

The brute is much more content with mere existence than man; the plant is wholly so; and man finds satisfaction in it just in proportion as he is dull and obtuse. Accordingly, the life of the brute carries less of sorrow with it, but also less of joy, when compared with the life of man; and while this may be traced, on the one side, to freedom from the torment of *care* and *anxiety*, it is also due to the fact that *hope*, in any real sense, is unknown to the brute. It is thus deprived of any share in that which gives us the most and best of our joys and pleasures, the mental anticipation of a happy future, and the inspiriting play of phantasy, both of which we owe to our power of imagination. If the brute is free from care, it is also, in this sense, without hope; in either case, because its consciousness is limited to the present moment, to what it can actually see before it. The brute is an embodiment of present impulses, and hence what elements of fear and hope exist in its nature—and they do not go very far—arise only in relation to objects that lie before it and within reach of those impulses: whereas a man's range of vision embraces the whole of his life, and extends far into the past and future.

Following upon this, there is one respect in which brutes show real wisdom when compared with us—I mean, their quiet, placid enjoyment of the present moment. The tranquillity of mind which this seems to give them often puts us to shame for the many times we allow our thoughts and our cares to make us restless and discontented. And, in fact, those pleasures of hope and anticipation which I have been mentioning are not to be had for nothing. The delight which a man has in hoping for and looking forward to some special satisfaction is a part of the real pleasure attaching to it enjoyed in advance. This is afterwards deducted; for the more we look forward to anything, the less satisfaction we find in it when it comes. But the brute's enjoyment is not anticipated, and therefore, suffers no deduction; so that the actual pleasure of the moment comes to it whole and unimpaired. In the same way, too, evil presses upon the brute only with its own intrinsic weight; whereas with us the fear of its coming often makes its burden ten times more grievous.

It is just this characteristic way in which the brute gives itself up entirely to the present moment that contributes so much to the delight we take in our domestic pets. They are the present moment personified, and in some respects they make us feel the value of every hour that is free from trouble and annoyance, which we, with our thoughts and preoccupations, mostly disregard. But man, that selfish and heartless creature, misuses this quality of the brute to be more content than we are with mere existence, and often works it to such an extent that he allows the brute absolutely nothing more than mere, bare life. The bird which was made so that it might rove over half of the world, he shuts up into the space of a cubic foot, there to die a slow death in longing and crying for freedom; for in a cage it does not sing for the pleasure of it. And when I see how man misuses the dog, his best friend; how he ties up this intelligent animal with a chain, I feel the deepest sympathy with the brute and burning indignation against its master.

We shall see later that by taking a very high standpoint it is possible to justify the sufferings of mankind. But this justification cannot apply to animals, whose sufferings, while in a great measure brought about by men, are often considerable even apart from their agency. And so we are forced to ask, Why and for what purpose does all this torment and agony exist? There is nothing here to give the will pause; it is not free to deny itself and so obtain redemption. There is only one consideration that may serve to explain the sufferings of animals. It is this: that the will to live, which underlies the whole world of phenomena, must, in their case satisfy its cravings by feeding upon itself. This it does by forming a gradation of phenomena, every one of which exists at the expense of another. I have shown, however, that the capacity for suffering is less in animals than in man. Any further explanation that may be given of their fate will be in the nature of hypothesis, if not actually mythical in its character; and I may leave the reader to speculate upon the matter for himself.

Brahma is said to have produced the world by a kind of fall or mistake; and in order to atone for his folly, he is bound to remain in it himself until he works out his redemption. As an account of the origin of things, that is admirable! According to the doctrines of *Buddhism,* the world came into being as the result of some inexplicable disturbance in the heavenly calm of Nirvana, that blessed state obtained by expiation, which had endured so long a time—the change taking place by a kind of fatality. This explanation must be understood as having at bottom some moral bearing; although it is illustrated by an exactly parallel theory in the domain of physical science, which places the origin of the sun in a primitive streak of mist, formed one knows not how. Subsequently, by a series of moral errors, the world became gradually worse and worse—true of the physical orders as well—until it assumed the dismal aspect it wears to-day. Excellent! The *Greeks* looked upon the world and the gods as the work of an inscrutable necessity. A passable explanation: we may be content with it until we can get a better. Again, *Ormuzd* and *Ahriman* are rival powers, continually at war. That is not bad. But that a God like Jehovah should have created this world of misery and woe, out of pure caprice, and because he enjoyed doing it, and should then have clapped his hands in praise of his own work, and declared everything to be very good—that will not do at all! In its explanation of the origin of the world, Judaism is inferior to any other form of religious doctrine professed by a civilized nation; and it is quite in keeping with this that it is the only one which presents no trace whatever of any belief in the immortality of the soul.

Even though Leibnitz' contention, that this is the best of all possible worlds, were correct, that would not justify God in having created it. For he is the Creator not of the world only, but of possibility itself; and, therefore, he ought to have so ordered possibility as that it would admit of something better.

There are two things which make it impossible to believe that this world is the successful work of an all-wise, all-good, and, at the same time, all-powerful Being; firstly, the misery which abounds in it everywhere; and secondly, the ob-

vious imperfection of its highest product, man, who is a burlesque of what he should be. These things cannot be reconciled with any such belief. On the contrary, they are just the
facts which support what I have been saying; they are our
authority for viewing the world as the outcome of our own
misdeeds, and therefore, as something that had better not have
been. Whilst, under the former hypothesis, they amount to a
bitter accusation against the Creator, and supply material for
sarcasm; under the latter they form an indictment against our
own nature, our own will, and teach us a lesson of humility.
They lead us to see that, like the children of a libertine, we
come into the world with the burden of sin upon us; and that
it is only through having continually to atone for this sin that
our existence is so miserable, and that its end is death.

There is nothing more certain than the general truth that it
is the grievous *sin of the world* which has produced the
grievous *suffering of the world*. I am not referring here to the
physical connection between these two things lying in the
realm of experience; my meaning is metaphysical. Accordingly, the sole thing that reconciles me to the Old Testament is
the story of the Fall. In my eyes, it is the only metaphysical
truth in that book, even though it appears in the form of an
allegory. There seems to me no better explanation of our existence than that it is the result of some false step, some sin of
which we are paying the penalty. I cannot refrain from recom-
mending the thoughtful reader a popular, but at the same
time, profound treatise on this subject by Claudius which exhibits the essentially pessimistic spirit of Christianity. It is entitled: *Cursed is the ground for thy sake.*

Between the ethics of the Greeks and the ethics of the Hin-
doos, there is a glaring contrast. In the one case (with the
exception, it must be confessed, of Plato), the object of ethics
is to enable a man to lead a happy life; in the other, it is to
free and redeem him from life altogether—as is directly stated
in the very first words of the *Sankhya Karika.*

Allied with this is the contrast between the Greek and the
Christian idea of death. It is strikingly presented in a visible
form on a fine antique sarcophagus in the gallery of Florence,
which exhibits, in relief, the whole series of ceremonies attending a wedding in ancient times, from the formal offer to

the evening when Hymen's torch lights the happy couple
home. Compare with that the Christian coffin, draped in
mournful black and surmounted with a crucifix! How much
significance there is in these two ways of finding comfort in
death. They are opposed to each other, but each is right. The
one points to the *affirmation* of the will to live, which remains
sure of life for all time, however rapidly its forms may change.
The other, in the symbol of suffering and death, points to the
denial of the will to live, to redemption from this world, the
domain of death and devil. And in the question between the
affirmation and the denial of the will to live, Christianity is in
the last resort right.

The contrast which the New Testament presents when compared with the Old, according to the ecclesiastical view of the
matter, is just that existing between my ethical system and the
moral philosophy of Europe. The Old Testament represents
man as under the dominion of Law, in which, however, there
is no redemption. The New Testament declares Law to have
failed, frees man from its dominion,[2] and in its stead preaches
the kingdom of grace, to be won by faith, love of neighbor
and entire sacrifice of self. This is the path of redemption from
the evil of the world. The spirit of the New Testament is undoubtedly asceticism, however your protestants and rationalists may twist it to suit their purpose. Asceticism is the denial
of the will to live; and the transition from the Old Testament
to the New, from the dominion of Law to that of Faith, from
justification by works to redemption through the Mediator,
from the domain of sin and death to eternal life in Christ,
means, when taken in its real sense, the transition from the
merely moral virtues to the denial of the will to live. My philosophy shows the metaphysical foundation of justice and the
love of mankind, and points to the goal to which these virtues
necessarily lead, if they are practised in perfection. At the same
time it is candid in confessing that a man must turn his back
upon the world, and that the denial of the will to live is the
way of redemption. It is therefore really at one with the spirit
of the New Testament, whilst all other systems are couched
in the spirit of the Old; that is to say, theoretically as well as

[2] Cf. Romans vii; Galatians ii, iii.

practically, their result is Judaism—mere despotic theism. In this sense, then, my doctrine might be called the only true Christian philosophy—however paradoxical a statement this may seem to people who take superficial views instead of penetrating to the heart of the matter.

If you want a safe compass to guide you through life, and to banish all doubt as to the right way of looking at it, you cannot do better than accustom yourself to regard this world as a penitentiary, a sort of a penal colony. Amongst the Christian Fathers, Origen, with praiseworthy courage, took this view,[3] which is further justified by certain objective theories of life. I refer, not to my own philosophy alone, but to the wisdom of all ages, as expressed in Brahmanism and Buddhism, and in the sayings of Greek philosophers like Empedocles and Pythagoras; as also by Cicero, in his remark that the wise men of old used to teach that we come into this world to pay the penalty of crime committed in another state of existence—a doctrine which formed part of the initiation into the mysteries.[4] And Vanini—whom his contemporaries burned, finding that an easier task than to confute him—puts the same thing in a very forcible way. *Man,* he says, *is so full of every kind of misery that, were it not repugnant to the Christian religion, I should venture to affirm that if evil spirits exist at all, they have passed into human form and are now atoning for their crimes.*[5] And true Christianity—using the word in its right sense—also regards our existence as the consequence of sin and error.

If you accustom yourself to this view of life you will regulate your expectations accordingly, and cease to look upon all its disagreeable incidents, great and small, its sufferings, its worries, its misery, as anything unusual or irregular; nay, you will find that everything is as it should be, in a world where each of us pays the penalty of existence in his own peculiar way. Amongst the evils of a penal colony is the society of those who form it; and if the reader is worthy of better company, he will need no words from me to remind him of what he has to put up with at present. If he has a soul above the common, or if he is a man of genius, he will occasionally feel like some

[3] Augustine, *De Civitate Dei,* L. xi. c. 23.
[4] Cf. *Fragmenta de philosophia.*
[5] *De admirandis naturæ arcanis;* dial. L. p. 35.

noble prisoner of state, condemned to work in the galleys with common criminals; and he will follow his example and try to isolate himself.

In general, however, it should be said that this view of life will enable us to contemplate the so-called imperfections of the great majority of men, their moral and intellectual deficiencies and the resulting base type of countenance, without any surprise, to say nothing of indignation; for we shall never cease to reflect where we are, and that the men about us are beings conceived and born in sin, and living to atone for it. That is what Christianity means in speaking of the sinful nature of man.

Pardon's the word to all![6] Whatever folly men commit, be their shortcomings or their vices what they may, let us exercise forbearance; remembering that when these faults appear in others, it is our follies and vices that we behold. They are the shortcomings of humanity, to which we belong; whose faults, one and all, we share; yes, even those very faults at which we now wax so indignant, merely because they have not yet appeared in ourselves. They are faults that do not lie on the surface. But they exist down there in the depths of our nature; and should anything call them forth, they will come and show themselves, just as we now see them in others. One man, it is true, may have faults that are absent in his fellow; and it is undeniable that the sum total of bad qualities is in some cases very large; for the difference of individuality between man and man passes all measure.

In fact, the conviction that the world and man is something that had better not have been, is of a kind to fill us with indulgence towards one another. Nay, from this point of view, we might well consider the proper form of address to be, not *Monsieur, Sir, mein Herr,* but *my fellow-sufferer, Socî malorum, compagnon de miseres!* This may perhaps sound strange, but it is in keeping with the facts; it puts others in a right light; and it reminds us of that which is after all the most necessary thing in life—the tolerance, patience, regard, and love of neighbor, of which everyone stands in need, and which, therefore, every man owes to his fellow.

[6] "Cymbeline," Act v. Sc. 5.

XIII

THE VANITY OF EXISTENCE

(*from* PARERGA)

This vanity finds expression in the whole way in which things exist; in the infinite nature of Time and Space, as opposed to the finite nature of the individual in both; in the ever-passing present moment as the only mode of actual existence; in the interdependence and relativity of all things; in continual Becoming without ever Being; in constant wishing and never being satisfied; in the long battle which forms the history of life, where every effort is checked by difficulties, and stopped until they are overcome. Time is that in which all things pass away; it is merely the form under which the will to live—the thing-in-itself and therefore imperishable—has revealed to it that its efforts are in vain; it is that agent by which at every moment all things in our hands become as nothing, and lose any real value they possess.

That which *has been* exists no more; it exists as little as that which has *never* been. But of everything that exists you must say, in the next moment, that it has been. Hence something of great importance now past is inferior to something of little importance now present, in that the latter is a *reality*, and related to the former as something to nothing.

A man finds himself, to his great astonishment, suddenly existing, after thousands and thousands of years of non-existence: he lives for a little while; and then, again, comes an equally long period when he must exist no more. The heart rebels against this, and feels that it cannot be true. The crudest intellect cannot speculate on such a subject without having a presentiment that Time is something ideal in its nature. This ideality of Time and Space is the key to every true system of metaphysics; because it provides for quite another order of things than is to be met with in the domain of nature. This is why Kant is so great.

Of every event in our life we can say only for one moment that it *is;* for ever after, that it *was.* Every evening we are poorer by a day. It might, perhaps, make us mad to see how rapidly our short span of time ebbs away; if it were not that in the furthest depths of our being we are secretly conscious of our share in the exhaustible spring of eternity, so that we can always hope to find life in it again.

Consideration of the kind, touched on above, might, indeed, lead us to embrace the belief that the greatest *wisdom* is to make the enjoyment of the present the supreme object of life; because that is the only reality, all else being merely the play of thought. On the other hand, such a course might just as well be called the greatest *folly:* for that which in the next moment exists no more, and vanishes utterly, like a dream, can never be worth a serious effort.

The whole foundation on which our existence rests is the present—the ever-fleeting present. It lies, then, in the very nature of our existence to take the form of constant motion, and to offer no possibility of our ever attaining the rest for which we are always striving. We are like a man running downhill, who cannot keep on his legs unless he runs on, and will inevitably fall if he stops; or, again, like a pole balanced on the tip of one's finger; or like a planet, which would fall into its sun the moment it ceased to hurry forward on its way. Unrest is the mark of existence.

In a world where all is unstable, and nought can endure, but is swept onwards at once in the hurrying whirlpool of change; where a man, if he is to keep erect at all, must always be advancing and moving, like an acrobat on a rope— in such a world, happiness is inconceivable. How can it dwell where, as Plato says, *continual Becoming and never Being* is the sole form of existence? In the first place, a man never is happy, but spends his whole life in striving after something which he thinks will make him so; he seldom attains his goal, and when he does, it is only to be disappointed; he is mostly shipwrecked in the end, and comes into harbor with masts and rigging gone. And then, it is all one whether he has been happy or miserable; for his life was never anything more than a present moment always vanishing; and now it is over.

At the same time it is a wonderful thing that, in the world of human beings as in that of animals in general, this manifold restless motion is produced and kept up by the agency of two simple impulses—hunger and the sexual instinct; aided a little, perhaps, by the influence of boredom, but by nothing else; and that, in the theatre of life, these suffice to form the *primum mobile* of how complicated a machinery, setting in motion how strange and varied a scene!

On looking a little closer, we find that inorganic matter presents a constant conflict between chemical forces, which eventually works dissolution; and on the other hand, that organic life is impossible without continual change of matter, and cannot exist if it does not receive perpetual help from without. This is the realm of *finality;* and its opposite would be *an infinite existence,* exposed to no attack from without, and needing nothing to support it; the realm of eternal peace; some timeless, changeless state, one and undiversified; the negative knowledge of which forms the dominant note of the Platonic philosophy. It is to some such state as this that the denial of the will to live opens up the way.

The scenes of our life are like pictures done in rough mosaic. Looked at close, they produce no effect. There is nothing beautiful to be found in them, unless you stand some distance off. So, to gain anything we have longed for is only to discover how vain and empty it is; and even though we are always living in expectation of better things, at the same time we often repent and long to have the past back again. We look upon the present as something to be put up with while it lasts, and serving only as the way towards our goal. Hence most people, if they glance back when they come to the end of life, will find that all along they have been living *ad interim:* they will be surprised to find that the very thing they disregarded and let slip by unenjoyed, was just the life in the expectation of which they passed all their time. Of how many a man may it not be said that hope made a fool of him until he danced into the arms of death!

Then again, how insatiable a creature is man! Every satisfaction he attains lays the seeds of some new desire, so that there is no end to the wishes of each individual will. And why is this? The real reason is simply that, taken in itself, Will is the lord of all worlds: everything belongs to it, and therefore no one single thing can ever give it satisfaction, but only the whole, which is endless. For all that, it must rouse our sympathy to think how very little the Will, this lord of the world, really gets when it takes the form of an individual; usually only just enough to keep the body together. This is why man is so very miserable.

Life presents itself chiefly as a task—the task, I mean, of subsisting at all, *gagner sa vie*. If this is accomplished, life is a burden, and then there comes the second task of doing something with that which has been won—of warding off boredom, which, like a bird of prey, hovers over us, ready to fall wherever it sees a life secure from need. The first task is to win something; the second, to banish the feeling that it has been won; otherwise it is a burden.

Human life must be some kind of mistake. The truth of this will be sufficiently obvious if we only remember that man is a compound of needs and necessities hard to satisfy; and that even when they are satisfied, all he obtains is a state of painlessness, where nothing remains to him but abandonment to boredom. This is direct proof that existence has no real value in itself; for what is boredom but the feeling of the emptiness of life? If life—the craving for which is the very essence of our being—were possessed of any positive intrinsic value, there would be no such thing as boredom at all: mere existence would satisfy us in itself, and we should want for nothing. But as it is, we take no delight in existence except when we are struggling for something; and then distance and difficulties to be overcome make our goal look as though it would satisfy us—an illusion which vanishes when we reach it; or else when we are occupied with some purely intellectual interest—when in reality we have stepped forth from life to look upon it from the outside, much after the manner of spectators at a play. And even sensual pleasure itself means nothing but a struggle and aspiration, ceasing the moment its aim is attained. Whenever we are not occupied in one of these ways, but cast upon existence itself, its vain and worthless nature is brought home to us; and this is what we mean by boredom. The hankering

after what is strange and uncommon—an innate and ineradicable tendency of human nature—shows how glad we are at any
interruption of that natural course of affairs which is so very
tedious.

That this most perfect manifestation of the will to live, the
human organism, with the cunning and complex working of
its machinery, must fall to dust and yield up itself and all its
strivings to extinction—this is the naive way in which Nature,
who is always so true and sincere in what she says, proclaims
the whole struggle of this will as in its very essence barren
and unprofitable. Were it of any value in itself, anything unconditioned and absolute, it could not thus end in mere
nothing.

If we turn from contemplating the world as a whole, and,
in particular, the generations of men as they live their little
hour of mock-existence and then are swept away in rapid succession; if we turn from this, and look at life in its small details,
as presented, say, in a comedy, how ridiculous it all seems!
It is like a drop of water seen through a microscope, a single
drop teeming with *infusoria;* or a speck of cheese full of mites
invisible to the naked eye. How we laugh as they bustle about
so eagerly, and struggle with one another in so tiny a space!
And whether here, or in the little span of human life, this
terrible activity produces a comic effect.

It is only in the microscope that our life looks so big. It is
an indivisible point, drawn out and magnified by the powerful
lenses of Time and Space.

XIV

ON THE COMPARATIVE PLACE OF INTEREST AND BEAUTY IN WORKS OF ART

(from posthumous writings)

In the productions of poetic genius, especially of the epic and dramatic kind, there is, apart from Beauty, another quality which is attractive: I mean Interest.

The beauty of a work of art consists in the fact that it holds up a clear mirror to certain *ideas* inherent in the world in general; the beauty of a work of poetic art in particular is that it renders the ideas inherent in mankind, and thereby leads it to a knowledge of these ideas. The means which poetry uses for this end are the exhibition of significant characters and the invention of circumstances which will bring about significant situations, giving occasion to the characters to unfold their peculiarities and show what is in them; so that by some such representation a clearer and fuller knowledge of the many-sided idea of humanity may be attained. Beauty, however, in its general aspect, is the inseparable characteristic of the idea when it has become known. In other words, everything is beautiful in which an idea is revealed; for to be beautiful means no more than clearly to express an idea.

Thus we perceive that beauty is always an affair of *knowledge*, and that it appeals to *the knowing subject*, and not to *the will*; nay, it is a fact that the apprehension of beauty on the part of the subject involves a complete suppression of the will.

On the other hand, we call drama or descriptive poetry interesting when it represents events and actions of a kind which necessarily arouse concern or sympathy, like that which we feel in real events involving our own person. The fate of the person represented in them is felt in just the same fashion as our own: we await the development of events with anxiety; we eagerly follow their course; our hearts quicken when the

hero is threatened; our pulse falters as the danger reaches its
acme, and throbs again when he is suddenly rescued. Until
we reach the end of the story we cannot put the book aside;
we lie away far into the night sympathising with our hero's
troubles as though they were our own. Nay, instead of finding
pleasure and recreation in such representations, we should feel
all the pain which real life often inflicts upon us, or at least
the kind which pursues us in our uneasy dreams, if in the act
of reading or looking at the stage we had not the firm ground
of reality always beneath our feet. As it is, in the stress of a
too violent feeling, we can find relief from the illusion of the
moment, and then give way to it again at will. Moreover, we
can gain this relief without any such violent transition as occurs in a dream, when we rid ourselves of its terrors only by
the act of awaking.

It is obvious that what is affected by poetry of this character is our *will*, and not merely our intellectual powers pure
and simple. The word *interest* means, therefore, that which
arouses the concern of the individual will, *quod nostrâ interest;*
and here it is that beauty is clearly distinguished from interest.
The one is an affair of the intellect, and that, too, of the purest
and simplest kind. The other works upon the will. Beauty,
then, consists in an apprehension of ideas; and knowledge of
this character is beyond the range of the principle that nothing
happens without a cause. Interest, on the other hand, has its
origin nowhere but in the course of events; that is to say, in
the complexities which are possible only through the action
of this principle in its different forms.

We have now obtained a clear conception of the essential
difference between the beauty and the interest of a work of
art. We have recognised that beauty is the true end of every
art, and therefore, also, of the poetic art. It now remains to
raise the question whether the interest of a work of art is a
second end, or a means to the exhibition of its beauty; or
whether the interest of it is produced by its beauty as an essential concomitant, and comes of itself as soon as it is beautiful;
or whether interest is at any rate compatible with the main
end of art; or, finally, whether it is a hindrance to it.

In the first place, it is to be observed that the interest of
a work of art is confined to works of poetic art. It does not

exist in the case of fine art, or of music or architecture. Nay, with these forms of art it is not even conceivable, unless, indeed, the interest be of an entirely personal character, and confined to one or two spectators; as, for example, where a picture is a portrait of some one whom we love or hate; the building, my house or my prison; the music, my wedding dance, or the tune to which I marched to the war. Interest of this kind is clearly quite foreign to the essence and purpose of art; it disturbs our judgment in so far as it makes the purely artistic attitude impossible. It may be, indeed, that to a smaller extent this is true of all interest.

Now, since the interest of a work of art lies in the fact that we have the same kind of sympathy with a poetic representation as with reality, it is obvious that the representation must deceive us for the moment; and this it can do only by its truth. But truth is an element in perfect art. A picture, a poem, should be as true as nature itself; but at the same time it should lay stress on whatever forms the unique character of its subject by drawing out all its essential manifestations, and by rejecting everything that is unessential and accidental. The picture or the poem will thus emphasize its *idea*, and give us that *ideal truth* which is superior to nature.

Truth, then, forms the point that is common both to interest and beauty in a work of art, as it is its truth which produces the illusion. The fact that the truth of which I speak is *ideal truth* might, indeed, be detrimental to the illusion, since it is just here that we have the general difference between poetry and reality, art and nature. But since it is possible for reality to coincide with the ideal, it is not actually necessary that this difference should destroy the illusion. In the case of fine arts there is, in the range of the means which art adopts, a certain limit, and beyond it illusion is impossible. Sculpture, that is to say, gives us mere colourless form; its figures are without eyes and without movement; and painting provides us with no more than a single view, enclosed within strict limits, which separate the picture from the adjacent reality. Here, then, there is no room for illusion, and consequently none for that interest or sympathy which resembles the interest we have in reality; the will is at once excluded, and the object alone is presented to us in a manner that frees it from any personal concern.

It is a highly remarkable fact that a spurious kind of fine art oversteps these limits, produces an illusion of reality, and arouses our interest; but at the same time it destroys the effect which fine art produces, and serves as nothing but a mere means of exhibiting the beautiful, that is, of communicating a knowledge of the ideas which it embodies. I refer to *waxwork*. Here, we might say, is the dividing line which separates it from the province of fine art. When waxwork is properly executed, it produces a perfect illusion; but for that very reason we approach a wax figure as we approach a real man, who, as such, is for the moment an object presented to our will. That is to say, he is an object of interest; he arouses the will, and consequently stills the intellect. We come up to a wax figure with the same reserve and caution as a real man would inspire in us: our will is excited; it waits to see whether he is going to be friendly to us, or the reverse, fly from us, or attack us; in a word, it expects some action of him. But as the figure, nevertheless, shows no sign of life, it produces the impression which is so very disagreeable, namely, of a corpse. This is a case where the interest is of the most complete kind, and yet where there is no work of art at all. In other words, interest is not in itself a real end of art.

The same truth is illustrated by the fact that even in poetry it is only the dramatic and descriptive kind to which interest attaches; for if interest were, with beauty, the aim of art, poetry of the lyrical kind would, for that very reason, not take half so great a position as the other two.

In the second place, if interest were a means in the production of beauty, every interesting work would also be beautiful. That, however, is by no means the case. A drama or a novel may often attract us by its interest, and yet be so utterly deficient in any kind of beauty that we are afterwards ashamed of having wasted our time on it. This applies to many a drama which gives no true picture of the real life of man; which contains characters very superficially drawn, or so distorted as to be actual monstrosities, such as are not to be found in nature; but the course of events and the play of the action are so intricate, and we feel so much for the hero in the situation in

which he is placed, that we are not content until we see the
knot untangled and the hero rescued. The action is so cleverly
governed and guided in its course that we remain in a state
of constant curiosity as to what is going to happen, and we
are utterly unable to form a guess; so that between eagerness
and surprise our interest is kept active; and as we are pleas-
antly entertained, we do not notice the lapse of time. Most of
Kotzebue's plays are of this character. For the mob this is the
right thing: it looks for amusement, something to pass the
time, not for intellectual perception. Beauty is an affair of
such perception; hence sensibility to beauty varies as much
as the intellectual faculties themselves. For the inner truth of
a representation, and its correspondence with the real nature
of humanity, the mob has no sense at all. What is flat and
superficial it can grasp, but the depths of human nature are
opened to it in vain.

It is also to be observed that dramatic representations which
depend for their value on their interest lose by repetition, because they are no longer able to arouse curiosity as to their
course, since it is already known. To see them often, makes
them stale and tedious. On the other hand, works of which
the value lies in their beauty gain by repetition, as they are
then more and more understood.

Most novels are on the same footing as dramatic representations of this character. They are creatures of the same sort of
imagination as we see in the story-teller of Venice and Naples,
who lays a hat on the ground and waits until an audience is
assembled. Then he spins a tale which so captivates his hearers
that, when he gets to the catastrophe, he makes a round of
the crowd, hat in hand, for contributions, without the least
fear that his hearers will slip away. Similar story-tellers ply
their trade in this country, though in a less direct fashion.
They do it through the agency of publishers and circulating
libraries. Thus they can avoid going about in rags, like their
colleagues elsewhere; they can offer the children of their imagination to the public under the title of novels, short stories,
romantic poems, fairy tales, and so on; and the public, in a
dressing-gown by the fireside, sits down more at its ease, but
also with a greater amount of patience, to the enjoyment of
the interest which they provide.

How very little æsthetic value there generally is in productions of this sort is well known; and yet it cannot be denied that many of them are interesting; or else how could they be so popular?

We see, then, in reply to our second question, that interest does not necessarily involve beauty; and, conversely, it is true that beauty does not necessarily involve interest. Significant characters may be represented, that open up the depths of human nature, and it may all be expressed in actions and sufferings of an exceptional kind, so that the real nature of humanity and the world may stand forth in the picture in the clearest and most forcible lines; and yet no high degree of interest may be excited in the course of events by the continued progress of the action, or by the complexity and unexpected solution of the plot. The immortal masterpieces of Shakespeare contain little that excites interest; the action does not go forward in one straight line, but falters, as in *Hamlet*, all through the play; or else it spreads out in breadth, as in *The Merchant of Venice*, whereas length is the proper dimension of interest; or the scenes hang loosely together, as in *Henry IV*. Thus it is that Shakespeare's dramas produce no appreciable effect on the mob.

The dramatic requirement stated by Aristotle, and more particularly the unity of action, have in view the interest of the piece rather than its artistic beauty. It may be said, generally, that these requirements are drawn up in accordance with the principle of sufficient reason to which I have referred above. We know, however, that the *idea*, and, consequently, the beauty of a work of art, exist only for the perceptive intelligence which has freed itself from the domination of that principle. It is just here that we find the distinction between interest and beauty; as it is obvious that interest is part and parcel of the mental attitude which is governed by the principle, whereas beauty is always beyond its range. The best and most striking refutation of the Aristotelian unities is Manzoni's. It may be found in the preface to his dramas.

What is true of Shakespeare's dramatic works is true also of Goethe's. Even *Egmont* makes little effect on the public, because it contains scarcely any complication or development; and if *Egmont* fails, what are we to say of *Tasso* or *Iphigenia?*

That the Greek tragedians did not look to interest as a means of working upon the public, is clear from the fact that the material of their masterpieces was almost always known to every one: they selected events which had often been treated dramatically before. This shows us how sensitive was the Greek public to the beautiful, as it did not require the interest of unexpected events and new stories to season its enjoyment.

Neither does the quality of interest often attach to masterpieces of descriptive poetry. Father Homer lays the world and humanity before us in its true nature, but he takes no trouble to attract our sympathy by a complexity of circumstance, or to surprise us by unexpected entanglements. His pace is lingering; he stops at every scene; he puts one picture after another tranquilly before us, elaborating it with care. We experience no passionate emotion in reading him; our demeanour is one of pure perceptive intelligence; he does not arouse our will, but sings it to rest; and it costs us no effort to break off in our reading, for we are not in condition of eager curiosity. This is all still more true of Dante, whose work is not, in the proper sense of the word, an epic, but a descriptive poem. The same thing may be said of the four immortal romances: *Don Quixote, Tristram Shandy, La Nouvelle Heloïse*, and *Wilhelm Meister*. To arouse our interest is by no means the chief aim of these works; in *Tristram Shandy* the hero, even at the end of the book, is only eight years of age.

On the other hand, we must not venture to assert that the quality of interest is not to be found in masterpieces of literature. We have it in Schiller's dramas in an appreciable degree, and consequently they are popular; also in the *Œdipus Rex* of Sophocles. Amongst masterpieces of description, we find it in Ariosto's *Orlando Furioso;* nay, an example of a high degree of interest, bound up with the beautiful, is afforded in an excellent novel by Walter Scott—*The Heart of Midlothian*. This is the most interesting work of fiction that I know, where all the effects due to interest, as I have given them generally in the preceding remarks, may be most clearly observed. At the same time it is a very beautiful romance throughout; it shows the most varied pictures of life, drawn with striking truth; and it exhibits highly different characters with great justice and fidelity.

Interest, then, is certainly compatible with beauty. That was our third question. Nevertheless, a comparatively small admixture of the element of interest may well be found to be most advantageous as far as beauty is concerned; for beauty is and remains the end of art. Beauty is in twofold opposition with interest; firstly, because it lies in the perception of the idea, and such perception takes its object entirely out of the range of the forms enunciated by the principle of sufficient reason; whereas interest has its sphere mainly in circumstance, and it is out of this principle that the complexity of circumstance arises. Secondly, interest works by exciting the will; whereas beauty exists only for the pure perceptive intelligence, which has no will. However, with dramatic and descriptive literature an admixture of interest is necessary, just as a volatile and gaseous substance requires a material basis if it is to be preserved and transferred. The admixture is necessary, partly, indeed, because interest is itself created by the events which have to be devised in order to set the characters in motion; partly because our minds would be weary of watching scene after scene if they had no concern for us, or of passing from one significant picture to another if we were not drawn on by some secret thread. It is this that we call interest; it is the sympathy which the event in itself forces us to feel, and which, by riveting our attention, makes the mind obedient to the poet, and able to follow him into all the parts of his story.

If the interest of a work of art is sufficient to achieve this result, it does all that can be required of it; for its only service is to connect the pictures by which the poet desires to communicate a knowledge of the idea, as if they were pearls, and interest were the thread that holds them together, and makes an ornament out of the whole. But interest is prejudicial to beauty as soon as it oversteps this limit; and this is the case if we are so led away by the interest of a work that whenever we come to any detailed description in a novel, or any lengthy reflection on the part of a character in a drama, we grow impatient and want to put spurs to our author, so that we may follow the development of events with greater speed. Epic and dramatic writings, where beauty and interest are both present in a high degree, may be compared to the working of a watch, where interest is the spring which keeps all the wheels in motion. If it worked unhindered, the watch would run down in a few minutes. Beauty, holding us in the spell of description and reflection, is like the barrel which checks its movement.

Or we may say that interest is the body of a poetic work, and beauty the soul. In the epic and the drama, interest, as a necessary quality of the action, is the matter; and beauty, the form that requires the matter in order to be visible.

XV

ON THE INNER NATURE OF ART[1]

(CHAPTER XXXIV *from the* SUPPLEMENTS)

Not merely philosophy but also the fine arts work at bottom towards the solution of the problem of existence. For in every mind that once gives itself up to the purely objective contemplation of nature a desire has been excited, however concealed and unconscious it may be, to comprehend the true nature of things, of life and existence. For this alone has interest for the intellect as such, *i.e.*, for the pure subject of knowledge which has become free from the aims of the will; as for the subject which knows as a mere individual the aims of the will alone have interest. On this account the result of the purely objective apprehension of things is an expression more of the nature of life and existence, more an answer to the question, "What is life?" Every genuine and successful work of art answers this question in its own way with perfect correctness. But all the arts speak only the naive and childish language of perception, not the abstract and serious language of *reflection;* their answer is therefore a fleeting image: not permanent and general knowledge. Thus for *perception* every work of art answers that question, every painting, every statue, every poem, every scene upon the stage: music also answers it; and indeed more profoundly than all the rest, for in its language, which is understood with absolute directness, but which is yet untranslatable into that of the reason, the inner nature of all life and existence expresses itself. Thus all the other arts hold up to the questioner a perceptible image, and say, "Look here, this is life." Their answer, however correct it may be, will yet always afford merely a temporary, not a complete and final,

[1] This chapter is connected with § 49 of THE WORLD AS WILL AND IDEA, Dolphin Books, Doubleday & Company, Inc., 1961.

satisfaction. For they always give merely a fragment, an example instead of the rule, not the whole, which can only be given in the universality of the *conception.* For this, therefore, thus for reflection and in the abstract, to give an answer which just on that account shall be permanent and suffice for always, is the task of philosophy. However, we see here upon what the relationship of philosophy to the fine arts rests, and can conclude from that to what extent the capacity of both, although in its direction and in secondary matters very different, is yet in its root the same.

Every work of art accordingly really aims at showing us life and things as they are in truth, but cannot be directly discerned by every one through the mist of objective and subjective contingencies. Art takes away this mist.

The works of the poets, sculptors, and representative artists in general contain an unacknowledged treasure of profound wisdom; just because out of them the wisdom of the nature of things itself speaks, whose utterances they merely interpret by illustrations and purer repetitions. On this account, however, every one who reads the poem or looks at the picture must certainly contribute out of his own means to bring that wisdom to light; accordingly he comprehends only so much of it as his capacity and culture admit of; as in the deep sea each sailor only lets down the lead as far as the length of the line will allow. Before a picture, as before a prince, every one must stand, waiting to see whether and what it will speak to him; and, as in the case of a prince, so here he must not himself address it, for then he would only hear himself. It follows from all this that in the works of the representative arts all truth is certainly contained, yet only *virtualiter* or *implicite;* philosophy, on the other hand, endeavours to supply the same truth *actualiter* and *explicite,* and therefore, in this sense, is related to art as wine to grapes. What it promises to supply would be, as it were, an already realised and clear gain, a firm and abiding possession; while that which proceeds from the achievements and works of art is one which has constantly to be reproduced anew. Therefore, however, it makes demands, not only upon those who produce its works, but also upon those who are to enjoy them which are discouraging and

hard to comply with. Therefore its public remains small, while
that of art is large.

The co-operation of the beholder, which is referred to above,
as demanded for the enjoyment of a work of art, depends
partly upon the fact that every work of art can only produce
its effect through the medium of the fancy; therefore it must
excite this, and can never allow it to be left out of the play
and remain inactive. This is a condition of the æsthetic effect,
and therefore a fundamental law of all fine arts. But it follows
from this that, through the work of art, everything must not
be directly given to the senses, but rather only so much as is
demanded to lead the fancy on to the right path; something,
and indeed the ultimate thing, must always be left over for the
fancy to do. Even the author must always leave something
over for the reader to think; for Voltaire has very rightly said,
"*Le secret d'être ennuyeux, c'est de tout dire.*" But besides
this, in art the best of all is too spiritual to be given directly
to the senses; it must be born in the imagination of the beholder, although begotten by the work of art. It depends upon
this that the sketches of great masters often effect more than
their finished pictures; although another advantage certainly
contributes to this, namely, that they are completed offhand
in the moment of conception; while the perfected painting is
only produced through continued effort, by means of skilful
deliberation and persistent intention, for the inspiration cannot
last till it is completed. From the fundamental æsthetical law
we are speaking of, it is further to be explained why wax figures never produce an æsthetic effect, and therefore are not
properly works of fine art, although it is just in them that the
imitation of nature is able to reach its highest grade. For they
leave nothing for the imagination to do. Sculpture gives merely
the form without the colour; painting gives the colour, but the
mere appearance of the form; thus both appeal to the imagination of the beholder. The wax figure, on the other hand, gives
all, form and colour at once; whence arises the appearance of
reality, and the imagination is left out of account. Poetry, on
the contrary, appeals indeed to the imagination alone, which
it sets in action by means of mere words.

An arbitrary playing with the means of art without a proper
knowledge of the end is, in every art, the fundamental char-

acteristic of the dabbler. Such a man shows himself in the
pillars that support nothing, aimless volutes, juttings and pro-
jections of bad architecture, in the meaningless runs and figures, together with the aimless noise of bad music, in the
jingling of the rhymes of senseless poetry, &c.

It follows from the preceding chapter, and from my whole
view of art, that its aim is the facilitating of the knowledge
of the Ideas of the world (in the Platonic sense, the only one
which I recognise for the word Idea). The Ideas, however,
are essentially something perceptible, which, therefore, in its
fuller determinations, is inexhaustible. The communication of
such an Idea can therefore only take place on the path of
perception, which is that of art. Whoever, therefore, is filled
with the comprehension of an Idea is justified if he chooses
art as the medium of its communication. The mere conception, on the other hand, is something completely determinable,
therefore exhaustible, and distinctly thought, the whole content of which can be coldly and dryly expressed in words. Now
to desire to communicate such a conception by means of a work
of art is a very useless circumlocution, indeed belongs to that
playing with the means of art without knowledge of its end
which has just been condemned. Therefore a work of art
which has proceeded from mere distinct conceptions is always
ungenuine. If now, in considering a work of plastic art, or in
reading a poem, or in hearing a piece of music (which aims
at describing something definite), we see, through all the rich
materials of art, the distinct, limited, cold, dry conception
shine out, and at last come to the front, the conception which
was the kernel of this work, the whole notion of which consequently consisted in the distinct thinking of it, and accordingly is absolutely exhausted by its communication, we feel
disgusted and indignant, for we see ourselves deceived and
cheated out of our interest and attention. We are only perfectly satisfied by the impression of a work of art when it
leaves something which, with all our thinking about it, we
cannot bring down to the distinctness of a conception. The
mark of that hybrid origin from mere conceptions is that the
author of a work of art could, before he set about it, give in
distinct words what he intended to present; for then it would
have been possible to attain his whole end through these

words. Therefore it is an undertaking as unworthy as it is absurd if, as has often been tried at the present day, one seeks
to reduce a poem of Shakspeare's or Goethe's to the abstract
truth which it was its aim to communicate. Certainly the artist
ought to think in the arranging of his work; but only that
thought which was *perceived* before it was thought has afterwards, in its communication, the power of animating or
rousing, and thereby becomes imperishable. We shall not refrain from observing here that certainly the work which is
done at a stroke, like the sketches of painters already referred
to, the work which is completed in the inspiration of its first
conception, and as it were unconsciously dashed off, like the
melody which comes entirely without reflection, and quite as
if by inspiration, and finally, also the lyrical poem proper, the
mere song, in which the deeply felt mood of the present, and
the impression of the surroundings, as if involuntarily, pours
itself forth in words, whose metre and rhyme come about
of their own accord—that all these, I say, have the great advantage of being purely the work of the ecstasy of the moment, the inspiration, the free movement of genius, without
any admixture of intention and reflection; hence they are
through and through delightful and enjoyable, without shell
and kernel, and their effect is much more inevitable than that
of the greatest works of art, of slower and more deliberate
execution. In all the latter, thus in great historical paintings,
in long epic poems, great operas, &c., reflection, intention, and
deliberate selection has had an important part; understanding,
technical skill, and routine must here fill up the gaps which
the conception and inspiration of genius has left, and must
mix with these all kinds of necessary supplementary work as
cement of the only really genuinely brilliant parts. This explains why all such works, only excepting the perfect masterpieces of the very greatest masters (as, for example, "Hamlet,"
"Faust," the opera of "Don Juan"), inevitably contain an admixture of something insipid and wearisome, which in some
measure hinders the enjoyment of them. Proofs of this are the
"Messiah," "*Gerusalemme liberata*," even "Paradise Lost" and
the "Æneid"; and Horace already makes the bold remark,
"*Quandoque dormitat bonus Homerus.*" But that this is the

case is the consequence of the limitation of human powers in general.

The mother of the useful arts is necessity; that of the fine arts superfluity. As their father, the former have understanding; the latter genius, which is itself a kind of superfluity, that of the powers of knowledge beyond the measure which is required for the service of the will.

XVI

THE WAY OF SALVATION

There is only one inborn error, and that is, that we exist in order to be happy. It is inborn in us because it is one with our existence itself, and our whole being is only a paraphrase of it, nay, our body is its monogram. We are nothing more than will to live and the successive satisfaction of all our volitions is what we think in the conception of happiness.

As long as we persist in this inborn error, indeed even become rigidly fixed in it through optimistic dogmas, the world appears to us full of contradictions. For at every step, in great things as in small, we must experience that the world and life are by no means arranged with a view to containing a happy existence. While now by this the thoughtless man only finds himself tormented in reality, in the case of him who thinks there is added to his real pain the theoretical perplexity why a world and a life which exist in order that one may be happy in them answer their end so badly. First of all it finds expression in pious ejaculations, such as, "Ah! why are the tears on earth so many?" &c. &c. But in their train come disquieting doubts about the assumptions of those preconceived optimistic dogmas. One may try if one will to throw the blame of one's individual unhappiness now upon the circumstances, now upon other men, now upon one's own bad luck, or even upon one's own awkwardness, and may know well how all these have worked together to produce it; but this in no way alters the result that one has missed the real end of life, which consists indeed in being happy. The consideration of this is, then, often very depressing, especially if life is already on the wane; hence the countenances of almost all elderly persons wear the expression of that which in English is called disappointment.

Besides this, however, hitherto every day of our life has taught us that joys and pleasures, even if attained, are in themselves delusive, do not perform what they promise, do not satisfy the heart, and finally their possession is at least embittered by the disagreeables that accompany them or spring from them; while, on the contrary, the pains and sorrows prove themselves very real, and often exceed all expectation. Thus certainly everything in life is calculated to recall us from that original error, and to convince us that the end of our existence is not to be happy. Indeed, if we regard it more closely and without prejudice, life rather presents itself as specially intended to be such that we shall *not* feel ourselves happy in it, for through its whole nature it bears the character of something for which we have no taste, which must be endured by us, and from which we have to return as from an error that our heart may be cured of the passionate desire of enjoyment, nay, of life, and turned away from the world. In this sense, it would be more correct to place the end of life in our woe than in our welfare. For the considerations at the conclusion of the preceding chapter [of SUPPLEMENTS TO THE FOURTH BOOK OF THE WORLD AS WILL AND IDEA] have shown that the more one suffers the sooner one attains to the true end of life, and that the more happily one lives the longer this is delayed. The conclusion of the last letter of Seneca corresponds with this: *bonum tunc habebis tuum, quum intelliges infelicissimos esse felices;* which certainly seems to show the influence of Christianity. The peculiar effect of the tragic drama also ultimately depends upon the fact that it shakes that inborn error by vividly presenting in a great and striking example the vanity of human effort and the nothingness of this whole existence, and thus discloses the profound significance of life; hence it is recognised as the sublimest form of poetry. Whoever now has returned by one or other path from that error which dwells in us *a priori* will soon see all in another light, and will now find the world in harmony with his insight, although not with his wishes. Misfortunes of every kind and magnitude, although they pain him, will no longer surprise him, for he has come to see that it is just pain and trouble that tend towards the true end of life, the turning away of the will from it. This will give him indeed a wonderful composedness in all that may happen,

similar to that with which a sick person who undergoes a long
and painful cure bears the pain of it as a sign of its efficacy.
In the whole of human existence suffering expresses itself
clearly enough as its true destiny. Life is deeply sunk in suffering, and cannot escape from it; our entrance into it takes
place amid tears, its course is at bottom always tragic, and its
end still more so. There is an unmistakable appearance of intention in this. As a rule man's destiny passes through his mind
in a striking manner, at the very summit of his desires and
efforts, and thus his life receives a tragic tendency by virtue of
which it is fitted to free him from the passionate desire of
which every individual existence is an example, and bring him
into such a condition that he parts with life without retaining
a single desire for it and its pleasures. Suffering is, in fact, the
purifying process through which alone, in most cases, the man
is sanctified, *i.e.*, is led back from the path of error of the will
to live. In accordance with this, the salutary nature of the
cross and of suffering is so often explained in Christian books
of edification, and in general the cross, an instrument of suffering, not of doing, is very suitably the symbol of the Christian
religion. Nay, even the Preacher, who is still Jewish, but so
very philosophical, rightly says: "Sorrow is better than laughter: for by the sadness of the countenance the heart is made
better" (Eccles. vii. 3). I have presented suffering as to a certain extent a substitute for virtue and holiness; but here I
must make the bold assertion that, taking everything into consideration, we have more to hope for our salvation and deliverance from what we suffer than from what we do. Precisely in this spirit Lamartine very beautifully says in his
"Hymne à la douleur," apostrophising pain:—

> *Tu me traites sans doute en favori des cieux,*
> *Car tu n'épargnes pas les larmes à mes yeux.*
> *Eh bien! je les reçois comme tu les envoies,*
> *Tes maux seront mes biens, et tes soupirs mes joies.*
> *Je sens qu'il est en toi, sans avoir combattu,*
> *Une vertu divine au lieu de ma vertu,*
> *Que tu n'es pas la mort l'âme, mais sa vie,*
> *Que ton bras, en frappant, guérit et vivifie.*

If, then, suffering itself has such a sanctifying power, this will belong in an even higher degree to death, which is more feared than any suffering. Answering to this, a certain awe, kindred to that which great suffering occasions us, is felt in the presence of every dead person, indeed every case of death presents itself to a certain extent as a kind of apotheosis or canonisation; therefore we cannot look upon the dead body of even the most insignificant man without awe, and indeed, extraordinary as the remark may sound in this place, in the presence of every corpse the watch goes under arms. Dying is certainly to be regarded as the real aim of life: in the moment of death all that is decided for which the whole course of life was only the preparation and introduction. Death is the result, the *Résumé* of life, or the added up sum which expresses at once the instruction which life gave in detail, and bit by bit; this, that the whole striving whose manifestation is life was a vain, idle, and self-contradictory effort, to have returned from which is a deliverance. As the whole, slow vegetation of the plant is related to the fruit, which now at a stroke achieves a hundredfold what the plant achieved gradually and bit by bit, so life, with its obstacles, deluded hopes, frustrated plans, and constant suffering, is related to death, which at one stroke destroys all, all that the man has willed, and so crowns the instruction which life gave him. The completed course of life upon which the dying man looks back has an effect upon the whole will that objectifies itself in this perishing individuality, analogous to that which a motive exercises upon the conduct of the man. It gives it a new direction, which accordingly is the moral and essential result of the life. Just because a sudden death makes this retrospect impossible, the Church regards such a death as a misfortune, and prays that it should be averted. Since this retrospect, like the distinct foreknowledge of death, as conditioned by the reason, is possible only in man, not in the brute, and accordingly man alone really drinks the cup of death, humanity is the only material in which the will can deny itself and entirely turn away from life. To the will that does not deny itself every birth imparts a new and different intellect,—till it has learned the true nature of life, and in consequence of this wills it no more.

In the natural course, in age the decay of the body coincides with that of the will. The desire for pleasures soon vanishes with the capacity to enjoy them. The occasion of the most vehement willing, the focus of the will, the sexual impulse, is first extinguished, whereby the man is placed in a position which resembles the state of innocence which existed before the development of the genital system. The illusions, which set up chimeras as exceedingly desirable benefits, vanish, and the knowledge of the vanity of all earthly blessings takes their place. Selfishness is repressed by the love of one's children, by means of which the man already begins to live more in the ego of others than in his own, which now will soon be no more. This course of life is at least the desirable one; it is the euthanasia of the will. In hope of this the Brahman is ordered, after he has passed the best years of his life, to forsake possessions and family, and lead the life of a hermit (*Menu*, B. 6). But if, conversely, the desire outlives the capacity for enjoyment, and we now regret particular pleasures in life which we miss, instead of seeing the emptiness and vanity of all; and if then gold, the abstract representative of the objects of desire for which the sense is dead, takes the place of all these objects themselves, and now excites the same vehement passions which were formerly more pardonably awakened by the objects of actual pleasure, and thus now with deadened senses a lifeless but indestructible object is desired with equally indestructible eagerness; or, also, if, in the same way, existence in the opinion of others takes the place of existence and action in the real world, and now kindles the same passions;—then the will has become sublimated and etherealised into avarice or ambition; but has thereby thrown itself into the last fortress, in which it can only now be besieged by death. The end of existence has been missed.

All these considerations afford us a fuller explanation of that purification, conversion of the will and deliverance, which is brought about by the suffering of life, and without doubt is the most frequent. For it is the way of sinners such as we all are. The other way, which leads to the same goal, by means of mere knowledge and the consequent appropriation of the suffering of a whole world, is the narrow path of the elect, the saints, and therefore to be regarded as a rare exception. Therefore without that first way for most of us there would be no salvation to hope for. However, we struggle against entering upon it, and strive rather to procure for ourselves a safe and agreeable existence, whereby we chain our will ever more firmly to life. The conduct of the ascetics is the opposite of this. They make their life intentionally as poor, hard, and empty of pleasure as possible, because they have their true and ultimate welfare in view. But fate and the course of things care for us better than we ourselves, for they frustrate on all sides our arrangements for an utopian life, the folly of which is evident enough from its brevity, uncertainty, and emptiness, and its conclusion by bitter death; they strew thorns upon thorns in our path, and meet us everywhere with healing sorrow, the panacea of our misery. What really gives its wonderful and ambiguous character to our life is this, that two diametrically opposite aims constantly cross each other in it; that of the individual will directed to chimerical happiness in an ephemeral, dream-like, and delusive existence, in which, with reference to the past, happiness and unhappiness are a matter of indifference, and the present is every moment becoming the past; and that of fate visibly enough directed to the destruction of our happiness, and thereby to the mortification of our will and the abolition of the illusion that holds us chained in the bonds of this world.

The prevalent and peculiarly Protestant view that the end of life lies solely and immediately in the moral virtues, thus in the practice of justice and benevolence, betrays its insufficiency even in the fact that so miserably little real and pure morality is found among men. I am not speaking at all of lofty virtue, nobleness, magnanimity, and self-sacrifice, which one hardly finds anywhere but in plays and novels, but only of those virtues which are the duty of every one. Let whoever is old think of all those with whom he has had to do; how many persons will he have met who were merely really and truly *honest?* Were not by far the greater number, in spite of their shameless indignation at the slightest suspicion of dishonesty or even untruthfulness, in plain words, the precise opposite? Were not abject selfishness, boundless avarice, well-concealed knavery, and also poisonous envy and fiendish delight in the misfortunes of others so universally prevalent that the slightest exception was met with surprise? And benevolence, how very rarely it extends beyond a gift of what is so superfluous that one never misses it. And is the whole end of existence to lie in such exceedingly rare and weak traces of morality? If we place it, on the contrary, in the entire reversal of this nature of ours (which bears the evil fruits just mentioned) brought about by suffering, the matter gains an appearance of probability and is brought into agreement with what actually lies before us. Life presents itself then as a purifying process, of which the purifying lye is pain. If the process is carried out, it leaves behind it the previous immorality and wickedness as refuse, and there appears what the Veda says: *"Finditur nodus cordis, dissolvuntur omnes dubitationes, ejusque opera evanescunt."* As agreeing with this view the fifteenth sermon of Meister Eckhard will be found very well worth reading.

FREE-WILL AND FATALISM

(from PARERGA)

No thoughtful man can have any doubt, after the conclusions reached in my prize-essay on *Moral Freedom,* that such freedom is to be sought, not anywhere in nature, but outside of it. The only freedom that exists is of a metaphysical character. In the physical world freedom is an impossibility. Accordingly, while our several actions are in no wise free, every man's individual character is to be regarded as a free act. He is such and such a man, because once for all it is his will to be that man. For the will itself, and in itself, and also in so far as it is manifest in an individual, and accordingly constitutes the original and fundamental desires of that individual, is independent of all knowledge, because it is antecedent to such knowledge. All that it receives from knowledge is the series of motives by which it successively develops its nature and makes itself cognisable or visible; but the will itself, as something that lies beyond time, and so long as it exists at all, never changes. Therefore every man, being what he is and placed in the circumstances which for the moment obtain, but which on their part also arise by strict necessity, can absolutely never do anything else than just what at that moment he does do. Accordingly, the whole course of a man's life, in all its incidents great and small, is as necessarily predetermined as the course of a clock.

The main reason of this is that the kind of metaphysical free act which I have described tends to become a knowing consciousness—a perceptive intuition, which is subject to the forms of space and time. By means of those forms the unity and indivisibility of the act are represented as drawn asunder into a series of states and events, which are subject to the

Principle of Sufficient Reason in its four forms—and it is this that is meant by *necessity*. But the result of it all assumes a moral complexion. It amounts to this, that by what we do we know what we are, and by what we suffer we know what we deserve.

Further, it follows from this that a man's *individuality* does not rest upon the principle of individuation alone, and therefore is not altogether phenomenal in its nature. On the contrary, it has its roots in the thing-in-itself, in the will which is the essence of each individual. The character of this individual is itself individual. But how deep the roots of individuality extend is one of the questions which I do not undertake to answer.

In this connection it deserves to be mentioned that even Plato, in his own way, represented the individuality of a man as a free act.[1] He represented him as coming into the world with a given tendency, which was the result of the feelings and character already attaching to him in accordance with the doctrine of metempsychosis. The Brahmin philosophers also express the unalterable fixity of innate character in a mystical fashion. They say that Brahma, when a man is produced, engraves his doings and sufferings in written characters on his skull, and that his life must take shape in accordance therewith. They point to the jagged edges in the sutures of the skull-bones as evidence of this writing; and the purport of it, they say, depends on his previous life and actions. The same view appears to underlie the Christian, or rather, the Pauline, dogma of Predestination.

But this truth, which is universally confirmed by experience, is attended with another result. All genuine merit, moral as well as intellectual, is not merely physical or empirical in its origin, but metaphysical; that is to say, it is given *a priori* and not *a posteriori;* in other words, it lies innate and is not acquired, and therefore its source is not a mere phenomenon, but the thing-in-itself. Hence it is that every man achieves only that which is irrevocably established in his nature, or is born with him. Intellectual capacity needs, it is true, to be developed just as many natural products need to be cultivated

[1] *Phædrus* and *Laws*, bk. x.

in order that we may enjoy or use them; but just as in the case of a natural product no cultivation can take the place of original material, neither can it do so in the case of intellect. That is the reason why qualities which are merely acquired, or learned, or enforced—that is, qualities *a posteriori*, whether moral or intellectual—are not real or genuine, but superficial only, and possessed of no value. This is a conclusion of true metaphysics, and experience teaches the same lesson to all who can look below the surface. Nay, it is proved by the great importance which we all attach to such innate characteristics as physiognomy and external appearance, in the case of a man who is at all distinguished; and that is why we are so curious to see him. Superficial people, to be sure,—and, for very good reasons, commonplace people too,—will be of the opposite opinion; for if anything fails them they will thus be enabled to console themselves by thinking that it is still to come.

The world, then, is not merely a battlefield where victory and defeat receive their due recompense in a future state. No! the world is itself the Last Judgment on it. Every man carries with him the reward and the disgrace that he deserves; and this is no other than the doctrine of the Brahmins and Buddhists as it is taught in the theory of metempsychosis.

The question has been raised, What two men would do, who lived a solitary life in the wilds and met each other for the first time. Hobbes, Pufendorf, and Rousseau have given different answers. Pufendorf believed that they would approach each other as friends; Hobbes, on the contrary, as enemies; Rousseau, that they would pass each other by in silence. All three are both right and wrong. This is just a case in which the incalculable difference that there is in innate moral disposition between one individual and another would make its appearance. The difference is so strong that the question here raised might be regarded as the standard and measure of it. For there are men in whom the sight of another man at once rouses a feeling of enmity, since their inmost nature exclaims at once: That is not me! There are others in whom the sight awakens immediate sympathy; their inmost nature says: *That is me over again!* Between the two there are countless degrees. That in this most important matter we are so totally different is a great problem, nay, a mystery.

In regard to this *a priori* nature of moral character there is matter for varied reflection in a work by Bastholm, a Danish writer, entitled *Historical Contributions to the Knowledge of Man in the Savage State*. He is struck by the fact that intellectual culture and moral excellence are shown to be entirely independent of each other, inasmuch as one is often found without the other. The reason of this, as we shall find, is simply that moral excellence in no wise springs from reflection, which is developed by intellectual culture, but from the will itself, the constitution of which is innate and not susceptible in itself of any improvement by means of education. Bastholm represents most nations as very vicious and immoral; and on the other hand he reports that excellent traits of character are found amongst some savage peoples; as, for instance, amongst the Orotchyses, the inhabitants of the island Savu, the Tunguses, and the Pelew islanders. He thus attempts to solve the problem, How it is that some tribes are so remarkably good, when their neighbours are all bad.

It seems to me that the difficulty may be explained as follows: Moral qualities, as we know, are heritable, and an isolated tribe, such as is described, might take its rise in some one family, and ultimately in a single ancestor who happened to be a good man, and then maintain its purity. Is it not the case, for instance, that on many unpleasant occasions, such as repudiation of public debts, filibustering raids and so on, the English have often reminded the North Americans of their descent from English penal colonists? It is a reproach, however, which can apply only to a small part of the population.

It is marvellous how *every man's individuality* (that is to say, the union of a definite character with a definite intellect) accurately determines all his actions and thoughts down to the most unimportant details, as though it were a dye which pervaded them; and how, in consequence, one man's whole course of life, in other words, his inner and outer history, turns out so absolutely different from another's. As a botanist knows a plant in its entirety from a single leaf; as Cuvier from a single bone constructed the whole animal, so an accurate knowledge of a man's whole character may be attained from a single characteristic act; that is to say, he himself may to some extent be constructed from it, even though the act in question is of very trifling consequence. Nay, that is the most perfect test of all, for in a matter of importance people are on their guard; in trifles they follow their natural bent without much reflection. That is why Seneca's remark, that even the smallest things may be taken as evidence of character, is so true: *argumenta morum ex minimis quoque licet capere.*[2] If a man shows by his absolutely unscrupulous and selfish behaviour in small things that a sentiment of justice is foreign to his disposition, he should not be trusted with a penny unless on due security. For who will believe that the man who every day shows that he is unjust in all matters other than those which concern property, and whose boundless selfishness everywhere protrudes through the small affairs of ordinary life which are subject to no scrutiny, like a dirty shirt through the holes of a ragged jacket—who, I ask, will believe that such a man will act honourably in matters of *meum* and *tuum* without any other incentive but that of justice? The man who has no conscience in small things will be a scoundrel in big things. If we neglect small traits of character, we have only ourselves to blame if we afterwards learn to our disadvantage what this character is in the great affairs of life. On the same principle, we ought to break with so-called friends even in matters of trifling moment, if they show a character that is malicious or bad or vulgar, so that we may avoid the bad turn which only waits for an opportunity of being done us. The same thing applies to servants. Let it always be our maxim: Better alone than amongst traitors.

Of a truth the first and foremost step in all knowledge of mankind is the conviction that a man's conduct, taken as a whole, and in all its essential particulars, is not governed by his reason or by any of the resolutions which he may make in virtue of it. No man becomes this or that by wishing to be it, however earnestly. His acts proceed from his innate and unalterable character, and they are more immediately and particularly determined by motives. A man's conduct, therefore, is the necessary product of both character and motive. It may be illustrated by the course of a planet, which is the result of the combined effect of the tangential energy with which it

[2] *Ep.*, 52.

is endowed, and the centripetal energy which operates from the sun. In this simile the former energy represents character, and the latter the influence of motive. It is almost more than a mere simile. The tangential energy which properly speaking is the source of the planet's motion, whilst on the other hand the motion is kept in check by gravitation, is, from a metaphysical point of view, the will manifesting itself in that body.

To grasp this fact is to see that we really never form anything more than a conjecture of what we shall do under circumstances which are still to happen; although we often take our conjecture for a resolve. When, for instance, in pursuance of a proposal, a man with the greatest sincerity, and even eagerness, accepts an engagement to do this or that on the occurrence of a certain future event, it is by no means certain that he will fulfil the engagement; unless he is so constituted that the promise which he gives, in itself and as such, is always and everywhere a motive sufficient for him, by acting upon him, through considerations of honour, like some external compulsion. But above and beyond this, what he will do on the occurrence of that event may be foretold from true and accurate knowledge of his character and the external circumstances under the influence of which he will fall; and it may with complete certainty be foretold from this alone. Nay, it is a very easy prophecy if he has been already seen in a like position; for he will inevitably do the same thing a second time, provided that on the first occasion he had a true and complete knowledge of the facts of the case. For, as I have often remarked, a final cause does not impel a man by being real, but by being known; *causa finalis non movet secundum suum esse reale, sed secundum esse cognitum.*[3] Whatever he failed to recognise or understand the first time could have no influence upon his will; just as an electric current stops when some isolating body hinders the action of the conductor. This unalterable nature of character, and the consequent necessity of our actions, are made very clear to a man who has not, on any given occasion, behaved as he ought to have done, by showing a lack either of resolution or endurance or courage, or some other quality demanded at the moment. Afterwards

[3] Suarez, *Disp. Metaph.*, xxiii., §§ 7 and 8.

he recognises what it is that he ought to have done; and, sincerely repenting of his incorrect behaviour, he thinks to himself, *If the opportunity were offered to me again, I should act differently.* It is offered once more; the same occasion recurs; and to his great astonishment he does precisely the same thing over again.

The best examples of the truth in question are in every way furnished by Shakespeare's plays. It is a truth with which he was thoroughly imbued, and his intuitive wisdom expressed it in a concrete shape on every page. I shall here, however, give an instance of it in a case in which he makes it remarkably clear, without exhibiting any design or affectation in the matter; for he was a real artist and never set out from general ideas. His method was obviously to work up to the psychological truth which he grasped directly and intuitively, regardless of the fact that few would notice or understand it, and without the smallest idea that some dull and shallow fellows in Germany would one day proclaim far and wide that he wrote his works to illustrate moral commonplaces. I allude to the character of the Earl of Northumberland, whom we find in three plays in succession, although he does not take a leading part in any one of them; nay, he appears only in a few scenes distributed over fifteen acts. Consequently, if the reader is not very attentive, a character exhibited at such great intervals, and its moral identity, may easily escape his notice, even though it has by no means escaped the poet's. He makes the earl appear everywhere with a noble and knightly grace, and talk in language suitable to it; nay, he sometimes puts very beautiful and even elevated passages into his mouth. At the same time he is very far from writing after the manner of Schiller, who was fond of painting the devil black, and whose moral approval or disapproval of the characters which he presented could be heard in their own words. With Shakespeare, and also with Goethe, every character, as long as he is on the stage and speaking, seems to be absolutely in the right, even though it were the devil himself. In this respect let the reader compare Duke Alba as he appears in Goethe with the same character in Schiller.

We make the acquaintance of the Earl of Northumberland in the play of *Richard II.*, where he is the first to hatch a plot

against the King in favour of Bolingbroke, afterwards Henry
IV., to whom he even offers some personal flattery (Act II.,
Sc. 3). In the following act he suffers a reprimand because,
in speaking of the King he talks of him as "Richard," without
more ado, but protests that he did it only for brevity's sake.
A little later his insidious words induce the King to surrender.
In the following act, when the King renounces the crown,
Northumberland treats him with such harshness and contempt
that the unlucky monarch is quite broken, and losing all patience once more exclaims to him: *Fiend, thou torment'st me
ere I come to hell!* At the close, Northumberland announces
to the new King that he has sent the heads of the former
King's adherents to London.

In the following tragedy, *Henry IV.*, he hatches a plot
against the new King in just the same way. In the fourth act
we see the rebels united, making preparations for the decisive
battle on the morrow, and only waiting impatiently for Northumberland and his division. At last there arrives a letter from
him, saying that he is ill, and that he cannot entrust his force
to any one else; but that nevertheless the others should go forward with courage and make a brave fight. They do so, but,
greatly weakened by his absence, they are completely defeated; most of their leaders are captured, and his own son,
the valorous Hotspur, falls by the hand of the Prince of Wales.

Again, in the following play, the *Second Part of Henry IV.*,
we see him reduced to a state of the fiercest wrath by the
death of his son, and maddened by the thirst for revenge.
Accordingly he kindles another rebellion, and the heads of it
assemble once more. In the fourth act, just as they are about
to give battle, and are only waiting for him to join them, there
comes a letter saying that he cannot collect a proper force,
and will therefore seek safety for the present in Scotland; that,
nevertheless, he heartily wishes their heroic undertaking the
best success. Thereupon they surrender to the King under a
treaty which is not kept, and so perish.

So far is character from being the work of reasoned choice
and consideration that in any action the intellect has nothing
to do but to present motives to the will. Thereafter it looks
on as a mere spectator and witness at the course which life
takes, in accordance with the influence of motive on the given

character. All the incidents of life occur, strictly speaking, with the same necessity as the movement of a clock. On this point let me refer to my prize-essay on *The Freedom of the Will.* I have there explained the true meaning and origin of the persistent illusion that the will is entirely free in every single action; and I have indicated the cause to which it is due. I will only add here the following teleological explanation of this natural illusion.

Since every single action of a man's life seems to possess the freedom and originality which in truth only belong to his character as he apprehends it, and the mere apprehension of it by his intellect is what constitutes his career; and since what is original in every single action seems to the empirical consciousness to be always being performed anew, a man thus receives in the course of his career the strongest possible moral lesson. Then, and not before, he becomes thoroughly conscious of all the bad sides of his character. Conscience accompanies every act with the comment: *You should act differently,* although its true sense is: *You could be other than you are.* As the result of this immutability of character on the one hand, and, on the other, of the strict necessity which attends all the circumstances in which character is successively placed, every man's course of life is precisely determined from Alpha right through to Omega. But, nevertheless, one man's course of life turns out immeasurably happier, nobler and more worthy than another's, whether it be regarded from a subjective or an objective point of view, and unless we are to exclude all ideas of justice, we are led to the doctrine which is well accepted in Brahmanism and Buddhism, that the subjective conditions in which, as well as the objective conditions under which, every man is born, are the moral consequences of a previous existence.

Macchiavelli, who seems to have taken no interest whatever in philosophical speculations, is drawn by the keen subtlety of his very unique understanding into the following observation, which possesses a really deep meaning. It shows that he had an intuitive knowledge of the entire necessity with which, characters and motives being given, all actions take place. He makes it at the beginning of the prologue to his comedy *Clitia.* If, he says, *the same men were to recur in the world in the way that the same circumstances recur, a hundred years would never elapse without our finding ourselves together once more, and doing the same things as we are doing now—Se nel mondo tornassino i medesimi uomini, como tornano i medesimi casi, non passarebbono mai cento anni che noi non ci trovassimo un altra volta insieme, a fare le medesime cose che hora.* He seems however to have been drawn into the remark by a reminiscence of what Augustine says in his *De Civitate Dei*, bk. xii., ch. xiii.

Again, Fate is nothing but the conscious certainty that all that happens is fast bound by a chain of causes, and therefore takes place with a strict necessity; that the future is already ordained with absolute certainty and can undergo as little alteration as the past. In the fatalistic myths of the ancients all that can be regarded as fabulous is the prediction of the future; that is, if we refuse to consider the possibility of magnetic clairvoyance and second sight. Instead of trying to explain away the fundamental truth of Fatalism by superficial twaddle and foolish evasion, a man should attempt to get a clear knowledge and comprehension of it; for it is demonstrably true, and it helps us in a very important way to an understanding of the mysterious riddle of our life. Predestination and Fatalism do not differ in the main. They differ only in this, that with Predestination the given character and external determination of human action proceed from a rational Being, and with Fatalism from an irrational one. But in either case the result is the same: that happens which must happen.

On the other hand the conception of *Moral Freedom* is inseparable from that of *Originality*. A man may be said, but he cannot be conceived, to be the work of another, and at the same time be free in respect of his desires and acts. He who called him into existence out of nothing in the same process created and determined his nature—in other words, the whole of his qualities. For no one can create without creating a something, that is to say, a being determined throughout and in all its qualities. But all that a man says and does necessarily proceeds from the qualities so determined; for it is only the qualities themselves set in motion. It is only some external impulse that they require to make their appearance. As a man is, so must he act; and praise or blame attaches, not to his separate acts, but to his nature and being.

That is the reason why Theism and the moral responsibility of man are incompatible; because responsibility always reverts to the creator of man and it is there that it has its centre. Vain attempts have been made to make a bridge from one of these incompatibles to the other by means of the conception of moral freedom; but it always breaks down again. What is *free* must also be *original*. If our will is *free*, our will is also *the original element*, and conversely. Pre-Kantian dogmatism tried to separate these two predicaments. It was thereby compelled to assume two kinds of freedom, one cosmological, of the first cause, and the other moral and theological, of human will. These are represented in Kant by the third as well as the fourth antinomy of freedom.

On the other hand, in my philosophy the plain recognition of the strictly necessary character of all action is in accordance with the doctrine that what manifests itself even in the organic and irrational world is *will*. If this were not so, the necessity under which irrational beings obviously act would place their action in conflict with will; if, I mean, there were really such a thing as the freedom of individual action, and this were not as strictly necessitated as every other kind of action. But, as I have just shown, it is this same doctrine of the necessary character of all acts of will which makes it needful to regard a man's existence and being as itself the work of his freedom, and consequently of his will. The will, therefore, must be self-existent; it must possess so-called *a-se-ity*. Under the opposite supposition all responsibility, as I have shown, would be at an end, and the moral like the physical world would be a mere machine, set in motion for the amusement of its manufacturer placed somewhere outside of it. So it is that truths hang together, and mutually advance and complete one another; whereas error gets jostled at every corner.

What kind of influence it is that *moral instruction* may exercise on conduct, and what are the limits of that influence, are questions which I have sufficiently examined in the twentieth section of my treatise on the *Foundation of Morality*. In all essential particulars an analogous influence is exercised by *example,* which, however, has a more powerful effect than doctrine, and therefore it deserves a brief analysis.

In the main, example works either by restraining a man or by encouraging him. It has the former effect when it determines him to leave undone what he wanted to do. He sees, I mean, that other people do not do it; and from this he judges, in general, that it is not expedient; that it may endanger his person, or his property, or his honour. He rests content, and gladly finds himself relieved from examining into the matter for himself. Or he may see that another man, who has not refrained, has incurred evil consequences from doing it; this is example of the deterrent kind. The example which encourages a man works in a twofold manner. It either induces him to do what he would be glad to leave undone, if he were not afraid lest the omission might in some way endanger him, or injure him in others' opinion; or else it encourages him to do what he is glad to do, but has hitherto refrained from doing from fear of danger or shame; this is example of the seductive kind. Finally, example may bring a man to do what he would have otherwise never thought of doing. It is obvious that in this last case example works in the main only on the intellect; its effect on the will is secondary, and if it has any such effect, it is by the interposition of the man's own judgment, or by reliance on the person who presented the example.

The whole influence of example—and it is very strong—rests on the fact that a man has, as a rule, too little judgment of his own, and often too little knowledge, to explore his own way for himself, and that he is glad, therefore, to tread in the footsteps of some one else. Accordingly, the more deficient he is in either of these qualities, the more is he open to the influence of example; and we find, in fact, that most men's guiding star is the example of others; that their whole course of life, in great things and in small, comes in the end to be mere imitation; and that not even in the pettiest matters do they act according to their own judgment. Imitation and custom are the spring of almost all human action. The cause of it is that men fight shy of all and any sort of reflection, and very properly mistrust their own discernment. At the same time this remarkably strong imitative instinct in man is a proof of his kinship with apes.

But the kind of effect which example exercises depends upon a man's character, and thus it is that the same example may possibly seduce one man and deter another. An easy opportunity of observing this is afforded in the case of certain social impertinences which come into vogue and gradually spread. The first time that a man notices anything of the kind, he may say to himself: *For shame! how can he do it! how selfish and inconsiderate of him! really, I shall take care never to do anything like that.* But twenty others will think: *Aha! if he does that, I may do it too.*

As regards morality, example, like doctrine, may, it is true, promote civil or legal amelioration, but not that inward amendment which is, strictly speaking, the only kind of moral amelioration. For example always works as a personal motive alone, and assumes, therefore, that a man is susceptible to this sort of motive. But it is just the predominating sensitiveness of a character to this or that sort of motive that determines whether its morality is true and real; though, of whatever kind it is, it is always innate. In general it may be said that example operates as a means of promoting the good and the bad qualities of a character, but it does not create them; and so it is that Seneca's maxim, *velle non discitur—will cannot be learned* —also holds good here. But the innateness of all truly moral qualities, of the good as of the bad, is a doctrine that consorts better with the metempsychosis of the Brahmins and Buddhists, according to which a man's good and bad deeds follow him from one existence to another like his shadow, than with Judaism. For Judaism requires a man to come into the world as a moral blank, so that, in virtue of an inconceivable free will, directed to objects which are neither to be sought nor avoided—*liberum arbitrium indifferentiæ*—and consequently as the result of reasoned consideration, he may choose whether he is to be an angel or a devil, or anything else that may lie between the two. Though I am well aware what the Jewish scheme is, I pay no attention to it; for my standard is truth. I am no professor of philosophy, and therefore I do not find my vocation in establishing the fundamental ideas of Judaism at any cost, even though they for ever bar the way to all and every kind of philosophical knowledge. *Liberum arbitrium indifferentiæ* under the name of *moral freedom* is a charming doll for professors of philosophy to dandle; and we must leave it to those intelligent, honourable and upright gentlemen.

XVIII

HUMAN NATURE

(from PARERGA*)*

Truths of the physical order may possess much external significance, but internal significance they have none. The latter is the privilege of intellectual and moral truths, which are concerned with the objectivation of the will in its highest stages, whereas physical truths are concerned with it in its lowest.

For example, if we could establish the truth of what up till now is only a conjecture, namely, that it is the action of the sun which produces thermoelectricity at the equator; that this produces terrestrial magnetism; and that this magnetism, again, is the cause of the *aurora borealis*, these would be truths externally of great, but internally of little, significance. On the other hand, examples of internal significance are furnished by all great and true philosophical systems; by the catastrophe of every good tragedy; nay, even by the observation of human conduct in the extreme manifestations of its morality and immorality, of its good and its evil character. For all these are expressions of that reality which takes outward shape as the world, and which, in the highest stages of its objectivation, proclaims its innermost nature.

To say that the world has only a physical and not a moral significance is the greatest and most pernicious of all errors, the fundamental blunder, the real perversity of mind and temper; and, at bottom, it is doubtless the tendency which faith personifies as Anti-Christ. Nevertheless, in spite of all religions —and they are systems which one and all maintain the opposite, and seek to establish it in their mythical way—this fundamental error never becomes quite extinct, but raises its head from time to time afresh, until universal indignation compels it to hide itself once more.

Yet, however certain we may feel of the moral significance of life and the world, to explain and illustrate it, and to resolve the contradiction between this significance and the world as it is, form a task of great difficulty; so great, indeed, as to make it possible that it has remained for me to exhibit the true and only genuine and sound basis of morality everywhere and at all times effective, together with the results to which it leads. The actual facts of morality are too much on my side for me to fear that my theory can ever be replaced or upset by any other.

However, so long as even my ethical system continues to be ignored by the professorial world, it is Kant's moral principle that prevails in the universities. Among its various forms the one which is most in favour at present is "the dignity of man." I have already exposed the absurdity of this doctrine in my treatise on the *Foundation of Morality*. Therefore I will only say here that if the question were asked on what the alleged dignity of man rests, it would not be long before the answer was made that it rests upon his morality. In other words, his morality rests upon his dignity, and his dignity rests upon his morality.

But apart from this circular argument it seems to me that the idea of dignity can be applied only in an ironical sense to a being whose will is so sinful, whose intellect is so limited, whose body is so weak and perishable as man's. How shall a man be proud, when his conception is a crime, his birth a penalty, his life a labour, and death a necessity!—

> *Quid superbit homo? cujus conceptio culpa,*
> *Nasci pœna, labor vita, necesse mori!*

Therefore, in opposition to the above-mentioned form of the Kantian principle, I should be inclined to lay down the following rule: When you come into contact with a man, no matter whom, do not attempt an objective appreciation of him according to his worth and dignity. Do not consider his bad will, or his narrow understanding and perverse ideas; as the former may easily lead you to hate and the latter to despise him; but fix your attention only upon his sufferings, his needs, his anxieties, his pains. Then you will always feel your kinship with him; you will sympathise with him; and instead of

hatred or contempt you will experience the commiseration that
alone is the peace to which the Gospel calls us. The way to
keep down hatred and contempt is certainly not to look for
a man's alleged "dignity," but, on the contrary, to regard him
as an object of pity.

The Buddhists, as the result of the more profound views
which they entertain on ethical and metaphysical subjects,
start from the cardinal vices and not the cardinal virtues; since
the virtues make their appearance only as the contraries or
negations of the vices. According to Schmidt's *History of the
Eastern Mongolians* the cardinal vices in the Buddhist scheme
are four: Lust, Indolence, Anger, and Avarice. But probably
instead of Indolence, we should read Pride; for so it stands
in the *Lettres édifiantes et curieuses*,[1] where Envy, or Hatred,
is added as a fifth. I am confirmed in correcting the statement
of the excellent Schmidt by the fact that my rendering agrees
with the doctrine of the Sufis, who are certainly under the
influence of the Brahmins and Buddhists. The Sufis also maintain that there are four cardinal vices, and they arrange them
in very striking pairs, so that Lust appears in connection with
Avarice, and Anger with Pride. The four cardinal virtues opposed to them would be Chastity and Generosity, together
with Gentleness and Humility.

When we compare these profound ideas of morality, as they
are entertained by oriental nations, with the celebrated cardinal virtues of Plato, which have been recapitulated again
and again—Justice, Valour, Temperance, and Wisdom—it is
plain that the latter are not based on any clear, leading idea,
but are chosen on grounds that are superficial and, in part,
obviously false. Virtues must be qualities of the will, but Wisdom is chiefly an attribute of the Intellect. *Sōphrosynē*, which
Cicero translates *Temperantia*, is a very indefinite and ambiguous word, and it admits, therefore, of a variety of applications: it may mean discretion, or abstinence, or keeping a level
head. Courage is not a virtue at all; although sometimes it is a
servant or instrument of virtue; but it is just as ready to become the servant of the greatest villainy. It is really a quality
of temperament. Even Geulinx (in the preface to this *Ethics*)

[1] Edit. of 1819, vol. vi., p. 372.

condemned the Platonic virtues and put the following in their place: Diligence, Obedience, Justice and Humility; which are obviously bad. The Chinese distinguish five cardinal virtues: Sympathy, Justice, Propriety, Wisdom, and Sincerity. The virtues of Christianity are theological, not cardinal: Faith, Love, and Hope.

Fundamental disposition towards others, assuming the character either of Envy or of Sympathy, is the point at which the moral virtues and vices of mankind first diverge. These two diametrically opposite qualities exist in every man; for they spring from the inevitable comparison which he draws between his own lot and that of others. According as the result of this comparison affects his individual character does the one or the other of these qualities become the source and principle of all his action. Envy builds the wall between *Thee* and *Me* thicker and stronger; Sympathy makes it slight and transparent; nay, sometimes it pulls down the wall altogether; and then the distinction between self and not-self vanishes.

Valour, which has been mentioned as a virtue, or rather the Courage on which it is based (for valour is only courage in war), deserves a closer examination. The ancients reckoned Courage among the virtues, and cowardice among the vices; but there is no corresponding idea in the Christian scheme, which makes for charity and patience, and in its teaching forbids all enmity or even resistance. The result is that with the moderns Courage is no longer a virtue. Nevertheless it must be admitted that cowardice does not seem to be very compatible with any nobility of character—if only for the reason that it betrays an overgreat apprehension about one's own person.

Courage, however, may also be explained as a readiness to meet ills that threaten at the moment, in order to avoid greater ills that lie in the future; whereas cowardice does the contrary. But this readiness is of the same quality as *patience*, for patience consists in the clear consciousness that greater evils than those which are present, and that any violent attempt to flee from or guard against the ills we have may bring the others upon us. Courage, then, would be a kind of patience; and since it is patience that enables us to practise forbearance and self control, Courage is, through the medium of patience, at least akin to virtue.

But perhaps Courage admits of being considered from a higher point of view. The fear of death may in every case be traced to a deficiency in that natural philosophy—natural, and therefore resting on mere feeling—which gives a man the assurance that he exists in everything outside him just as much as in his own person; so that the death of his person can do him little harm. But it is just this very assurance that would give a man heroic Courage; and therefore, as the reader will recollect from my *Ethics*, Courage comes from the same source as the virtues of Justice and Humanity. This is, I admit, to take a very high view of the matter; but apart from it I cannot well explain why cowardice seems contemptible, and personal courage a noble and sublime thing; for no lower point of view enables me to see why a finite individual who is everything to himself—nay, who is himself even the very fundamental condition of the existence of the rest of the world—should not put his own preservation above every other aim. It is, then, an insufficient explanation of Courage to make it rest only on utility, to give it an empirical and not a transcendental character. It may have been for some such reason that Calderon once uttered a sceptical but remarkable opinion in regard to Courage, nay, actually denied its reality; and put his denial into the mouth of a wise old minister, addressing his young sovereign. "Although," he observed, "natural fear is operative in all alike, a man may be brave in not letting it be seen; and it is this that constitutes Courage":

> *Que aunque el natural temor*
> *En todos obra igualmente,*
> *No mostrarle es ser valiente*
> *Y esto es lo que hace el valor.*[2]

In regard to the difference which I have mentioned between the ancients and the moderns in their estimate of Courage as a virtue, it must be remembered that by Virtue, *virtus*, ἀρετή, the ancients understood every excellence or quality that was praiseworthy in itself, it might be moral or intellectual, or possibly only physical. But when Christianity demonstrated that the fundamental tendency of life was moral, it was moral superiority alone than henceforth attached to the notion of Vir-

[2] *La Hija del Aire*, ii., 2.

tue. Meanwhile the earlier usage still survived in the elder Latinists, and also in Italian writers, as is proved by the well-known meaning of the word *virtuoso*. The special attention of students should be drawn to this wider range of the idea of Virtue amongst the ancients, as otherwise it might easily be a source of secret perplexity. I may recommend two passages preserved for us by Stobæus, which will serve this purpose. One of them is apparently from the Pythagorean philosopher Metopos, in which the fitness of every bodily member is declared to be a virtue. The other pronounces that the virtue of a shoemaker is to make good shoes. This may also serve to explain why it is that in the ancient scheme of ethics virtues and vices are mentioned which find no place in ours.

As the place of Courage amongst the virtues is a matter of doubt, so is that of Avarice amongst the vices. It must not, however, be confounded with greed, which is the most immediate meaning of the Latin word *avaritia*. Let us then draw up and examine the arguments *pro et contra* in regard to Avarice, and leave the final judgment to be formed by every man for himself.

On the one hand it is argued that it is not Avarice which is a vice, but extravagance, its opposite. Extravagance springs from a brutish limitation to the present moment, in comparison with which the future, existing as it does only in thought, is as nothing. It rests upon the illusion that sensual pleasures possess a positive or real value. Accordingly, future need and misery is the price at which the spendthrift purchases pleasures that are empty, fleeting, and often no more than imaginary; or else feeds his vain, stupid self-conceit on the bows and scrapes of parasites who laugh at him in secret, or on the gaze of the mob and those who envy his magnificence. We should, therefore, shun the spendthrift as though he had the plague, and on discovering his vice break with him betimes, in order that later on, when the consequences of his extravagance ensue, we may neither have to help to bear them, nor, on the other hand, have to play the part of the friends of Timon of Athens.

At the same time it is not to be expected that he who foolishly squanders his own fortune will leave another man's intact, if it should chance to be committed to his keeping; nay, *sui profusus* and *alieni appetens* are by Sallust very rightly conjoined. Hence it is that extravagance leads not only to impoverishment but also to crime; and crime amongst the moneyed classes is almost always the result of extravagance. It is accordingly with justice that the *Koran* declares all spendthrifts to be "brothers of Satan."

But it is superfluity that Avarice brings in its train, and when was superfluity ever unwelcome? That must be a good vice which has good consequences. Avarice proceeds upon the principle that all pleasure is only negative in its operation and that the happiness which consists of a series of pleasures is a chimæra; that, on the contrary, it is pains which are positive and extremely real. Accordingly, the avaricious man foregoes the former in order that he may be the better preserved from the latter, and thus it is that *bear and forbear—sustine et abstine*—is his maxim. And because he knows, further, how inexhaustible are the possibilities of misfortune, and how innumerable the paths of danger, he increases the means of avoiding them, in order, if possible, to surround himself with a triple wall of protection. Who, then, can say where precaution against disaster begins to be exaggerated? He alone who knows where the malignity of fate reaches its limit. And even if precaution were exaggerated it is an error which at the most would hurt the man who took it, and not others. If he will never need the treasures which he lays up for himself, they will one day benefit others whom nature has made less careful. That until then he withdraws the money from circulation is no misfortune; for money is not an article of consumption: it only represents the good things which a man may actually possess, and is not one itself. Coins are only counters; their value is what they represent; and what they represent cannot be withdrawn from circulation. Moreover, by holding back the money, the value of the remainder which is in circulation is enhanced by precisely the same amount. Even though it be the case, as is said, that many a miser comes in the end to love money itself for its own sake, it is equally certain that many a spendthrift, on the other hand, loves spending and squandering for no better reason. Friendship with a miser is not only without danger, but it is profitable, because of the great advantages it can bring. For it is doubtless those who are nearest and dearest to the miser who on his death will reap the fruits of the self-control which he exercised; but even in his lifetime, too, something may be expected of him in cases of great need. At any rate one can always hope for more from him than from the spendthrift, who has lost his all and is himself helpless and in debt. *Mas dà el duro que el desnudo,* says a Spanish proverb; the man who has a hard heart will give more than the man who has an empty purse. The upshot of all this is that Avarice is not a vice.

On the other side, it may be said that Avarice is the quintessence of all vices. When physical pleasures seduce a man from the right path, it is his sensual nature—the animal part of him —which is at fault. He is carried away by its attractions, and, overcome by the impression of the moment, he acts without thinking of the consequences. When, on the other hand, he is brought by age or bodily weakness to the condition in which the vices that he could never abandon end by abandoning him, and his capacity for physical pleasure dies—if he turns to Avarice, the intellectual desire survives the sensual. Money, which represents all the good things of this world, and is these good things in the abstract, now becomes the dry trunk overgrown with all the dead lusts of the flesh, which are egoism in the abstract. They come to life again in the love of the Mammon. The transient pleasure of the senses has become a deliberate and calculated lust of money, which, like that to which it is directed, is symbolical in its nature, and, like it, indestructible.

This obstinate love of the pleasures of the world—a love which, as it were, outlives itself; this utterly incorrigible sin, this refined and sublimated desire of the flesh, is the abstract form in which all lusts are concentrated, and to which it stands like a general idea to individual particulars. Accordingly, Avarice is the vice of age, just as extravagance is the vice of youth.

This *disputatio in utramque partem*—this debate for and against—is certainly calculated to drive us into accepting the *juste milieu* morality of Aristotle; a conclusion that is also supported by the following consideration.

Every human perfection is allied to a defect into which it threatens to pass; but it is also true that every defect is allied to a perfection. Hence it is that if, as often happens, we make a mistake about a man, it is because at the beginning of our acquaintance with him we confound his defects with the kinds of perfection to which they are allied. The cautious man seems to us a coward; the economical man, a miser; the spendthrift seems liberal; the rude fellow, downright and sincere; the fool-hardy person looks as if he were going to work with a noble self-confidence; and so on in many other cases.

No one can live among men without feeling drawn again and again to the tempting supposition that moral baseness and intellectual incapacity are closely connected, as though they both sprang direct from one source. That that, however, is not so, I have shown in detail. That it seems to be so is merely due to the fact that both are so often found together; and the circumstance is to be explained by the very frequent occur-rence of each of them, so that it may easily happen for both to be compelled to live under one roof. At the same time it is not to be denied that they play into each other's hands to their mutual benefit; and it is this that produces the very un-edifying spectacle which only too many men exhibit, and that makes the world to go as it goes. A man who is unintelligent is very likely to show his perfidy, villainy and malice; whereas a clever man understands how to conceal these qualities. And how often, on the other hand, does a perversity of heart pre-vent a man from seeing truths which his intelligence is quite capable of grasping!

Nevertheless, let no one boast. Just as every man, though he be the greatest genius, has very definite limitations in some one sphere of knowledge, and thus attests his common origin with the essentially perverse and stupid mass of mankind, so also has every man something in his nature which is positively evil. Even the best, nay the noblest, character will sometimes surprise us by isolated traits of depravity; as though it were to acknowledge his kinship with the human race, in which villainy—nay, cruelty—is to be found in that degree. For it was just in virtue of this evil in him, this bad principle, that of necessity he became a man. And for the same reason the world in general is what my clear mirror of it has shown it to be.

But in spite of all this the difference even between one man and another is incalculably great, and many a one would be horrified to see another as he really is. Oh, for some Asmodeus of morality, to make not only roofs and walls transparent to his favourites, but also to lift the veil of dissimulation, fraud, hypocrisy, pretence, falsehood and deception, which is spread over all things! to show how little true honesty there is in the world, and how often, even where it is least to be expected, behind all the exterior outwork of virtue, secretly and in the innermost recesses, unrighteousness sits at the helm! It is just on this account that so many men of the better kind have four-footed friends: for, to be sure, how is a man to get relief from the endless dissimulation, falsity and malice of mankind, if there were no dogs into whose honest faces he can look without distrust?

For what is our civilised world but a big masquerade? where you meet knights, priests, soldiers, men of learning, barristers, clergymen, philosophers, and I don't know what all! But they are not what they pretend to be; they are only masks, and, as a rule, behind the masks you will find money-makers. One man, I suppose, puts on the mask of law, which he has borrowed for the purpose from a barrister, only in order to be able to give another man a sound drubbing; a second has chosen the mask of patriotism and the public welfare with a similar intent; a third takes religion or purity of doctrine. For all sorts of purposes men have often put on the mask of philosophy, and even of philanthropy, and I know not what besides. Women have a smaller choice. As a rule they avail themselves of the mask of morality, modesty, domesticity, and humility. Then there are general masks, without any particular character attaching to them like dominoes. They may be met with everywhere; and of this sort is the strict rectitude, the courtesy, the sincere sympathy, the smiling friendship, that people profess. The whole of these masks as a rule are merely, as I have said, a disguise for some industry, commerce, or speculation. It is merchants alone who in this respect constitute any honest class. They are the only people who give themselves out to be what they are; and therefore they go about without any mask at all, and consequently take a humble rank.

It is very necessary that a man should be apprised early in life that it is a masquerade in which he finds himself. For

otherwise there are many things which he will fail to understand and put up with, nay, at which he will be completely
puzzled, and that man longest of all whose heart is made of
better clay—

Et meliore luto finxit prœcordia Titan.[3]

Such for instance is the favour that villainy finds; the neglect
that merit, even the rarest and the greatest, suffers at the hands
of those of the same profession; the hatred of truth and great
capacity; the ignorance of scholars in their own province; and
the fact that true wares are almost always despised and the
merely specious ones in request. Therefore let even the young
be instructed betimes that in this masquerade the apples are
of wax, the flowers of silk, the fish of pasteboard, and that all
things—yes, all things—are toys and trifles; and that of two
men whom he may see earnestly engaged in business, one is
supplying spurious goods and the other paying for them in
false coin.

But there are more serious reflections to be made, and worse
things to be recorded. Man is at bottom a savage, horrible
beast. We know it, if only in the business of taming and restraining him which we call civilisation. Hence it is that we
are terrified if now and then his nature breaks out. Wherever
and whenever the locks and chains of law and order fall off
and give place to anarchy, he shows himself for what he is.
But it is unnecessary to wait for anarchy in order to gain enlightenment on this subject. A hundred records, old and new,
produce the conviction that in his unrelenting cruelty man is
in no way inferior to the tiger and the hyæna. A forcible
example is supplied by a publication of the year 1841 entitled
*Slavery and the Internal Slave Trade in the United States of
North America: being replies to questions transmitted by the
British Anti-slavery Society to the American Anti-slavery Society.* This book constitutes one of the heaviest indictments
against the human race. No one can put it down without a feeling of horror, and few without tears. For whatever the reader
may have ever heard, or imagined, or dreamt, of the unhappy
condition of slavery, or indeed of human cruelty in general, it
will seem small to him when he reads of the way in which those

[3] Juvenal, *Sat.* 14, 34.

devils in human form, those bigoted, church-going, strictly Sabbatarian rascals—and in particular the Anglican priests among them—treated their innocent black brothers, who by wrong and violence had got into their diabolical clutches.

Other examples are furnished by Tshudi's *Travels in Peru*, in the description which he gives of the treatment of the Peruvian soldiers at the hands of their officers; and by Macleod's *Travels in Eastern Africa*, where the author tells of the cold-blooded and truly devilish cruelty with which the Portuguese in Mozambique treat their slaves. But we need not go for examples to the New World, that obverse side of our planet. In the year 1848 it was brought to life that in England, not in one, but apparently in a hundred cases within a brief period, a husband had poisoned his wife or *vice versa*, or both had joined in poisoning their children, or in torturing them slowly to death by starving and ill-treating them, with no other object than to get the money for burying them which they had insured in the Burial Clubs against their death. For this purpose a child was often insured in several, even in as many as twenty clubs at once.[4]

Details of this character belong, indeed, to the blackest pages in the criminal records of humanity. But, when all is said, it is the inward and innate character of man, this god *par excellence* of the Pantheists, from which they and everything like them proceed. In every man there dwells, first and foremost, a colossal egoism, which breaks the bounds of right and justice with the greatest freedom, as everyday life shows on a small scale, and as history on every page of it on a large. Does not the recognised need of a balance of power in Europe, with the anxious way in which it is preserved, demonstrate that man is a beast of prey, who no sooner sees a weaker man near him than he falls upon him without fail? and does not the same hold good of the affairs of ordinary life?

But to the boundless egoism of our nature there is joined more or less in every human breast a fund of hatred, anger, envy, rancour and malice, accumulated like the venom in a serpent's tooth, and waiting only for an opportunity of venting itself, and then, like a demon unchained, of storming and rag-

[4] Cf. *The Times*, 20th, 22nd and 23rd Sept., 1848, and also 12th Dec., 1853.

ing. If a man has no great occasion for breaking out, he will end by taking advantage of the smallest, and by working it up into something great by the aid of his imagination; for, however small it may be, it is enough to rouse his anger—

Quantulacunque adeo est occasio, sufficit irae[5]—

and then he will carry it as far as he can and may. We see this in daily life, where such outbursts are well known under the name of "venting one's gall on something." It will also have been observed that if such outbursts meet with no opposition the subject of them feels decidedly the better for them afterwards. That anger is not without its pleasure is a truth that was recorded even by Aristotle;[6] and he quotes a passage from Homer, who declares anger to be sweeter than honey. But not in anger alone—in hatred too, which stands to anger like a chronic to an acute disease, a man may indulge with the greatest delight:

> Now hatred is by far the longest pleasure,
> Men love in haste, but they detest at leisure.[7]

Gobineau in his work *Les Races Humaines* has called man *l'animal méchant par excellence*. People take this very ill, because they feel that it hits them; but he is quite right, for man is the only animal which causes pain to others without any further purpose than just to cause it. Other animals never do it except to satisfy their hunger, or in the rage of combat. If it is said against the tiger that he kills more than eats, he strangles his prey only for the purpose of eating it; and if he cannot eat it, the only explanation is, as the French phrase has it, that *ses yeux sont plus grands que son estomac*. No animal ever torments another for the mere purpose of tormenting, but man does it, and it is this that constitutes the diabolical feature in his character which is so much worse than the merely animal. I have already spoken of the matter in its broad aspect; but it is manifest even in small things, and every reader has a daily opportunity of observing it. For instance, if two little dogs are playing together—and what a genial and charming

5 Juvenal, *Sat.* 13, 183.
6 *Rhet.*, i., 11; ii., 2.
7 Byron, *Don Juan*, c. xiii. 6.

sight it is—and a child of three or four years joins them, it is almost inevitable for it to begin hitting them with a whip or stick, and thereby show itself, even at that age, *l'animal méchant par excellence.* The love of teasing and playing tricks, which is common enough, may be traced to the same source. For instance, if a man has expressed his annoyance at any interruption or other petty inconvenience, there will be no lack of people who for that very reason will bring it about: *animal méchant par excellence!* This is so certain that a man should be careful not to express any annoyance at small evils. On the other hand he should also be careful not to express his pleasure at any trifle, for, if he does so, men will act like the jailer who, when he found that his prisoner had performed the laborious task of taming a spider, and took a pleasure in watching it, immediately crushed it under his foot: *l'animal méchant par excellence!* This is why all animals are instinctively afraid of the sight, or even of the track of a man, that *animal méchant par excellence!* nor does their instinct play them false; for it is man alone who hunts game for which he has no use and which does him no harm.

It is a fact, then, that in the heart of every man there lies a wild beast which only waits for an opportunity to storm and rage, in its desire to inflict pain on others, or, if they stand in his way, to kill them. It is this which is the source of all the lust of war and battle. In trying to tame and to some extent hold it in check, the intelligence, its appointed keeper, has always enough to do. People may, if they please, call it the radical evil of human nature—a name which will at least serve those with whom a word stands for an explanation. I say, however, that it is the will to live, which, more and more embittered by the constant sufferings of existence, seeks to alleviate its own torment by causing torment in others. But in this way a man gradually develops in himself real cruelty and malice. The observation may also be added that as, according to Kant, matter subsists only through the antagonism of the powers of expansion and contraction, so human society subsists only by the antagonism of hatred, or anger, and fear. For there is a moment in the life of all of us when the malignity of our nature might perhaps make us murderers, if it were not accompanied by a due admixture of fear to keep it within bounds; and this fear, again, would make a man the sport and laughing stock of every boy, if anger were not lying ready in him, and keeping watch.

But it is *Schadenfreude*, a mischievous delight in the misfortunes of others, which remains the worst trait in human nature. It is a feeling which is closely akin to cruelty, and differs from it, to say the truth, only as theory from practice. In general, it may be said of it that it takes the place which pity ought to take—pity which is its opposite, and the true source of all real justice and charity.

Envy is also opposed to pity, but in another sense; envy, that is to say, is produced by a cause directly antagonistic to that which produces the delight in mischief. The opposition between pity and envy on the one hand, and pity and the delight in mischief on the other, rests, in the main, on the occasions which call them forth. In the case of envy it is only as a direct effect of the cause which excites it that we feel it at all. That is just the reason why envy, although it is a reprehensible feeling, still admits of some excuse, and is, in general, a very human quality; whereas the delight in mischief is diabolical, and its taunts are the laughter of hell.

The delight in mischief, as I have said, takes the place which pity ought to take. Envy, on the contrary, finds a place only where there is no inducement to pity, or rather an inducement to its opposite; and it is just as this opposite that envy arises in the human breast; and so far, therefore, it·may still be reckoned a human sentiment. Nay, I am afraid that no one will be found to be entirely free from it. For that a man should feel his own lack of things more bitterly at the sight of another's delight in the enjoyment of them, is natural; nay, it is inevitable; but this should not rouse his hatred of the man who is happier than himself. It is just this hatred, however, in which true envy consists. Least of all should a man be envious, when it is a question, not of the gifts of fortune, or chance, or another's favour, but of the gifts of nature; because everything that is innate in a man rests on a metaphysical basis, and possesses justification of a higher kind; it is, so to speak, given him by Divine grace. But, unhappily, it is just in the case of personal advantages that envy is most irreconcilable. Thus it is that intelligence, or even genius, cannot get

on in the world without begging pardon for its existence,
wherever it is not in a position to be able, proudly and boldly,
to despise the world.

In other words, if envy is aroused only by wealth, rank, or
power, it is often kept down by egoism, which perceives that,
on occasion, assistance, enjoyment, support, protection, advancement, and so on, may be hoped for from the object of
envy or that at least by intercourse with him a man may himself win honour from the reflected light of his superiority; and
here, too, there is the hope of one day attaining all those advantages himself. On the other hand, in the envy that is directed to natural gifts and personal advantages, like beauty in
women, or intelligence in men, there is no consolation or hope
of one kind or the other; so that nothing remains but to indulge
a bitter and irreconcilable hatred of the person who possesses
these privileges; and hence the only remaining desire is to take
vengeance on him.

But here the envious man finds himself in an unfortunate
position; for all his blows fall powerless as soon as it is known
that they come from him. Accordingly he hides his feelings
as carefully as if they were secret sins, and so becomes an
inexhaustible inventor of tricks and artifices and devices for
concealing and masking his procedure, in order that, unper-
ceived, he may wound the object of his envy. For instance,
with an air of the utmost unconcern he will ignore the advantages which are eating his heart out; he will neither see
them, nor know them, nor have observed or even heard of
them, and thus make himself a master in the art of dissimulation. With great cunning he will completely overlook the man
whose brilliant qualities are gnawing at his heart, and act as
though he were quite an unimportant person; he will take no
notice of him, and, on occasion, will have even quite forgotten
his existence. But at the same time he will before all things
endeavour by secret machination carefully to deprive those
advantages of any opportunity of showing themselves and becoming known. Then out of his dark corner he will attack these
qualities with censure, mockery, ridicule and calumny, like
the toad which spurts its poison from a hole. No less will he
enthusiastically praise unimportant people, or even indifferent
or bad performances in the same sphere. In short, he will be-

come a Proteas in stratagem, in order to wound others without showing himself. But what is the use of it? The trained eye recognises him in spite of it all. He betrays himself, if by nothing else, by the way in which he timidly avoids and flies from the object of his envy, who stands the more completely alone, the more brilliant he is; and this is the reason why pretty girls have no friends of their own sex. He betrays himself, too, by the causeless hatred which he shows—a hatred which finds vent in a violent explosion at any circumstance however trivial, though it is often only the product of his imagination. How many such men there are in the world may be recognised by the universal praise of modesty, that is, of a virtue invented on behalf of dull and commonplace people. Nevertheless, it is a virtue which, by exhibiting the necessity for dealing considerately with the wretched plight of these people, is just what calls attention to it.

For our self-consciousness and our pride there can be nothing more flattering than the sight of envy lurking in its retreat and plotting its schemes; but never let a man forget that where there is envy there is hatred, and let him be careful not to make a false friend out of any envious person. Therefore it is important to our safety to lay envy bare; and a man should study to discover its tricks, as it is everywhere to be found and always goes about *incognito;* or as I have said, like a venomous toad it lurks in dark corners. It deserves neither quarter nor sympathy; but as we can never reconcile it let our rule of conduct be to scorn it with a good heart, and as our happiness and glory is torture to it we may rejoice in its sufferings:

> *Den Neid wirst nimmer du versöhnen;*
> *So magst du ihn getrost verhöhnen.*
> *Dein Glück, dein Ruhm ist ihm ein Leiden:*
> *Magst drum an seiner Quaal dich weiden.*

We have been taking a look at the *depravity* of man, and it is a sight which may well fill us with horror. But now we must cast our eyes on the *misery* of his existence; and when we have done so, and are horrified by that too, we must look back again at his depravity. We shall then find that they hold the balance to each other. We shall perceive the eternal justice of things; for we shall recognise that the world is itself the Last

Judgment on it, and we shall begin to understand why it is that everything that lives must pay the penalty of its existence, first in living and then in dying. Thus the evil of the penalty accords with the evil of the sin—*malum pœnæ* with *malum culpæ*. From the same point of view we lose our indignation at that intellectual incapacity of the great majority of mankind which in life so often disgusts us. In this *Sansara*, as the Buddhists call it, human misery, human depravity and human folly correspond with one another perfectly, and they are of like magnitude. But if, on some special inducement, we direct our gaze to one of them, and survey it in particular, it seems to exceed the other two. This, however, is an illusion, and merely the effect of their colossal range.

All things proclaim this *Sansara;* more than all else, the world of mankind; in which, from a moral point of view, villainy and baseness, and from an intellectual point of view, incapacity and stupidity, prevail to a horrifying extent. Nevertheless, there appear in it, although very spasmodically, and always as a fresh surprise, manifestations of honesty, of goodness, nay, even of nobility; and also of great intelligence, of the thinking mind of genius. They never quite vanish, but like single points of light gleam upon us out of the great dark mass. We must accept them as a pledge that this *Sansara* contains a good and redeeming principle, which is capable of breaking through and of filling and freeing the whole of it.

The readers of my *Ethics* know that with me the ultimate foundation of morality is the truth which in the *Vedas* and the *Vedanta* receives its expression in the established, mystical formula, *Tat twam asi* (*This is thyself*), which is spoken with reference to every living thing, be it man or beast, and is called the *Mahavakya*, the great word.

Actions which proceed in accordance with this principle, such as those of the philanthropist, may indeed be regarded as the beginning of mysticism. Every benefit rendered with a pure intention proclaims that the man who exercises it acts in direct conflict with the world of appearance; for he recognises himself as identical with another individual, who exists in complete separation from him. Accordingly, all disinterested kindness is inexplicable; it is a mystery; and hence in order to explain it a man has to resort to all sorts of fictions. When Kant had demolished all other arguments for theism, he admitted one only, that it gave the best interpretation and solution of such mysterious actions, and of all others like them. He therefore allowed it to stand as a presumption unsusceptible indeed of theoretical proof, but valid from a practical point of view. I may, however, express my doubts whether he was quite serious about it. For to make morality rest on theism is really to reduce morality to egoism; although the English, it is true, as also the lowest classes of society with us, do not perceive the possibility of any other foundation for it.

The above-mentioned recognition of a man's own true being in another individual objectively presented to him, is exhibited in a particularly beautiful and clear way in the cases in which a man, already destined to death beyond any hope of rescue, gives himself up to the welfare of others with great solicitude and zeal, and tries to save them. Of this kind is the well-known story of a servant who was bitten in a courtyard at night by a mad dog. In the belief that she was beyond hope, she seized the dog and dragged it into a stable, which she then locked, so that no one else might be bitten. Then again there is the incident in Naples, which Tischbein has immortalised in one of his *aquarelles.* A son, fleeing from the lava which is rapidly streaming toward the sea, is carrying his aged father on his back. When there is only a narrow strip of land left between the devouring elements, the father bids the son put him down, so that the son may save himself by flight, as otherwise both will be lost. The son obeys, and as he goes casts a glance of farewell on his father. This is the moment depicted. The historical circumstance which Scott represents in his masterly way in *The Heart of Midlothian,* chap. ii., is of a precisely similar kind; where, of two delinquents condemned to death, the one who by his awkwardness caused the capture of the other happily sets him free in the chapel by overpowering the guard after the execution-sermon, without at the same time making any attempt on his own behalf. Nay, in the same category must also be placed the scene which is represented in a common engraving, which may perhaps be objectionable to western readers—I mean the one in which a soldier, kneeling

to be shot, is trying by waving a cloth to frighten away his
dog who wants to come to him.

In all these cases we see an individual in the face of his
own immediate and certain destruction no longer thinking of
saving himself, so that he may direct the whole of his efforts
to saving some one else. How could there be a clearer expression of the consciousness that what is being destroyed is only
a phenomenon, and that the destruction itself is only a phenomenon; that, on the other hand, the real being of the man
who meets his death is untouched by that event, and lives on
in the other man, in whom even now, as his action betrays, he
so clearly perceives it to exist? For if this were not so, and it
was his real being which was about to be annihilated, how
could that being spend its last efforts in showing such an ardent
sympathy in the welfare and continued existence of another?

There are two different ways in which a man may become
conscious of his own existence. On the one hand, he may have
an empirical perception of it, as it manifests itself externally—
something so small that it approaches vanishing point; set in
a world which, as regards time and space, is infinite; one only
of the thousand millions of human creatures who run about
on this planet for a very brief period and are renewed every
thirty years. On the other hand, by going down into the depths
of his own nature, a man may become conscious that he is all
in all; that, in fact, he is the only real being; and that, in
addition, this real being perceives itself again in others, who
present themselves from without, as though they formed a
mirror of himself.

Of these two ways in which a man may come to know what
he is, the first grasps the phenomenon alone, the mere product
of *the principle of individuation;* whereas the second makes a
man immediately conscious that he is *the thing-in-itself.* This
is a doctrine in which, as regards the first way, I have Kant,
and as regards both, I have the *Vedas,* to support me.

There is, it is true, a simple objection to the second method.
It may be said to assume that one and the same being can
exist in different places at the same time, and yet be complete
in each of them. Although, from an empirical point of view,
this is the most palpable impossibility—nay, absurdity—it is
nevertheless perfectly true of the thing-in-itself. The impossi-

bility and the absurdity of it, empirically, are only due to the forms which phenomena assume, in accordance with the principle of individuation. For the thing-in-itself, the will to live, exists whole and undivided in every being, even in the smallest, as completely as in the sum-total of all things that ever were or are or will be. This is why every being, even the smallest, says to itself, So long as I am safe, let the world perish—*dum ego salvus sim, pereat mundus*. And, in truth, even if only one individual were left in the world, and all the rest were to perish, the one that remained would still possess the whole self-being of the world, uninjured and undiminished, and would laugh at the destruction of the world as an illusion. This conclusion *per impossible* may be balanced by the counter-conclusion, which is on all fours with it, that if that last individual were to be annihilated in and with him the whole world would be destroyed. It was in this sense that the mystic Angelus Silesius declared that God could not live for a moment without him, and that if he were to be annihilated God must of necessity give up the ghost:

Ich weiss dass ohne mich Gott nicht ein Nu kann leben;
Werd' ich zunicht, er muss von Noth den Geist aufgeben.

But the empirical point of view also to some extent enables us to perceive that it is true, or at least possible, that our self can exist in other beings whose consciousness is separated and different from our own. That this is so is shown by the experience of somnambulists. Although the identity of their ego is preserved throughout, they know nothing, when they awake, of all that a moment before they themselves said, did or suffered. So entirely is the individual consciousness a phenomenon that even in the same ego two consciousnesses can arise of which the one knows nothing of the other.

XIX

OF WOMEN

(from PARERGA*)*

Schiller's poem in honor of women, *Würde der Frauen,* is the result of much careful thought, and it appeals to the reader by its antithetic style and its use of contrast; but as an expression of the true praise which should be accorded to them, it is, I think, inferior to these few words of Jouy's: *Without women, the beginning of our life would be helpless; the middle, devoid of pleasure; and the end, of consolation.* The same thing is more feelingly expressed by Byron in *Sardanapalus:*

> The very first
> Of human life must spring from woman's breast,
> Your first small words are taught you from her lips,
> Your first tears quench'd by her, and your last sighs
> Too often breathed out in a woman's hearing,
> When men have shrunk from the ignoble care
> Of watching the last hour of him who led them.
> (Act I. Scene 2.)

These two passages indicate the right standpoint for the appreciation of women.

You need only look at the way in which she is formed, to see that woman is not meant to undergo great labor, whether of the mind or of the body. She pays the debt of life not by what she does, but by what she suffers; by the pains of child-bearing and care for the child, and by submission to her husband, to whom she should be a patient and cheering companion. The keenest sorrows and joys are not for her, nor is she called upon to display a great deal of strength. The current of her life should be more gentle, peaceful and trivial than man's, without being essentially happier or unhappier.

Women are directly fitted for acting as the nurses and teachers of our early childhood by the fact that they are themselves childish, frivolous and short-sighted; in a word, they are big children all their life long—a kind of intermediate stage between the child and the full-grown man, who is man in the strict sense of the word. See how a girl will fondle a child for days together, dance with it and sing to it; and then think what a man, with the best will in the world, could do if he were put in her place.

With young girls Nature seems to have had in view what, in the language of the drama, is called *a striking effect;* as for a few years she dowers them with a wealth of beauty and is lavish in her gift of charm, at the expense of all the rest of their life; so that during those years they may capture the fantasy of some man to such a degree that he is hurried away into undertaking the honorable care of them, in some form or other, as long as they live—a step for which there would not appear to be any sufficient warranty if reason only directed his thoughts. Accordingly, Nature has equipped woman, as she does all her creatures, with the weapons and implements requisite for the safeguarding of her existence, and for just as long as it is necessary for her to have them. Here, as elsewhere, Nature proceeds with her usual economy; for just as the female ant, after fecundation, loses her wings, which are then superfluous, nay, actually a danger to the business of breeding; so, after giving birth to one or two children, a woman generally loses her beauty; probably, indeed, for similar reasons.

And so we find that young girls, in their hearts, look upon domestic affairs or work of any kind as of secondary importance, if not actually as a mere jest. The only business that really claims their earnest attention is love, making conquests, and everything connected with this—dress, dancing, and so on.

The nobler and more perfect a thing is, the later and slower it is in arriving at maturity. A man reaches the maturity of his reasoning powers and mental faculties hardly before the age of twenty-eight; a woman at eighteen. And then, too, in the case of woman, it is only reason of a sort—very niggard in its dimensions. That is why women remain children their whole life long; never seeing anything but what is quite close to them, cleaving to the present moment, taking appearance for reality, and preferring trifles to matters of the first importance. For it is by virtue of his reasoning faculty that man does not live in the present only, like the brute, but looks about him and considers the past and the future; and this is the origin of prudence, as well as of that care and anxiety which so many people exhibit. Both the advantages and the disadvantages which this involves, are shared in by the woman to a smaller extent because of her weaker power of reasoning. She may, in fact, be described as intellectually short-sighted, because, while she has an intuitive understanding of what lies quite close to her, her field of vision is narrow and does not reach to what is remote; so that things which are absent, or past, or to come, have much less effect upon women than upon men. This is the reason why women are more often inclined to be extravagant, and sometimes carry their inclination to a length that borders upon madness. In their hearts, women think that it is men's business to earn money and theirs to spend it—if possible during their husband's life, but, at any rate, after his death. The very fact that their husband hands them over his earnings for purposes of housekeeping, strengthens them in this belief.

However many disadvantages all this may involve, there is at least this to be said in its favor; that the woman lives more in the present than the man, and that, if the present is at all tolerable, she enjoys it more eagerly. This is the source of that cheerfulness which is peculiar to women, fitting her to amuse man in his hours of recreation, and, in case of need, to console him when he is borne down by the weight of his cares.

It is by no means a bad plan to consult women in matters of difficulty, as the Germans used to do in ancient times; for their way of looking at things is quite different from ours, chiefly in the fact that they like to take the shortest way to their goal, and, in general, manage to fix their eyes upon what lies before them; while we, as a rule, see far beyond it, just because it is in front of our noses. In cases like this, we need to be brought back to the right standpoint, so as to recover the near and simple view.

Then, again, women are decidedly more sober in their judgment than we are, so that they do not see more in things than is really there; whilst, if our passions are aroused, we are apt to see things in an exaggerated way, or imagine what does not exist.

The weakness of their reasoning faculty also explains why it is that women show more sympathy for the unfortunate than men do, and so treat them with more kindness and interest; and why it is that, on the contrary, they are inferior to men in point of justice, and less honorable and conscientious. For it is just because their reasoning power is weak that present circumstances have such a hold over them, and those concrete things, which lie directly before their eyes, exercise a power which is seldom counteracted to any extent by abstract principles of thought, by fixed rules of conduct, firm resolutions, or, in general, by consideration for the past and the future, or regard for what is absent and remote. Accordingly, they possess the first and main elements that go to make a virtuous character, but they are deficient in those secondary qualities which are often a necessary instrument in the formation of it.[1]

Hence, it will be found that the fundamental fault of the female character is that it has *no sense of justice*. This is mainly due to the fact, already mentioned, that women are defective in the powers of reasoning and deliberation; but it is also traceable to the position which Nature has assigned to them as the weaker sex. They are dependent, not upon strength, but upon craft; and hence their instinctive capacity for cunning, and their ineradicable tendency to say what is not true. For as lions are provided with claws and teeth, and elephants and boars with tusks, bulls with horns, and cuttle fish with its clouds of inky fluid, so Nature has equipped woman, for her defence and protection, with the arts of dissimulation; and all the power which Nature has conferred upon man in the shape of physical strength and reason, has been bestowed upon women in this form. Hence, dissimulation is innate in woman, and almost as much a quality of the stupid as of the clever. It is as natural for them to make use of it on every

[1] In this respect they may be compared to an animal organism which contains a liver but no gall-bladder. Here let me refer to what I have said in my treatise on *The Foundation of Morals,* § 17.

occasion as it is for those animals to employ their means of defence when they are attacked; they have a feeling that in doing so they are only within their rights. Therefore a woman who is perfectly truthful and not given to dissimulation is perhaps an impossibility, and for this very reason they are so quick at seeing through dissimulation in others that it is not a wise thing to attempt it with them. But this fundamental defect which I have stated, with all that it entails, gives rise to falsity, faithlessness, treachery, ingratitude, and so on. Perjury in a court of justice is more often committed by women than by men. It may, indeed, be generally questioned whether women ought to be sworn in at all. From time to time one finds repeated cases everywhere of ladies, who want for nothing, taking things from shop-counters when no one is looking, and making off with them.

Nature has appointed that the propagation of the species shall be the business of men who are young, strong and handsome; so that the race may not degenerate. This is the firm will and purpose of Nature in regard to the species, and it finds its expression in the passions of women. There is no law that is older or more powerful than this. Woe, then, to the man who sets up claims and interests that will conflict with it; whatever he may say and do, they will be unmercifully crushed at the first serious encounter. For the innate rule that governs women's conduct, though it is secret and unformulated, nay, unconscious in its working, is this: *We are justified in deceiving those who think they have acquired rights over the species by paying little attention to the individual, that is, to us. The constitution and, therefore, the welfare of the species have been placed in our hands and committed to our care, through the control we obtain over the next generation, which proceeds from us; let us discharge our duties conscientiously.* But women have no abstract knowledge of this leading principle; they are conscious of it only as a concrete fact; and they have no other method of giving expression to it than the way in which they act when the opportunity arrives. And then their conscience does not trouble them so much as we fancy; for in the darkest recesses of their heart, they are aware that in committing a breach of their duty towards the indi-

vidual, they have all the better fulfilled their duty towards
the species, which is infinitely greater.

And since women exist in the main solely for the propagation of the species, and are not destined for anything else, they
live, as a rule, more for the species than for the individual,
and in their hearts take the affairs of the species more seriously
than those of the individual. This gives their whole life and
being a certain levity; the general bent of their character is
in a direction fundamentally different from that of man; and it
is this to which produces that discord in married life which is
so frequent, and almost the normal state.

The natural feeling between men is mere indifference, but
between women it is actual enmity. The reason of this is that
trade-jealousy—*odium figulinum*—which, in the case of men
does not go beyond the confines of their own particular pursuit; but, with women, embraces the whole sex; since they
have only one kind of business. Even when they meet in the
street, women look at one another like Guelphs and Ghibel-
lines. And it is a patent fact that when two women make first
acquaintance with each other, they behave with more constraint and dissimulation than two men would show in a like
case; and hence it is that an exchange of compliments between
two women is a much more ridiculous proceeding than between two men. Further, whilst a man will, as a general rule,
always preserve a certain amount of consideration and humanity in speaking to others, even to those who are in a very inferior position, it is intolerable to see how proudly and disdain-
fully a fine lady will generally behave towards one who is
in a lower social rank (I do not mean a woman who is in her
service), whenever she speaks to her. The reason of this may
be that, with women, differences of rank are much more pre-
carious than with us; because, while a hundred considerations
carry weight in our case, in theirs there is only one, namely,
with which man they have found favor; as also that they stand
in much nearer relations with one another than men do, in
consequence of the one-sided nature of their calling. This
makes them endeavor to lay stress upon differences of rank.

It is only the man whose intellect is clouded by his sexual
impulses that could give the name of *the fair sex* to that under-
sized, narrow-shouldered, broad-hipped, and short-legged

race; for the whole beauty of the sex is bound up with this impulse. Instead of calling them beautiful, there would be more warrant for describing women as the unæsthetic sex. Neither for music, nor for poetry, nor for fine art, have they really and truly any sense or susceptibility; it is a mere mockery if they make a pretence of it in order to assist their endeavor to please. Hence, as a result of this, they are incapable of taking a *purely objective interest* in anything; and the reason of it seems to me to be as follows. A man tries to acquire *direct* mastery over things, either by understanding them, or by forcing them to do his will. But a woman is always and everywhere reduced to obtaining this mastery *indirectly,* namely, through a man; and whatever direct mastery she may have is entirely confined to him. And so it lies in woman's nature to look upon everything only as a means for conquering man; and if she takes an interest in anything else, it is simulated—a mere roundabout way of gaining her ends by coquetry, and feigning what she does not feel. Hence, even Rousseau declared: *Women have, in general, no love for any art; they have no proper knowledge of any; and they have no genius.*[2]

No one who sees at all below the surface can have failed to remark the same thing. You need only observe the kind of attention women bestow upon a concert, an opera, or a play— the childish simplicity, for example, with which they keep on chattering during the finest passages in the greatest masterpieces. If it is true that the Greeks excluded women from their theatres they were quite right in what they did; at any rate you would have been able to hear what was said upon the stage. In our day, besides, or in lieu of saying, *Let a woman keep silence in the church,* it would be much to the point to say *Let a woman keep silence in the theatre.* This might, perhaps, be put up in big letters on the curtain.

And you cannot expect anything else of women if you consider that the most distinguished intellects among the whole sex have never managed to produce a single achievement in the fine arts that is really great, genuine, and original; or given to the world any work of permanent value in any sphere. This

[2] Lettre à d'Alembert. Note xx.

is most strikingly shown in regard to painting, where mastery of technique is at least as much within their power as within ours—and hence they are diligent in cultivating it; but still, they have not a single great painting to boast of, just because they are deficient in that objectivity of mind which is so directly indispensable in painting. They never get beyond a subjective point of view. It is quite in keeping with this that ordinary women have no real susceptibility for art at all; for Nature proceeds in strict sequence—*non facit saltum*. And Huarte in his *Examen de ingenios para las scienzias*—a book which has been famous for three hundred years—denies women the possession of all the higher faculties. The case is not altered by particular and partial exceptions; taken as a whole, women are, and remain, thorough-going Philistines, and quite incurable. Hence, with that absurd arrangement which allows them to share the rank and title of their husbands they are a constant stimulus to his ignoble ambitions. And, further, it is just because they are Philistines that modern society, where they take the lead and set the tone, is in such a bad way. Napoleon's saying—that *women have no rank*—should be adopted as the right standpoint in determining their position in society; and as regards their other qualities Chamfort makes the very true remark: *They are made to trade with our own weaknesses and our follies, but not with our reason. The sympathies that exist between them and men are skin-deep only, and do not touch the mind or the feelings or the character.* They form the *sexus sequior*—the second sex, inferior in every respect to the first; their infirmities should be treated with consideration; but to show them great reverence is extremely ridiculous, and lowers us in their eyes. When Nature made two divisions of the human race, she did not draw the line exactly through the middle. These divisions are polar and opposed to each other, it is true; but the difference between them is not qualitative merely, it is also quantitative.

This is just the view which the ancients took of woman, and the view which people in the East take now; and their judgment as to her proper position is much more correct than ours, with our old French notions of gallantry and our preposterous system of reverence—that highest product of Teutonico-Christian stupidity. These notions have served only to make

women more arrogant and overbearing; so that one is occasionally reminded of the holy apes in Benares, who in the
consciousness of their sanctity and inviolable position, think
they can do exactly as they please.

But in the West, the woman, and especially the *lady*, finds
herself in a false position; for woman, rightly called by the
ancients, *sexus sequior*, is by no means fit to be the object of
our honor and veneration, or to hold her head higher than
man and be on equal terms with him. The consequences of
this false position are sufficiently obvious. Accordingly, it
would be a very desirable thing if this Number-Two of the
human race were in Europe also relegated to her natural place,
and an end put to that lady nuisance, which not only moves
all Asia to laughter, but would have been ridiculed by Greece
and Rome as well. It is impossible to calculate the good effects
which such a change would bring about in our social, civil
and political arrangements. There would be no necessity for
the Salic law: it would be a superfluous truism. In Europe
the *lady*, strictly so-called, is a being who should not exist at
all; she should be either a housewife or a girl who hopes to
become one; and she should be brought up, not to be arrogant, but to be thrifty and submissive. It is just because there
are such people as *ladies* in Europe that the women of the
lower classes, that is to say, the great majority of the sex, are
much more unhappy than they are in the East. And even Lord
Byron says: *Thought of the state of women under the ancient
Greeks—convenient enough. Present state, a remnant of the
barbarism of the chivalric and the feudal ages—artificial and
unnatural. They ought to mind home—and be well fed and
clothed—but not mixed in society. Well educated, too, in religion—but to read neither poetry nor politics—nothing but
books of piety and cookery. Music—drawing—dancing—also a
little gardening and ploughing now and then. I have seen them
mending the roads in Epirus with good success. Why not, as
well as hay-making and milking?*

The laws of marriage prevailing in Europe consider the
woman as the equivalent of the man—start, that is to say, from
a wrong position. In our part of the world where monogamy
is the rule, to marry means to halve one's rights and double
one's duties. Now, when the laws gave women equal rights

with man, they ought to have also endowed her with a masculine intellect. But the fact is, that just in proportion as the honors and privileges which the laws accord to women, exceed the amount which nature gives, is there a diminution in the number of women who really participate in these privileges; and all the remainder are deprived of their natural rights by just so much as is given to the others over and above their share. For the institution of monogamy, and the laws of marriage which it entails, bestow upon the woman an unnatural position of privilege, by considering her throughout as the full equivalent of the man, which is by no means the case; and seeing this, men who are shrewd and prudent very often scruple to make so great a sacrifice and to acquiesce in so unfair an arrangement.

Consequently, whilst among polygamous nations every woman is provided for, where monogamy prevails the number of married women is limited; and there remains over a large number of women without stay or support, who, in the upper classes, vegetate as useless old maids, and in the lower succumb to hard work for which they are not suited; or else become *filles de joie,* whose life is as destitute of joy as it is of honor. But under the circumstances they become a necessity; and their position is openly recognized as serving the special end of warding off temptation from those women favored by fate, who have found, or may hope to find, husbands. In London alone there are 80,000 prostitutes. What are they but the women, who, under the institution of monogamy have come off worse? Theirs is a dreadful fate: they are human sacrifices offered up on the altar of monogamy. The women whose wretched position is here described are the inevitable set-off to the European lady with her arrogance and pretension. Polygamy is therefore a real benefit to the female sex if it is taken as a whole. And, from another point of view, there is no true reason why a man whose wife suffers from chronic illness, or remains barren, or has gradually become too old for him, should not take a second. The motives which induce so many people to become converts to Mormonism appear to be just those which militate against the unnatural institution of monogamy.

Moreover, the bestowal of unnatural rights upon women has

imposed upon them unnatural duties, and, nevertheless, a breach of these duties makes them unhappy. Let me explain. A man may often think that his social or financial position will suffer if he marries, unless he makes some brilliant alliance. His desire will then be to win a woman of his own choice under conditions other than those of marriage, such as will secure her position and that of the children. However fair, reasonable, fit and proper these conditions may be, and the woman consents by foregoing that undue amount of privilege which marriage alone can bestow, she to some extent loses her honor, because marriage is the basis of civic society; and she will lead an unhappy life, since human nature is so constituted that we pay an attention to the opinion of other people which is out of all proportion to its value. On the other hand, if she does not consent, she runs the risk either of having to be given in marriage to a man whom she does not like, or of being landed high and dry as an old maid; for the period during which she has a chance of being settled for life is very short. And in view of this aspect of the institution of monogamy, Thomasius' profoundly learned treatise, *de Concubinatu,* is well worth reading; for it shows that, amongst all nations and in all ages, down to the Lutheran Reformation, concubinage was permitted; nay, that it was an institution which was to a certain extent actually recognized by law, and attended with no dishonor. It was only the Lutheran Reformation that degraded it from this position. It was seen to be a further justification for the marriage of the clergy; and then, after that, the Catholic Church did not dare to remain behind-hand in the matter.

There is no use arguing about polygamy; it must be taken as *de facto* existing everywhere, and the only question is as to how it shall be regulated. Where are there, then, any real monogamists? We all live, at any rate, for a time, and most of us, always, in polygamy. And so, since every man needs many women, there is nothing fairer than to allow him, nay, to make it incumbent upon him, to provide for many women. This will reduce woman to her true and natural position as a subordinate being; and the *lady*—that monster of European civilization and Teutonico-Christian stupidity—will disappear from the world, leaving only *women,* but no more *unhappy women,* of whom Europe is now full.

In India, no woman is ever independent, but in accordance with the law of Manu,[3] she stands under the control of her father, her husband, her brother or her son. It is, to be sure, a revolting thing that a widow should immolate herself upon her husband's funeral pyre; but it is also revolting that she should spend her husband's money with her paramours—the money for which he toiled his whole life long, in the consoling belief that he was providing for his children. Happy are those who have kept the middle course—*medium tenuere beati.*

The first love of a mother for her child is, with the lower animals as with men, of a purely *instinctive* character, and so it ceases when the child is no longer in a physically helpless condition. After that, the first love should give way to one that is based on habit and reason; but this often fails to make its appearance, especially where the mother did not love the father. The love of a father for his child is of a different order, and more likely to last; because it has its foundation in the fact that in the child he recognizes his own inner self; that is to say, his love for it is metaphysical in its origin.

In almost all nations, whether of the ancient or the modern world, even amongst the Hottentots,[4] property is inherited by the male descendants alone; it is only in Europe that a departure has taken place; but not amongst the nobility, however. That the property which has cost men long years of toil and effort, and been won with so much difficulty, should afterwards come into the hands of women, who then, in their lack of reason, squander it in a short time, or otherwise fool it away, is a grievance and a wrong as serious as it is common, which should be prevented by limiting the right of women to inherit. In my opinion, the best arrangement would be that by which women, whether widows or daughters, should never receive anything beyond the interest for life on property secured by mortgage, and in no case the property itself, or the capital, except where all male descendants fail. The people who make money are men, not women; and it follows from this that women are neither justified in having unconditional posses-

[3] Ch. V., v. 148.
[4] Leroy, *Lettres philosophiques sur l'intelligence et la perfectibilité des animaux, avec quelques lettres sur l'homme,* p. 298, Paris, 1802.

sion of it, nor fit persons to be entrusted with its administration. When wealth, in any true sense of the word, that is to say, funds, houses or land, is to go to them as an inheritance they should never be allowed the free disposition of it. In their case a guardian should always be appointed; and hence they should never be given the free control of their own children, wherever it can be avoided. The vanity of women, even though it should not prove to be greater than that of men, has this much danger in it, that it takes an entirely material direction. They are vain, I mean, of their personal beauty, and then of finery, show and magnificence. That is just why they are so much in their element in society. It is this, too, which makes them so inclined to be extravagant, all the more as their reasoning power is low. But with men vanity often takes the direction of non-material advantages, such as intellect, learning, courage.

In the *Politics*[5] Aristotle explains the great disadvantage which accrued to the Spartans from the fact that they conceded too much to their women, by giving them the right of inheritance and dower, and a great amount of independence; and he shows how much this contributed to Sparta's fall. May it not be the case in France that the influence of women, which went on increasing steadily from the time of Louis XIII., was to blame for that gradual corruption of the Court and the Government, which brought about the Revolution of 1789, of which all subsequent disturbances have been the fruit? However that may be, the false position which women occupy, demonstrated as it is, in the most glaring way, by the institution of the *lady*, is a fundamental defect in our social scheme, and this defect, proceeding from the very heart of it, must spread its baneful influence in all directions.

That woman is by nature meant to obey may be seen by the fact that every woman who is placed in the unnatural position of complete independence, immediately attaches herself to some man, by whom she allows herself to be guided and ruled. It is because she needs a lord and master. If she is young, it will be a lover; if she is old, a priest.

[5] Bk. I., ch. 9.

THE CHRISTIAN SYSTEM

(from PARERGA*)*

When the Church says that, in the dogmas of religion, reason is totally incompetent and blind, and its use to be reprehended, it is in reality attesting the fact that these dogmas are allegorical in their nature, and are not to be judged by the standard which reason, taking all things *sensu proprio,* can alone apply. Now the absurdities of a dogma are just the mark and sign of what is allegorical and mythical in it. In the case under consideration, however, the absurdities spring from the fact that two such heterogeneous doctrines as those of the Old and New Testaments had to be combined. The great allegory was of gradual growth. Suggested by external and adventitious circumstances, it was developed by the interpretation put upon them, an interpretation in quiet touch with certain deep-lying truths only half realized. The allegory was finally completed by Augustine, who penetrated deepest into its meaning, and so was able to conceive it as a systematic whole and supply its defects. Hence the Augustinian doctrine, confirmed by Luther, is the complete form of Christianity; and the Protestants of to-day, who take Revelation *sensu proprio* and confine it to a single individual, are in error in looking upon the first beginnings of Christianity as its most perfect expression. But the bad thing about all religions is that, instead of being able to confess their allegorical nature, they have to conceal it; accordingly, they parade their doctrine in all seriousness as true *sensu proprio,* and as absurdities form an essential part of these doctrines, you have the great mischief of a continual fraud. And, what is worse, the day arrives when they are no longer true *sensu proprio,* and then there is an end of them; so that, in that respect, it would be better to admit their allegorical nature at once. But the difficulty is to teach the multitude that something can be both true and untrue at the same time. And as all religions are in a greater or less degree of this nature, we must recognize the fact that mankind cannot get on without a certain amount of absurdity, that absurdity is an element in its existence, and illusion indispensable; as indeed other aspects of life testify.

I have said that the combination of the Old Testament with the New gives rise to absurdities. Among the examples which illustrate what I mean, I may cite the Christian doctrine of Predestination and Grace, as formulated by Augustine and adopted from him by Luther; according to which one man is endowed with grace and another is not. Grace, then, comes to be a privilege received at birth and brought ready into the world; a privilege, too, in a matter second to none in importance. What is obnoxious and absurd in this doctrine may be traced to the idea contained in the Old Testament, that man is the creation of an external will, which called him into existence out of nothing. It is quite true that genuine moral excellence is really innate; but the meaning of the Christian doctrine is expressed in another and more rational way by the theory of metempsychosis, common to Brahmans and Buddhists. According to this theory, the qualities which distinguish one man from another are received at birth, are brought, that is to say, from another world and a former life; these qualities are not an external gift of grace, but are the fruits of the acts committed in that other world. But Augustine's dogma of Predestination is connected with another dogma, namely, that the mass of humanity is corrupt and doomed to eternal damnation, that very few will be found righteous and attain salvation, and that only in consequence of the gift of grace, and because they are predestined to be saved; whilst the remainder will be overwhelmed by the perdition they have deserved, viz., eternal torment in hell. Taken in its ordinary meaning, the dogma is revolting, for it comes to this: it condemns a man, who may be, perhaps, scarcely twenty years of age, to expiate his errors, or even his unbelief, in everlasting torment; nay, more, it makes this almost universal damnation the natural effect of original sin, and therefore the necessary consequence of the Fall. This is a result which must have been foreseen by him who made mankind, and who, in the first place, made them not better than they are, and secondly, set a trap for them into which he must have known they would fall; for he made the whole world, and nothing is hidden from him. According to this doctrine, then, God created out of nothing a weak race prone to sin, in order to give them over to endless torment. And, as a last characteristic, we are told that this God, who prescribes forbearance and forgiveness of every fault, exercises none himself, but does the exact opposite; for a punishment which comes at the end of all things, when the world is over and done with, cannot have for its object either to improve or deter, and is therefore pure vengeance. So that, on this view, the whole race is actually destined to eternal torture and damnation, and created expressly for this end, the only exception being those few persons who are rescued by election of grace, from what motive one does not know.

Putting these aside, it looks as if the Blessed Lord had created the world for the benefit of the devil! it would have been so much better not to have made it at all. So much, then, for a dogma taken *sensu proprio*. But look at it *sensu allegorico*, and the whole matter becomes capable of a satisfactory interpretation. What is absurd and revolting in this dogma is, in the main, as I said, the simple outcome of Jewish theism, with its "creation out of nothing," and really foolish and paradoxical denial of the doctrine of metempsychosis which is involved in that idea, a doctrine which is natural, to a certain extent self-evident, and, with the exception of the Jews, accepted by nearly the whole human race at all times. To remove the enormous evil arising from Augustine's dogma, and to modify its revolting nature, Pope Gregory I., in the sixth century, very prudently matured the doctrine of *Purgatory*, the essence of which already existed in Origen (cf. Bayle's article on Origen, note B.). The doctrine was regularly incorporated into the faith of the Church, so that the original view was much modified, and a certain substitute provided for the doctrine of metempsychosis; for both the one and the other admit a process of purification. To the same end, the doctrine of "the Restoration of all things" was established, according to which, in the last act of the Human Comedy, the sinners one and all will be reinstated *in integrum*. It is only

Protestants, with their obstinate belief in the Bible, who cannot be induced to give up eternal punishment in hell. If one were spiteful, one might say, "much good may it do them," but it is consoling to think that they really do not believe the doctrine; they leave it alone, thinking in their hearts, "It can't be so bad as all that."

The rigid and systematic character of his mind led Augustine, in his austere dogmatism and his resolute definition of doctrines only just indicated in the Bible and, as a matter of fact, resting on very vague grounds, to give hard outlines to these doctrines and to put a harsh construction on Christianity: the result of which is that his views offend us, and just as in his day Pelagianism arose to combat them, so now in our day Rationalism does the same. Take, for example, the case as he states it generally in the *De Civitate Dei*, Bk. xii. ch. 21. It comes to this: God creates a being out of nothing, forbids him some things, and enjoins others upon him; and because these commands are not obeyed, he tortures him to all eternity with every conceivable anguish; and for this purpose, binds soul and body inseparably together, so that, instead of the torment destroying this being by splitting him up into his elements, and so setting him free, he may live to eternal pain. This poor creature, formed out of nothing! At least, he has a claim on his original nothing: he should be assured, as a matter of right, of this last retreat, which, in any case, cannot be a very evil one: it is what he has inherited. I, at any rate, cannot help sympathizing with him. If you add to this Augustine's remaining doctrines, that all this does not depend on the man's own sins and omissions, but was already predestined to happen, one really is at a loss what to think. Our highly educated Rationalists say, to be sure, "It's all false, it's a mere bugbear; we're in a state of constant progress, step by step raising ourselves to ever greater perfection." Ah! what a pity we didn't begin sooner; we should already have been there.

In the Christian system the devil is a personage of the greatest importance. God is described as absolutely good, wise and powerful; and unless he were counterbalanced by the devil, it would be impossible to see where the innumerable and measureless evils, which predominate in the world, come from, if

there were no devil to account for them. And since the Rationalists have done away with the devil, the damage inflicted on
the other side has gone on growing, and is becoming more
and more palpable; as might have been foreseen, and was
foreseen, by the orthodox. The fact is, you cannot take away
one pillar from a building without endangering the rest of it.
And this confirms the view, which has been established on
other grounds, that Jehovah is a transformation of Ormuzd,
and Satan of the Ahriman who must be taken in connection
with him. Ormuzd himself is a transformation of Indra.

Christianity has this peculiar disadvantage, that, unlike
other religions, it is not a pure system of doctrine: its chief and
essential feature is that it is a history, a series of events, a collection of facts, a statement of the actions and sufferings of
individuals: it is this history which constitutes dogma, and
belief in it is salvation. Other religions, Buddhism, for instance,
have, it is true, historical appendages, the life, namely, of their
founders: this, however, is not part and parcel of the dogma
but is taken along with it. For example, the Lalitavistara may
be compared with the Gospel so far as it contains the life of
Sakya-muni, the Buddha of the present period of the world's
history: but this is something which is quite separate and different from the dogma, from the system itself: and for this
reason; the lives of former Buddhas were quite other, and
those of the future will be quite other, than the life of the
Buddha of to-day. The dogma is by no means one with the
career of its founder; it does not rest on individual persons or
events; it is something universal and equally valid at all times.
The Lalitavistara is not, then, a gospel in the Christian sense of
the word; it is not the joyful message of an act of redemption;
it is the career of him who has shown how each one may
redeem himself. The historical constitution of Christianity
makes the Chinese laugh at missionaries as story-tellers.

I may mention here another fundamental error of Christianity, an error which cannot be explained away, and the
mischievous consequences of which are obvious every day: I
mean the unnatural distinction Christianity makes between
man and the animal world to which he really belongs. It sets
up man as all-important, and looks upon animals as merely

things. Brahmanism and Buddhism, on the other hand, true to the facts, recognize in a positive way that man is related generally to the whole of nature, and specially and principally to animal nature; and in their systems man is always represented by the theory of metempsychosis and otherwise, as closely connected with the animal world. The important part played by animals all through Buddhism and Brahmanism, compared with the total disregard of them in Judaism and Christianity, puts an end to any question as to which system is nearer perfection, however much we in Europe may have become accustomed to the absurdity of the claim. Christianity contains, in fact, a great and essential imperfection in limiting its precepts to man, and in refusing rights to the entire animal world. As religion fails to protect animals against the rough, unfeeling and often more than bestial multitude, the duty falls to the police; and as the police are unequal to the task, societies for the protection of animals are now formed all over Europe and America. In the whole of uncircumcised Asia, such a procedure would be the most superfluous thing in the world, because animals are there sufficiently protected by religion, which even makes them objects of charity. How such charitable feelings bear fruit may be seen, to take an example, in the great hospital for animals at Surat, whither Christians, Mohammedans and Jews can send their sick beasts, which, if cured, are very rightly not restored to their owners. In the same way when a Brahman or a Buddhist has a slice of good luck, a happy issue in any affair, instead of mumbling a *Te Deum,* he goes to the market-place and buys birds and opens their cages at the city gate; a thing which may be frequently seen in Astrachan, where the adherents of every religion meet together: and so on in a hundred similar ways. On the other hand, look at the revolting ruffianism with which our Christian public treats its animals; killing them for no object at all, and laughing over it, or multilating or torturing them: even its horses, who form its most direct means of livelihood, are strained to the utmost in their old age, and the last strength worked out of their poor bones until they succumb at last under the whip. One might say with truth, Mankind are the devils of the earth, and the animals the souls they torment. But what can you expect from the masses, when there are

men of education, zoologists even, who, instead of admitting
what is so familiar to them, the essential identity of man and
animal, are bigoted and stupid enough to offer a zealous opposition to their honest and rational colleagues, when they
class man under the proper head as an animal, or demonstrate
the resemblance between him and the chimpanzee or ourang-
outang. It is a revolting thing that a writer who is so pious
and Christian in his sentiments as Jung Stilling should use a
simile like this, in his *Scenen aus dem Geisterreich*. (Bk. II.
sc. i., p. 15.) "Suddenly the skeleton shriveled up into an
indescribably hideous and dwarf-like form, just as when you
bring a large spider into the focus of a burning glass, and watch
the purulent blood hiss and bubble in the heat." This man of
God then was guilty of such infamy! or looked on quietly
when another was committing it! in either case it comes to
the same thing here. So little harm did he think of it that he
tells us of it in passing, and without a trace of emotion. Such
are the effects of the first chapter of Genesis, and, in fact, of
the whole of the Jewish conception of nature. The standard
recognized by the Hindus and Buddhists is the Mahavakya
(the great word),—"tat-twam-asi" (this is thyself), which may
always be spoken of every animal, to keep us in mind of the
identity of his inmost being with ours. Perfection of morality,
indeed! Nonsense.

The fundamental characteristics of the Jewish religion are
realism and optimism, views of the world which are closely
allied; they form, in fact, the conditions of theism. For theism
looks upon the material world as absolutely real, and regards
life as a pleasant gift bestowed upon us. On the other hand,
the fundamental characteristics of the Brahman and Buddhist
religions are idealism and pessimism, which look upon the
existence of the world as in the nature of a dream, and life as
the result of our sins. In the doctrines of the Zendavesta, from
which, as is well known, Judaism sprang, the pessimistic element is represented by Ahriman. In Judaism, Ahriman has as
Satan only a subordinate position; but, like Ahriman, he is the
lord of snakes, scorpions, and vermin. But the Jewish system
forthwith employs Satan to correct its fundamental error of
optimism, and in the *Fall* introduces the element of pessimism,

a doctrine demanded by the most obvious facts of the world. There is no truer idea in Judaism than this, although it transfers to the course of existence what must be represented as its foundation and antecedent.

The New Testament, on the other hand, must be in some way traceable to an Indian source: its ethical system, its ascetic view of morality, its pessimism, and its Avatar, are all thoroughly Indian. It is its morality which places it in a position of such emphatic and essential antagonism to the Old Testament, so that the story of the Fall is the only possible point of connection between the two. For when the Indian doctrine was imported into the land of promise, two very different things had to be combined: on the one hand the consciousness of the corruption and misery of the world, its need of deliverance and salvation through an Avatar, together with a morality based on self-denial and repentance; on the other hand the Jewish doctrine of Monotheism, with its corollary that "all things are very good." And the task succeeded as far as it could, as far, that is, as it was possible to combine two such heterogeneous and antagonistic creeds.

As ivy clings for the support and stay it wants to a rough-hewn post, everywhere conforming to its irregularities and showing their outline, but at the same time covering them with life and grace, and changing the former aspect into one that is pleasing to the eye; so the Christian faith, sprung from the wisdom of India, overspreads the old trunk of rude Judaism, a tree of alien growth; the original form must in part remain, but it suffers a complete change and becomes full of life and truth, so that it appears to be the same tree, but is really another.

Judaism had presented the Creator as separated from the world, which he produced out of nothing. Christianity identifies this Creator with the Saviour, and through him, with humanity: he stands as their representative; they are redeemed in him, just as they fell in Adam, and have lain ever since in the bonds of iniquity, corruption, suffering and death. Such is the view taken by Christianity in common with Buddhism; the world can no longer be looked at in the light of Jewish optimism, which found "all things very good": nay, in the Christian scheme, the devil is named as its Prince or Ruler (John

12, 33). The world is no longer an end, but a means: and the realm of everlasting joy lies beyond it and the grave. Resignation in this world and direction of all our hopes to a better, form the spirit of Christianity. The way to this end is opened by the Atonement, that is the Redemption from this world and its ways. And in the moral system, instead of the law of vengeance, there is the command to love your enemy; instead of the promise of innumerable posterity, the assurance of eternal life; instead of visiting the sins of the fathers upon the children to the third and fourth generations, the Holy Spirit governs and overshadows all.

We see, then, that the doctrines of the Old Testament are rectified and their meaning changed by those of the New, so that, in the most important and essential matters, an agreement is brought about between them and the old religions of India. Everything which is true in Christianity may also be found in Brahmanism and Buddhism. But in Hinduism and Buddhism you will look in vain for any parallel to the Jewish doctrines of "a nothing quickened into life," or of "a world made in time," which cannot be humble enough in its thanks and praises to Jehovah for an ephemeral existence full of misery, anguish and need.

Whoever seriously thinks that superhuman beings have ever given our race information as to the aim of its existence and that of the world, is still in his childhood. There is no other revelation than the thoughts of the wise, even though these thoughts, liable to error as is the lot of everything human, are often clothed in strange allegories and myths under the name of religion. So far, then, it is a matter of indifference whether a man lives and dies in reliance on his own or another's thoughts; for it is never more than human thought, human opinion, which he trusts. Still, instead of trusting what their own minds tell them, men have as a rule a weakness for trusting others who pretend to supernatural sources of knowledge. And in view of the enormous intellectual inequality between man and man, it is easy to see that the thoughts of one mind might appear as in some sense a revelation to another.

XXI

ON GENIUS

(from PARERGA*)*

No difference of rank, position, or birth, is so great as the gulf that separates the countless millions who use their head only in the service of their belly, in other words, look upon it as an instrument of the will, and those very few and rare persons who have the courage to say: No! it is too good for that; my head shall be active only in its own service; it shall try to comprehend the wondrous and varied spectacle of this world, and then reproduce it in some form, whether as art or as literature, that may answer to my character as an individual. These are the truly noble, the real *noblesse* of the world. The others are serfs and go with the soil—*glebæ adscripti*. Of course, I am here referring to those who have not only the courage, but also the call, and therefore the right, to order the head to quit the service of the will; with a result that proves the sacrifice to have been worth the making. In the case of those to whom all this can only partially apply, the gulf is not so wide; but even though their talent be small, so long as it is real, there will always be a sharp line of demarcation between them and the millions.[1]

The works of fine art, poetry and philosophy produced by a nation are the outcome of the superfluous intellect existing in it.

[1] The correct scale for adjusting the hierarchy of intelligences is furnished by the degree in which the mind takes merely individual or approaches universal views of things. The brute recognizes only the individual as such: its comprehension does not extend beyond the limits of the individual. But man reduces the individual to the general; herein lies the exercise of his reason; and the higher his intelligence reaches, the nearer do his general ideas approach the point at which they become universal.

For him who can understand aright—*cum grano salis*—the relation between the genius and the normal man may, perhaps, be best expressed as follows: A genius has a double intellect, one for himself and the service of his will; the other for the world, of which he becomes the mirror, in virtue of his purely objective attitude towards it. The work of art or poetry or philosophy produced by the genius is simply the result, or quintessence, of this contemplative attitude, elaborated according to certain technical rules.

The normal man, on the other hand, has only a single intellect, which may be called *subjective* by contrast with the *objective* intellect of genius. However acute this subjective intellect may be—and it exists in very various degrees of perfection—it is never on the same level with the double intellect of genius; just as the open chest notes of the human voice, however high, are essentially different from the falsetto notes. These, like the two upper octaves of the flute and the harmonics of the violin, are produced by the column of air dividing itself into two vibrating halves, with a node between them; while the open chest notes of the human voice and the lower octave of the flute are produced by the undivided column of air vibrating as a whole. This illustration may help the reader to understand that specific peculiarity of genius which is unmistakably stamped on the works, and even on the physiognomy, of him who is gifted with it. At the same time it is obvious that a double intellect like this must, as a rule, obstruct the service of the will; and this explains the poor capacity often shown by genius in the conduct of life. And what specially characterizes genius is that it has none of that sobriety of temper which is always to be found in the ordinary simple intellect, be it acute or dull.

The brain may be likened to a parasite which is nourished as a part of the human frame without contributing directly to its inner economy; it is securely housed in the topmost story, and there leads a self-sufficient and independent life. In the same way it may be said that a man endowed with great mental gifts leads, apart from the individual life common to all, a second life, purely of the intellect. He devotes himself to the constant increase, rectification and extension, not of mere learning, but of real systematic knowledge and insight; and remains untouched by the fate that overtakes him personally, so long as it does not disturb him in his work. It is thus a life which raises a man and sets him above fate and its changes. Always thinking, learning, experimenting, practicing his knowledge, the man soon comes to look upon this second life as the chief mode of existence, and his merely personal life as something subordinate, serving only to advance ends higher than itself.

An example of this independent, separate existence is furnished by Goethe. During the war in the Champagne, and amid all the bustle of the camp, he made observations for his theory of color; and as soon as the numberless calamities of that war allowed of his retiring for a short time to the fortress of Luxembourg, he took up the manuscript of his *Farbenlehre*. This is an example which we, the salt of the earth, should endeavor to follow, by never letting anything disturb us in the pursuit of our intellectual life, however much the storm of the world may invade and agitate our personal environment; always remembering that we are the sons, not of the bondwoman, but of the free. As our emblem and coat of arms, I propose a tree mightily shaken by the wind, but still bearing its ruddy fruit on every branch; with the motto *Dum convellor mitescunt*, or *Conquassata sed ferax*.

That purely intellectual life of the individual has its counterpart in humanity as a whole. For there, too, the real life is the life of the *will*, both in the empirical and in the transcendental meaning of the word. The purely intellectual life of humanity lies in its effort to increase knowledge by means of the sciences, and its desire to perfect the arts. Both science and art thus advance slowly from one generation to another, and grow with the centuries, every race as it hurries by furnishing its contribution. This intellectual life, like some gift from heaven, hovers over the stir and movement of the world; or it is, as it were, a sweet-scented air developed out of the ferment itself —the real life of mankind, dominated by will; and side by side with the history of nations, the history of philosophy, science and art takes its innocent and bloodless way.

The difference between the genius and the ordinary man is, no doubt, a *quantitative* one, in so far as it is a difference of degree; but I am tempted to regard it also as *qualitative*, in view of the fact that ordinary minds, notwithstanding individual variation, have a certain tendency to think alike. Thus on similar occasions their thoughts at once all take a similar direction, and run on the same lines; and this explains why their judgments constantly agree—not, however, because they are based on truth. To such lengths does this go that certain fundamental views obtain amongst mankind at all times, and are always being repeated and brought forward anew, whilst the great minds of all ages are in open or secret opposition to them.

A genius is a man in whose mind the world is presented as an object is presented in a mirror, but with a degree more of clearness and a greater distinction of outline than is attained by ordinary people. It is from him that humanity may look for most instruction; for the deepest insight into the most important matters is to be acquired, not by an observant attention to detail, but by a close study of things as a whole. And if his mind reaches maturity, the instruction he gives will be conveyed now in one form, now in another. Thus genius may be defined as an eminently clear consciousness of things in general, and therefore, also of that which is opposed to them, namely, one's own self.

The world looks up to a man thus endowed, and expects to learn something about life and its real nature. But several highly favorable circumstances must combine to produce genius, and this is a very rare event. It happens only now and then, let us say once in a century, that a man is born whose intellect so perceptibly surpasses the normal measure as to amount to that second faculty which seems to be accidental, as it is out of all relation to the will. He may remain a long time without being recognized or appreciated, stupidity preventing the one and envy the other. But should this once come to pass, mankind will crowd round him and his works, in the hope that he may be able to enlighten some of the darkness of their existence or inform them about it. His message is, to some extent, a revelation, and he himself a higher being, even though he may be but little above the ordinary standard.

Like the ordinary man, the genius is what he is chiefly for himself. This is essential to his nature: a fact which can neither be avoided nor altered. What he may be for others remains a matter of chance and of secondary importance. In no case can people receive from his mind more than a reflection, and then only when he joins with them in the attempt to get his thought into their heads; where, however, it is never anything but an exotic plant, stunted and frail.

In order to have original, uncommon, and perhaps even immortal thoughts, it is enough to estrange oneself so fully from the world of things for a few moments, that the most ordinary objects and events appear quite new and unfamiliar. In this way their true nature is disclosed. What is here demanded cannot, perhaps, be said to be difficult; it is not in our power at all, but is just the province of genius.

By itself, genius can produce original thoughts just as little as a woman by herself can bear children. Outward circumstances must come to fructify genius, and be, as it were, a father to its progeny.

The mind of genius is among other minds what the carbuncle is among precious stones: it sends forth light of its own, while the others reflect only that which they have received. The relation of the genius to the ordinary mind may also be described as that of an idio-electrical body to one which merely is a conductor of electricity.

The mere man of learning, who spends his life in teaching what he has learned, is not strictly to be called a man of genius; just as idio-electrical bodies are not conductors. Nay, genius stands to mere learning as the words to the music in a song. A man of learning is a man who has learned a great deal; a man of genius, one from whom we learn something which the genius has learned from nobody. Great minds, of which there is scarcely one in a hundred millions, are thus the lighthouses of humanity; and without them mankind would lose itself in the boundless sea of monstrous error and bewilderment.

And so the simple man of learning, in the strict sense of the word—the ordinary professor, for instance—looks upon the genius much as we look upon a hare, which is good to eat after it has been killed and dressed up. So long as it is alive, it is only good to shoot at.

He who wishes to experience gratitude from his contemporaries, must adjust his pace to theirs. But great things are never produced in this way. And he who wants to do great things must direct his gaze to posterity, and in firm confidence

elaborate his work for coming generations. No doubt, the result may be that he will remain quite unknown to his contemporaries, and comparable to a man who, compelled to
spend his life upon a lonely island, with great effort sets up a
monument there, to transmit to future sea-farers the knowledge of his existence. If he thinks it a hard fate, let him console
himself with the reflection that the ordinary man who lives for
practical aims only, often suffers a like fate, without having
any compensation to hope for; inasmuch as he may, under
favorable conditions, spend a life of material production, earn-
ing, buying, building, fertilizing, laying out, founding, establishing, beautifying with daily effort and unflagging zeal, and
all the time think that he is working for himself; and yet in the
end it is his descendants who reap the benefit of it all, and
sometimes not even his descendants. It is the same with the
man of genius; he, too, hopes for his reward and for honor at
least; and at last finds that he has worked for posterity alone.
Both, to be sure, have inherited a great deal from their ancestors.

The compensation I have mentioned as the privilege of
genius lies, not in what it is to others, but in what it is to itself.
What man has in any real sense lived more than he whose
moments of thought make their echoes heard through the
tumult of centuries? Perhaps, after all, it would be the best
thing for a genius to attain undisturbed possession of himself,
by spending his life in enjoying the pleasure of his own
thoughts, his own works, and by admitting the world only as
the heir of his ample existence. Then the world would find the
mark of his existence only after his death, as it finds that of
the Ichnolith.

It is not only in the activity of his highest powers that the
genius surpasses ordinary people. A man who is unusually well-
knit, supple and agile, will perform all his movements with
exceptional ease, even with comfort, because he takes a direct
pleasure in an activity for which he is particularly well-
equipped, and therefore often exercises it without any object.
Further, if he is an acrobat or a dancer, not only does he
take leaps which other people cannot execute, but he also betrays rare elasticity and agility in those easier steps which
others can also perform, and even in ordinary walking. In

the same way a man of superior mind will not only produce thoughts and works which could never have come from another; it will not be here alone that he will show his greatness; but as knowledge and thought form a mode of activity natural and easy to him, he will also delight himself in them at all times, and so apprehend small matters which are within the range of other minds, more easily, quickly and correctly than they. Thus he will take a direct and lively pleasure in every increase of knowledge, every problem solved, every witty thought, whether of his own or another's; and so his mind will have no further aim than to be constantly active. This will be an inexhaustible spring of delight; and boredom, that spectre which haunts the ordinary man, can never come near him.

Then, too, the masterpieces of past and contemporary men of genius exist in their fullness for him alone. If a great product of genius is recommended to the ordinary, simple mind, it will take as much pleasure in it as the victim of gout receives in being invited to a ball. The one goes for the sake of formality, and the other reads the book so as not to be in arrear. For La Bruyère was quite right when he said: *All the wit in the world is lost upon him who has none.* The whole range of thought of a man of talent, or of a genius, compared with the thoughts of the common man, is, even when directed to objects essentially the same, like a brilliant oil-painting, full of life, compared with a mere outline or a weak sketch in water-color.

All this is part of the reward of genius, and compensates him for a lonely existence in a world with which he has nothing in common and no sympathies. But since size is relative, it comes to the same thing whether I say, Caius was a great man, or Caius has to live amongst wretchedly small people: for Brobdingnack and Lilliput vary only in the point from which they start. However great, then, however admirable or instructive, a long posterity may think the author of immortal works, during his lifetime he will appear to his contemporaries small, wretched, and insipid in proportion. This is what I mean by saying that as there are three hundred degrees from the base of a tower to the summit, so there are exactly three hundred from the summit to the base. Great minds thus owe

little ones some indulgence; for it is only in virtue of these little
minds that they themselves are great.

Let us, then, not be surprised if we find men of genius generally unsociable and repellent. It is not their want of sociabil-
ity that is to blame. Their path through the world is like that
of a man who goes for a walk on a bright summer morning. He
gazes with delight on the beauty and freshness of nature, but
he has to rely wholly on that for entertainment; for he can
find no society but the peasants as they bend over the earth
and cultivate the soil. It is often the case that a great mind
prefers soliloquy to the dialogue he may have in this world.
If he condescends to it now and then, the hollowness of it
may possibly drive him back to his soliloquy; for in forgetful-
ness of his interlocutor, or caring little whether he understands or not, he talks to him as a child talks to a doll.

Modesty in a great mind would, no doubt, be pleasing to
the world; but, unluckily, it is a *contradictio in adjecto*. It
would compel a genius to give the thoughts and opinions, nay,
even the method and style, of the million preference over his
own; to set a higher value upon them; and, wide apart as they
are, to bring his views into harmony with theirs, or even
suppress them altogether, so as to let the others hold the field.
In that case, however, he would either produce nothing at all,
or else his achievements would be just upon a level with theirs.
Great, genuine and extraordinary work can be done only in
so far as its author disregards the method, the thoughts, the
opinions of his contemporaries, and quietly works on, in spite
of their criticism, on his side despising what they praise. No
one becomes great without arrogance of this sort. Should his
life and work fall upon a time which cannot recognize and
appreciate him, he is at any rate true to himself; like some
noble traveler forced to pass the night in a miserable inn; when
morning comes, he contentedly goes his way.

A poet or philosopher should have no fault to find with his
age if it only permits him to do his work undisturbed in his
own corner; nor with his fate if the corner granted him allows
of his following his vocation without having to think about
other people.

For the brain to be a mere laborer in the service of the
belly, is indeed the common lot of almost all those who do not

live on the work of their hands; and they are far from being discontented with their lot. But it strikes despair into a man of great mind, whose brain-power goes beyond the measure necessary for the service of the will; and he prefers, if need be, to live in the narrowest circumstances, so long as they afford him the free use of his time for the development and application of his faculties; in other words, if they give him the leisure which is invaluable to him.

It is otherwise with ordinary people: for them leisure has no value in itself, nor is it, indeed, without its dangers, as these people seem to know. The technical work of our time, which is done to an unprecedented perfection, has, by increasing and multiplying objects of luxury, given the favorites of fortune a choice between more leisure and culture upon the one side, and additional luxury and good living, but with increased activity, upon the other; and, true to their character, they choose the latter, and prefer champagne to freedom. And they are consistent in their choice; for, to them, every exertion of the mind which does not serve the aims of the will is folly. Intellectual effort for its own sake, they call eccentricity. Therefore, persistence in the aims of the will and the belly will be concentricity; and, to be sure, the will is the centre, the kernel of the world.

But in general it is very seldom that any such alternative is presented. For as with money, most men have no superfluity, but only just enough for their needs, so with intelligence; they possess just what will suffice for the service of the will, that is, for the carrying on of their business. Having made their fortune, they are content to gape or to indulge in sensual pleasures or childish amusements, cards or dice; or they will talk in the dullest way, or dress up and make obeisance to one another. And how few are those who have even a little superfluity of intellectual power! Like the others they too make themselves a pleasure; but it is a pleasure of the intellect. Either they will pursue some liberal study which brings them in nothing, or they will practice some art; and in general, they will be capable of taking an objective interest in things, so that it will be possible to converse with them. But with the others it is better not to enter into any relations at all; for, except when they tell the results of their own experience or

give an account of their special vocation, or at any rate impart what they have learned from some one else, their conversation will not be worth listening to; and if anything is
said to them, they will rarely grasp or understand it aright,
and it will in most cases be opposed to their own opinions.
Balthazar Gracian describes them very strikingly as men who
are not men—*hombres che non lo son*. And Giordano Bruno
says the same thing: *What a difference there is in having to
do with men compared with those who are only made in their
image and likeness!*[2] And how wonderfully this passage agrees
with that remark in the Kurral: *The common people look like
men but I have never seen anything quite like them*. If the
reader will consider the extent to which these ideas agree in
thought and even in expression, and in the wide difference
between them in point of date and nationality, he cannot doubt
but that they are at one with the facts of life. It was certainly not under the influence of those passages that, about
twenty years ago, I tried to get a snuff-box made, the lid of
which should have two fine chestnuts represented upon it, if
possible in mosaic; together with a leaf which was to show
that they were horse chestnuts. This symbol was meant to keep
the thought constantly before my mind. If anyone wishes for
entertainment, such as will prevent him feeling solitary even
when he is alone, let me recommend the company of dogs,
whose moral and intellectual qualities may almost afford delight and gratification.

Still, we should always be careful to avoid being unjust. I
am often surprised by the cleverness, and now and again by
the stupidity of my dog; and I have similar experiences with
mankind. Countless times, in indignation at their incapacity,
their total lack of discernment, their bestiality, I have been
forced to echo the old complaint that folly is the mother and
the nurse of the human race:

> *Humani generis mater nutrixque profecto*
> *Stultitia est.*

But at other times I have been astounded that from such a
race there could have gone forth so many arts and sciences,

[2] Opera: ed. Wagner, I. 224.

abounding in so much use and beauty, even though it has always been the few that produce them. Yet these arts and
sciences have struck root, established and perfected themselves: and the race has with persistent fidelity preserved
Homer, Plato, Horace and others for thousands of years, by
copying and treasuring their writings, thus saving them from
oblivion, in spite of all the evils and atrocities that have happened in the world. Thus the race has proved that it appre-
ciates the value of these things, and at the same time it can
form a correct view of special achievements or estimate signs
of judgment and intelligence. When this takes place amongst
those who belong to the great multitude, it is by a kind of
inspiration. Sometimes a correct opinion will be formed by the
multitude itself; but this is only when the chorus of praise has
grown full and complete. It is then like the sound of un-
trained voices; where there are enough of them, it is always
harmonious.

Those who emerge from the multitude, those who are called
men of genius, are merely the *lucida intervalla* of the whole
human race. They achieve that which others could not possibly achieve. Their originality is so great that not only is their
divergence from others obvious, but their individuality is expressed with such force, that all the men of genius who have
ever existed show, every one of them, peculiarities of character and mind; so that the gift of his works is one which he
alone of all men could ever have presented to the world. This
is what makes that simile of Ariosto's so true and so justly
celebrated: *Natura lo fece e poi ruppe lo stampo.* After Nature stamps a man of genius, she breaks the die.

But there is always a limit to human capacity; and no one
can be a great genius without having some decidedly weak
side, it may even be, some intellectual narrowness. In other
words, there will be some faculty in which he is now and then
inferior to men of moderate endowments. It will be a faculty
which, if strong, might have been an obstacle to the exercise
of the qualities in which he excels. What this weak point is,
it will always be hard to define with any accuracy even in a
given case. It may be better expressed indirectly; thus Plato's
weak point is exactly that in which Aristotle is strong, and

vice versa; and so, too, Kant is deficient just where Goethe is great.

Now, mankind is fond of venerating something; but its veneration is generally directed to the wrong object, and it remains so directed until posterity comes to set it right. But the educated public is no sooner set right in this, than the honor which is due to genius degenerates; just as the honor which the faithful pay to their saints easily passes into a frivolous worship of relics. Thousands of Christians adore the relics of a saint whose life and doctrine are unknown to them; and the religion of thousands of Buddhists lies more in veneration of the Holy Tooth or some such object, or the vessel that contains it, or the Holy Bowl, or the fossil footstep, or the Holy Tree which Buddha planted, than in the thorough knowledge and faithful practice of his high teaching. Petrarch's house in Arqua; Tasso's supposed prison in Ferrara; Shakespeare's house in Stratford, with his chair; Goethe's house in Weimar, with its furniture; Kant's old hat; the autographs of great men; these things are gaped at with interest and awe by many who have never read their works. They cannot do anything more than just gape.

The intelligent amongst them are moved by the wish to see the objects which the great man habitually had before his eyes; and by a strange illusion, these produce the mistaken notion that with the objects they are bringing back the man himself, or that something of him must cling to them. Akin to such people are those who earnestly strive to acquaint themselves with the subject-matter of a poet's works, or to unravel the personal circumstances and events in his life which have suggested particular passages. This is as though the audience in a theatre were to admire a fine scene and then rush upon the stage to look at the scaffolding that supports it. There are in our day enough instances of these critical investigators, and they prove the truth of the saying that mankind is interested, not in the *form* of a work, that is, in its manner of treatment, but in its actual matter. All it cares for is the theme. To read a philosopher's biography, instead of studying his thoughts, is like neglecting a picture and attending only to the style of its frame, debating whether it is carved well or ill, and how much it cost to gild it.

This is all very well. However, there is another class of persons whose interest is also directed to material and personal considerations, but they go much further and carry it to a point where it becomes absolutely futile. Because a great man has opened up to them the treasures of his inmost being, and, by a supreme effort of his faculties, produced works which not only redound to their elevation and enlightenment, but will also benefit their posterity to the tenth and twentieth generation; because he has presented mankind with a matchless gift, these varlets think themselves justified in sitting in judgment upon his personal morality, and trying if they cannot discover here or there some spot in him which will soothe the pain they feel at the sight of so great a mind, compared with the overwhelming feeling of their own nothingness.

This is the real source of all those prolix discussions, carried on in countless books and reviews, on the moral aspect of Goethe's life, and whether he ought not to have married one or other of the girls with whom he fell in love in his young days; whether, again, instead of honestly devoting himself to the service of his master, he should not have been a man of the people, a German patriot, worthy of a seat in the *Paulskirche*, and so on. Such crying ingratitude and malicious detraction prove that these self-constituted judges are as great knaves morally as they are intellectually, which is saying a great deal.

A man of talent will strive for money and reputation; but the spring that moves genius to the production of its works is not as easy to name. Wealth is seldom its reward. Nor is it reputation or glory; only a Frenchman could mean that. Glory is such an uncertain thing, and, if you look at it closely, of so little value. Besides it never corresponds to the effort you have made:

Responsura tuo nunquam est par fama labori.

Nor, again, is it exactly the pleasure it gives you; for this is almost outweighed by the greatness of the effort. It is rather a peculiar kind of instinct, which drives the man of genius to give permanent form to what he sees and feels, without being conscious of any further motive. It works, in the main, by a necessity similar to that which makes a tree bear its fruit; and no external condition is needed but the ground upon which it is to thrive.

On a closer examination, it seems as though, in the case of a genius, the will to live, which is the spirit of the human species, were conscious of having, by some rare chance, and for a brief period, attained a greater clearness of vision, and were now trying to secure it, or at least the outcome of it, for the whole species, to which the individual genius in his inmost being belongs; so that the light which he sheds about him may pierce the darkness and dullness of ordinary human consciousness and there produce some good effect.

Arising in some such way, this instinct drives the genius to carry his work to completion, without thinking of reward or applause or sympathy; to leave all care for his own personal welfare; to make his life one of industrious solitude, and to strain his faculties to the utmost. He thus comes to think more about posterity than about contemporaries; because, while the latter can only lead him astray, posterity forms the majority of the species, and time will gradually bring the discerning few who can appreciate him. Meanwhile it is with him as with the artist described by Goethe; he has no princely patron to prize his talents, no friend to rejoice with him:

> *Ein Fürst der die Talente schätzt,*
> *Ein Freund, der sich mit mir ergötzt,*
> *Die haben leider mir gefehlt.*

His work is, as it were, a sacred object and the true fruit of his life, and his aim in storing it away for a more discerning posterity will be to make it the property of mankind. An aim like this far surpasses all others, and for it he wears the crown of thorns which is one day to bloom into a wreath of laurel. All his powers are concentrated in the effort to complete and secure his work; just as the insect, in the last stage of its development, uses its whole strength on behalf of a brood it will never live to see; it puts its eggs in some place of safety, where, as it well knows, the young will one day find life and nourishment, and then dies in confidence.

XXII

❧ ❧

THE ART OF CONTROVERSY

(from PARERGA*)*
PRELIMINARY: LOGIC AND DIALECTIC

By the ancients, Logic and Dialectic were used as synonymous terms; although *logizesthai*, "to think over, to consider, to calculate," and *dialegesthai*, "to converse," are two very different things.

The name Dialectic was, as we are informed by Diogenes Laertius, first used by Plato; and in the *Phædrus, Sophist, Republic*, bk. vii., and elsewhere, we find that by Dialectic he means the regular employment of the reason, and skill in the practice of it. Aristotle also uses the word in this sense; but, according to Laurentius Valla, he was the first to use Logic too in a similar way. Dialectic, therefore, seems to be an older word than Logic. Cicero and Quintilian use the words in the same general signification.[1]

This use of the words and synonymous terms lasted through the Middle Ages into modern times; in fact, until the present day. But more recently, and in particular by Kant, Dialectic has often been employed in a bad sense, as meaning "the art of sophistical controversy"; and hence Logic has been preferred, as of the two the more innocent designation. Nevertheless, both originally meant the same thing; and in the last few years they have again been recognised as synonymous.

It is a pity that the words have thus been used from of old,

[1] Cic. *in Lucullo: Dialecticam inventam esse, veri et falsi quasi disceptatricem. Topica*, c. 2: *Stoici enim judicandi vias diligenter persecuti sunt, ea scientia, quam* Dialecticen *appellant.* Quint., lib. ii., 12: *Itaque hæc pars dialecticæ, sive illam disputatricem dicere malimus;* and with him this latter word appears to be the Latin equivalent for Dialectic. (So far according to "Petri Rami dialectica, Audomari Talaei praelectionibus illustrata." 1569.)

and that I am not quite at liberty to distinguish their meanings. Otherwise, I should have preferred to define *Logic* as "the science of the laws of thought, that is, of the method of reason"; and *Dialectic* as "the art of disputation," in the modern sense of the word. It is clear, then, that Logic deals with a subject of a purely *a priori* character, separable in definition from experience, namely, the laws of thought, the process of reason; the laws, that is, which reason follows when it is left to itself and not hindered, as in the case of solitary thought on the part of a rational being who is in no way misled. Dialectic, on the other hand, would treat of the intercourse between two rational beings who, because they are rational, ought to think in common, but who, as soon as they cease to agree like two clocks keeping exactly the same time, create a disputation, or intellectual contest. Regarded as purely rational beings, the individuals would, I say, necessarily be in agreement, and their variation springs from the difference essential to individuality; in other words, it is drawn from experience.

Logic, therefore, as the science of thought, or the science of the process of pure reason, should be capable of being constructed *a priori*. Dialectic, for the most part, can be constructed only *a posteriori;* that is to say, we may learn its rules by an experiential knowledge of the disturbance which pure thought suffers through the difference of individuality manifested in the intercourse between two rational beings, and also by acquaintance with the means which disputants adopt in order to make good against one another their own individual thought, and to show that it is pure and objective. For human nature is such that if A. and B. are engaged in thinking in common, and are communicating their opinions to one another on any subject, so long as it is not a mere fact of history, and A. perceives that B.'s thoughts on one and the same subject are not the same as his own, he does not begin by revising his own process of thinking, so as to discover any mistake which he may have made, but he assumes that the mistake has occurred in B.'s. In other words, man is naturally obstinate; and this quality in him is attended with certain results, treated of in the branch of knowledge which I should like to call Dialectic, but which, in order to avoid misunderstanding, I shall call Controversial or Eristical Dialectic. Accordingly, it is the branch of knowledge which treats of the obstinacy natural to man. Eristic is only a harsher name for the same thing.

Controversial Dialectic is the art of disputing, and of disputing in such a way as to hold one's own, whether one is in the right or the wrong—*per fas et nefas*.[2] A man may be objectively in the right, and nevertheless in the eyes of bystanders, and sometimes in his own, he may come off worst. For example, I may advance a proof of some assertion, and my adversary may refute the proof, and thus appear to have refuted the assertion, for which there may, nevertheless, be other proofs. In this case, of course, my adversary and I change places: he comes off best, although, as a matter of fact, he is in the wrong.

If the reader asks how this is, I reply that it is simply the natural baseness of human nature. If human nature were not base, but thoroughly honourable, we should in every debate have no other aim than the discovery of truth; we should not in the least care whether the truth proved to be in favour of the opinion which we had begun by expressing, or of the opin-

[2] According to Diogenes Laertius, v., 28, Aristotle put Rhetoric and Dialectic together, as aiming at persuasion; and Analytic and Philosophy as aiming at truth. Aristotle does, indeed, distinguish between (1) *Logic*, or Analytic, as the theory or method of arriving at true or apodeictic conclusions; and (2) *Dialectic* as the method of arriving at conclusions that are accepted or pass current as true, *probabilia;* conclusions in regard to which it is not taken for granted that they are false, and also not taken for granted that they are true in themselves, since that is not the point. What is this but the art of being in the right, whether one has any reason for being so or not, in other words, the art of attaining the appearance of truth, regardless of its substance? That is, then, as I put it above.

Aristotle divides all conclusions into logical and dialectical, in the manner described, and then into eristical. (3) *Eristic* is the method by which the form of the conclusion is correct, but the premisses, the materials from which it is drawn, are not true, but only appear to be true. Finally (4) *Sophistic* is the method in which the form of the conclusion is false, although it seems correct. These three last properly belong to the art of Controversial Dialectic, as they have no objective truth in view, but only the appearance of it, and pay no regard to truth itself; that is to say, they aim at victory. Aristotle's book on *Sophistic Conclusions* was edited apart from the others, and at a later date. It was the last book of his *Dialectic*.

ion of our adversary. That we should regard as a matter of
no moment, or, at any rate, of very secondary consequence;
but, as things are, it is the main concern. Our innate vanity,
which is particularly sensitive in reference to our intellectual
powers, will not suffer us to allow that our first position was
wrong and our adversary's right. The way out of this difficulty
would be simply to take the trouble always to form a correct
judgment. For this a man would have to think before he spoke.
But, with most men, innate vanity is accompanied by loquacity
and innate dishonesty. They speak before they think; and even
though they may afterwards perceive that they are wrong,
and that what they assert is false, they want it to seem the
contrary. The interest in truth, which may be presumed to
have been their only motive when they stated the proposition
alleged to be true, now gives way to the interests of vanity:
and so, for the sake of vanity, what is true must seem false,
and what is false must seem true.

However, this very dishonesty, this persistence in a proposition which seems false even to ourselves, has something to be
said for it. It often happens that we begin with the firm conviction of the truth of our statement; but our opponent's argument appears to refute it. Should we abandon our position at
once, we may discover later on that we were right after all;
the proof we offered was false, but nevertheless there was a
proof for our statement which was true. The argument which
would have been our salvation did not occur to us at the moment. Hence we make it a rule to attack a counter-argument,
even though to all appearances it is true and forcible, in the
belief that its truth is only superficial, and that in the course
of the dispute another argument will occur to us by which we
may upset it, or succeed in confirming the truth of our statement. In this way we are almost compelled to become dishonest; or, at any rate, the temptation to do so is very great.
Thus it is that the weakness of our intellect and the perversity
of our will lend each other mutual support; and that, generally, a disputant fights not for truth, but for his proposition,
as though it were a battle *pro aris et focis*. He sets to work
per fas et nefas; nay, as we have seen, he cannot easily do
otherwise. As a rule, then, every man will insist on maintaining

whatever he has said, even though for the moment he may consider it false or doubtful.[3]

To some extent every man is armed against such a procedure by his own cunning and villainy. He learns by daily experience, and thus comes to have his own *natural Dialectic*, just as he has his own *natural Logic*. But his Dialectic is by no means as safe a guide as his Logic. It is not so easy for any one to think or draw an inference contrary to the laws of Logic; false judgments are frequent, false conclusions very rare. A man cannot easily be deficient in natural Logic, but he may very easily be deficient in natural Dialectic, which is a gift apportioned in unequal measure. In so far natural Dialectic resembles the faculty of judgment, which differs in degree with every man; while reason, strictly speaking, is the same. For it often happens that in a matter in which a man is really in the right, he is confounded or refuted by merely superficial arguments; and if he emerges victorious from a contest, he owes it very often not so much to the correctness of his judgment in stating his proposition, as to the cunning and address with which he defended it.

Here, as in all other cases, the best gifts are born with a man; nevertheless, much may be done to make him a master of this art by practice, and also by a consideration of the tactics which may be used to defeat an opponent, or which he uses himself for a similar purpose. Therefore, even though

[3] Machiavelli recommends his Prince to make use of every moment that his neighbour is weak, in order to attack him; as otherwise his neighbour may do the same. If honour and fidelity prevailed in the world, it would be a different matter; but as these are qualities not to be expected, a man must not practise them himself, because he will meet with a bad return. It is just the same in a dispute: if I allow that my opponent is right as soon as he seems to be so, it is scarcely probable that he will do the same when the position is reversed; and as he acts wrongly, I am compelled to act wrongly too. It is easy to say that we must yield to truth, without any prepossession in favour of our own statements; but we cannot assume that our opponent will do it, and therefore we cannot do it either. Nay, if I were to abandon the position on which I had previously bestowed much thought, as soon as it appeared that he was right, it might easily happen that I might be misled by a momentary impression, and give up the truth in order to accept an error.

Logic may be of no very real, practical use, Dialectic may certainly be so; and Aristotle, too, seems to me to have drawn up his Logic proper, or Analytic, as a foundation and preparation for his Dialectic, and to have made this his chief business. Logic is concerned with the mere form of propositions; Dialectic, with their contents or matter—in a word, with their substance. It was proper, therefore, to consider the general form of all propositions before proceeding to particulars.

Aristotle does not define the object of Dialectic as exactly as I have done it here; for while he allows that its principal object is disputation, he declares at the same time that it is also the discovery of truth.[4] Again, he says, later on, that if, from the philosophical point of view, propositions are dealt with according to their truth, Dialectic regards them according to their plausibility, or the measure in which they will win the approval and assent of others.[5] He is aware that the objective truth of a proposition must be distinguished and separated from the way in which it is pressed home, and approbation won for it; but he fails to draw a sufficiently sharp distinction between these two aspects of the matter, so as to reserve Dialectic for the latter alone.[6] The rules which he

[4] *Topica*, bk. i., 2.

[5] *Ib.*, 12.

[6] On the other hand, in his book *De Sophisticis Elenchis*, he takes too much trouble to separate *Dialectic* from *Sophistic* and *Eristic*, where the distinction is said to consist in this, that dialectical conclusions are true in their form and their contents, while sophistical and eristical conclusions are false.

Eristic so far differs from Sophistic that, while the master of Eristic aims at mere victory, the Sophist looks to the reputation, and with it, the monetary rewards which he will gain. But whether a proposition is true in respect of its contents is far too uncertain a matter to form the foundation of the distinction in question; and it is a matter on which the disputant least of all can arrive at certainty; nor is it disclosed in any very sure form even by the result of the disputation. Therefore, when Aristotle speaks of *Dialectic*, we must include in it Sophistic, Eristic, and Peirastic, and define it as "the art of getting the best of it in a dispute," in which, unquestionably, the safest plan is to be in the right to begin with; but this in itself is not enough in the existing disposition of mankind, and, on the other hand, with the weakness of the human intellect, it is not altogether necessary. Other expedients are required, which, just because they are unnecessary to the attain-

often gives for Dialectic contain some of those which properly belong to Logic; and hence it appears to me that he has not provided a clear solution of the problem.

We must always keep the subject of one branch of knowledge quite distinct from that of any other. To form a clear idea of the province of Dialectic, we must pay no attention to objective truth, which is an affair of Logic; we must regard it simply as *the art of getting the best of it in a dispute,* which, as we have seen, is all the easier if we are actually in the right. In itself Dialectic has nothing to do but to show how a man may defend himself against attacks of every kind, and especially against dishonest attacks; and, in the same fashion, how he may attack another man's statement without contradicting himself, or generally without being defeated. The discovery of objective truth must be separated from the art of winning acceptance for propositions; for objective truth is an entirely different matter: it is the business of sound judgment, reflection and experience, for which there is no special art.

Such, then, is the aim of Dialectic. It has been defined as the Logic of appearance; but the definition is a wrong one, as in that case it could only be used to repel false propositions. But even when a man has the right on his side, he needs Dialectic in order to defend and maintain it; he must know what the dishonest tricks are, in order to meet them; nay, he must

---

ment of objective truth, may also be used when a man is objectively in the wrong; and whether or not this is the case, is hardly ever a matter of complete certainty.

I am of opinion, therefore, that a sharper distinction should be drawn between Dialectic and Logic than Aristotle has given us; that to Logic we should assign objective truth as far as it is merely formal, and that Dialectic should be confined to the art of gaining one's point, and contrarily, that Sophistic and Eristic should not be distinguished from Dialectic in Aristotle's fashion, since the difference which he draws rests on objective and material truth; and in regard to what this is, we cannot attain any clear certainty before discussion; but we are compelled, with Pilate, to ask, *What is truth?* Two men often engage in a warm dispute, and then return to their homes each of the other's opinion, which he has exchanged for his own. It is easy to say that in every dispute we should have no other aim than the advancement of truth; but before dispute no one knows where it is, and through his opponent's arguments and his own a man is misled.

often make use of them himself, so as to beat the enemy with
his own weapons.

Accordingly, in a dialectical contest we must put objective
truth aside, or, rather, we must regard it as an accidental circumstance, and look only to the defence of our own position
and the refutation of our opponent's.

In following out the rules to this end, no respect should be
paid to objective truth, because we usually do not know where
the truth lies. As I have said, a man often does not himself
know whether he is in the right or not; he often believes it,
and is mistaken: both sides often believe it. Truth is in the
depths. At the beginning of a contest each man believes, as a
rule, that right is on his side; in the course of it, both become
doubtful, and the truth is not determined or confirmed until
the close.

Dialectic, then, need have nothing to do with truth, as little
as the fencing master considers who is in the right when a
dispute leads to a duel. Thrust and parry is the whole business.
Dialectic is the art of intellectual fencing; and it is only when
we so regard it that we can erect it into a branch of knowledge.
For if we take purely objective truth as our aim, we are reduced to mere Logic; if we take the maintenance of false propositions, it is mere Sophistic; and in either case it would have
to be assumed that we were aware of what was true and what
was false; and it is seldom that we have any clear idea of the
truth beforehand. The true conception of Dialectic is, then,
that which we have formed: it is the art of intellectual fencing
used for the purpose of getting the best of it in a dispute;
and, although the name *Eristic* would be more suitable, it is
more correct to call it controversial Dialectic, *Dialectica eristica*.

Dialectic in this sense of the word has no other aim but to
reduce to a regular system and collect and exhibit the arts
which most men employ when they observe, in a dispute, that
truth is not on their side, and still attempt to gain the day.
Hence, it would be very inexpedient to pay any regard to objective truth or its advancement in a science of Dialectic; since
this is not done in that original and natural Dialectic innate
in men, where they strive for nothing but victory. The science
of Dialectic, in one sense of the word, is mainly concerned to
tabulate and analyse dishonest stratagems, in order that in a

real debate they may be at once recognised and defeated. It is for this very reason that Dialectic must admittedly take victory, and not objective truth, for its aim and purpose.

I am not aware that anything has been done in this direction, although I have made inquiries far and wide. It is, therefore, an uncultivated soil. To accomplish our purpose, we must draw from our experience; we must observe how in the debates which often arise in our intercourse with our fellow-men this or that stratagem is employed by one side or the other. By finding out the common elements in tricks repeated in different forms, we shall be enabled to exhibit certain general stratagems which may be advantageous, as well for our own use, as for frustrating others if they use them.

What follows is to be regarded as a first attempt.

THE BASIS OF ALL DIALECTIC

First of all, we must consider the essential nature of every dispute: what it is that really takes place in it.

Our opponent has stated a thesis, or we ourselves,—it is all one. There are two modes of refuting it, and two courses that we may pursue.

I. The modes are (1) *ad rem*, (2) *ad hominem* or *ex concessis*. That is to say: We may show either that the proposition is not in accordance with the nature of things, *i.e.*, with absolute, objective truth; or that it is inconsistent with other statements or admissions of our opponent, *i.e.*, with truth as it appears to him. The latter mode of arguing a question produces only a relative conviction, and makes no difference whatever to the objective truth of the matter.

II. The two courses that we may pursue are (1) the direct, and (2) the indirect refutation. The direct attacks the reason for the thesis; the indirect, its results. The direct refutation shows that the thesis is not true; the indirect, that it cannot be true.

The direct course admits of a twofold procedure. Either we may show that the reasons for the statement are false (*nego majorem, minorem*); or we may admit the reasons or premisses, but show that the statement does not follow from them (*nego consequentiam*); that is, we attack the conclusion or form of the syllogism.

The direct refutation makes use either of the *diversion* or of the *instance*.

(*a*) The *diversion*.—We accept our opponent's proposition as true, and then show what follows from it when we bring it into connection with some other proposition acknowledged to be true. We use the two propositions as the premisses of a syllogism giving a conclusion which is manifestly false, as contradicting either the nature of things,[7] or other statements of our opponent himself; that is to say, the conclusion is false either *ad rem* or *ad hominem*.[8] Consequently, our opponent's proposition must have been false; for, while true premisses can give only a true conclusion, false premisses need not always give a false one.

(*b*) The *instance*, or the example to the contrary.—This consists in refuting the general proposition by direct reference to particular cases which are included in it in the way in which it is stated, but to which it does not apply, and by which it is therefore shown to be necessarily false.

Such is the framework or skeleton of all forms of disputation; for to this every kind of controversy may be ultimately reduced. The whole of a controversy may, however, actually proceed in the manner described, or only appear to do so; and it may be supported by genuine or spurious arguments. It is just because it is not easy to make out the truth in regard to this matter, that debates are so long and so obstinate.

Nor can we, in ordering the argument, separate actual from apparent truth, since even the disputants are not certain about it beforehand. Therefore I shall describe the various tricks or stratagems without regard to questions of objective truth or falsity; for that is a matter on which we have no assurance, and which cannot be determined previously. Moreover, in every disputation or argument on any subject we must agree about something; and by this, as a principle, we must be willing to judge the matter in question. We cannot argue with

[7] If it is in direct contradiction with a perfectly undoubted truth, we have reduced our opponent's position *ad absurdum*.

[8] Socrates, in *Hippia Maj. et alias*.

those who deny principles: *Contra negantem principia non est disputandum.*

STRATAGEMS

I

The *Extension.*—This consists in carrying your opponent's proposition beyond its natural limits; in giving it as general a signification and as wide a sense as possible, so as to exaggerate it; and, on the other hand, in giving your own proposition as restricted a sense and as narrow limits as you can, because the more general a statement becomes, the more numerous are the objections to which it is open. The defence consists in an accurate statement of the point or essential question at issue.

Example 1.—I asserted that the English were supreme in drama. My opponent attempted to give an instance to the contrary, and replied that it was a well-known fact that in music, and consequently in opera, they could do nothing at all. I repelled the attack by reminding him that music was not included in dramatic art, which covered tragedy and comedy alone. This he knew very well. What he had done was to try to generalise my proposition, so that it would apply to all theatrical representations, and, consequently, to opera and then to music, in order to make certain of defeating me. Contrarily, we may save our proposition by reducing it within narrower limits than we had first intended, if our way of expressing it favours this expedient.

Example 2.—A. declares that the Peace of 1814 gave back their independence to all the German towns of the Hanseatic League. B. gives an instance to the contrary by reciting the fact that Dantzig, which received its independence from Buonaparte, lost it by that Peace. A. saves himself thus: "I said 'all German towns,' and Dantzig was in Poland."

This trick was mentioned by Aristotle in the *Topica* (bk. viii., cc. 11, 12).

Example 3.—Lamarck, in his *Philosophie Zoologique* (vol. i., p. 203), states that the polype has no feeling, because it has no nerves. It is certain, however, that it has some sort of perception; for it advances towards light by moving in an ingenious fashion from branch to branch, and it seizes its prey.

Hence it has been assumed that its nervous system is spread over the whole of its body in equal measure, as though it were blended with it; for it is obvious that the polype possesses some faculty of perception without having any separate organs of sense. Since this assumption refutes Lamarck's position, he argues thus: "In that case all parts of its body must be capable of every kind of feeling, and also of motion, of will, of thought. The polype would have all the organs of the most perfect animal in every point of its body; every point could see, smell, taste, hear, and so on; nay, it could think, judge, and draw conclusions; every particle of its body would be a perfect animal and it would stand higher than man, as every part of it would possess all the faculties which man possesses only in the whole of him. Further, there would be no reason for not extending what is true of the polype to all monads, the most imperfect of all creatures, and ultimately to the plants, which are also alive, etc., etc." By using dialectical tricks of this kind a writer betrays that he is secretly conscious of being in the wrong. Because it was said that the creature's whole body is sensitive to light, and is therefore possessed of nerves, he makes out that its whole body is capable of thought.

II

The *Homonymy.*—This trick is to extend a proposition to something which has little or nothing in common with the matter in question but the similarity of the word; then to refute it triumphantly, and so claim credit for having refuted the original statement.

It may be noted here that synonyms are two words for the same conception; homonyms, two conceptions which are covered by the same word. (See Aristotle, *Topica*, bk. i., c. 13.) "Deep," "cutting," "high," used at one moment of bodies, at another of tones, are homonyms; "honourable" and "honest" are synonyms.

This is a trick which may be regarded as identical with the sophism *ex homonymia;* although, if the sophism is obvious, it will deceive no one.

> Every light can be extinguished.
> The intellect is a light.
> Therefore it can be extinguished.

Here it is at once clear that there are four terms in the syllogism, "light" being used both in a real and in a metaphorical sense. But if the sophism takes a subtle form, it is, of course, apt to mislead, especially where the conceptions which are covered by the same word are related, and inclined to be interchangeable. It is never subtle enough to deceive, if it is used intentionally; and therefore cases of it must be collected from actual and individual experience.

It would be a very good thing if every trick could receive some short and obviously appropriate name, so that when a man used this or that particular trick, he could be at once reproached for it.

I will give two examples of the homonymy.

Example 1.—A.: "You are not yet initiated into the mysteries of the Kantian philosophy."

B.: "Oh, if it's mysteries you're talking of, I'll have nothing to do with them."

Example 2.—I condemned the principle involved in the word *honour* as a foolish one; for, according to it, a man loses his honour by receiving an insult, which he cannot wipe out unless he replies with a still greater insult, or by shedding his adversary's blood or his own. I contended that a man's true honour cannot be outraged by what he suffers, but only and alone by what he does; for there is no saying what may befall any one of us. My opponent immediately attacked the reason I had given, and triumphantly proved to me that when a tradesman was falsely accused of misrepresentation, dishonesty, or neglect in his business, it was an attack upon his honour, which in this case was outraged solely by what he suffered, and that he could only retrieve it by punishing his aggressor and making him retract.

Here, by a homonymy, he was foisting *civic honour*, which is otherwise called *good name*, and which may be outraged by libel and slander, on to the conception of *knightly honour*, also called *point d'honneur*, which may be outraged by insult. And since an attack on the former cannot be disregarded, but must be repelled by public disproof, so, with the same justification, an attack on the latter must not be disregarded either, but it must be defeated by still greater insult and a duel. Here we have a confusion of two essentially different things through

the homonymy in the word *honour,* and a consequent alteration of the point in dispute.

III

Another trick is to take a proposition which is laid down
relatively, and in reference to some particular matter, as
though it were uttered with a general or absolute application;
or, at least, to take it in some quite different sense, and then
refute it. Aristotle's example is as follows:

A Moor is black; but in regard to his teeth he is white;
therefore, he is black and not black at the same moment. This
is an obvious sophism, which will deceive no one. Let us contrast it with one drawn from actual experience.

In talking of philosophy, I admitted that my system upheld
the Quietists, and commended them. Shortly afterwards the
conversation turned upon Hegel, and I maintained that his
writings were mostly nonsense; or, at any rate, that there were
many passages in them where the author wrote the words,
and it was left to the reader to find a meaning for them. My
opponent did not attempt to refute this assertion *ad rem,* but
contented himself by advancing the *argumentum ad hominem,*
and telling me that I had just been praising the Quietists, and
that they had written a good deal of nonsense too.

This I admitted; but, by way of correcting him, I said that
I had praised the Quietists, not as philosophers and writers,
that is to say, for their achievements in the sphere of *theory,*
but only as men, and for their conduct in mere matters of
practice; and that in Hegel's case we were talking of theories.
In this way I parried the attack.

The first three tricks are of a kindred character. They have
this in common, that something different is attacked from that
which was asserted. It would therefore be an *ignoratio elenchi*
to allow oneself to be disposed of in such a manner.

For in all the examples that I have given, what the opponent
says is true, but it stands in apparent and not in real contradiction with the thesis. All that the man whom he is attacking
has to do is to deny the validity of his syllogism; to deny,
namely, the conclusion which he draws, that because his proposition is true, ours is false. In this way his refutation is itself
directly refuted by a denial of his conclusion, *per negationem*

consequentiae. Another trick is to refuse to admit true premisses because of a foreseen conclusion. There are two ways of defeating it, incorporated in the next two sections.

IV

If you want to draw a conclusion, you must not let it be foreseen, but you must get the premisses admitted one by one, unobserved, mingling them here and there in your talk; otherwise, your opponent will attempt all sorts of chicanery. Or, if it is doubtful whether your opponent will admit them, you must advance the premisses of these premisses; that is to say, you must draw up pro-syllogisms, and get the premisses of several of them admitted in no definite order. In this way you conceal your game until you have obtained all the admissions that are necessary, and so reach your goal by making a circuit. These rules are given by Aristotle in his *Topica,* bk. viii., c. 1. It is a trick which needs no illustration.

V

To prove the truth of a proposition, you may also employ previous propositions that are not true, should your opponent refuse to admit the true ones, either because he fails to perceive their truth, or because he sees that the thesis immediately follows from them. In that case the plan is to take propositions which are false in themselves but true for your opponent, and argue from the way in which he thinks, that is to say, *ex concessis*. For a true conclusion may follow from false premisses, but not *vice versa*. In the same fashion your opponent's false propositions may be refuted by other false propositions, which he, however, takes to be true; for it is with him that you have to do, and you must use the thoughts that he uses. For instance, if he is a member of some sect to which you do not belong, you may employ the declared opinions of this sect against him, as principles.[9]

VI

Another plan is to beg the question in disguise by postulating what has to be proved, either (1) under another name; for instance, "good repute" instead of "honour"; "virtue" in-

[9] Aristotle, *Topica,* bk. viii., chap. 2.

stead of "virginity," etc.; or by using such convertible terms
as "red-blooded animals" and "vertebrates"; or (2) by making
a general assumption covering the particular point in dispute;
for instance, maintaining the uncertainty of medicine by postulating the uncertainty of all human knowledge. (3) If, *vice
versa,* two things follow one from the other, and one is to be
proved, you may postulate the other. (4) If a general proposition is to be proved, you may get your opponent to admit
every one of the particulars. This is the converse of the
second.[10]

VII

Should the disputation be conducted on somewhat strict
and formal lines, and there be a desire to arrive at a very clear
understanding, he who states the proposition and wants to
prove it may proceed against his opponent by question, in
order to show the truth of the statement from his admissions.
The erotematic, or Socratic, method was especially in use
among the ancients; and this and some of the tricks following
later on are akin to it.[11]

The plan is to ask a great many wide-reaching questions at
once, so as to hide what you want to get admitted, and, on
the other hand, quickly propound the argument resulting from
the admissions; for those who are slow of understanding cannot follow accurately, and do not notice any mistakes or gaps
there may be in the demonstration.

VIII

This trick consists in making your opponent angry; for when
he is angry he is incapable of judging aright, and perceiving
where his advantage lies. You can make him angry by doing
him repeated injustice, or practising some kind of chicanery,
and being generally insolent.

IX

Or you may put questions in an order different from that
which the conclusion to be drawn from them requires, and

[10] *Idem,* chap. 11. The last chapter of this work contains some
good rules for the practice of Dialectics.

[11] They are all a free version of chap. 15 of Aristotle's *De
Sophistici Elenchis.*

transpose them, so as not to let him know at what you are
aiming. He can then take no precautions. You may also use
his answers for different or even opposite conclusions, according to their character. This is akin to the trick of masking your
procedure.

X

If you observe that your opponent designedly returns a negative answer to the questions which, for the sake of your proposition, you want him to answer in the affirmative, you must
ask the converse of the proposition, as though it were that
which you were anxious to see affirmed; or, at any rate, you
may give him his choice of both, so that he may not perceive
which of them you are asking him to affirm.

XI

If you make an induction, and your opponent grants you
the particular cases by which it is to be supported, you must
refrain from asking him if he also admits the general truth
which issues from the particulars, but introduce it afterwards
as a settled and admitted fact; for, in the meanwhile, he will
himself come to believe that he has admitted it, and the same
impression will be received by the audience, because they will
remember the many questions as to the particulars, and suppose that they must, of course, have attained their end.

XII

If the conversation turns upon some general conception
which has no particular name, but requires some figurative
or metaphorical designation, you must begin by choosing a
metaphor that is favourable to your proposition. For instance,
the names used to denote the two political parties in Spain,
Serviles and *Liberales,* are obviously chosen by the latter. The
name *Protestants* is chosen by themselves, and also the name
Evangelicals; but the Catholics call them *heretics.* Similarly,
in regard to the names of things which admit of a more exact
and definite meaning: for example, if your opponent proposes
an *alteration,* you can call it an *innovation,* as this is an in-
vidious word. If you yourself make the proposal, it will be
the converse. In the first case, you can call the antagonistic

principle "the existing order," in the second, "antiquated prejudice." What an impartial man with no further purpose to
serve would call "public worship" or a "system of religion," is
described by an adherent as "piety," "godliness": and by an
opponent as "bigotry," "superstition." This is, at bottom, a
subtle *petitio principii*. What is sought to be proved is, first of
all, inserted in the definition, whence it is then taken by mere
analysis. What one man calls "placing in safe custody," another calls "throwing into prison." A speaker often betrays his
purpose beforehand by the names which he gives to things.
One man talks of "the clergy"; another, of "the priests."

Of all the tricks of controversy, this is the most frequent,
and it is used instinctively. You hear of "religious zeal," or
"fanaticism"; a *"faux pas,"* a "piece of gallantry," or "adultery"; an "equivocal," or a "bawdy" story; "embarrassment,"
or "bankruptcy"; "through influence and connection," or by
"bribery and nepotism"; "sincere gratitude," or "good pay."

XIII

To make your opponent accept a proposition, you must give
him the counter-proposition as well, leaving him his choice of
the two; and you must render the contrast as glaring as you
can, so that to avoid being paradoxical he will accept the
proposition, which is thus made to look quite probable. For
instance, if you want to make him admit that a boy must do
everything that his father tells him to do, ask him "whether
in all things we must obey or disobey our parents." Or, if a
thing is said to occur "often," ask whether by "often" you are
to understand few or many cases; and he will say "many." It
is as though you were to put grey next black, and call it white;
or next white, and call it black.

XIV

This, which is an impudent trick, is played as follows: When
your opponent has answered several of your questions without
the answers turning out favourable to the conclusion at which
you are aiming, advance the desired conclusion,—although it
does not in the least follow,—as though it had been proved,
and proclaim it in a tone of triumph. If your opponent is shy
or stupid, and you yourself possess a great deal of impudence

and a good voice, the trick may easily succeed. It is akin to the fallacy *non causae ut causae.*

XV

If you have advanced a paradoxical proposition and find a difficulty in proving it, you may submit for your opponent's acceptance or rejection some true proposition, the truth of which, however, is not quite palpable, as though you wished to draw your proof from it. Should he reject it because he suspects a trick, you can obtain your triumph by showing how absurd he is; should he accept it, you have got reason on your side for the moment, and must now look about you; or else you can employ the previous trick as well, and maintain that your paradox is proved by the proposition which he has accepted. For this an extreme degree of impudence is required; but experience shows cases of it, and there are people who practise it by instinct.

XVI

Another trick is to use arguments *ad hominem*, or *ex concessis*.[12] When your opponent makes a proposition, you must try to see whether it is not in some way—if needs be, only apparently—inconsistent with some other proposition which he has made or admitted, or with the principles of a school or sect which he has commended and approved, or with the ac-

---

[12] The truth from which I draw my proof may be either (1) of an objective and universally valid character; in that case my proof is veracious, *secundum veritatem;* and it is such proof alone that has any genuine validity. Or (2) it may be valid only for the person to whom I wish to prove my proposition, and with whom I am disputing. He has, that is to say, either taken up some position once for all as a prejudice, or hastily admitted it in the course of the dispute; and on this I ground my proof. In that case, it is a proof valid only for this particular man, *ad hominem.* I compel my opponent to grant my proposition, but I fail to establish it as a truth of universal validity. My proof avails for my opponent alone, but for no one else. For example, if my opponent is a devotee of Kant's, and I ground my proof on some utterance of that philosopher, it is a proof which in itself is only *ad hominem.* If he is a Mohammedan, I may prove my point by reference to a passage in the Koran, and that is sufficient for him; but here it is only a proof *ad hominem.*

tions of those who support the sect, or else of those who give it only an apparent and spurious support, or with his own actions or want of action. For example, should he defend suicide, you may at once exclaim, "Why don't you hang yourself?" Should he maintain that Berlin is an unpleasant place to live in, you may say, "Why don't you leave by the first train?" Some such claptrap is always possible.

XVII

If your opponent presses you with a counter-proof, you will often be able to save yourself by advancing some subtle distinction, which, it is true, had not previously occurred to you; that is, if the matter admits of a double application, or of being taken in any ambiguous sense.

XVIII

If you observe that your opponent has taken up a line of argument which will end in your defeat, you must not allow him to carry it to its conclusion, but interrupt the course of the dispute in time, or break it off altogether, or lead him away from the subject, and bring him to others. In short, you must effect the trick which will be noticed later on, the *mutatio controversiae*. (See § xxix.)

XIX

Should your opponent expressly challenge you to produce any objection to some definite point in his argument, and you have nothing much to say, you must try to give the matter a general turn, and then talk against that. If you are called upon to say why a particular physical hypothesis cannot be accepted, you may speak of the fallibility of human knowledge, and give various illustrations of it.

XX

When you have elicited all your premisses, and your opponent has admitted them, you must refrain from asking him for the conclusion, but draw it at once for yourself; nay, even though one or other of the premisses should be lacking, you may take it as though it too had been admitted, and draw the conclusion. This trick is an application of the fallacy *non causae ut causae.*

XXI

When your opponent uses a merely superficial or sophistical argument and you see through it, you can, it is true, refute it by setting forth its captious and superficial character; but it is better to meet him with a counter-argument which is just as superficial and sophistical, and so dispose of him; for it is with victory that you are concerned, and not with truth. If, for example, he adopts an *argumentum ad hominem,* it is sufficient to take the force out of it by a counter *argumentum ad hominem* or *argumentum ex concessis;* and, in general, instead of setting forth the true state of the case at equal length, it is shorter to take this course if it lies open to you.

XXII

If your opponent requires you to admit something from which the point in dispute will immediately follow, you must refuse to do so, declaring that it is a *petitio principii.* For he and the audience will regard a proposition which is near akin to the point in dispute as identical with it, and in this way you deprive him of his best argument.

XXIII

Contradiction and contention irritate a man into exaggerating his statement. By contradicting your opponent you may drive him into extending beyond its proper limits a statement which, at all events within those limits and in itself, is true; and when you refute this exaggerated form of it, you look as though you had also refuted his original statement. Contrarily, you must take care not to allow yourself to be misled by contradictions into exaggerating or extending a statement of your own. It will often happen that your opponent will himself directly try to extend your statement further than you meant it; here you must at once stop him, and bring him back to the limits which you set up: "That's what I said, and no more."

XXIV

This trick consists in stating a false syllogism. Your opponent makes a proposition, and by false inference and distortion of his ideas you force from it other propositions which it does not contain and he does not in the least mean; nay, which are absurd or dangerous. It then looks as if his proposition gave rise to others which are inconsistent either with themselves or with some acknowledged truth, and so it appears to be indirectly refuted. This is the *diversion*, and it is another application of the fallacy *non causae ut causae.*

XXV

This is a case of the *diversion* by means of an *instance to the contrary.* With an induction a great number of particular instances are required in order to establish it as a universal proposition; but with the *diversion* a single instance, to which the proposition does not apply, is all that is necessary to overthrow it. This is a controversial method known as the *instance —instantia.* For example, "all ruminants are horned" is a proposition which may be upset by the single instance of the camel. The *instance* is a case in which a universal truth is sought to be applied, and something is inserted in the fundamental definition of it which is not universally true, and by which it is upset. But there is room for mistake; and when this trick is employed by your opponent, you must observe (1) whether the example which he gives is really true; for there are problems of which the only true solution is that the case in point is not true—for example, many miracles, ghost stories, and so on; and (2) whether it really comes under the conception of the truth thus stated; for it may only appear to do so, and the matter is one to be settled by precise distinctions; and (3) whether it is really inconsistent with this conception; for this again may be only an apparent inconsistency.

XXVI

A brilliant move is the *retorsio argumenti,* or turning of the tables, by which your opponent's argument is turned against himself. He declares, for instance, "So-and-so is a child, you must make allowance for him." You retort, "Just because he is a child, I must correct him; otherwise he will persist in his bad habits."

XXVII

Should your opponent surprise you by becoming particularly angry at an argument, you must urge it with all the more zeal; not only because it is a good thing to make him angry, but because it may be presumed that you have here put your finger on the weak side of his case, and that just here he is more open to attack than even for the moment you perceive.

XXVIII

This is chiefly practicable in a dispute between scholars in the presence of the unlearned. If you have no argument *ad rem*, and none either *ad hominem*, you can make one *ad auditores*; that is to say, you can start some invalid objection, which, however, only an expert sees to be invalid. Now your opponent is an expert, but those who form your audience are not, and accordingly in their eyes he is defeated; particularly if the objection which you make places him in any ridiculous light. People are ready to laugh, and you have the laughers on your side. To show that your objection is an idle one, would require a long explanation on the part of your opponent, and a reference to the principles of the branch of knowledge in question, or to the elements of the matter which you are discussing; and people are not disposed to listen to it.

For example, your opponent states that in the original formation of a mountain-range the granite and other elements in its composition were, by reason of their high temperature, in a fluid or molten state; that the temperature must have amounted to some 480° Fahrenheit; and that when the mass took shape it was covered by the sea. You reply, by an argument *ad auditores*, that at that temperature—nay, indeed, long before it had been reached, namely, at 212° Fahrenheit—the sea would have been boiled away, and spread through the air in the form of steam. At this the audience laughs. To refute the objection, your opponent would have to show that the boiling-point depends not only on the degree of warmth, but also on the atmospheric pressure; and that as soon as about half the sea-water had gone off in the shape of steam, this pres-

sure would be so greatly increased that the rest of it would fail
to boil even at a temperature of 480°. He is debarred from
giving this explanation, as it would require a treatise to demonstrate the matter to those who had no acquaintance with
physics.

XXIX

If you find that you are being worsted, you can make a
diversion—that is, you can suddenly begin to talk of something
else, as though it had a bearing on the matter in dispute, and
afforded an argument against your opponent. This may be
done without presumption if the diversion has, in fact, some
general bearing on the matter; but it is a piece of impudence
if it has nothing to do with the case, and is only brought in
by way of attacking your opponent.

For example, I praised the system prevailing in China,
where there is no such thing as hereditary nobility, and offices
are bestowed only on those who succeed in competitive ex-
aminations. My opponent maintained that learning, as little
as the privilege of birth (of which he had a high opinion) fits a
man for office. We argued, and he got the worst of it. Then he
made a diversion, and declared that in China all ranks were
punished with the bastinado, which he connected with the
immoderate indulgence in tea, and proceeded to make both
of them a subject of reproach to the Chinese. To follow him
into all this would have been to allow oneself to be drawn
into a surrender of the victory which had already been won.

The diversion is mere impudence if it completely abandons
the point in dispute, and raises, for instance, some such objection as "Yes, and you also said just now," and so on. For then
the argument becomes to some extent personal; of the kind
which will be treated of in the last section. Strictly speaking,
it is half-way between the *argumentum ad personam*, which
will there be discussed, and the *argumentum ad hominem*.

How very innate this trick is, may be seen in every quarrel
between common people. If one of the parties makes some
personal reproach against the other, the latter, instead of answering it by refuting it, allows it to stand,—as it were, admits
it; and replies by reproaching his antagonist on some other
ground. This is a stratagem like that pursued by Scipio when

he attacked the Carthaginians, not in Italy, but in Africa. In war, diversions of this kind may be profitable; but in a quarrel they are poor expedients, because the reproaches remain, and those who look on hear the worst that can be said of both parties. It is a trick that should be used only *faute de mieux*.

XXX

This is the *argumentum ad verecundiam*. It consists in making an appeal to authority rather than reason, and in using such an authority as may suit the degree of knowledge possessed by your opponent.

Every man prefers belief to the exercise of judgment, says Seneca; and it is therefore an easy matter if you have an authority on your side which your opponent respects. The more limited his capacity and knowledge, the greater is the number of the authorities who weigh with him. But if his capacity and knowledge are of a high order, there are very few; indeed, hardly any at all. He may, perhaps, admit the authority of professional men versed in a science or an art or a handicraft of which he knows little or nothing; but even so he will regard it with suspicion. Contrarily, ordinary folk have a deep respect for professional men of every kind. They are unaware that a man who makes a profession of a thing loves it not for the thing itself, but for the money he makes by it; or that it is rare for a man who teaches to know his subject thoroughly; for if he studies it as he ought, he has in most cases no time left in which to teach it.

But there are very many authorities who find respect with the mob, and if you have none that is quite suitable, you can take one that appears to be so; you may quote what some said in another sense or in other circumstances. Authorities which your opponent fails to understand are those of which he generally thinks the most. The unlearned entertain a peculiar respect for a Greek or a Latin flourish. You may also, should it be necessary, not only twist your authorities, but actually falsify them, or quote something which you have invented entirely yourself. As a rule, your opponent has no books at hand, and could not use them if he had. The finest illustration of this is furnished by the French *curé*, who, to avoid being compelled, like other citizens, to pave the street in front of his house, quoted a saying which he described as biblical: *paveant illi, ego non pavebo.* That was quite enough for the municipal officers.

A universal prejudice may also be used as an authority; for most people think with Aristotle that that may be said to exist which many believe. There is no opinion, however absurd, which men will not readily embrace as soon as they can be brought to the conviction that it is generally adopted. Example affects their thought just as it affects their action. They are like sheep following the bell-wether just as he leads them. They would sooner die than think. It is very curious that the universality of an opinion should have so much weight with people, as their own experience might tell them that its acceptance is an entirely thoughtless and merely imitative process. But it tells them nothing of the kind, because they possess no self-knowledge whatever.

But to speak seriously, the universality of an opinion is no proof, nay, it is not even a probability, that the opinion is right. Those who maintain that it is so must assume (1) that length of time deprives a universal opinion of its demonstrative force, as otherwise all the old errors which were once universally held to be true would have to be recalled; for instance, the Ptolemaic system would have to be restored, or Catholicism re-established in all Protestant countries. They must assume (2) that distance of space has the same effect; otherwise the respective universality of opinion among the adherents of Buddhism, Christianity, and Islam will put them in a difficulty.

When we come to look into the matter, so-called universal opinion is the opinion of two or three persons; and we should be persuaded of this if we could see the way in which it really arises.

We should find that it is two or three persons who, in the first instance, accepted it, or advanced and maintained it; and of whom people were so good as to believe that they had thoroughly tested it. Then a few other persons, persuaded beforehand that the first were men of the requisite capacity, also accepted the opinion. These, again, were trusted by many others, whose laziness suggested to them that it was better to believe at once, than to go through the troublesome task of testing the matter for themselves. Thus the number of these lazy and credulous adherents grew from day to day; for the opinion had no sooner obtained a fair measure of support than its further supporters attributed this to the fact that the opinion could only have obtained it by the cogency of its arguments. The remainder were then compelled to grant what was universally granted, so as not to pass for unruly persons who resisted opinions which every one accepted, or pert fellows who thought themselves cleverer than any one else.

When opinion reaches this stage, adhesion becomes a duty; and henceforward the few who are capable of forming a judgment hold their peace. Those who venture to speak are such as are entirely incapable of forming any opinions or any judgment of their own, being merely the echo of others' opinions; and, nevertheless, they defend them with all the greater zeal and intolerance. For what they hate in people who think differently is not so much the different opinions which they profess, as the presumption of wanting to form their own judgment; a presumption of which they themselves are never guilty, as they are very well aware. In short, there are very few who can think, but every man wants to have an opinion; and what remains but to take it ready-made from others, instead of forming opinions for himself?

Since this is what happens, where is the value of the opinion even of a hundred millions? It is no more established than an historical fact reported by a hundred chroniclers who can be proved to have plagiarised it from one another; the opinion in the end being traceable to a single individual.[13] It is all what I say, what you say, and, finally, what he says; and the whole of it is nothing but a series of assertions:

> *Dico ego, tu dicis, sed denique dixit et ille;*
> *Dictaque post toties, nil nisi dicta vides.*

Nevertheless, in a dispute with ordinary people, we may employ universal opinion as an authority. For it will generally be found that when two of them are fighting, that is the weapon which both of them choose as a means of attack. If a man of the better sort has to deal with them, it is most advisable for him to condescend to the use of this weapon too, and to

[13] See Bayle's *Pensées sur les Comètes*, i., p. 10.

select such authorities as will make an impression on his opponent's weak side. For, *ex hypothesi,* he is as insensible to all rational argument as a horny-hided Siegfried, dipped in the flood of incapacity, and unable to think or judge.

Before a tribunal the dispute is one between authorities alone,—such authoritative statements, I mean, as are laid down by legal experts; and here the exercise of judgment consists in discovering what law or authority applies to the case in question. There is, however, plenty of room for Dialectic; for should the case in question and the law not really fit each other, they can, if necessary, be twisted until they appear to do so, or *vice versa.*

XXXI

If you know that you have no reply to the arguments which your opponent advances, you may, by a fine stroke of irony, declare yourself to be an incompetent judge: "What you now say passes my poor powers of comprehension; it may be all very true, but I can't understand it, and I refrain from any expression of opinion on it." In this way you insinuate to the bystanders, with whom you are in good repute, that what your opponent says is nonsense. Thus, when Kant's *Kritik* appeared, or, rather, when it began to make a noise in the world, many professors of the old ecclectic school declared that they failed to understand it, in the belief that their failure settled the business. But when the adherents of the new school proved to them that they were quite right, and had really failed to understand it, they were in a very bad humour.

This is a trick which may be used only when you are quite sure that the audience thinks much better of you than of your opponent. A professor, for instance, may try it on a student.

Strictly, it is a case of the preceding trick: it is a particularly malicious assertion of one's own authority, instead of giving reasons. The counter-trick is to say: "I beg your pardon; but, with your penetrating intellect, it must be very easy for you to understand anything; and it can only be my poor statement of the matter that is at fault"; and then go on to rub it into him until he understands it *nolens volens,* and sees for himself that it was really his own fault alone. In this way you parry his attack. With the greatest politeness he wanted to insinuate that you were talking nonsense; and you, with equal courtesy, prove to him that he is a fool.

XXXII

If you are confronted with an assertion, there is a short way of getting rid of it, or, at any rate, of throwing suspicion on it, by putting it into some odious category; even though the connection is only apparent, or else of a loose character. You can say, for instance, "That is Manichæism," or "It is Arianism," or "Pelagianism," or "Idealism," or "Spinozism," or "Pantheism," or "Brownianism," or "Naturalism," or "Atheism," or "Rationalism," "Spiritualism," "Mysticism," and so on. In making an objection of this kind, you take it for granted (1) that the assertion in question is identical with, or is at least contained in, the category cited—that is to say, you cry out, "Oh, I have heard that before"; and (2) that the system referred to has been entirely refuted, and does not contain a word of truth.

XXXIII

"That's all very well in theory, but it won't do in practice." In this sophism you admit the premises but deny the conclusion, in contradiction with a well-known rule of logic. The assertion is based upon an impossibility: what is right in theory *must* work in practice; and if it does not, there is a mistake in the theory; something has been overlooked and not allowed for; and, consequently, what is wrong in practice is wrong in theory too.

XXXIV

When you state a question or an argument, and your opponent gives you no direct answer or reply, but evades it by a counter-question or an indirect answer, or some assertion which has no bearing on the matter, and, generally, tries to turn the subject, it is a sure sign that you have touched a weak spot, sometimes without knowing it. You have, as it were, reduced him to silence. You must, therefore, urge the point all the more, and not let your opponent evade it, even when you do not know where the weakness which you have hit upon really lies.

XXXV

There is another trick which, as soon as it is practicable, makes all others unnecessary. Instead of working on your opponent's intellect by argument, work on his will by motive; and he, and also the audience if they have similar interests, will at once be won over to your opinion, even though you got it out of a lunatic asylum; for, as a general rule, half an ounce of will is more effective than a hundredweight of insight and intelligence. This, it is true, can be done only under peculiar circumstances. If you succeed in making your opponent feel that his opinion, should it prove true, will be distinctly prejudicial to his interest, he will let it drop like a hot potato, and feel that it was very imprudent to take it up.

A clergyman, for instance, is defending some philosophical dogma; you make him sensible of the fact that it is in immediate contradiction with one of the fundamental doctrines of his Church, and he abandons it.

A landed proprietor maintains that the use of machinery in agricultural operations, as practised in England, is an excellent institution, since an engine does the work of many men. You give him to understand that it will not be very long before carriages are also worked by steam, and that the value of his large stud will be greatly depreciated; and you will see what he will say.

In such cases every man feels how thoughtless it is to sanction a law unjust to himself—*quam temere in nosmet legem sancimus iniquam!* Nor is it otherwise if the bystanders, but not your opponent, belong to the same sect, guild, industry, club, etc., as yourself. Let his thesis be never so true, as soon as you hint that it is prejudicial to the common interests of the said society, all the bystanders will find that your opponent's arguments, however excellent they be, are weak and contemptible; and that yours, on the other hand, though they were random conjecture, are correct and to the point; you will have a chorus of loud approval on your side, and your opponent will be driven out of the field with ignominy. Nay, the bystanders will believe, as a rule, that they have agreed with you out of pure conviction. For what is not to our interest mostly seems absurd to us; our intellect being no *siccum lumen*.

This trick might be called "taking the tree by its root"; its usual name is the *argumentum ab utili.*

XXXVI

You may also puzzle and bewilder your opponent by mere bombast; and the trick is possible, because a man generally supposes that there must be some meaning in words:

Gewöhnlich glaubt der Mensch, wenn er nur Worte hört,
Es müsse sich dabei doch auch was denken lassen.

If he is secretly conscious of his own weakness, and accustomed to hear much that he does not understand, and to make as though he did, you can easily impose upon him by some serious fooling that sounds very deep or learned, and deprives him of hearing, sight, and thought; and by giving out that it is the most indisputable proof of what you assert. It is a well-known fact that in recent times some philosophers have practised this trick on the whole of the public with the most brilliant success. But since present examples are odious, we may refer to *The Vicar of Wakefield* for an old one.

XXXVII

Should your opponent be in the right, but, luckily for your contention, choose a faulty proof, you can easily manage to refute it, and then claim that you have thus refuted his whole position. This is a trick which ought to be one of the first; it is, at bottom, an expedient by which an *argumentum ad hominem* is put forward as an *argumentum ad rem.* If no accurate proof occurs to him or to the bystanders, you have won the day. For example, if a man advances the ontological argument by way of proving God's existence, you can get the best of him, for the ontological argument may easily be refuted. This is the way in which bad advocates lose a good case, by trying to justify it by an authority which does not fit it, when no fitting one occurs to them.

XXXVIII

A last trick is to become personal, insulting, rude, as soon as you perceive that your opponent has the upper hand, and that you are going to come off worst. It consists in passing from the subject of dispute, as from a lost game, to the disputant himself, and in some way attacking his person. It may be called the *argumentum ad personam,* to distinguish it from the *argumentum ad hominem,* which passes from the objective discussion of the subject pure and simple to the statements or admissions which your opponent has made in regard to it. But in becoming personal you leave the subject altogether, and turn your attack to his person, by remarks of an offensive and spiteful character. It is an appeal from the virtues of the intellect to the virtues of the body, or to mere animalism. This is a very popular trick, because every one is able to carry it into effect; and so it is of frequent application. Now the question is, What counter-trick avails for the other party? for if he has recourse to the same rule, there will be blows, or a duel, or an action for slander.

It would be a great mistake to suppose that it is sufficient not to become personal yourself. For by showing a man quite quietly that he is wrong, and that what he says and thinks is incorrect—a process which occurs in every dialectical victory —you embitter him more than if you used some rude or insulting expression. Why is this? Because, as Hobbes observes,[14] all mental pleasure consists in being able to compare oneself with others to one's own advantage. Nothing is of greater moment to a man than the gratification of his vanity, and no wound is more painful than that which is inflicted on it. Hence such phrases as "Death before dishonour," and so on. The gratification of vanity arises mainly by comparison of oneself with others, in every respect, but chiefly in respect of one's intellectual powers; and so the most effective and the strongest gratification of it is to be found in controversy. Hence the embitterment of defeat, apart from any question of injustice; and hence recourse to that last weapon, that last trick, which you cannot evade by mere politeness. A cool demeanour may, however, help you here, if, as soon as your opponent becomes personal, you quietly reply, "That has no bearing on the point in dispute," and immediately bring the conversation back to it, and continue to show him that he is wrong, without taking any notice of his insults. Say, as Themistocles said

[14] *Elementa philosophica de Cive.*

to Eurybiades—*Strike, but hear me.* But such demeanour is not given to every one.

As a sharpening of wits, controversy is often, indeed, of mutual advantage, in order to correct one's thoughts and awaken new views. But in learning and in mental power both disputants must be tolerably equal. If one of them lacks learning, he will fail to understand the other, as he is not on the same level with his antagonist. If he lacks mental power, he will be embittered, and led into dishonest tricks, and end by being rude.

The only safe rule, therefore, is that which Aristotle mentions in the last chapter of his *Topica*: not to dispute with the first person you meet, but only with those of your acquaintance of whom you know that they possess sufficient intelligence and self-respect not to advance absurdities; to appeal to reason and not to authority, and to listen to reason and yield to it; and, finally, to cherish truth, to be willing to accept reason even from an opponent, and to be just enough to bear being proved to be in the wrong, should truth lie with him. From this it follows that scarcely one man in a hundred is worth your disputing with him. You may let the remainder say what they please, for every one is at liberty to be a fool —*desipere est jus gentium.* Remember what Voltaire says: *La paix vaut encore mieux que la vérité.* Remember also an Arabian proverb which tells us that *on the tree of silence there hangs its fruit, which is peace.*